CRITIQUE

OF

RELIGION AND PHILOSOPHY

CRITIQUE
of RELIGION
and PHILOSOPHY

by
Walter Kaufmann

PRINCETON UNIVERSITY PRESS
PRINCETON, NEW JERSEY

Copyright © 1958 by Walter Kaufmann
Published by Princeton University Press, Princeton, New Jersey
In the U. K. : Princeton University Press, Chichester, West Sussex

LCC 78-424
ISBN 0-691-02001-9 (paperback edition)
ISBN 0-691-07230-2 (hardcover edition)

First PRINCETON PAPERBACK printing, 1978

Fifth printing, 1990

12 13 14 15 16 17 18

Princeton University Press books are printed on acid-free paper
and meet the guidelines for permanence and durability of the
Committee on Production Guidelines for Book Longevity of the
Council on Library Resources

Originally published by Harper & Row, 1958
Harper Torchbook edition published 1972

Printed in the United States of America

ISBN-13: 978-0-691-02001-3

ISBN-10: 0-691-02001-9

TO
BRUNO KAUFMANN
1881–1956

CONTENTS

Contents

Contents

X. SCRIPTURES AND POETRY, OR HOW TO READ THE BIBLE

XI. REASON AND EROS

PREFACE TO THE PRINCETON
PAPERBACK EDITION

REMBRANDT's "Large Self-Portrait" in the Vienna art museum cast a spell on me when I first saw it. But it spoke to me even more when I saw it again in 1962 after three weeks in Poland. In Warsaw I had virtually smelled the blood of the Jews killed there in 1943, and I had also spent an afternoon in Auschwitz. The portrait looked more powerful than ever after these experiences. Rembrandt had been twelve when the Thirty Years War began, and this painting was done four years after the devastation of Europe had ended. In those days there was no market for Rembrandt's many self-portraits. They were not painted for clients nor with any hope of a sale. Here was integrity incarnate. But how could one pass the muster of these eyes? One has to do something for a living, especially if one has a family, but I felt that I wanted to write only in the spirit in which Rembrandt had painted himself, without regard for what might pay or advance my career. And whenever I think about the millions killed during the second World War and ask myself what I have done with the life granted to me but not to so many others, the books I have written spell some small comfort.

Critique of Religion and Philosophy is very different from most scholarly books. Perhaps others felt like Dwight Mac-Donald who told me before he actually read it that he had seen it at somebody's house and it had struck him as "really crazy." It certainly did not fail to impede my career, but I have never regretted writing and publishing it. What keeps surprising me is how many people, including even reviewers, understood and appreciated it. Yet the immediate reception of a book, whether it is ignored or wins a great deal of praise, means little. The true test is whether it endures.

The survival of a human being creates no presumption whatsoever in his favor. Many of the finest die early. It is different with books and works of art. Most die in their infancy, and there is no good reason to feel ambivalent about the survival of one's works. I feel unalloyed gratitude to the publisher for keeping *Critique* in print more than twenty years after it first appeared.

The reader has a right to ask why I have not revised and updated it like my first book, *Nietzsche*. The nature of *Critique* did not make this feasible. It is a voyage of discovery in which the author comes to grips with a multitude of points of view that seemed to call for a response. It would not do to doctor the log and insert additional ports of call; the less so because the book also has the kind of unity that one associates with works of art. One cannot expect a painter to update his paintings, least of all a self-portrait. Of course, *Critique* is nowhere near that personal, and I have continued my researches into some of the questions broached here. But the results have appeared in other books; notably in *The Faith of a Heretic* (1961, reprinted with a new preface in 1978), in *Religions in Four Dimensions* (1976), and in *Man's Lot: A Trilogy* (1978). The trilogy consists of *Life at the Limits, Time Is an Artist*, and *What is Man?* It is even more unconventional than *Critique* and contains more than 330 color photographs as well as many in black and white.

Looking back on *Critique* now, I find that today I would do countless things differently. There are some ports at which I would no longer stop at all—because of what I discovered when I called there. And that information may still be worth sharing. The aspect of the book about which I don't have any second thoughts at all is that I feel more than ever that humanists should be concerned less with the opinions of their peers and elders than with the challenge of Rembrandt's eyes.

September 1978   W.K.

PREFACE TO
THE 1972 EDITION

THIS NEW EDITION IS UNCHANGED. What needed to be added I put into the sequel, *The Faith of a Heretic*. But the publisher's request for a new preface evokes reflections on what has happened since the original edition appeared in 1958. Consider my central intentions, as stated in the original preface: "To get many small suggestions accepted—say, about the interpretation of Hegel—is far less intriguing than the hope of pricking some pervasive prejudices and thus changing not only one's readers but also, if only a little, the whole intellectual climate."

Since then the intellectual climate has changed so dramatically that one might suppose that the battle is won, and the book dated or at most of historical interest now. This change, of course, had a multitude of causes. It took ten thousand Greeks to stem the Persian tide at Marathon. Even so, Aeschylus was prouder of having been one of these ten thousand than he was of his tragedies. But in the realm of the spirit triumphs are double-edged. The battle that this book helped to win was no Marathon; neither is this book dated.

It is convenient to distinguish three groups of readers. First, there are those who were changed by this book. They comprise much the smallest group, but letters from many countries still assure me occasionally that it exists. If this should be accounted a triumph, I do not know enough about most of these readers to tell whether and how it is double-edged.

Then there is the far larger group of those who were not affected by this book nor by the change in our intellectual

climate. This group includes a great many professional philosophers. Although those who welcomed this book included many
distinguished philosophers, professional philosophy has become
even more scholastic since the fifties. Among professors the
sixties actually witnessed a revival of keen interest in the
medieval arguments for God's existence.

This development is balanced to some extent by the growth
of interest in Hegel, Nietzsche, and existentialism. With that we
have come to the third group; for this interest might be accounted a triumph. But among professional philosophers these
new concerns are rarely informed by the spirit of this book.
Whatever professors of philosophy take up nowadays tends to
become scholastic, and the rigor of the scholastics is *rigor
mortis.*

Goethe's Mephistopheles urged the student who sought
advice about courses "to start with Logic":

For thus your mind is trained and braced,
In Spanish boots it will be laced,
That on the road of thought maybe
It henceforth creep more thoughtfully . . .
Who would study and describe the living, starts
By driving the spirit out of the parts:
In the palm of his hand he holds all the sections,
Lacks nothing, except the spirit's connections.

Scholasticism has not changed its ways. Rigor sets in after the
life has been driven out of the parts. To creep is a virtue, to leap
a vice, and speed the sin of the spirit. As for "The Philosophic
Flight" (the title of the first chapter of this book), that is to the
scholastic a contradiction in terms.

The change in our intellectual climate is only beginning to
affect philosophy. There is a growing interest in substantive
questions, but so far most philosophers can still think of only
two ways of dealing with them: either scholastically or by protesting their convictions after hours. As yet few philosophers
have found the courage for an attack on their own convictions.
The rigor required for a relentless examination of our own
faith, morals, and methods is still alien to most of the profes-

sion. One hesitates to ask what speaks against one's dearest beliefs and to seek out alternatives. The scholastic operates within a consensus and abhors all forms of culture shock. Where historical philosophers are studied, it is not considered sufficient that they are dead, but special pains are taken lest an individual might yet confront us with a challenge. The individual is therefore spirited away, and one deals only with assorted arguments, preferably under a microscope. That is also true of much recent work on Hegel, Nietzsche, and existentialism.

Religion has changed far more since the fifties than has philosophy, and much of this change has been, at least superficially, in the spirit of this book. Consider two of its targets: Christianity and theology. The lack of reverence for Christinaity in this book gave deep offense to many Christians but was experienced as liberating by many non-Christians here and abroad. By overthrowing a few taboos this book helped to change attitudes toward Christianity. Earlier critiques had usually attacked religion in general; here, however, the relation of Christianity to other religions, and especially to Buddhism and Judaism, was seen in a new perspective. Now it seems scarcely credible that Franz Rosenzweig should actually have suggested that Gentiles could find the way to God only through Christianity. There has been a change, and this book contributed to it; but we need only see my critique in a larger setting to realize how double-edged this triumph is.

Much the longest chapter in my *Nietzsche: Philosopher, Psychologist, Antichrist* (1950) was devoted to "Nietzsche's Repudiation of Christianity," and another chapter dealt with "The Death of God." Four years later I published a volume of new translations, including *The Antichrist*. Earlier it had been easy and customary to dismiss Nietzsche's attacks on Christianity as simply mad. Now some Protestant theologians discovered in these two volumes that "God is dead," and my translation of the passage in which Nietzsche first made this pronouncement was reprinted in innumerable volumes. At the same time the news media publicized the paradoxical attempt to base a new theology on this discovery. In the sixties, when the prime mover of this predictably stillborn theology once spoke from the same platform as I did, he was shocked and disappointed that I took no pride in his progeny.

Still, this might be seen as the last gasp of theology, and it is possible that my work has contributed to the death of theology. This book distinguished sharply and unfashionably between theology and "The Core of Religion." It called for more concern with religious experience and religious scriptures. In the fifties theology was still very prestigious, and this call seemed quixotic. But during the sixties this concern spread rapidly. It even entered our colleges, as the challenge of a new generation of students led more and more professors to try new approaches. But again it would be folly to suppose that the battle has been won.

While the interest in non-theological religion spread, "the Need for Negative Thinking," mentioned in the original preface, also came to be widely felt, and "critique" became once again a term of honor. Yet both the religious seekers and the negative thinkers are for the most part neo-romantics. They tend to be uncritical of what is dear to them: their own convictions, sentiments, experiences, and above all the fashions that they share with their peers. The rigor needed to examine our own methods and beliefs is as rare in the younger generation as it is among their teachers.

That this book anticipated or helped to bring about some far-reaching changes is no ground for elation. Fashion is false. There is much in this book that is timelier now than when it was written; for example, the sections on Buddhism, Zen, mysticism, and the relation of scriptures to poetry, as well as the paragraphs on Hermann Hesse. Then, few readers had ever heard of Hesse, and hardly any had taken up Buddhism or Zen. Now there are multitudes.

The fight continues. For the neo-romantics as well as the scholastics this still untimely book may still be timely.

January 1, 1972   W. K.

PREFACE TO
THE FIRST EDITION

I

FOR ALL. Philosophers examine their life, ideas, and assumptions not only occasionally but full time. Some do it playfully and feign perplexity to create suspense, while allaying any apprehensions by reminding us now and then that what they are doing has no bearing on the conduct of their life. This approach is fashionable in the English-speaking world today. One can learn a great deal from philosophers of this kind, but one can learn even more from Socrates: three lessons, for example.

First, that playfulness is quite compatible with seriousness. Socrates' playfulness, his wit, his frank delight in verbal contests and shrewd, unexpected moves, all meet the eye; but in his *Apology* his seriousness is hardly less in evidence. Both qualities are blended perfectly.

Secondly, the philosopher's seriousness need not consist in the unhumorous insistence that he must be right. He need not even attach ultimate significance to right opinions. He may be serious in his determination to change other men by making them less irrational and in his willingness to be changed himself in the course of his inquiries.

Thirdly, a critique need not be less serious than a positive construction. There is something playful about systems. Whether novel or codifications of previous beliefs, they generally represent merely one alternative among others. This is equally true of external criticism, which depends on standards that are not acknowledged by those criticized. But internal criticism can be definitive. Directed at trivialities, it will be trivial. Directed at enduring dangers that confront men in all ages, it may be of lasting importance. The critic who attacks idolatry does the most serious thing of which a man is capable.

Here the two major sources of our civilization are at one. The ethos of Elijah's challenge "How long will you limp on both legs?" is not far different from Socrates'. In their attempt to expose the perennial inconsistencies of their contemporaries and in their opposition to the idols of the age, not only the prophets agreed with Socrates but the Buddha did, too.

Although our time bows in these three directions, too, this critical ethos is ill represented. Reading Amos and the Buddha, the *Apology* and Job, few feel that dissatisfaction with themselves which, according to the end of the *Symposion,* Socrates induced in some of his contemporaries. This discontent, once felt, is not allayed by scholarship: "What is the use of doing over again what other people have done already, or what I myself have done already, or what other people might do?" Gide asks in *The Counterfeiters* (170); and in the accompanying *Journal* he notes: "To disturb is my function. The public always prefers to be reassured. There are those whose job this is. There are only too many" (416).

We need not choose between disturbing and offering something positive. One can try to sustain a consistent positive outlook and define it in terms of a critique of idol upon idol.

Inverting the Latin adage, *de mortuis nil nisi bene,* the temper of the time brooks cavalier dismissals of such men as Plato, Hegel, and Nietzsche, while one treats the living reverentially. For all their influence, Niebuhr, Tillich, Toynbee, and the Thomists have evoked little criticism in America. Ancient Judaism and medieval Catholicism may be submitted to sweeping strictures, but of living Protestantism one speaks *nil nisi bene,* nothing but well.

"He that sees but does not bear witness, be accursed," says the Book of Jubilees (4.5). Nor need one choose between bearing witness and enjoying one's work. To get many small suggestions accepted—say, about the interpretation of Hegel —is far less intriguing than the hope of pricking some pervasive prejudices and thus changing not only one's readers but also, if only a little, the whole intellectual climate.

II

FOR SCHOLARS. The great danger that confronts any such ambitious attempt is that it may become slovenly in detail and thus an example of intellectual sluggishness on a different plane. It is safer to deal with one small question at a time, seeking protection behind footnotes; and many of the best philosophers prefer solid papers in scholarly journals.

The present book contains no footnotes, but page references are given after quotations in the text, and the books cited— and only these—are listed in the Bibliography. (Poems that are not credited—nor creditable—are my own.)

What is gained by presenting a whole view in a single volume of manageable size is cross-illumination. Instead of developing an idea very fully and surrounding it with a vast apparatus, one can show its relation to other ideas. Instead of burying it, one can try to bring it to life.

For this one has to make sacrifices and omit more than one says. But this price is dearer to the author than to most readers. If the writer finds a place for only a fraction of his material on three religions and has to omit Hinduism altogether, it hurts him more than you.

There is a moral. The arrangement of this book with its many sections with individual titles may suggest that it is meant for browsing. It is not. Superficially, each section can be understood by itself; but many, including the three dialogues, are likely to be misunderstood out of context. If it were not for that, they could and should have been developed separately.

Emphatically, this book is meant to be read in the order in which it is presented. Those who merely wish to be diverted may disregard this counsel. But serious readers and all who care to understand the author's views should heed it.

III

FOR THE CURIOUS. The godly reader who disregards the sentence in italics in the previous section may soon find his charity endangered. But if he follows the path mapped out for him, he may well find himself in basic sympathy with what he reads, although scarcely in complete agreement.

For those whom a prohibition tempts to sin, like Eve in Eden, there is this provision. Though it were better if they did not peek—if peek they must, let them steal a glimpse, not immediately but when temptation has become too great, at the long Biblical quotation in Section 79. And if that does not suffice them, let them read Section 25. "But," as St. Paul says, "I speak this by permission, and not of commandment."

IV

BIRD'S-EYE VIEW. Whatever one says, most readers begin by browsing, which is fun, then skip what they have already read, which is understandable, and in the end are put off by a lack of organization. To save them from such injustice, one is expected to tell them in the beginning what they would find out for themselves if they took the trouble. If the author refuses, reviewers feel that they might just as well have skipped the Preface, too.

Critique, in the title, means an effort not to debunk but to show the limits of what is criticized, what it can and cannot do, its value and abuses. This, as well as the book's opposition to theology, may justify the Kantian word. In its tone and positive suggestions, however, the book is far from Kantian.

Religion means primarily, but not only, Christianity, Judaism, and Buddhism, which are all discussed in some detail.

Philosophy is dealt with not only in the first three chapters, which are devoted to it entirely, but throughout the book. No historical or systematic survey is attempted, but in the context of specific problems whole sections are devoted to Plato, St. Thomas, Kant, James, and Wittgenstein; and many other philosophers are discussed, too. A positive conception of philosophy is sketched in Chapter I, and related to positivism and existentialism in Chapter II. These are considered not merely as two fashions but as two timeless tendencies. Thus Chapter II advances the critique of philosophy. Chapter III develops a conception of truth which is important for the following critique of religion. Then the conception of philosophy worked out so far is developed further through a sustained effort to practice what has been preached.

Those who skip the chapter on truth or the section on Zen Buddhism will not fully understand the critique of theology. The last chapter points back to the beginning of the book almost as overtly as in *Finnegans Wake*, and perhaps the first two sections cannot be fully understood until one has finished the book; but the prose, unlike Heidegger's, is as far from Joyce's as it is from Kant's.

"How to Go to Hell" is the subtitle of one chapter and could be the title of the whole book. If it were, the subtitle might be "The Need for Negative Thinking." But that would sound flippant; and in spite of the current vogue of Kierkegaard, people expect a book to be either serious or humorous, not both. If the book had a funny title, people might be disappointed to find it dead serious in a sense. It is better to surprise them the other way around.

V

DEBTS AND POLEMICS. Discussions with colleagues and students on three continents have helped me greatly. A very few ideas were tried out first in undergraduate courses; many more in seminars and occasional lectures at two dozen institutions. The ensuing discussions and the comments of some colleagues who read parts of my manuscript at various stages have been most beneficial. Above all, I am indebted to Princeton University and to my colleagues Hugo Bedau and Gregory Vlastos (Princeton) and Warner Wick (Chicago) who, out of sheer kindness, read the entire manuscript and offered detailed criticisms. My wife, Hazel, has for once less aided than abetted me.

My debts to some of the writers whom I criticize, especially the immortals, should be plain. I have also profited from oral discussions with many of the living with whom I take issue. The effect of personal acquaintance is often disarming. It takes a deliberate effort to resume the critic's stance. But this effort is called for where a man has ceased to be a private individual and become an idol, albeit without half trying.

If certain polemical sections were omitted, some readers would, no doubt, confuse the outlook of this book with the position of Fromm or Niebuhr, Jaspers or Tillich. In a syncretistic age, one must fight the comfortable blurring of all contours and the growing inability to say No. One must insist on important differences.

It would have added little if I had softened my criticisms by spelling out in detail my agreement with other things these men have said. It goes without saying that one does not disagree on everything. And any statement, however silly, can be backed up with a quotation from some great man, not to speak of men *thought* to be great. Such citations have little value.

Discussion of views one rejects is important for yet another reason. If one simply ignores alternative suggestions, any outline of one's views becomes dogmatic and tedious. Polemic recaptures the excitement of the search for truth. There are those who consider mere correctness trite. Polemic may remind them of the difficulty of achieving correctness and of the high adventure of the search for truth.

W. K.

CRITIQUE
OF
RELIGION AND PHILOSOPHY

The unexamined life is not worth living.

SOCRATES

One does not pour new wine into old skins.

JESUS

Superstition, idolatry, and hypocrisy have ample wages, but truth goes begging.

LUTHER

A very popular error: having the courage of one's convictions; rather it is a matter of having the courage for an attack on one's convictions!

NIETZSCHE

Courage will not save you; but it will shew that your souls are still alive.

SHAW

Laughter also has this subtle advantage, that it need not remain without an overtone of sympathy and brotherly understanding; as the laughter that greets Don Quixote's absurdities and misadventures does not mock the hero's intent.

SANTAYANA

I. THE PHILOSOPHIC FLIGHT

1. PHILOSOPHICAL PSYCHOLOGY. Modern philosophy, unlike medieval philosophy, begins with man. Bacon and Descartes repeated the feat of Socrates and brought philosophy down to earth again. Or rather, this had been the accomplishment of the Sophists, a generation before Socrates, and was essentially a critical enterprise. With Descartes, doubt came into its own once more, and the analysis of human knowledge made cosmic and theological speculations problematic.

On the continent, Spinoza and Leibniz still developed their imposing metaphysics, while the British Empiricists determined the pattern of modern philosophy with their essays "concerning human understanding," "concerning the principles of human knowledge," and "concerning the principles of morals." With Kant's critiques of reason and judgment, man became the center of continental philosophy, too. Hegel's speculative philosophy could not halt this development which is continued in our time by pragmatism and positivism, analysis and existentialism.

In spite of this expense of brilliancy, modern philosophy has not yielded any remotely acceptable picture of man. The thinkers of the Enlightenment showed too little understanding of religion and art, feeling, passion, and the imagination; and neither romanticism nor any modern philosophy has produced a conception of man that would even tempt us to assent.

Today many philosophers would object that such an attempt would be psychology, not philosophy—as if there had ever been a great philosopher who did not offer a psychology and a picture of man. As if Plato and Aristotle had worried about trespassing into psychology. Or Spinoza. Or Hume. Or the utilitarians. Or Nietzsche. In our time, this trespass into psychology is one of the few things that the existentialists have in common with William James and John Dewey. If modern psychology has produced major insights, let the philosopher use them. If it has accomplished what the philosophers have tried to do, this will come as a surprise not only to philosophers.

Psychology is not a single field of study, and there is no psychological method. Investigation ranges from physiological psychology (which is sometimes indistinguishable from physiology) to psychoanalysis, from ethics to population research, from medicine and sociology to statistics and the behavior of rats in mazes. All this does not involve the least criticism of psychology, but it raises doubts about the meaning of the question with which some philosophers like to confound their colleagues: Is not that psychology? It would make far more sense to confront Freud's conception of ego, id, and superego with the question: Is not that philosophy? But any such morbid fear of trespasses across academic borderlines deserves disparagement.

Philosophers can perform a major service by clarifying concepts which are often confused and breed further confusion. But the philosopher neither has a monopoly of this art nor is he condemned to ignore all empirical data. In some of the most interesting philosophic works, psychological analysis and analysis of concepts illuminate each other.

Indeed, any philosophic work that pursues one to the exclusion of the other does so at its peril. Psychological speculation without careful attention to the concepts used is likely to be philosophically naïve—and Freud's so-called metapsychology is a case in point. But what is overlooked by many contemporary philosophers is that conceptual analyses divorced from all psychology are frequently no less naïve.

This fault is one of the few things that the British school of linguistic analysis today has in common with the British

Idealism of yesterday. Thus T. H. Green's Idealistic defense
of the retributive function of punishment was vitiated by his
disregard for psychological observation. That "the state cannot be supposed capable of vindictive passion" may be true as
far as ordinary language goes; but Green's peremptory claim
that "Indignation against wrong done to another has nothing
in common with a desire to revenge a wrong done to oneself"
(183 f.) flouts the psychological insights of the Buddha, Nietzsche, and Freud.

Ordinary language philosophy, like Idealism, is often guilty
of rationalization—or, as another Idealist, Bradley, put it very
beautifully, "the finding of bad reasons for what we believe on
instinct" (xii). Indeed, there are few great philosophers to
whom this dictum is as applicable as it is to G. E. Moore,
whose revolt against Bradley ten years later, in 1903, inaugurated the development that has culminated in ordinary language philosophy. (See Chapter II.) If, as Bradley added,
"the finding of these reasons is no less an instinct," it ought
to be the aim of philosophy to teach men to master this instinct and become housebroken.

Few philosophers have mastered this propensity completely.
We remember Descartes' resolve to doubt and Kant's devastating attack on theology and generally ignore the bad reasons
they offered for belief in God and immortality. Idealism went
so far in rationalizing that it is hard to forget this. And ordinary language philosophy is well on its way toward succeeding Idealism as the prime apologist for Christianity and
bourgeois morals. While psychologists, following Freud, Nietzsche, and Spinoza, *question* traditional beliefs, more and more
philosophers assume that philosophy must avoid contamina-
tion by psychology and concentrate on studying the rationale
of ordinary moral and religious language.

Philosophers who have not repudiated psychology as a matter of principle have often shown a flagrant disregard for observation and developed strangely unempirical psychologies.
This is true not only of some British philosophers, most notably Bentham, but even more of German philosophers from
Kant to Heidegger. Much philosophic psychology is simply
poor psychology. But great psychologists are exceedingly rare,

and many of them have been philosophers. Even so, psychology has been the heel of Achilles for too many philosophers.

2. THE PSYCHOLOGY OF TRUTH.   An attempt to understand man need not proceed by way of a study of rats. One can also proceed by considering man's most distinctive endeavors: art, religion, philosophy, morality, and science. The point is not that rat psychology is less elevating but that it does not lead to any understanding of these phenomena—or of psychology itself.

Philosophers love to discuss the nature of philosophy. Historians have shown great interest in the history of history and have traced the rise of the historical consciousness and the development of historiography. But the psychology of psychology is a subject of which most psychologists prefer not to think—unless they try to debunk the theories of their rivals by psychologizing them; for example, by pointing out that Adler was a very small man and *therefore* insisted on the inferiority complex, masculine protest, and overcompensation.

The subject matter of modern psychology is not homo sapiens but, for the most part, man's irrationality and abundant subhumanity. As far as psychoanalysis is concerned, Freud himself emphasized this in 1914 in the context of *his* critique of Adler. (IV, 460 f. He did *not* mention Adler's size.) Psychoanalysis, said Freud, "has never claimed that it offered a complete theory of man's psychic life; it only demanded that its results should be used to supplement and correct the knowledge acquired elsewhere. Alfred Adler's theory, however, goes far beyond this goal. . . ." So did Freud's own speculations later on.

Modern psychology—Pavlov's and Watson's as well as Freud's—began as a revolt against what seemed an infamous conspiracy to cover up some of the most striking features of human behavior and motivation. In fact, it was no conspiracy any more than was men's blindness to the actual behavior of external objects—a state of guilty innocence that, according to a widely accepted legend, Galileo attacked when he dropped

weights from the Leaning Tower. It is a slow process to learn
to see straight, and—Descartes' influential superstition notwithstanding—we gained some certainty about the outside
world centuries before we learned to see ourselves. Slowly we
worked our way from the stars down to man. And when we
finally got that far, what was more natural than that we should
have concentrated first of all on what was new because it had
been systematically ignored: man's similarity to animals, con-
ditioned reflexes, abnormal psychology, and the psychopathology of everyday life.

The psychology of error has now been given a great deal of
attention and is fascinating. The psychology of truth has
scarcely come into view. The psychologist likes to play God:
he assumes a privileged position high above that human folly
which he studies. He illuminates the thinking of others and
ignores his own. And if, like Freud, he draws much of his
material from his own experience, he draws on his dreams
and on that considerable portion of his life when he is not
doing psychology: he throws little or no light on his thinking
as a psychologist insofar as it is presumably sound. But what
are we doing when we search for truth?

An inspirational answer would lead us back to pleasant
prejudice; and some of the cheerful neo-Freudians who think
they have outgrown the master's stern suggestions have all but
become lay preachers. Freud was not at all too critical or
gloomy; but his attempts to analyze the psychological foundations of religion, art, and science were abortive.

By all means, let the psychologist tell us how similar religious people are to neurotics and how closely some great
artists resemble his patients. But there *are* differences, and
perhaps the pursuits of normal and even abnormal men contain some elements which are brought out most clearly in the
works of the great—including the work, the devotion, the scientific hunger of a Freud.

That no Plato, not to speak of Socrates, could have arisen
in the city he describes in the *Republic,* is one of the most
serious internal criticisms of Plato's social thought. And it is
a crucial criticism of Freud's psychology that it cannot account

for the phenomenon of Freud himself—indeed, that on its presuppositions Freud's work could never have been accomplished. These suggestions will be developed in the last chapter.

One need not extol man's distinctive endeavors simply because they are distinctive. On the contrary: one can study them as aspirations which usually fall short of what is wanted. If one asks in this spirit about the relation of philosophy and religion to truth, the implicit foci of the discussion are two questions which have been at the center of philosophy since Socrates—questions which are found in the Bible, too, albeit with a different accent: "What is man?" and "What is truth?"

3. STYLE.   One begins by considering the style of a book a peculiarity of the author; then one fancies that it is a feature of the age.

James Joyce began his last work in the middle of a sentence and furnished the beginning of that sentence in the final words of the book, to bring out the essential integrity of the work which, in a sense, has neither beginning nor end. What seems sheer eccentricity at first glance appears in a different light as soon as it is put side by side with modern painting—and perhaps also philosophy.

When did this contemporary predicament begin? Hegel already did not know where to begin because every sentence was bound to presuppose all the rest. Nietzsche's major works lack the kind of structure one expects of pupils. Wittgenstein's logistic arrangement in his *Tractatus* often differs only superficially from a very loose aphoristic style, and in the end he found himself literally unable to complete a book containing his philosophy. Heidegger has given us a fragment of one book, and then lectures and essays.

The problem transcends the age. A philosophic book is almost a contradiction in terms. Socrates knew this and did not even try to write; Plato knew it and wrote dialogues—in which arguments alternate with myths, and epigrams with digressions—as well as a letter in which he insisted that his dialogues did not really contain his philosophy. In a sense, Plato's dialogues, however artfully organized, are fragments of the mind's soliloquy: invitations to a philosophic life.

Spinoza put down his philosophy in a single volume, apparently *ordine geometrico*, but had recourse to a stunning diversity of styles. Much of Leibniz' philosophy has to be gleaned from his letters. Kant could write brilliant essays, but his *magnum opus*, the *Critique of Pure Reason*, is one of the worst-written great books of all time. And yet it would be impertinent to ridicule the style, for the problem is universal.

What, then, of the British philosophers? Do their often brilliantly written books lack greatness? What of Hobbes, Berkeley, and Hume, or of Russell, who can boast of a hundred books? Two kinds of relatively neat philosophic books *can* be written. First, critical analyses of arguments, positions, and conceits; and the British have contributed some of the best of these. Secondly, sketches of constructive suggestions, outlines of new positions. But these are possible in book form only if one is content to leave out some of the most interesting and important areas of human experience, as Hobbes did in his *Leviathan*, and as others have done since to an even greater extent. This is also true of Leibniz' *Monadology* and of Berkeley, who combined criticism and construction with true brilliancy.

What seems impossible is to organize in the same manner a record of a philosophic life after the manner of Plato, Spinoza, and Nietzsche, or to deal so neatly with the *substance* of philosophy and religion—not merely with a few arguments. If one wants to cope with man's most far-flung aspirations, one must give up the relatively petty aspiration of writing a strait-laced book.

4. THE PHILOSOPHER'S DILEMMA. Style is often considered a merely literary matter. But one major problem of style that confronts the philosopher is a question not only of art but also of truth.

The scientist's originality may at times consist in simply

noting something new. To a lesser extent this is also true of the historian; but he must integrate his discoveries with previous knowledge. At this point the question of style becomes inescapable: should he press his new insights one-sidedly to provoke discussion and fertilize the field, or should he eschew radicalism for the sake of balance and bury his insights under a bushel of old knowledge?

For the philosopher the same problem is even more acute because he deals with questions which have long been discussed by some of the wisest and most brilliant men of all time; and even if he raises new problems, he must always relate them to the old ones and show how his insights affect the thought of Plato. Should soundness be incompatible with fertility?

If a philosopher argues in some detail that ultimate reality is will, or matter, or spirit, he is honored as the protagonist of a major metaphysic; and if he claims that the meaning of an idea consists in its practical effects, or that only what is verifiable is meaningful, or that the meaning of a word or expression must be gleaned from its use, he is hailed as a revolutionary. But if he gives limited credit to each suggestion, he is plainly eclectic and not really important.

Aristotle alone has escaped this odium, owing to uniquely favorable circumstances. The views he integrated are known to us for the most part only through him: as we read him, therefore, we experience the excitement of the many radical views which he rejects as one-sided. And coming so near the beginning of Western philosophy, he was the first to map out the whole field with systematic vision. Ever since, it may seem at this point, the question has been one of becoming either an Aristotelian, adding a few footnotes, or a heretic—radical, one-sided, and unsound.

No one can present all sides of a question. But one can try to do justice to most and be, at worst, pedantic and pedestrian; at best, encyclopedic—and in neither case a good philosopher —or one can be radical and wrong. Or is there a way out?

5. THE PHILOSOPHIC FLIGHT.   Philosophy, like poetry, deals
with ancient themes: poetry with experiences, philosophy with
problems known for centuries. Both must add a new precision
born of passion.

The intensity of great philosophy and poetry is abnormal
and subversive: it is the enemy of habit, custom, and all
stereotypes. The motto is always that what is well known is
not known at all well.

Great poetry often deals with hackneyed themes. Sophocles
and Shakespeare chose well-known stories, Goethe wrote on
love, Dostoevsky on murder. Yet what is new each time is not
merely the language. The poet's passion cracks convention:
the chains of custom drop; the world of our everyday experience is exposed as superficial appearance; the person we had
seemed to be and our daily contacts and routines appear as
shadows on a screen, without depth; while the poet's myth
reveals reality.

Newspaper reports, and even scenes we have seen with our
own eyes, are like distorted images in muddy waters of that
reality which we encounter in *Oedipus Tyrannus, Lear* or *The
Brothers Karamazov*. We live upon the surface; we are like
ants engaged in frantic aimlessness—and that one talent which
is death to hide, lodged with us useless till the artist comes,
restoring vision, freeing us from living death.

Philosophy, as Plato and Aristotle said, begins in wonder.
This wonder means a dim awareness of the useless talent,
some sense that antlikeness is a betrayal. But what are the
alternatives? Bacon suggested: being bees or spiders. Some
thinkers, like the ant, collect; some, like the spider, spin; some,
like the bee, collect, transform by adding of their substance,
and create.

Vary the metaphor. Men are so many larvae, crawling, wrig-
gling, eating—living in two dimensions. Many die while in this
state. Some are transformed and take a single flight before
they settle down to live as ants. Few become butterflies and
revel in their new-found talent, a delight to all.

Philosophy means liberation from the two dimensions of
routine, soaring above the well known, seeing it in new per-

spectives, arousing wonder and the wish to fly. Philosophy sub-
verts man's satisfaction with himself, exposes custom as a
questionable dream, and offers not so much solutions as a different life.

A great deal of philosophy, including truly subtle and ingenious works, was not intended as an edifice for men to live
in, safe from sun and wind, but as a challenge: don't sleep
on! there are so many vantage points; they change in flight:
what matters is to leave off crawling in the dust.

A philosopher's insight may be a photograph taken in flight.
Those who have never flown think they are wise when noting
that two such pictures are not alike: they contradict each
other; flying is no good; hail unto all that crawls! The history
of philosophy is a photo album with snapshots of the life of
the spirit. Adherents of a philosophy mistake a few snapshots
for the whole of life.

6. A SERIES OF ETCHINGS. Can a philosopher communicate
the sense of flight? Parmenides tried it in a philosophic poem,
using the image of a chariot ride, leaving the earth. Plato
sought to recapture the life of the spirit in dialogues, and at
its best his prose suggests the transport of the soul. In some of
the dialogues it takes a historian of philosophy to mistake a
fleeting perspective for a position.

The great philosopher generally captures something of his
wonder; he communicates his own experience how the seemingly familiar appears differently from new perspectives; and
he infuses the delight of his flight into his suggestions for a
new map.

One need not be either one-sided or dull. Many-sidedness
is not pedestrian unless the tempo is plodding. If passion is
lacking, and the intensity of personal experience—if their
place is taken by a pedantic determination to cover the field
—then it is indeed likely that justice will be done to no side:
the presentation of each will be weakened by endless qualifications. We are offered a series of retouched pictures and denied both truth and participation in the philosophic flight.

To present everything is impossible; but one can present several images, each boldly etched to bring out what truth there is in it, unretouched, as sharp as possible. One can also offer criticisms of retouched pictures. At its best, philosophy offers a great deal of truth and an invitation to a different way of life. It does not give us all of the truth, but that may be safely left to the legal imagination.

7. HEGEL AND NIETZSCHE. The two modern philosophers who have come closest to saying what has been suggested here are Hegel and Nietzsche. Hegel said that it was the task of philosophy, *was bekannt ist, zu erkennen:* to attain knowledge of what is known by acquaintance, what is familiar. Like Socrates, he saw that philosophy cannot abide unquestioning acquaintance.

Moreover, Hegel's *Phenomenology of the Spirit* represents the most sustained attempt ever made to show how different philosophic positions are merely stages in the life of the spirit. Yet the result is bizarre. For Hegel tried to deduce each stage in turn from the preceding one, and his deductions are often grotesque. But even where we understand how a man who identifies himself passionately with a position, taking it more seriously than its previous proponents, is driven beyond it to the next position, the question remains: Could the same position be reached in another way? Would it look different in that case, appearing in a different perspective? And could one proceed from it in a direction that did not occur to Hegel? To cite his own words, Hegel recorded his own voyage of discovery.

Nietzsche, who loved Genoa, occasionally compared himself with Columbus and asked his readers to embark on the high seas in search of yet uncharted distances. But where Hegel produced a painstaking log, allowing us to follow the stations of his Odyssey, Nietzsche's sharp vignettes often lack detail, as if he had flown rather than sailed and had found time only for rapid sketches. And sometimes it seems as if his papers had got mixed up to boot and were offered in random order.

If Hegel doctored his log, Nietzsche seems to have kept none at all. If Hegel forces things into his system, Nietzsche writes like a man who wants to get things out of his system.

In fact, Nietzsche had lost any belief that his flights had followed the course of a world spirit or that the sequence was sacrosanct. He was not one of those who take a single flight before they settle down. Nietzsche was like the butterfly: the sun and air were his medium, not the dust, and he spent his life in flight and sometimes saw the same views in different perspectives.

The image of the butterfly may seem inappropriate, but Goethe often used it in serious contexts, most significantly in his poem *Selige Sehnsucht*, "Blessed Yearning." And if Goethe was guilty of a scientific error in this poem and ought to have written "moth," that only shows how attached he was to the butterfly.

> *Tell it none except the wise,*
> *for the common crowd defames:*
> *of the living I shall praise*
> *that which longs for death in flames.*
>
> *In the love night which created*
> *you where you create, a yearning*
> *wakes: you see, intoxicated,*
> *far away a candle burning.*
>
> *Darkness now no longer snares you,*
> *shadows lose their ancient force,*
> *as a new desire tears you*
> *up to higher intercourse.*
>
> *Now no distance checks your flight,*
> *charmed you come and you draw nigh*
> *till, with longing for the light,*
> *you are burnt, O butterfly.*
>
> *And until you have possessed*
> *dying and rebirth,*
> *you are but a sullen guest*
> *on the gloomy earth.*

For Nietzsche, as for Goethe, the rebirth did not involve any traditional faith. It meant rising above the darkness in which most men live—or rather do not live—and creating life out of the suffering of which others die. Dying and rebirth was for both the heartbeat of the creative life. In Nietzsche's phrase: "One pays dearly for immortality: one must die several times while still alive" (660).

The saturnine aspect of German existentialism was as alien to Nietzsche as it was to Goethe. The thought of death and the experience of failure did not fill them with dread like Heidegger or with intimations of the divine like Jaspers.

In some ways, Jaspers' position is similar to that suggested here; but, like Heidegger, he abandons close conceptual analysis and argument without realizing that these are quite indispensable to guard against arbitrariness—we shall have to invoke them in due time—and his magisterial gravity easily equals that of the professors whom he scorns. Nietzsche, too, appreciated the importance of argument insufficiently; but what strikes one first in his work is his wealth of fruitful suggestions, his lighthearted derision of the spirit of gravity, and his exhortation to laugh.

8. WHY MOST PHILOSOPHERS CANNOT LAUGH.   Why did so few of the great philosophers laugh? Were they frightened by Socrates' death, or perhaps awed by Aristotle? Descartes, Spinoza, Hobbes, and Locke are as serious as Kant and the German professors of philosophy who came after him. And Hegel, who was far from humorless, concealed his jokes behind so many pronouns that they have to be construed.

Is all this due to the weight of tradition, or perhaps related to the prohibition of laughter in church? After all, the young Plato could laugh, and so could Shakespeare, even in *Lear* and *Macbeth*. And Goethe. And Dostoevsky. But if one can laugh in *Lear*, why not in the *Critique of Practical Reason?* Is the mad Lear funnier than Kant's postulate of God?

If Goethe could laugh at his Faust through the mouth of Mephistopheles, why can't any philosopher laugh at himself, except only the allegedly austere author of *Zarathustra*, Part Four? And even Nietzsche's humor was promptly buried in the most dismal interpretations and translations.

One reason for the scarcity of laughter in philosophy has been suggested by Andersen in his fairy tale, "The Emperor's Clothes." If one must pretend to see something one doesn't see, lest one be considered incompetent, is one in any position to laugh? That alone illuminates a vast literature, including many commentaries, not to speak of lecturers and students who would not dare to publish their careful paraphrases of texts they do not understand.

But what of the great philosophers? Perhaps all too many of them had seen very little and required the most serious application to extract a system from so little insight. They had to ask themselves what followed from their previous writings, and relied on parallels and extrapolations: who could laugh doing that? Hegel had seen enough to laugh but felt ashamed to and hid his humor. Russell and Santayana laugh —if not at themselves, at least at each other.

9. WHAT LONG APHORISMS CAN MEAN.   If Nietzsche's aphorisms reflect the experimentalist's determination to remain unprejudiced by any system, critics will still feel that the power is lacking to fashion a comprehensive image. Even at his best, the aphorist seems a literary miniaturist.

What condemned Nietzsche to writing long aphorisms, however, was an excess rather than a deficiency—perhaps even two excesses. The first was a superabundance of insights. Homer, being blind, can organize what he has seen and fashion it into a comprehensive epic. The philosopher who has gone blind has all his life to create his system. Nietzsche was a writer who kept seeing things while writing.

The other excess was in penetration. To cover an outline, neatly taking up each topic in turn, one must not see too deeply anywhere. In fact, it helps if one sees next to nothing: then one can apply a single insight—either one's own of many years ago or even that of another man who never thought of applying it in this manner—to one topic after another till the book is long enough or the system complete. If one sees deeply, a passage originally intended for one section will suddenly appear to be no less relevant to several other topics; and as this happens to passage after passage, the outline disintegrates, any hope of a system evaporates, and a series of long aphorisms appears.

Nietzsche is the outstanding example of such an embarrassment of riches, but Plato was beset by the same excesses. In writing the *Republic*, for example, he kept seeing things; and because he was penetrating, here as elsewhere, the same passages are equally relevant to metaphysics and ethics, education, poetry, politics, and religion, and whatever else few other men have understood so well. And where there is such abundance there is laughter, too.

The laughter of Plato and Shakespeare, Goethe and Nietzsche, is the frolicsome foam on the waves of an inexhaustible sea: it is power that delights in itself and mocks in advance the myopia of the scholars who miss the spirit's flight.

Aphorisms, to be sure, *may* signify the lack of strength to build up a coherent structure; and a glittering mosaic of epigrams is apt to be brilliant but lacking in depth. In few styles are the extremes so far from each other, ranging from mere lack of discipline to diverting wit, and from the suggestive to the profound.

A system is like a sonnet which is relatively safe for the poet who is not too sure of himself and content to express mainly one thought and at most two emotions. There is safety in the form. But systematic philosophers rarely follow the example of the sonneteer and compose one system after another. Bertrand Russell may be an exception; and his laughter, too, is born of abundance.

There are two kinds of philosophers. Both go out with similar hopes and acquire some competence. But to one kind you must give a topic. (After a while he may learn to think up his own.) The topic may be small or nothing less than a system: what matters is that it is primary, and the writer then brings to bear on it what competence he has. The other kind of writer has something to say before he is sure to what topic it will be most relevant. He writes first, and the outline comes afterward if at all—not to help him decide what to say but to assist him in organizing what he has said.

At that point great improvements may be effected—the rewriting may actually be harder than the writing—and parallels and extrapolations may play their part after all: if so, we get an intermediate style, well exemplified by Spinoza and Kant. Spinoza found a place for insights and arguments, epigrams and diatribes, in the austere mansions of his geometric temple. Kant accumulated notes for over a dozen years and then, in about six months, fashioned them into his first *Critique*. He had somewhat pedantic ideas about organization, and the result was stylistically bizarre. But this could not obscure his profound originality, and the impact of the book was immediate and unparalleled. So Kant naturally felt that he must model his second and third *Critiques* after the first one.

If Kant and Spinoza occupy an intermediate position, and Nietzsche is the classical representative of one extreme, the other extreme, which is most common, is incompatible with ultimate excellence and therefore cannot be illustrated with names of equal rank. At his worst, however, Hegel furnishes a good example, particularly in parts of his philosophy of nature which he found it necessary to include in his *Encyclopaedia of the Philosophical Sciences* to fill the gap between the first part and the last.

Bertrand Russell admits that his firsthand acquaintance with Hegel depends largely on Hegel's treatment of mathematics. His opinion of Hegel is therefore comparable to an opinion of Russell based on the sections on Hegel and Nietzsche, and easily half a dozen others, in his *History of Western Philosophy*. To complete his ambitious outline, Russell, too, had to stretch his competence and write about many things of which he lacked sufficient knowledge. It might have been better after all to leave the gaps unfilled. And that is what long aphorisms can mean.

10. RELATIVITY AND CRITICISM. However one writes, some selection is imperative. Does selection, then, imply relativity? Most so-called historical relativists base their case on the impossibility of reporting everything. Is not the situation the same in philosophy?

The relativists overestimate their case. The image of the map gives it away at a glance. Maps are selective, but it would be misleading to call them relative in the sense of "merely subjective." One map may concentrate on mountains, valleys, and rivers; another on railroads; a third on highways. In terms of its purpose, each can be evaluated critically. A book on a thinker and a book on ethics must also be judged in terms of their implicit purposes. Neither can be expected to cover the field.

No good book on a philosopher wants to tell us everything he said: he himself did that. It may aim to outline his finished system and, judged in terms of this intention, may be excellent without doing justice to his development or his influence. A highway map may be accurate but fail us if we want a railroad map. Or a book on a philosopher may seek to correct misconceptions—either his own or those of others about him, or both. Or it may concentrate on one particular work, or on his method. Most likely it will be intended to fulfill several of these functions. It can always be criticized in relation to each; there is no need for relativistic resignation.

A book may also reflect the author's emotional reaction to the man on whom he writes. Here it may reveal the author's stature or stupidity: it is no longer comparable to a map, but a piece of self-expression. As such it is subject to different standards from those applying to a map, but relativism is again the wrong word. The fact that different painters would paint the same scene differently does not establish the impossibility of an accurate map.

Most books on philosophers combine self-expression with the attempt to advance certain problems to a solution; and the author's personal reactions are not usually confined to a separate chapter. But this does not mean that such books cannot be judged objectively. Those intent on such judgment must disentangle the author's various problems and purposes, including those which are never explicitly stated.

Often a book on a philosopher contains such fundamental mistakes that certain oversimplications become pardonable: "the book is altogether worthless," or "the author uses his subject as a mere foil," or "this is a reduction to the absurd of the psychoanalytic approach."

Everything here said may be transposed to make it applicable to nonhistorical works on philosophy, whether they deal with ethics or philosophy of religion. Such essays, too, seek to solve problems or explicate insights. If a philosopher had no problems and no insights, his work—to borrow David Hume's apt phrase—should be committed to the flames.

An accurate map may mislead us. All the highways may be there, but no indication that our car will be unable to make the grade at one point. Or we may have assumed that there were no trains when a cheap train could actually have got us to our destination in half the time. Often the author himself is unaware of what he omits.

Some of the most important philosophic criticism consists simply in determining what features a map portrays and what it leaves out. Measuring a man's performance against his intentions is relatively secondary.

To give two examples: Mill's ethics differs from Kant's. While Kant proposed that moral goodness in any concrete instance depends on the maxim which the agent had in mind, John Stuart Mill suggested that it depends on the consequences of the act. Both saw something significant: the ethics of Kant and Mill may be compared to two maps which record different features. Kant noted something about the meaning of "morally good" when applied to an agent, Mill about the meaning of a morally good *act*. In line with this distinction, an act which is praiseworthy, taken in itself, may be performed by a man who, under the circumstances, deserves no moral approbation for performing it.

Suppose two philosophers pass different value judgments: one considers pity the crown of the virtues while another condemns it. Here the metaphor of the map may seem to break down; but it does not. As long as the two men merely pit preference against preference, this is not philosophy; but if they offer arguments of any merit, then they record some observations—perhaps about the motivation or the effects of pity, or possibly about its compatibility with justice or some other virtue. In each case, some feature of pity is recorded on the map, not necessarily correctly.

One can criticize a philosophic position without the benefit of a rival position and, of course, without knowledge of the world spirit or the wave of the future. Philosophic criticism is usually internal criticism and not arbitrary: one cannot take it or leave it; it does not depend on external standards.

Some external standards are so plausible that one does not hesitate to invoke them. But future criticism may either find them mutually inconsistent or define the limits of their relevance. And a popular standard may be a mere label hiding a hornets' nest of confusion.

Relevant criticism may be offered by those who have never taken a philosophic flight. One can tell a rotten egg without being able to lay a fresh one. And a philosophic essay involves more than new insights; it also requires exposition and arguments which may be objectionable.

Clever criticisms can be stupid: those who see only the errors of Plato may be brilliant, but they are blind. Every great philosophic work says, like Rilke's "Archaic Torso of Apollo": "You must change your life." The critic who does not realize this is a Philistine—or possibly a positivist: he has a very inadequate notion of philosophy. But those who see only this challenge may also be positivists, in which case they are likely to discount it as merely emotive; or they may be *Schwärmer* —romantic souls—or possibly existentialists. And their notion of philosophy is inadequate, too. For not every call to change one's life is philosophic: religion, art, and morality embody a similar challenge. What distinguishes philosophy is that it lives in the tension between challenge and analysis, between positivism and existentialism.

But aren't positivism and existentialism merely modern phenomena? Timely at best, and possibly almost dated? Is philosophy itself perhaps dated?

II. POSITIVISM AND
EXISTENTIALISM

11. TWO REVOLTS. Contemporary philosophy is largely a philosophy of revolt, or rather two philosophies of revolt. It is convenient to call them positivism and existentialism, though both labels are problematic and justifiable only as stenographic devices. The so-called positivists usually repudiate this label, even as Jaspers and Heidegger spurn "existentialism." Only the French seem to like the pose that goes with such a banner. Yet it is not Comte and Sartre alone that shall be considered here but two larger movements which make problematic traditional philosophy as we know it from the works of Plato and Aristotle, Descartes and Hobbes, Berkeley, Kant, and Hegel, among others.

Comte (1798–1857) is rarely mentioned by the positivists of today, and their lack of admiration for him is, no doubt, one reason why they do not care to be called positivists, even as Jaspers' and Heidegger's protest that they are not existentialists is motivated in part by their dislike for Sartre. And yet modern positivism is close to Comte in a number of ways.

Contemporary positivism has split into two movements of revolt: one relies heavily on symbolic logic, the other on "ordinary language." What both have in common with Comte is a deeply unhistorical, even antihistorical outlook. Empathy and that virtuosity of understanding past positions which was cultivated by romantics and Hegelians are not the forte of

Carnap and Reichenbach or of the ordinary language philosophers any more than of Comte. On the contrary, theirs is a
decided lack of respect for the past. Where they concern themselves with previous thinkers it is generally not to learn but
criticize.

Comte inaugurated positivism with his law of the three
stages: the first stage of every culture is theological, and theology is for him practically a synonym for superstition. Next
comes metaphysics, which is scarcely less superstitious: it substitutes principles and forces for the ancient gods. Finally, positivism brings scientific knowledge in place of honored errors.

Contemporary positivists rarely mention Comte's stages, but
when they deal with the past they almost always concentrate
on errors and confusions, and they have even retained something of Comte's messianic airs. Thus Wittgenstein said in the
Preface of his first book, published after World War I, that
he had solved all the major philosophic problems—though he
added characteristically that one could now see how little was
done when all problems were solved; and in his second phase,
in his posthumous *Investigations,* he sharply criticized his first
book.

To the existentialists, the positivists would deny the very
name of philosophers: when they do not, as usual, ignore them
altogether, they stigmatize them as muddleheads. The existentialists return the compliment: one of the few things on which
they are agreed is that positivism means the renunciation of
philosophy. When a famous existentialist left Einstein, whose
philosophic attitude was close to positivism, and his wife said,
"Einstein has not changed at all," the existentialist replied:
"No, as childish as ever—*noch immer der selbe alte Kindskopf.*"
The positivists consider the existentialists *Wirrköpfe,* and the
existentialists take the positivists for *Kindsköpfe.* Logically,
both could be right, but it takes a good deal of *parti pris* to
see nothing but confusion or childishness in the other camp.
In fact, both movements have renounced philosophy in the
traditional sense—possibly with reason.

More's the pity that they can no longer communicate with
each other. Their neat geographical separation today is due to

Hitler rather than to cultural origins: many of the leading positivists originally wrote in German. But the complete breakdown of communication between both camps marks a major
bar to international understanding and merits rather more concern than it receives. Paradoxically, this lack of mutual understanding and this downright contempt for each other are
due largely to what both camps have in common: both have
repudiated most traditional philosophy and thus lost common
ground; both have messianic overtones, and rival messiahs can
scarcely be expected to be sympathetic toward each other; and
both are often all but untranslatable.

What is wanted is some idea of what each of them is doing
and not doing—not external criticism but some notes for a map.
An etching of each may make some of their failings plain. All
that is needed is a little acid. (Cf. §§ 6, 10.)

If either movement were devoid of insights it would little
deserve study. In fact, each has got hold of something of first-
rate importance, and this is what ultimately matters in the
present context.

12. ANALYTIC PHILOSOPHY.   Of the two kinds of positivism,
the more formal type, which is usually instantly recognizable
by its profuse use of symbolic logic, need not be considered
here. Its remoteness from traditional philosophy and from the
problems of religious truth to be considered here is obvious.
Unquestionably, men like Carnap, Reichenbach, and others
have done work of great importance on problems, for example,
that relate to probability; but it is the other type of positivism
that shall concern us here. For want of a better name, it may
be called analytic philosophy.

This movement is almost as heavily indebted to G. E. Moore
as existentialism is to Kierkegaard. Both men began by fighting the shadow of Hegel—not Hegel himself. In his "Autobiography," Moore tells us how, as an undergraduate, he "was
obliged to read some Hegel," but "never thought it worth
while to read him again." But "following McTaggart," his
teacher, he became an "enthusiastic admirer" of Bradley; and

it was against Bradley and McTaggart that he revolted eventually, in the opening years of the twentieth century.

Here were philosophers—hardly among the greatest, but
still philosophers, and there were other, lesser men like them
—whose dialectic seemed to have led them into merely verbal
problems. That must never happen again. Words must be considered more carefully. The main target of this attack is neither
the ordinary man nor the man who has taken a philosophic
flight: it is the don who has no problems but has made it his
profession to deal with problems. There is no end to the problem of how to guard him against spurious problems.

To be sure, the don, being a human being, must have problems; but these he keeps to himself: it would be a breach of
good manners to do otherwise, if not downright existentialist.
As a result, he has no philosophic problems. To cite Moore's
"Autobiography": "I do not think that the world or the sciences would ever have suggested to me any philosophic problems. What has suggested philosophical problems to me is
things which other philosophers have said about the world or
the sciences."

What could be more remote from existentialism and more
academic? Looking for problems in this manner, one need
never fear that one will not find enough—especially if one is
not content with what other philosophers have actually said.
No doubt, Moore's problems were "suggested" to him by what
others had said, but his famous "Refutation of Idealism"
(1903), for example, "purported to be a criticism of Berkeley.
Now the position actually criticized in that article is not Berkeley's position; indeed, in certain important respects it is the
exact position which Berkeley was controverting." This is the
judgment of two philosophers, Collingwood (22) and McKeon
(456), who have little in common except a strong interest in
the history of ideas. Indeed, McKeon says: "I also agree" with
Moore's "frequent statements of suspicion that no one ever
held the propositions which he refutes"; and he gives examples (455).

Surely, there is a comic element in this situation, but there
is nothing glib or facile about Moore's misunderstandings of

the propositions that he criticizes. He conveys a profound sense
of the difficulty of the subject matter, and he is not in the
least condescending. Many of those who have followed in his
footsteps criticize muddles without realizing that their own
prose, approached in the same surgical spirit, is no less vulnerable than the texts they criticize.

Moore's attitude is quite different. Modesty and honesty are
among his most outstanding characteristics. Although he is
quite generally credited with a decisive influence on Bertrand
Russell, he is capable of saying: "I do not know that Russell
has ever owed to me anything except mistakes." Comparing
his own widely celebrated *Principia Ethica* with his little book
on *Ethics,* published in the Home University Library, he says:
"This book [*Ethics*] I myself like better than *Principia Ethica,*
because it seems to me to be much clearer and far less full
of confusions and invalid arguments." And in an essay on
"Moore's Influence" Susan Stebbing illustrates his attitude toward his own work: "At a symposium of the Aristotelian Society, on 'Internal Relations,' the two symposiasts based their
remarks on Moore's well-known paper on that subject. Moore
expressed genuine surprise that they should do so. He expressed himself as unable to understand what he could *possibly* have meant by the views he had previously stated, and
was quite convinced that they were wrong."

Seeing that Moore prefers even pedantry to lack of clarity,
how could one expect him to understand Heidegger's prose or
Sartre's *L'être et le néant?* Or Jaspers on "the Encompassing"?

In yet another sense: what could be more remote from existentialism? Can one imagine Heidegger or Jaspers saying that
they prefer one of their smaller books to one widely considered
their chef-d'oeuvre because it is "far less full of confusions and
invalid arguments"? Or would they ever say—though confronted with their prose it would be much more understandable—that they did not know what they "could *possibly* have
meant"? But at this point Moore differs not only from the existentialists. Did Kant, Fichte, Schelling, or Schopenhauer dis-
claim their own contributions to say that their colleagues really
did not owe to them "anything except mistakes"? Or did they

not rather insist that whatever was good in another man's work was really *their* contribution, and that only the mistakes were original?

Moore means a new point of departure in philosophy. What at first seems comic or pedantic is in fact impassioned honesty and modesty and has revolutionized the atmosphere of English-speaking philosophy. What philosophers have learned from Moore's modesty is a certain moderation: they have learned to limit themselves to tackling single arguments and questions.

What precisely is involved is best shown by a contrast, necessarily a little oversimplified, with the way philosophy is studied at German universities, where Moore's name is scarcely known. There are chiefly two alternatives. Either one studies past philosophers with a reverent determination to rethink their thoughts and resents the question whether these philosophers were right on this point and their arguments sound there as being philosophically naïve and impertinent, or one condemns a Kant out of hand as dated by Idealism or by existentialism. Either, in short, questions of truth or soundness are declined as impudent or they are settled wholesale by appeals to history.

Analytic philosophy does not only develop the intellectual conscience, train the mind, and combine subtlety with scrupulous precision; above all, it teaches people to think critically and makes them instinctively antiauthoritarian. There is something democratic in this way of thinking: a proposition is a proposition, whether written by a student, a professor, or a Plato; the laws of logic are no respecters of persons. At this point, however, all modesty is suddenly abandoned, and every student can tell you what is wrong with Kant without troubling to read more than a few pages. Refutations and discoveries of confusions are the order of the day.

All this is preferable to blind authoritarianism, but one may recall the words of Hegel: "To judge what has content and solidity is easiest; to comprehend it is more difficult; but what is most difficult is to combine both functions and produce an account of it."

We shall have to return to the shortcomings of analytic philosophy. Suffice it now to say that Moore attacked the fog that secondhand Hegelians had spread over the British universities. A therapeutic effort was unquestionably called for; but the cure of a disease should not be taken for a panacea, let alone salvation. The limits of its applicability should be recognized.

13. EXISTENTIALISM. Existentialism is not a philosophy but a label for several different revolts against traditional philosophy: the so-called existentialists share a preoccupation with dread, death, despair, and dauntlessness as well as the conviction that English-speaking philosophy does not deserve the name of philosophy, and, finally, a heartfelt aversion for each other.

The movement begins with Kierkegaard's attack on Hegel's shadow, which the Dane mistook for Hegel himself. In fact, it was, if not the shadow, the caricature which the old, embittered Schelling had sketched in his Berlin lectures, ten years after the death of his erstwhile friend. Trendelenburg's critique of Hegel had supplied some further features. Kierkegaard broadened the attack into a grand revolt against all academic philosophy, indeed against philosophy in general. Philosophy undermines faith; careful, critical thinking is, to Kierkegaard, "insubordination"; and painstaking analytic efforts are frivolity as long as our salvation is at stake. He did not claim to be a philosopher, was deeply opposed to philosophy, and wished he could leap into faith. (Cf. the first chapter of my *Existentialism from Dostoevsky to Sartre* and the chapters on Kierkegaard, Jaspers, and Heidegger in my *From Shakespeare to Existentialism*.)

It is fashionable to give a sociological "explanation" of existentialism. But the origin of ideas is one thing, and the cause of their popularity another. Most Marxist interpretations of history—and many non-Marxist ones, too—overlook this distinction. Popularity is indeed determined in part by economic factors and heavily influenced by the over-all situation in which a society finds itself. But great spirits usually think against their age or apart from their age.

In Kierkegaard's Denmark and Nietzsche's Germany, prosperity and security were the order of the day—and their writings had no resonance. They became popular in Germany after the First World War when insecurity and anguish were common experiences. Nietzsche had begun to catch the popular fancy twenty years earlier, but the existential aspect of his thought was not discovered till the Empire had collapsed. Existentialism came into its own in Germany after the First World War and in France during the Second, each time marking the breakdown of the old order. Jaspers, Heidegger, and Sartre— unlike Kierkegaard and Nietzsche—were timely from the beginning, men who gave a voice to what millions felt less articulately. In this, and by no means only in this, they manifest far less originality and independence; and if it were not for Kierkegaard and Nietzsche one might easily commit the error of writing off existentialism as a mere fashion.

Defeat in war is no absolute prerequisite for the popularity of existentialism, though it helps. Under the prolonged strain of the Second World War, Kierkegaard finally found a public in the United States; and the insecurity of the cold war coupled with the threat of atomic war has elicited some further interest in existentialism. But prosperity reduces this interest to the level of a fad; and the German economic "miracle" undercuts Heidegger's influence more than any philosophic criticism. For most men are incapable of being existentialists with a full belly, except perhaps for one or two years of their youth. It is only the uncommon individual, like Kierkegaard, whose "dread" and "sickness unto death" and "fear and trembling" are not lessened by a regular supply of food. The success of existentialism with a large public depends on a widespread mood of despair and the feeling that a radical breach is required; and its implicit motto is: You must change your life.

Seeing that Jaspers, Heidegger, and Sartre do not share the central Christian inspiration of Kierkegaard and do not speak of insubordination and salvation, it may be far from obvious how existentialism represents a revolt against traditional philosophy. And yet these three men represent three revolts.

Jaspers notes in an early work, without apparent reason and

without comment, that Jacob Burckhardt despised Aristotle. In a late work he enumerates the great Greeks and omits the very name of Aristotle, while a third passage, toward the end of Jaspers' *Einführung in die Philosophie* (translated as *The Way to Wisdom!*) shows what is at stake: "From *Aristotle* one learns the categories which have ever since dominated the whole of occidental thinking. He determined the language (the terminology) of philosophizing, whether one thinks with him or against him or in such a manner that one overcomes this whole plane of philosophizing" (147). Jaspers wants to overcome the whole plane of traditional philosophy with its conceptual analyses and its attempts to offer knowledge of a sort. The desire for knowledge is in Jaspers' eyes the original sin of the philosophers. That is the central theme of his book-length critique of Schelling; that is also the core of his many books, lectures, and essays about Nietzsche, whose conclusions he dismisses wholesale as "a pile of vacuities and absurdities" (*Nietzsche und das Christentum*, 71). Every content is disparaged, in Jaspers' systematic works, too, and what remains is "philosophizing": the impetus, the movement beyond every content, the dissatisfaction with all knowledge, whether science or theology or philosophic pseudo knowledge—the suspense in "philosophic faith." (The book that bears this title, *Der philosophische Glaube*, has been translated as *The Perennial Scope of Philosophy*.)

That the great philosophers invited us to rise above our present state, to leave the dust and become butterflies, Jaspers sees clearly. But he is so concerned with the great effort to get off the ground and so determined to clear every rock of knowledge out of the way that he never sees how, once up in the air, we gain new knowledge, seeing things in new perspectives, and are able to make contributions for a new map. He sees how some professors of philosophy, of whom he speaks with great contempt, stay in the dust, and against them he would like to champion a magnificent tradition; but he sees only one aspect of this great tradition, and when he insists on this exclusively he rebels, like Kierkegaard, not only against some academicians but against traditional philosophy.

Heidegger's revolt against traditional philosophy becomes self-conscious and outspoken only in his later works. With the above evaluation of the work of Jaspers he might well agree, and in his praise of Aristotle, Heidegger will yield to none. Nietzsche, moreover, is for Heidegger not the archphilosophizer but the last metaphysician. Jaspers' strictures of Schelling, in turn, are taken for a critique of Heidegger by many readers. Clearly, Heidegger's revolt differs from Jaspers'; but in him, too, the negative impetus is clearer than the goal.

From the beginning it was Heidegger's radicalism that persuaded: his concern with care and guilt and dread and death seemed revolutionary. His apparent carefulness, which really mistakes mnemonic devices for arguments and verbal similarities and doubtful etymologies for proofs, gave people with an academic background a good conscience as they followed him. It was always his intensity that mattered to his followers, not the changing contents of his views or his many modes of expression, ranging from his own essays to interpretations of Kant and Hegel, Nietzsche, Hölderlin, and Rilke, and the famous 48-page essay on Anaximander's one surviving sentence. That the master's interpretations are generally repudiated by the specialists, that his etymologies are often artificial and his style is sometimes parodied with wit, does not dissuade his admirers. His style and etymologies communicate a need to go back to the roots and suggest that most traditional philosophy stayed at the surface: Latin mistranslations of the old Greek terms are like a thick crust that we have to penetrate, and even the thought of the later Greeks, beginning with Plato's alleged great confusion of truth and correctness, keeps us from the insights of the first philosophers, who were not guilty of the fateful bifurcation of philosophy and poetry.

This quest for a new sensibility and new knowledge, and the overwhelming trust in a few poets and the pre-Socratics, distinguish Heidegger's revolt from Jaspers'. Yet the chief concern of both is to clear rocks of pseudo knowledge out of our way—Jaspers as a preliminary for some future flight, Heidegger to prepare the descent into unknown depths.

Their efforts are at best propaedeutic, and in this they re-

semble the efforts of the analytic school: all we are offered is a
therapy to cure some of the ills of traditional philosophy.
Heidegger sees the propaedeutic nature of his own attempts
and speaks repeatedly of being on the way and of trying to
find the way to some place where the proper questions may
be asked one day.

Both Jaspers and Heidegger have abandoned argument after
the manner of traditional philosophers. Jaspers alternates between exposition and exhortation, or between what in German
one might call *referieren* and what he himself calls *apellieren*.
Heidegger openly spurns the thinking of traditional philosophers as "representational" (*vorstellend*) and champions a new
kind of thinking which tries to "recall" (*andenken*). Logical
argument is a poor guide for philosophers, he thinks, though
he is less explicit about what he would put in its place. He
is trying to develop an intuitive and hermeneutic thinking
which recalls what others have said—above all, the pre-
Socratics and Hölderlin. His thinking is associative rather than
analytical and even more arbitrary than Jaspers' book-length
interpretations. Like Jaspers, Heidegger systematically ignores
the intellectual development of the men with whom he deals.
Indeed, the texts he "interprets" are "used merely as material
for an idol that he molds out of lines picked arbitrarily from
here and there" (98), to cite Professor Muschg of Basel, whose
essay on "Zerschwatzte Dichtung" offers a devastating critique
of Heidegger.

In Sartre's work the impatience with traditional philosophy
that ultimately leads to the renunciation of philosophy meets
the eye. What all three men want is to change our attitudes;
and Sartre has recourse to art and then, impatient with art,
too, resorts to politics.

According to the analytic school, traditional philosophy was
not analytical enough; according to the existentialists, it was
too analytic. Both are right, and between them they make us
aware of the shortcomings of most traditional philosophy. Even
the greatest philosophers were guilty of innumerable fallacies,
errors, and confusions; but when all this is exposed or we are
offered a neat piece of flawless reasoning, we realize, as Witt-

genstein put it so well in the Preface to his first book, how little has been done.

Both movements are bothered by the abstractness and artificiality of so much traditional philosophy and try to bring philosophy down to earth again: that is what the appeals to ordinary language and extraordinary language, to common sense and uncommon experiences, have in common. They have, all of them, kindled their flame from the fire lit by Socrates.

14. TWO TIMELESS TENDENCIES.   What is unprecedented is not the emergence of these two divergent movements but only their neat geographical separation, which is partly due to the Nazis' expulsion of the positivists. The two tendencies have been notable in philosophy from the beginning. Hence John Burnet, in the most influential English book on the pre-Socratics, was able to present them as early natural scientists of a positivistic bent, while Werner Jaeger, in a more recent work of comparable scope, pictures them as theologians, and Heidegger can read his own thought into them. Plainly, the analytic and the existential tendencies were fused in pre-Socratic philosophy—and in Socrates and Plato.

In the Middle Ages we encounter a partial dissociation of sensibility. On the one hand, we have the philosophy of the schools—rigorous and subtle at its best, and pedantic and arid at its worst—and on the other, individuals who, conscious of these faults, insist that what truly matters is changing one's life. In Eckhart and some others both tendencies are fused again.

In Kierkegaard's attack on Hegelianism it is easy to recognize the mystic's protest against scholasticism; and the same antipathy survives in the enmity of existentialism and analysis. Except for their Gothic setting, the Oxford philosophers may seem to have little in common with the scholastics, but on reflection their way of life is not altogether different. More important: in craftsmanship, precision, and sobriety, no modern philosophic movement can compare with positivism. One must go back of the flowering of romanticism to find anything like it. How much like the proverbial question, how many angels could dance on the point of a needle, are such modern problems as whether I have a headache when I am not aware of it! How far from real angels and headaches!

Both questions turn on definitions. Progress becomes possible: the problem can be filed once it is seen that definition D_1 leads to solution S_1, D_2 to S_2, and so forth. In this way, scrupulous analysis reduces seemingly large questions to a lot of small ones, and abstractness gives way to concrete detail.

Impassioned and impatient thinkers stand aside, *see* angels or *feel* anguish, and find this mode of thinking highly abstract, frivolous, and childish. Earnestly they address the individual, point out these faults, and call attention to what such analysis can never grasp. But when they speak of anguish or of angels, God, the ground of being, or the Encompassing, their rivals find *their* way of speaking abstract, vague, and hopelessly confused.

The difference is partly one of temperament. One tendency is rooted in gregariousness: a social game for brilliant minds. The other one is born of solitude and the intensity that courts it. And each suspects the other, often with a strong dose of contempt.

Between these extremes, philosophy is lost. We can still accord the name to mystic and scholastic, analyst and existentialist; but the great philosopher does not merely excel in two genres: he masters two talents which is death to split.

Undisciplined vision, unexamined intuition, and sheer passion are the fountainheads of madness, superstition, and fanaticism. And cleverness and patience without vision are the expense of spirit in a waste of subtlety.

Great philosophy lives in the tension between these extremes. Kierkegaard and G. E. Moore are each only half a Socrates.

Kierkegaard often compared himself with Socrates; and his moral earnestness, his irony, and his attempt to overcome the cleavage between life and thought help to explain his meaning. Yet a central element of Socrates was lacking: the insistence that no moral life or true belief could justify poor arguments, vague concepts, or confusions.

It is this heritage of Socrates that Moore has resurrected with a moral earnestness that matches Kierkegaard's. Moore's faith in common sense, on the other hand, is strikingly at odds with Socrates' resolve to show up its confusions; and in Moore's whole approach to philosophic problems, as was shown before, there is something definitely academic; also, an un-Socratic loss of eloquence and, more important, of dimension.

Moore and Kierkegaard have become mentors of two different philosophic movements in which their partiality is crystallized. Socrates, in whom the extremes were fused, became the mentor of Antisthenes, the Cynic, and of Plato; Aristotle, Epicurus, and the Stoics; and all subsequent philosophers. His life was the life of dialogue, even to the exclusion of the lonely art of writing; and not only Plato but the history of Western thought records the dialogue he set in motion.

The analytic philosophers and the existentialists can no longer communicate with each other or with any truly different point of view; they have lost the art of dialogue.

Existentialism, like mysticism, is always in danger of becoming nothing but poor poetry, suggestive but arbitrary; or, when it renounces its poetic garbs, a sermon. The other type of thinking is in danger of degenerating into superficial criticastry of previous philosophers, void of real understanding, or it may culminate in the codification and rationalization of the common sense of an age.

Hegel offered some similar criticisms of the Enlightenment and of romanticism in the Preface of his *Phenomenology,* without naming them. Surely, the Enlightenment is the grandmother of positivism, and romanticism that of existentialism; and many of Hegel's comments are as timely one hundred and fifty years after he wrote them as they were in 1807. They are always timely because these two tendencies are timeless.

It may seem like an advance critique of Kierkegaard and Jaspers when Hegel speaks of those who want "not so much knowledge as edification," but Hegel's comments are applica-

ble to some men in every age: "The beautiful, the holy, the
eternal, religion, and love are the bait that is demanded to
arouse the desire to bite; not conceptual analysis but ecstasy,
not the coldly progressing necessity of the matter at hand but
fermenting enthusiasm."

Was Hegel, then, an analyst? No more so than Nietzsche,
whose repudiation of romanticism was frequently savage. In
principle, both took the stand of Socrates and Plato and Spinoza and protested against any bifurcation of intense experience and the analytic intellect.

The great philosopher is a poet with an intellectual conscience. If his imagination is too strong, it will outsoar his conscience. But if his conscience is too rigid, there will be no
vision. What is wanted is a wealth of intuitions, observations,
and insights, and the relentless passion to examine them. Under rational scrutiny, hunches are abandoned, insights modified, and observations found out to be partial. As Nietzsche
put it in one of his notes: "A very popular error: having the
courage of one's convictions; rather it is a matter of having
the courage for an *attack* on one's convictions!"

15. EMPIRICISM AS EMPIRICIDE.   The critical acumen and
scrupulous precision of analytic writing at its rare best cannot
be praised too highly; and yet the failings of this movement
are the consequences of its virtues. In the first place, these
virtues have become ends in themselves. Instead of employing
them to sift one's own wheat from one's chaff, one has abandoned any effort to grow wheat. Philosophy becomes a game
of skill, or a kind of shadowboxing. One attacks imaginary
views and arguments, ascribes them to a great philosopher, but
scarcely cares if the ascription is untenable. In fact, any sustained effort to determine what a great philosopher believed
is apt to be dismissed as "tombstone-polishing," to use one of
the favorite phrases of Professor Gilbert Ryle of Oxford.

Another consequence of the quest of precision is the flight
from rough and stony fields. Because the emotions, for example, tend to be a trifle messy and these men prefer to deal

with what is clean and neat, they have, on the whole, ignored large areas of experience and dealt very partially with art, religion, and morality.

Unquestionably, most so-called morality is a matter of habit, and in at least nine situations out of ten, members of the same social group will agree that they "know" right from wrong and good from evil. But occasionally some of us experience genuine perplexity. The analysts, continuing a trend long notable in British moral philosophy, have concentrated almost exclusively on habitual morality, avoiding moral perplexity, which is charged with emotion. Meanwhile, the existentialists leave out of account precisely what the analysts consider. Hence the difference in their maps.

Following in the footsteps of a long "empiricist" tradition, analytic philosophy shows little concern with aesthetic and religious experience. Usually, it ignores experience altogether and studies the relations between concepts, words, or propositions, without regard for the nonacademic experiences and problems from which these linguistic structures derive their meaning and significance.

Paradoxically, this has been the manner of empiricism from the start. The greatest empiricist yet, David Hume, in one of the finest works of this tradition and, beyond a doubt, the best it has contributed to the philosophy of religion, the famous *Dialogues Concerning Natural Religion,* a brilliant, witty, and incisive work, shows no awareness whatsoever of religious experience. Hume's critique of the argument for God's existence from the design of the world is unimpeachable: he shows its faulty logic. But what in all this is "empiricist"?

Many modern philosophers would reply: the thesis that all our ideas can be logically reconstructed from the single sense impressions of experience. This retort can mean one of two things. Either it is assumed that sense experience really consists of a series of distinct and clear impressions: in spite of Bergson and Gestalt psychology, this mechanistic fallacy is still so prevalent among philosophers that it is widely assumed that anyone who refuses to accept it must be unempirical. Or all this is condescendingly admitted: psychological reduction is out of the picture, and what counts is only logical reconstruction. A game, in other words. We see which of our ideas can be logically constructed out of single sense impressions. Who could object to that? But in that case, if we find ideas which cannot be reconstructed in this way, this is no longer an objection to ideas of this sort but a question mark concerning the significance of our game. And should empiricism really be defined as an attempt at logical reconstruction of our ideas out of elements which are, in fact, not the constituents of our experience? In that case we should ask again: but what in all this is "empiricist"?

In any case, empiricist philosophers down to the analysts of our day prefer not to discuss experience—prefer, in fact, not even to consider it. In this, the ordinary language philosophers and Carnap and his followers are as one. Could it be that the "empiricists," almost as much as Plato and the great metaphysicians, are at bottom otherworldly—motivated by the quest for security from the turmoil of experience? Is "empiricism" an attempt to escape from experience?

If "empiricism" resembles metaphysics in its flight from *this* world and its resolve to attain security in another, constructed world, this is not the first time that a movement of opposition has unwittingly taken over the most distinctive presuppositions of those whom it attacked. How similar the analysts are to the scholastics! How close "empiricism" is to rationalism!

Contemporary empiricism, no less than rationalism, strives for scientific precision. But can physics or mathematics furnish the norms for inquiries concerning art, religion, and morality? Or concerning ourselves? Because they cannot, the empiricists forsake experience and deal with probability instead, or analyze the arguments of others, or try, more and more, to settle messy empirical questions by recourse to ordinary language.

Thus the penchant for precision, in itself a virtue, has led more and more of the most brilliant young philosophers to devote their talents either to the otherworldly realms of logic or to high-level discussions of modern English usage. Conscious of the many blunders of the great philosophers, of their fallacies and follies, but without all love of a magnificent tradition, many of the brightest lose all contact with philosophy; and the aspiration for precision, not to speak of worldly motives, leads them to become consultants or computers for some corporation.

While the analysts thus seek a haven, the vast ocean of experience is left to the existentialists, who are not daunted by lack of precision. But, unlike Nietzsche and Wittgenstein, the existentialists from Kierkegaard to Heidegger lack the courage for an attack on their own convictions.

We need a new empiricism which neither flees experience nor ravishes it but tries to do justice to it. Why must we either ignore anguish or treat it as man's central experience? Why must we spurn experience, either because it is too messy or because it is not messy enough?

Allowing fully for the different purposes of Ryle's *Concept of Mind* and Heidegger's *Sein und Zeit,* are not both strangely remote from actual experience? Iris Murdoch in her little book on Sartre has said well: "The world of *The Concept of Mind* is the world in which people play cricket, cook cakes, make simple decisions, remember their childhood and go to the circus; not the world in which they commit sins, fall in love, say prayers or join the Communist Party" (35). And the world of existentialism is a world in which a man in dread who does not immediately realize what it is that he dreads, exults in the imprecision of his state of mind and takes it for a revelation of the Nothing. Neither positivism nor existentialism stoops to analyze confused states of mind; and since experience is for the most part confused, it is exposed like Oedipus to die of neglect. Let the philosopher beware!

16. PLATO'S VISION OF MAN. Great philosophies involve not only a conception of man as he is thought to be but also a vision of man as he ought to be. This is obvious in the case of the Cynics, Stoics, and Epicureans. It is scarcely less plain in the thought of Nietzsche and Spinoza. But it can also be shown in the work of Plato.

In his *Republic* the image of man's possible enhancement is central: the ideal commonwealth provides the necessary setting for it, and other forms of government are criticized because they prevent the development of the higher man and breed inferior types.

Most interpreters of Plato take it for granted that his metaphysics with its doctrine of two worlds is primary, that his theory of knowledge with its distinction between knowledge and belief is secondary, that his high esteem of mathematics and his apprehensions about art represent specific applications of his theory of knowledge; and his vision of what man might be is all but forgotten. But it was the image of the ideal man that marked the beginning of Plato's philosophy.

In the *Apology* of Socrates, we behold the ideal man of Plato, as yet unencumbered by metaphysics and epistemology. It is similar in *Crito* and the other early dialogues. It was the personality and life of Socrates no less than his teaching that suggested to Plato what man might be like, and converted him from writing poetry to writing philosophic dialogues.

Later contacts with Pythagoreans also made a deep impression on him: they believed in transmigration, in three types of men, in equality of men and women, and pursued mathematics and philosophy as means of salvation because these studies helped to elevate the soul above all earthly ties. The *Republic* describes a state in which each of the three Pythagorean types has its place: the Pythagoreans already had said that humanity could be divided, no less than those present at an Olympic game, into buyers and sellers, competitors, and —noblest of all—contemplators.

Plato's conviction that man ought to free himself from the tyranny of the senses and be ruled by reason was primary, and his interpretation of the four cardinal virtues explicates his central vision of what could be made of man. His ethics and psychology were primary and represented his original attempts to deal with the phenomenon of Socrates, and his attitudes toward art and mathematics, his distinction between knowledge and belief, and his hypostatizing of two worlds to correspond to these came later. Beginning with a contempt for unexamined beliefs and a thirst for certain knowledge, beginning with the ideal of a man who would be satisfied with nothing less, beginning with a contempt for the senses and an extreme admiration for reason, Plato arrived at his curious bifurcation of the world.

The bifurcation of the world is always rooted in a prior bifurcation of mankind and man. Wherever two worlds have been postulated, man was first divided into two parts—senses and reason, body and soul, phenomenon and noumenon—and often there were also thought to be two kinds of men: the mass and the elite. The doctrine of two worlds goes hand in hand with a superior valuation of the other world, the unseen one; and prior to Kant the central theme of all such teachings was the path by which a man could hope to reach this other world.

What makes Plato a philosopher, and not merely the founder of a quasi-religious sect, is that his metaphysics with its theory of Forms is based on logical argumentation. But the hypostatizing of the Forms, the bold assertion that there is another world in which they have their being, the depreciation of the world of sense in favor of this other world—all this is not required by logic.

The approach here suggested facilitates the solution of a puzzle which has plagued Plato scholars. In the *Phaedo,* within the framework of an unforgettable account of the last hours of Socrates and his death, Plato has Socrates discuss the soul in his last conversation, and among other things Socrates offers proofs of immortality and introduces the theory of Forms. A. E. Taylor and John Burnet argued that in view of the solemnity of the setting of this dialogue we must infer that Socrates himself said substantially what is here ascribed to him; but their suggestion has not found acceptance and may even be said to have been conclusively demolished by others. It is the consensus of almost all Plato scholars today that the agnosticism concerning any afterlife which finds such eloquent expression toward the end of the *Apology* reflects the views of the historical Socrates. In that case, however, it remains perplexing that Plato should have blandly mixed a faithful account of Socrates' last day and death with doctrines which bore no relation to Socrates at all. Yet most Plato scholars today are resigned to this assumption.

Probably, Plato's theory of Forms was initially inseparably connected with his conception of the relation of body and soul and with the person, rather than the explicit teaching, of Socrates. In the *Phaedo,* Plato has Socrates converse with two Pythagoreans, and the dialogue is narrated in the house of yet another Pythagorean, and there are many allusions to Pythagorean doctrines, beginning with explicit references to the Pythagorean conception of the body as the prison of the soul. The Pythagoreans in the dialogue do not fully understand their own ancient lore and ask Socrates to explain it to them. Perhaps Plato felt, when he encountered Pythagorean doctrines, that Socrates had been the most perfect embodiment of the Pythagorean ideal, much more impressive than any Pythagorean. Perhaps Socrates' complete equanimity in the face of death reminded him of the Pythagorean, originally Orphic, dictum that the body is the prison of the soul: death is not— may not be, cannot be—the end. There must be another world: the world of the soul, where the soul has its being before birth and after death. And having fallen back on these ancient religious ideas, Plato had made room for a world in which absolute justice and absolute beauty could have real existence instead of being mere concepts. His more strictly logical inquiries had convinced him of the crucial importance of these concepts, but the postulation of another world in which these "Ideas" were at home was not necessitated by logic. This theory had religious roots; but it was probably the impression that Socrates had made on him that led him to it.

The account here proposed receives important confirmation in one of Plato's later dialogues, the *Parmenides,* where the question is posed whether there must not be Forms or Ideas not only "of the just and the beautiful and the good, and of all that class" but also of man "or of fire and water" and, alas, of "such things as hair, mud, dirt, or anything else which is vile and paltry" (130). Plato found it hard to reconcile himself to any such conclusion; but what is most significant is that this very possibility occurred to him only late, as an after-thought. Plainly, it was not epistemology or logic that had led him to his theory of Forms to begin with. Rather, it had been reflection on man and his conduct, on body and soul and ethics —on man as he might and should be, on Socrates.

It would be silly to attempt a derivation of all of Plato's arguments from his conception of the ideal man: a problem once posed carries its own logic with it, and Plato was at all times singularly willing to face problems that came up and to try to advance them toward a solution. But once we go beyond such separate investigations and consider Plato's over-all philosophy we find a comprehensive world, and at its center Plato's vision of what man might be. Single arguments can be appraised without all reference to this, but Plato's thought as an organic whole cannot.

What has all this to do with existentialism or positivism? They, too, involve a vision of what man might be. In the case of existentialism this is obvious. Kierkegaard said of his own work as a whole: "This is a literary work in which the whole thought is the task of becoming a Christian." In Jaspers' books the author's appeal to the reader to become a different kind of man is scarcely less strong, while in Heidegger a superficial reader might conceivably ignore it—at the cost of failing utterly to comprehend what Heidegger attempts to do. The contrast between two modes of life, one authentic and one unauthentic, is of the essence of existentialism. But that positivism, too, involves a normative vision of man, that has to be shown.

17. THE BRITISH VISION OF MAN. What emotion is it that prompts some philosophers when they disparage the emotions much as Plato once disparaged sense experience? Again we are confronted with a bifurcation of man; again reason is on one side; but the emotions have taken the place of the senses.

Plato's attitude toward the emotions had been more tolerant. We need only recall what he says of love and its relation to philosophy in the *Symposion* and the *Phaedrus*. The dissociation of intellect and emotion would have been incomprehensible to him.

In its extreme form, the dissociation of intellect and emotion was the triumph of logical positivism; but in a more subtle form it has distinguished a good deal of British philosophy for centuries. Compare Berkeley with Spinoza, Hume with Voltaire, or Ryle with Sartre. The issue is not merely stylistic. Although Spinoza, Kant, and Hegel wrote less gracefully than Berkeley, Hume, and Ryle, their major philosophic works were, in a sense, less academic: they did not hesitate to deal with questions and experiences in which human emotions are involved. And that is why they have excited poets, theologians, social scientists, and wide circles of readers rather more than any purely philosophic work by any British thinker since Locke.

Even as Plato's disparagement of the senses prevented him from doing justice to certain areas of experience, notably art, and possibly impeded the development of the natural sciences, the fear of the realm of the emotions has kept many philosophers from doing justice to art and religion, and has led to a bizarre psychology. It is not as if Hume and Bentham opposed psychology; on the contrary, much of their philosophy is psychology, but inadequate psychology.

It is of the essence of empiricism and its offspring, positivism, that small, single questions are pursued rather than a comprehensive vision. These investigations cannot be reduced to a central image of man. Many an individual in this tradition does not have "a philosophy" in the sense in which Aristotle or Spinoza, Kant or Hegel, and even Plato and Nietzsche did. Nevertheless, the empiricist tradition offers more than single inquiries or monographs: it adds up to a philosophic world, and in this a vision of man is once again found at the center.

Of course, one cannot safely generalize about British philosophy, and what follows is at best suggestive and not literally applicable to all the thinkers in this great tradition. With this reservation, the man that is here made the norm of ethics and epistemology is strikingly different from Plato's Socrates.

Compared to Plato or the people of the Romance countries, he is exceedingly unemotional. He has a feeling for nature as far as it is visually apprehended, but much less for music; a strong sense of propriety and little sympathy with mysticism; and not much appreciation of the difference between moral perplexity and indecency, passion and bad manners. This may help to explain why this philosophy has never won many adherents in France, Italy, Spain, Latin America, Russia, or Germany, and why it has some influence today in Scandinavia.

One of the most important functions of philosophy is to scrutinize beliefs and arguments, and to exercise a certain skill in showing up fallacies. From Berkeley and Hume to Broad and Ryle, British philosophy has excelled in this work. It is easy to underestimate its significance, and nonphilosophers have generally given in to this temptation. The charge against this tradition should not be that it has been too critical—on the contrary, its critical power has been its chief excellence—but that it has avoided an awareness of its relevance to experience, or indeed of the nature of the experiences to which various beliefs and arguments owe their significance. In this they have been un-Socratic and aloof.

Professor Broad of Cambridge has given us the classical portrait of this image of man; and at the same time he has shown that he is a philosopher who can smile, if not laugh: "It is perhaps fair to warn the reader," he says in the Preface to his *Five Types of Ethical Theory*, "that my range of experience, both practical and emotional, is rather exceptionally narrow even for a don. Fellows of Colleges, in Cambridge at any rate, have few temptations to heroic virtue or spectacular vice; and I could wish that the rest of mankind were as fortunately situated. Moreover, I find it difficult to excite myself very much over right and wrong in practice. I have, *e.g.,* no clear idea of what people have in mind when they say that they labour under a sense of sin; yet I do not doubt that, in some cases, this is a genuine experience, which seems vitally important to those who have it, and may really be of profound ethical and metaphysical significance. I realize that these practical and emotional limitations may make me blind to certain important aspects of moral experience. Still, people who feel very strongly about any subject are liable to over-estimate its importance in the scheme of things. A healthy appetite for righteousness, kept in due control by good manners, is an excellent thing; but to 'hunger and thirst after' it is often merely a symptom of spiritual diabetes."

With its delightful humor this passage has a personal quality, like a portrait that shows the master's hand. What it shows is not the features of a single individual alone but an image of man that helps us understand a great tradition. Nothing like this passage could have been written by Plato, but it recalls Hume's famous autobiographic sketch: "I was, I say, a man of mild dispositions, of command of temper, of an open, social and cheerful humour, capable of attachment, but little susceptible of enmity, and of great moderation in all my passions. Even my love of literary fame, my ruling passion, never soured my temper." And Hume might well have added, like Broad: "and I could wish that the rest of mankind were as fortunately situated."

G. E. Moore's "Autobiography" may help complete the picture. He tells us modestly, as always, how fellowships and invitations extracted "a respectable amount of work" from him. "*Respectable,* I think; but, I am afraid, not more than respectable. . . . There is almost always something which I would much rather be doing than working: more often than not, *what* I would much rather be doing is reading some novel or some history or biography—some *story,* in fact; for stories, whether purporting to be true or avowedly mere fiction, have a tremendous fascination for me. The consequence is that I have always been having constantly to struggle to force myself to work, and constantly suffering from a more or less bad conscience for not succeeding better. This state of things seems to me so natural, that *I find it difficult to believe that it is not the same with everyone.*" (Italics in the last sentence are mine.)

Allowing for a dash of Socratic irony, the contrast with Socrates' *Apology* cannot be missed. Or with Plato. Or consider Nietzsche's mode of life. Tortured by migraine headaches, frequently knocked out by a rebellious stomach, cursed with almost blind eyes, pensioned off without any commitment, he writes day and night. He has every possible excuse for not working, but nothing else matters to him, not even the fearful price which his relentless work exacts from him in sheer physical pain.

What stories has Moore been reading, what novels, what biographies, that he should "find it difficult to believe" that his own disposition is not the quintessence of human nature? Certainly not the writers whom the existentialists admire: not Malraux, nor Dostoevsky. Nor the lives of Alexander, Hannibal, or Caesar; nor of Rembrandt or Van Gogh; or, to take gentler souls, of Mozart or of Schubert. What Moore has, or has not, read does not invalidate his often shrewd analyses of faulty arguments. But perhaps his "range of experience," to use Broad's apt phrase, explains some oddities of his ethics.

This conclusion is corroborated by the affectionate but ironic portrait of the young Moore in Lord Keynes' delightful essay "My Early Beliefs." Consider the following passage, for example: "How did we know what states of mind were good? This was a matter of direct inspection, of direct unanalysable intuition about which it was useless and impossible to argue. In that case who was right when there was a difference of opinion? . . . It might be that some people had an acuter sense of judgment, just as some people can judge a vintage port and others cannot. On the whole, so far as I remember, this explanation prevailed. In practice, victory was with those who could speak with the greatest appearance of clear, undoubting conviction and could best use the accents of infallibility. Moore at this time was a master of this method—greeting one's remarks with a gasp of incredulity—*Do you really think that,* an expression of face as if to hear such a thing said reduced him to a state of wonder verging on imbecility, with his mouth wide open and wagging his head in the negative so violently that his hair shook. *Oh!* he would say, goggling at you as if either you or he must be mad; and no reply was possible." Keynes' whole essay is relevant and, moreover, one of the finest bits of high comedy ever written.

The point at issue transcends any one person or clique. The whole philosophical tradition of which Moore forms an important link is not nourished on the reading mentioned; and reading would be the most obvious means to remedy a narrow range of experience, if that were considered pertinent. But the movement that is generally called empiricist really spurns experience.

It might be said that there are two traditions in British philosophy: the donnish strain represented by Broad and Moore does not encompass Bentham, Mill, or Russell. Russell, with a hundred volumes to his credit, obviously does not have to "force" himself "to work"; and, like Bentham and Mill, too, he clearly does not "find it difficult to excite" himself about justice, but considers it his duty to endorse social reforms. Still, there is a marked difference between these men, too, and Plato, Nietzsche, or Spinoza. The 'zeal for social reforms does not sensitize a Russell, Mill, or Bentham to the experience of a moral quandary—on the contrary—and these men have shown no more concern with aesthetic or religious experience than Berkeley and Hume, Moore, Broad, and Ryle. The difference between the two traditions of British philosophy is not as profound as it seems at first glance. We are justified in speaking of a single tradition, with the proviso that some of these men, unlike others, have taken a lively interest in social reforms.

The intense experiences of individuals—the lust for knowledge, the passion to create, the deep disturbance of the confrontation with great works of art, moral despair, or any inkling of the numinous—all this is foreign to empiricism. The world of empiricism is a desiccated world.

Personally, of course, some empiricists may be emotional, and it is a fact that some British philosophers love music. Nor should we criticize Plato for not having been sensuous (which, in fact, he may have been). The point is rather that large areas of experience are ignored.

Positivism and existentialism operate with different normative conceptions of man and make different contributions to the philosophic map. The existentialists concentrate almost exclusively on the most intense experiences.

The analysts are generally most reliable in single sharp analyses; but when they attempt to construct a larger picture, whether of ethics or the mind, their partiality stands revealed. Existentialism, on the other hand, suffers from two great dangers. First, it tends to ignore the ordinary for the extraordinary and to mistake the uncommon for the rule. Secondly, it does not demand of itself, let alone achieve, the greatest possible clarity of which its often difficult subject matter is capable.

Obviously, existentialism is more interesting for nonphilosophers, while professionals can learn more from the analysts.

18. DONNISH DOUBT. Autonomous philosophy, not dominated by theology, mysticism, or the desire for mere edification, has flourished only among the Greeks, the British, and the Germans—and, to a lesser extent, the French. All the great Western philosophers whose thought is recorded in our histories belong to one or another of these cultures, except only Spinoza, who was born in Holland of a Jewish family that had come from Portugal. Like Descartes and Leibniz, he was a European phenomenon; but the striking fact remains that all the other great philosophers, including Leibniz and Descartes, belonged to cultures which developed continuous philosophical traditions, and there are only four of these. The Romans produced no major philosopher but were in the main satisfied with Greek schools; and in the European Middle Ages, philosophy was fused with theology or mysticism as it always was in India. In the United States philosophy is thriving, but as yet the country has produced no Plato, no Spinoza, no Kant; and there has not yet developed a tradition comparable to the great succession of philosophers from Thales to the Stoics, from Leibniz to Nietzsche, from Descartes to Sartre, or from Bacon to Russell.

Of the four philosophical traditions, each has its distinctive character. French and British philosophy, for example, are not only utterly different today but have always been quite different. In France philosophy has been so closely allied with literature that it is nearly impossible to tell them apart. In fact, French philosophy has had a slightly existentialist flavor from the beginning. Montaigne, Pascal, Montesquieu, Voltaire, Rousseau, Comte (who tried to turn positivism into a religion), Bergson, and Sartre represent a remarkable continuity in this respect; and even Descartes does not fall entirely outside it. In his *Meditations* doubt never becomes merely academic.

To be sure, Descartes says that his doubt shall not affect his practice; but that is largely what Lovejoy once called, in another context, "the usual lightning-rod against ecclesiastical thunderbolts" (18). Admittedly, Descartes' doubt never becomes fully existential any more than did, say, Voltaire's: their ethics remains untouched; but in this respect only Nietzsche marks a decisive break with the past. In any case, the *Meditations* are not only superficially cast in an autobiographic form: the decision to doubt marks a turning point in Descartes' life, a resolve not to go on living as before, a dedication to meditate and criticize, the beginning of a new, a philosophic life.

British philosophy, by contrast, has cultivated donnish doubt, a philosophy of ingenuity and virtuosity which prides itself on its irrelevance to life. This is not yet true of Bacon, Hobbes, and Locke. Berkeley is the first great exponent of the new tradition in philosophy, and in sheer ingenuity and virtuosity he has perhaps never been equaled. What was with him a brilliant tour de force, Hume, a generation later, turned into a method and an influential precedent.

It is only in British philosophy—certainly not among the Greeks, the Germans, or the French—that merely intellectual doubt, unaccompanied by any deep emotion, and playful perplexity in the presence of preposterous puzzles have established themselves as a cultural tradition and achieved a degree of intellectual and literary excellence which commands profound respect.

Alas, "philosophical *problems*" remain, as Abraham Kaplan

has put it, "after we have disentangled ourselves from the philosophical *puzzles.* . . . One can resolve Ryle's dilemmas—as he conceives of such resolution—in virtual ignorance of the content of science and in virtual innocence of the depths of artistic, moral and religious experience. But knots yet remain to be untangled. . . . Ryle resolves the fatalistic 'What is, always was to be' into a tautology and a false imputation of logical inevitability. This is excellent so far as it goes. . . . But there is a problem which the puzzle conceals: assessing the moral implications of the fact that our conduct is enmeshed in a network of causal necessitation. This is the problem faced by Spinoza, say; and it is a problem which calls for a knowledge of psychodynamics and society, as Zeno's does of mathematics." And Kaplan also notes, rightly, that "the growth of knowledge, and reflection on our experience, generate new concepts and force changes on old ones; philosophy periodically sums up and systematizes such growth" (645 f.).

"Pure" philosophy is a chimera. Whether philosophic reflection takes off from confusions of past philosophers or from those of ordinary people, from problems posed by a work of literature, like *Antigone,* or from problems that arise in one's own life, the decision to confine oneself to linguistic analysis is arbitrary. Yet there are a great many British and American philosophers who accept the conclusion of Ryle's pioneering essay on "Systematically Misleading Expressions"; namely, that the diagnosis of such expressions "is what philosophical analysis is, and that this is the sole and whole function of philosophy." The motivation of this curious view is at least fourfold.

First, a careful analysis of the terms in which a problem is posed often does effect considerable clarification, and occasionally it leads, if not to the dissolution of the problem, to a fruitful reformulation. A hopelessly big problem, for example, may be broken down into several subproblems. So far, so good. Here the analytic philosophers can make, and have made, fine contributions; and no critic need claim that this is not an important part of philosophy.

Secondly, analytic philosophers frequently remark in con-

versation that the problems that remain after linguistic analysis are better handled by scientists. Indeed, anyone who refuses to restrict philosophy to linguistic analysis is generally
met with the charge—not to say, the ploy—that he evidently
wants philosophers to solve scientific problems in an armchair, without venturing into the laboratory. If no scientists
at the present time are in fact handling certain problems better than philosophers—or, for that matter, at all—we are generally told that we must wait for such scientists—psychologists,
for example—to appear in the future.

This calls for a twofold answer. First, by the same token,
we might just as well desist from linguistic analysis, too, and
wait for superior philologists to do a better job a hundred years
hence. The position of the ordinary language philosophers is
inconsistent at this point. On the one hand, they tell us that
philosophers have no business making empirical statements
which are confirmable by observation; on the other hand, their
articles consist largely of empirical statements that are confirmable by observing how educated people employ certain
words. The objection here is not to what the analysts are doing
but only to what they tell other philosophers they must not
do. Their position, though inconsistent, is understandable:
they are ashamed of the false empirical statements made by
previous philosophers; they see philosophy gradually retreating
as science advances; and they would like to stop this process
by retreating once and for all to a nook of traditional philosophy where they feel relatively safe from the advances of
science. An unsympathetic critic might say that they have
picked an area that is so dull and unrewarding that the chance
that any scientist might follow them to take it over is indeed
exceedingly small. But a more sympathetic critic might well
admit that the best practitioners are sometimes doing interesting work, exhibiting a skill that no philologist without a training in philosophy is likely to excel. This leads to the second
part of our answer.

While it is true that the acquisition of pertinent empirical
information requires some specialized competence, the use of
empirical data to advance philosophic problems toward a solu-

tion also requires some synopsis, some evaluation, and some training in philosophy. The philosopher who does not want to confine himself to linguistic analysis must acquire some non-philosophic competence, too, depending on the area of his study, in order to be able to evaluate and utilize the findings of nonphilosophic scholars. If he submits to the necessary discipline, he may be able to contribute something that nonphilosophic specialists are not at all likely to bring off. In this context it should be noted that most of the great philosophers were scholars in fields other than philosophy, too. And one may suspect that ordinary language philosophy proves attractive to so many bright young men because one can participate in most discussions and even publish contributions without developing any extraphilosophic competence.

Third, many of the philosophers who would confine philosophy to linguistic analysis are obsessed by the distinction between the moral philosopher, or analyst of moral terms, and the moralist—although almost all the great moral philosophers of the past were moralists, too. They fail to see the distinction between the moralist and the preacher. But we should not confound preaching with the careful and detailed development of a view and its implications, whether in morals or elsewhere.

Fourth, it would seem that a strong element of conformism plays some part in the motivation of the view that philosophers must confine themselves to linguistic analysis. There is a deep reluctance to stick out one's neck: there is safety in numbers, in belonging to a group, in employing a common method, and in not developing a position of one's own that would bring one into open conflict with more people than would be likely to be pleased. There is safety, too, in divorcing doubt from life and in maintaining an untouched and tranquil center outside philosophic scrutiny—a fortress from which, to use the current phrase, one "does" philosophy. One also plays the violin and loves one's wife, but one keeps these things separate.

Until recently, most British philosophers felt called upon to make respectable their radicalism in the theory of knowledge by showing that it had no influence whatever on

their morals. One was reminded of one of Jonathan Swift's
"Thoughts on Religion": "Violent zeal for truth hath an hundred and one odds to be either petulancy, ambition, or pride."
Also, of Swift's advice that, confronted with doubts, I should
see to it that "they have no influence on the conduct of my
life." But in the current phase of British philosophy scarcely
any doubt at all seems left.

19. WITTGENSTEIN. Against this background one may understand one of the great anomalies of modern philosophy.
Wittgenstein, a Viennese who succeeded to Moore's chair at
Cambridge but continued to write in German, has been almost completely ignored on the Continent but is hailed as the
greatest philosopher since Kant by many of the Oxonians
whom he himself considered "more linguists than philosophers"
(*AJP*, 80).

The son of a Roman Catholic mother and a Protestant father of Jewish descent, he was baptized in the Catholic Church;
but according to the illuminating biographical sketch of Professor Von Wright, his first successor at Cambridge, "certainly
he did not have a Christian faith." Indeed, he "was not, it
seems clear, in any conventional sense a religious man" (*AJP*,
78). But unlike Spinoza, Kant, and Nietzsche, whom he
equaled in his passionate intensity and his dedicated, lonely,
simple way of life, he did not in any way criticize traditional
religious beliefs. Indeed, one of his closest disciples, Miss Anscombe, who is also one of his executors and the editor and
translator of his posthumous books, is a loyal Roman Catholic,
while another disciple is an orthodox Calvinist, and a third has
embraced Episcopalianism. There would be nothing at all
strange about that, if Wittgenstein's philosophy had been
clearly academic and detached from life. But almost everything about Wittgenstein was unacademic, even anti-academic.

When he inherited his father's fortune, he gave it away; and
when his vastly influential *Tractatus Logico-Philosophicus* was
published in England, the Latin title being due to Moore, Wittgenstein was a village schoolmaster in Lower Austria. Later

he served as a gardener's assistant with the monks in another village. And no sooner had he become a professor at Cambridge than he decided to leave for London to serve as a hospital porter during the "blitz." In spite of his high professional competence in mathematics, he read little academic philosophy. As a young man, he found some inspiration in Schopenhauer. "From Spinoza, Hume, and Kant he said that he could get only occasional glimpses of understanding," according to Von Wright, who adds: "I do not think that he could have enjoyed Aristotle or Leibniz, two great logicians before him. But it is significant that he did read and enjoy Plato." And he was deeply impressed by Augustine, Kierkegaard, Dostoevsky, and Tolstoy. Of such a philosopher one might expect that his greatest influence would be on the *lives* of other men. Yet it is his impact on *academic* philosophy that is almost unequaled.

Wittgenstein had learned philosophy from men like Russell, taken seriously their problems, and suffered through them. But if you were in earnest when you asked, for example, whether there are other minds besides your own, that was an unbearable perplexity, and something had to be done about it. The young Wittgenstein proposed the so-called verification principle and tried to show that the most perplexing philosophic questions were "nonsense." And, as we have seen, "the author of the *Tractatus* thought he had solved all philosophical problems." (Von Wright, 536; cf. § 11 above.) Probably, one of the things that soon made him uneasy about this fond hope was confrontation with a generation of positivists who accepted his ideas almost as dogmas. Most men become convinced that they are right only after other people agree with them. But some of us find nothing more unsettling than our own words on the lips of others. Suddenly, we become keenly aware of what we failed to say.

"When the 'Verification Principle' was fashionable in many quarters, he remarked at the Moral Sciences Club: 'I used at one time to say that, in order to get clear how a certain sentence is used, it was a good idea to ask oneself the question: How would one try to verify such an assertion? But that's just one way among others. . . . For example, another question which is often very useful is to ask oneself: How is this word learnt? How would one set about teaching a child to use this word? But some people have turned this suggestion about asking for the verification into a dogma . . .'" (*AJP*, 79).

Soon Wittgenstein's second suggestion—"Don't ask for the meaning [analysis], ask for the use" (cited by Wisdom, 117) —was all but turned "into a dogma" at Cambridge and Oxford, fused with Moore's regard for common sense—and much to his surprise, Wittgenstein had designed a new pastime for the dons. His cure for a profound affliction lent itself perfectly to social cultivation. One could talk about the use of words, brilliantly even, without ever having suffered on account of any philosophic problem.

According to Moore, who attended Wittgenstein's lectures at Cambridge from 1930 to 1933, Wittgenstein himself heralded the advent of his later phase by announcing "that there was now, in philosophy, a 'kink' in the 'development of human thought'" and "that a 'new method' had been discovered, as had happened when 'chemistry was developed out of alchemy'; and that it was now possible for the first time that there should be 'skilful' philosophers, though of course there had been in the past 'great philosophers.' He went on to say that though philosophy had now been 'reduced to a matter of skill,' yet this skill, like other skills, is very difficult to acquire" (26). One can hardly blame his younger colleagues for trying as hard as they did to learn and practice this new method.

The nature of this new method made the development which he found so uncongenial all but inevitable. Here is a highly sympathetic picture of his own practice of this method: "Nearly every single thing said was easy to follow and was usually not the sort of thing anyone would wish to dispute." But "it was hard to see where all this often rather repetitive concrete detailed talk was leading to—how the examples were interconnected and how all this bore on the problem which one was accustomed to put to oneself in abstract terms" (*AJP*, 75). "At first one didn't see where all the talk was leading to. . . . And then, sometimes, one did, suddenly. All at once, sometimes, the solution to one's problem became clear and everything fell into place" (*AJP*, 77).

Moore relates that Wittgenstein "also said that he was not trying to teach us any new facts: that he would only tell us 'trivial' things—'things which we all know already'; but that the difficult thing was to get a 'synopsis' of these trivialities, and that our 'intellectual discomfort' can only be removed by a synopsis of *many* trivialities . . ." (27). The danger of this sort of thing, when it is practiced by lesser men, hardly needs to be spelled out.

Readers of Wittgenstein's posthumously published *Philosophical Investigations,* however, will agree that in *his* hands the many more or less trivial examples which succeed each other indefatigably come to a point again and again, and that these points, though often very simple, sometimes spell liberation from futile problems. He weans us from looking for definitions of the supposed essence of games, for example: "Do not say: 'They *must* have something in common; else they would not be called "games"'—but *look* whether all of them have something in common. . . . And the result of this reflection is: we behold a complicated net of similarities which overlap and intersect" (66). And Wittgenstein introduces the term "family resemblances" (67). This, too, may seem to be a trivial point and hardly worth making—unless you have spent years trying to define the essence of religion or philosophy, of the good or the beautiful. To see the enormous philosophical significance of this simple point, one needs only to read the discussion about beauty in one of Plato's most charming dialogues, the *Greater Hippias.*

Wittgenstein's approach may often seem needlessly indirect: at times a brief straightforward argument might spell a great relief. But he wants to communicate the experience of his flight. (Cf. §§ 5 ff. above. They were written independently of Wittgenstein's Preface, which makes some very similar points.) Above all, to cite his Preface: "I should not want my writing to relieve others from thinking. Rather, if it were possible, stimulate someone to thoughts of his own."

20. WITTGENSTEIN AND SOCRATES. The similarities are obvious by now. If Moore and Kierkegaard were each only half a Socrates (§14), Wittgenstein fused, far better than either of them, the existential pathos and the analytic carefulness of Socrates; he also wanted to teach a method rather than specific results; and the last quotation is, of course, the quintessence of Socrates. Finally, Wittgenstein, too, was in the best sense of that word a man possessed.

It is his *influence* that first awakens us to the important differences. Many English-speaking philosophers have come to call philosophic only those problems which disappear after the kind of linguistic analysis taught by Wittgenstein. German and French philosophers as well as most men who are not professional philosophers have no inclination to accept this usage nor much interest in the work of those who do. As a result, Wittgenstein has, in effect, removed philosophy from the market place.

He was not altogether innocent of this development. He himself confined his teachings to a few professionals and deliberately excluded many who would have liked to hear him. No doubt, he was motivated by his very seriousness; and we need only contrast his attitude with that of Heidegger, who fills the aula of his university as well as two other large auditoriums to which his lectures are carried by a public address system, to realize that Wittgenstein, who stressed discussion, was not as far from Socrates even in these matters as might appear at first glance. Nor was he as oracular as Heidegger. And yet, compared to Socrates, he *was* oracular, secretive, and esoteric.

Moreover, the problems that concerned Wittgenstein were those studied by some of his British predecessors—and the most academic of these. He took these problems terribly seriously, but not many people could be expected to do likewise. And whatever one says about the foundations of mathematics or about sense data, and whatever reasons one considers best for saying that sometimes I *know* that you are angry or bored, at that level our most persistent quandaries are ignored, the challenge to change one's life is not heeded, and a void remains—to be filled, unfortunately, without the benefit of philosophy.

Whether it is Kierkegaard that rushes in, extolling the "absurd," or rather common sense, whether it is Calvinism or Catholicism or the fashions of the day, philosophy has abdicated its responsibility.

Wittgenstein, like Socrates, compared the philosopher with a physician. Their differences can be clarified further in terms of this metaphor. According to Wittgenstein, "The philosopher treats a question—like a disease" (255). "There is no *one* method of philosophy, but there are methods—as it were, different therapies" (133). "Wittgenstein once said that he *'holds no opinions in philosophy'* and, again that he tries to remove *'a feeling of puzzlement, to cure a sort of mental cramp'*" (Wisdom, 169).

To vary the metaphor, problems are like nightmares, and one cannot compromise with them. Wittgenstein writes: "The clarity for which we strive is indeed *complete* clarity. But that means merely that philosophic problems ought to disappear *completely*. The real discovery is that which enables me to stop philosophizing whenever I want to" (133). Having a problem is like being caught in a dream. I must wake up and get out of the problem completely. The image of being caught in a room recurs several times (e.g., *AJP*, 77, 78)—most powerfully in the *Investigations:* "What is your aim in philosophy? —To show the fly the way out of the fly-bottle" (309); "An *image* held us imprisoned. And we could not get out, for it lay in our language which merely seemed to repeat it to us, inexorably" (115). And this metaphor, too, reminds one of a Kafkaesque nightmare: "We feel as if we had to fix a torn spider web with our fingers" (106). The diagnosis is always the same: "The questions that concern us originate, as it were, when language idles, not when it works" (132). The disease is due to a queer use of language—words like queer and odd recur often in Wittgensteinian philosophy—and the cure is always the same, too. We ask how the key terms are used and how we acquired their use.

The implication is—more emphatically in the works of most of his followers, who are also indebted to Moore: ordinary language is a pristine paradise of clarity, and confusion is an occupational disease of philosophers who misuse language more or less systematically. One disciple, Professor John Wisdom, the incumbent of Moore's and Wittgenstein's chair at Cambridge, repudiates this notion; for example, in his essay on "Philosophical Perplexity" in which he says: "With horrible ingenuity Moore can rapidly reduce any metaphysical theory to a ridiculous story. For he is right, they are false—only there *is* good in them, poor things." Going quite expressly beyond Wittgenstein, who "too much represents them as merely symptoms of linguistic confusion," Wisdom proposes that they are "also symptoms of linguistic penetration" (41).

"But the philosopher must pacify everyone," Wisdom says (46)—and there's the rub. This half-humorous but deeply anti-Socratic remark, made in passing, comes uncomfortably close to being the motto of Wisdom's philosophy. Far from attacking the confusions of ordinary language which he concedes in principle, Wisdom wants to "pacify those philosophers who are pleased with" metaphysical statements (46); and his famous essay on "Gods" culminates in an attempt to pacify the religious.

Wittgenstein confined his attention to the confusions of philosophers and tried to clear them up; Wisdom occasionally suggests that "there *is* good in them, poor things." Unlike Socrates, neither attacks the fateful confusions of theologians, statesmen, and whatever other oracles we have. It was by concentrating on the latter, and by exposing them in public, that Socrates invited that hostility which led to his trial and condemnation on the charges of impiety and corrupting youth.

The point at issue here is not Socrates' courage but the patent fact that confusion is not merely an occupational disease of philosophers, and that a philosopher can be of some service by exposing the rank confusions of nonphilosophers. If he doesn't, nobody else will.

Confusion among our politicians reaches to the very top, and muddles about the meaning of democracy, God, and good are common. Professional philosophers may wonder whether to stress liberty or equality in analyzing democracy, but our so-called statesmen often talk as if the essence of democracy were theism, as if its most potent weapon were prayer, and as if all opposition to democracy stemmed from atheism. Therefore, a man writing on political philosophy abdicates his most important responsibility if he confines himself *exclusively* to analyzing the confusions of some of his colleagues. If he thinks that ordinary men, including politicians and theologians, are less confused than Plato, Aristotle, Hobbes, or Mill, he is simply wrong as a matter of fact.

In their moral and religious beliefs and their attempts to state and defend these, most men contradict themselves even without the benefit of Socrates' persistent questions. Nor are all their confusions due to departures from ordinary language. The many conflicting uses of words like democracy, equality, freedom, God, and good are both ever new sources and faithful mirrors of the confusions encountered among ordinary people.

It is worth emphasizing that most things worth saying by a philosopher can be said in plain ordinary language; that some philosophers have had recourse to needless jargon; and that such jargon is very apt to lead to gross confusion. The same point applies to literary criticism and sociology. Reading a great deal of such prose, one often has to ask oneself as a matter of honesty: What does this mean in plain language? And the answer is often devastating.

For all that, one need not embrace what Bertrand Russell stigmatizes as "The Cult of 'Common Usage.'" Without accepting all the mordant objections to it which he has assembled in three witty and malicious essays, one may safely agree with him that this cult "makes almost inevitable the perpetuation among philosophers of the muddle-headedness they have taken over from common sense" (166). And one may add, as Russell does not: especially in religion.

Wittgenstein said: "Philosophy must not in any way, however slight, interfere with the ordinary use of language; in the end, philosophy can only describe it. . . . It leaves everything as it is" (124). But if a philosopher exposes the confusions of ordinary discourse about God or democracy, he may occasionally find it helpful to introduce novel distinctions and, more rarely, new terms, though new terms should be mere mnemonic devices. And in an important and obvious sense, a philosopher like Socrates, Spinoza, or Kant does *not* leave "everything as it is."

If Wittgenstein had a tendency to be too respectful before
the wisdom of simple people and perhaps actually felt some
slight nostalgia for the strong faith of Augustine or at least
Kierkegaard's faith in faith, Socrates, albeit in the market
place, went to the opposite extreme and tended to view with
scorn his intellectual inferiors. He came close to despising the
common people, and one might well call him arrogant—if that
were not an understatement for that confidence in his mission
which found expression in his *Apology,* and if his subordination of his whole existence to his mission were not the epitome
of humility. He had no personal life at all: his life was the life
of dialogue, and the aim of every dialogue was to turn common men into uncommon men. He did not want them to return
unchanged, nor did he wish to convert them to his own views.
He wanted them to become superior, each in his own way.
Such superiority, however, involved some break with the religion and morality of their elders.

Not only Antisthenes and Aristippus and Plato were his pupils, but also Aristotle, Zeno, and Epicurus—and Descartes and
Spinoza, Hume and Kant. All philosophers have in their various ways responded to his call. In Nietzsche we find Socrates'
protestant spirit and sarcasm; in Mill, the concern for free inquiry; in Moore, the passion for intellectual cleanliness; in
Kierkegaard, the existential pathos; in Jaspers, the opposition
to any definitive philosophy; and in Wittgenstein, the search
for a new method, the revolt against tradition, and—more obviously in his life than in his writings—the nonconformist. But
Wittgenstein's hard-won techniques still await sustained employment in the service of that idea for which Socrates died:
"The unexamined life is not worth living."

21. FOLLOWERS.   The difference between great philosophers
who disagree is perhaps less considerable than that which separates them from their followers. Members of philosophic
schools or coteries live on what others have seen, and the dis-

ciple usually applies his master's insights with a confidence which, most of the time, the master lacked.

The adherent of a philosopher is often a man who at first did not understand him at all and then staked several years on a tireless attempt to prove to himself that he did not lack the ability to gain an understanding. By the end of that time he sees clearly that his master's critics simply fail to understand him.

Whether one becomes a follower of Wittgenstein or Jaspers, Heidegger or Carnap, Thomas, Kierkegaard, or Hegel is almost accidental in some cases: what all such followers have in common is that after their initial great expenditure no capital remains for a second, third, or fourth investment of comparable magnitude, let alone a novel enterprise.

What such people rarely realize is that with equal effort they themselves could easily rebut their present strictures of their master's rivals. They could protest the crude misunderstandings of Heidegger with the very voice with which they now rebut extraordinary misconceptions of the ordinary language movement.

What has been suggested here about the two revolts against traditional philosophy will not convince the followers of either movement, even as their criticisms have failed to persuade the Thomists. Followers are people with no wish to be convinced, and great philosophers rarely understand the criticisms urged against them.

There are many more who are neither great philosophers nor followers and who stand appalled at the present situation in philosophy. There may also be some who would agree with André Gide "that the importance of . . . a new explanation of certain phenomena is not gauged only by its accuracy, but also, and above all, by the impetus it gives to the mind . . . by the new vistas it opens and the barriers it breaks down, by the weapons it forges. It is important that it should propose something new and, at the same time, oppose what is old" (77). If that should apply in some small measure to the present profile in counterpoint of two revolts against traditional philosophy, how much truer is it when applied to these revolts themselves!

III. TRUTH, LANGUAGE, AND EXPERIENCE

22.

Truth

What is truth? Something of which we rarely speak;
something some men seek;
something flouted by those who lie;
something of which Christ said, it is I;
something without which one goes to hell;
something judges expect one to tell;
a word of honor, a word of praise,
but not a very transparent phrase.

Truth does not exist, it is merely discussed,
but true is whatever we can trust,
whether a man or a piece of gold,
a Titian or something we are told,
a likeness or something we are taught—
and the noun, the truth, is an afterthought.

True and False

Propositions and pearls
and answers and girls
can be true or false,
while a Vienna waltz

and north and blue
can only be true:
there is no false north,
waltz, blue, and so forth;
but a true politician
is as false as a false proposition.

23. THE ASPIRATION FOR TRUTH.   What is the aspiration for truth that animates the philosopher, and not only the philosopher? What does he really want?

Man resents convention and wants to escape from it because he experiences it as a prison. This generalization may seem to apply only to some men, only to the few, only to ourselves. But convention is imposed ipon a child by force, and if anybody should be completely satisfied with it, without reservation, this would surely show that not only his will had been broken, which was an avowed aim of education until recently, but also his spirit.

Part of the excitement of the quest for truth comes from the scent of freedom; what is wanted is what is new, different, original: a hitherto unknown fact, a novel distinction, or an unconventional perspective. We want to break the tyranny of custom and see it at the mercy of our discoveries. We want to dislodge as much as possible of what had seemed firmly established.

In Plato and Nietzsche the aspiration for truth becomes comparable to the ambition to climb Everest or Annapurna: a downright contempt for the conventional life, the wish to dare, the quest of the dreadful power of loneliness felt in standing where no man before has stood and in seeing what no man has seen.

The desire for the unconventional, however, is compatible with falsehoods. A proposition can be original without being true. Why, then, does one want truth?

There are a number of reasons. First, what is utterly easy soon loses interest, becomes boring, and precludes any sense of accomplishment. It becomes as dull as any routine. So we contrive difficulties, we make rules, we impose some discipline and thus provide a framework within which originality can be achieved, but only at the cost of effort and with skill and scheming. The craving for originality could be indulged by simply claiming that Plato was brought up in India or that two and two is five. But assertions of this sort give no sense of accomplishment. The demand for evidence introduces the desired difficulty.

Moreover, we feel delight in overcoming not only difficulties but also the resistance of other men. In games both features are obvious: we devise rules to establish some degree of difficulty, and we pit our skill against opponents.

Beyond that, we try to play well by some objective standard; we try to achieve excellence, as it were, absolutely. To win over a poor player gives small satisfaction. In chess we want our victory to be due not to our rival's ignorance or absent-mindedness but to our own good play. In philosophy we want to conduct our argument in such a way that any adversary, however brilliant, would have to concede our triumph. The demand for evidence and logical consistency—for truth, in short—introduces not only the desired difficulty but also this objective standard.

We do not only want to achieve excellence, break the power of convention, and command the allegiance of other men: above all, we want to triumph over falsehood and deception. What is most humiliating about custom and convention is that they appear inseparable from ignorance, misinformation, and hypocrisy. To have to accept a whole world of beliefs, forced on us by our environment, without the chance to choose or build our own world of beliefs would mean a thousandfold frustration even if all that is forced on us were based on painstaking research. But soon we find that people lie to us complacently, whether they know the facts or have not bothered to determine them. The power that constrains our freedom is seen to be arbitrary and indifferent, a slothful despotism of surpassing cynicism. Every truth we discover makes this tyranny unsafe and is a blow for freedom, and the more of our previous so-called knowledge it affects, the better!

Every child likes to create his own world. As he grows up he has to abandon it and move into the public world where he has no palace of his own and must share whatever he is offered. The aspiration for truth is a fire that consumes this public world, constructed badly by the others. It represents a bold effort to create a public world that is ours. If we must all live together, let there be some rooms at least that we have fashioned, where, although we have to share them, we can feel at home!

Some truths are useful, and this has been emphasized more than enough by the pragmatists. Many truths are not useful, and even if they turn out to be, their utility may have been of little or no concern to the men who discovered them.

Some truths win approbation, some are resented. Some are mere pebbles on the streets of our public world, and some are highways; some are gardens, rafters, pegs, or mansions. Scientist, historian, and philosopher, poring over telescopes, diggings, documents, or dreams, analyzing concepts or the thoughts of others, seek to crack the ice of custom, to win their fellow men's assent, and to make some small contribution to that public world in which they are condemned to live. The quest for truth is the quest to fashion what is not bounded by the sense of sight or sound nor even by language.

There are lonely truths: not only those we come by without any wish but truths we seek without the least desire to communicate them; truths about ourselves, for instance. Here, too, we pit our efforts against manifold conventions, we reject the images of others, and we seek a contest with the one opponent who is omnipresent: our self. We want to face up to this uncanny presence; we refuse to be deceived. If we cannot be the lords of our own house, our self-respect is threatened: we must know the premises and all their wiles to enjoy secure possession and consider changes.

The aspiration for truth is not the desire to receive a present in a passive state; it involves self-assertion and rebellion. We refuse to be imposed upon; we refuse to be like objects; we aspire toward a higher state of being.

24. TRUTH AND CORRECTNESS. Because the aspiration for
truth is an aspiration for a higher state of being, it is often held
that truth cannot be mere correctness, which seems far too
trivial. Any homely proposition may well be correct; but truth,
it is supposed, must be much bigger—not a quality of propositions but elusive vastness: perhaps *King Lear* is true, or *Antigone;* but such a proposition as *"Antigone* was written by a
man named Sophocles" can be correct at best but never true,
according to some people. This suggestion sounds profound,
but is merely romantic. It belongs to that synthetic softening
of all contours in the twilight of nostalgic sentiment which
found its classical expression in the lines of a romantic poet:

> *"Beauty is truth, truth beauty,"—that is all
> Ye know on earth, and all ye need to know.*

If these lines were beautiful, they would refute themselves; for
Keats himself knew more than the phrase in quotes.

To say that these two lines are not correct but nevertheless
true would be a needless paradox inviting rank confusion. Far
more would be gained by saying, without any effort at profundity, that Keats' assertion is a half-truth and by specifying
what truth there is in it.

The assertion that *King Lear* or *Antigone* is "true" is not far
different from the gushing tribute that they are "divine." One
gathers that praise is intended, but the rest is vagueness. We
can say that these plays are beautiful, profound, or deeply
moving, that they change our attitudes or valuations, that they
broaden our understanding of man's nature or of man's condition, or that every time we read them we make new discoveries.
There is no lack of words, and a profound account is not one
that misuses the word "true," albeit systematically, but one
that introduces some precision, *explains* our admiration, and
brings out something we did not see so well before.

Shakespeare's Sonnet XCIV concludes: "Lilies that fester
smell far worse than weeds." Whether this is true would be a
question for a botanist. Of course, this is a metaphorical expression: Shakespeare's point is similar to an epigram in the
Babylonian Talmud (Sukkah 52a): "The greater the man, the

more powerful his evil impulse." Whether this is true is quite another question. Whether the sonnet is beautiful, that is a third question. And whether it is profound is a fourth question. These questions are independent of each other. I, for example, do not know whether the botanical statement is true; the psychological statement intended may need some qualification to be wholly true; but I think that this is one of Shakespeare's most beautiful sonnets, partly because it is one of the few that has a strong ending; and, seeing that it compresses Shakespeare's vision of ideal manhood into fourteen lines and thus illuminates his tragedies, I should call it one of the most profound poems in the English language. These opinions are arguable and would need to be substantiated by detailed analysis. Those, however, who would call the sonnet as a whole "true" blur important distinctions, distract attention from interesting questions, and raise pseudo problems.

The nonidiomatic extension of the epithet "true" to nonlinguistic structures, such as paintings, only adds further confusion. To call a late Van Gogh picture of cypresses and stars "true" involves a confusion of categories just like saying that my sleep was "slow." It sounds expressive, but it invites futile investigations.

If we say "truth" when we mean such things as passionate sincerity or adequacy to one's personal experience, including one's most intimate associations and emotions, we become involved in pointless problems about the relations between scientific and religious truth. If that is what is meant by "truth," then there need be no more conflict between religion and science than between astronomy and Van Gogh.

A picture may remind us of certain truths; for example, that the scientist's way of looking at nature is not the only one, or that colors can communicate emotion in a way of which many of us had not been aware. Such truths, however, are simply correct.

The most professional attack on the use of "true" as synonymous with "correct" has been based on the Greek word for truth: ἀλήθεια. Heidegger, and many another German writer in his wake, has pointed out that originally this meant un-

concealedness. Then it is argued that the Latin *veritas* has led
us away from the all-important notion of that which uncon-
ceals itself—or, as one might say just a little more idiomatically,
that which reveals itself. All this makes it appropriate to call a
work of art true, and Hoffmeister's German dictionary of philosophy says in the article on truth: "Thus the truth of Hellenism [*Griechentum,* of course, is more profound than Hellen-
ism] is Greek sculpture because here the Greek man gave
himself perfect expression." In Greek sculpture, in other words,
the Greek character stands unconcealed.

Naturally, the word "truth" can be redefined in this way.
But why should its usage be determined by a Greek etymology
rather than the etymology of "truth," which, exactly like the
German *Wahrheit,* is related to a root that means "trustworthy"?

That the redefinition of "truth" is arbitrary is the first objection to it. Secondly, it is unnecessary: we have too many
labels as it is, and what we need is not another big word but
judicious use of lots of little words. Third, this use of "true" and
"truth" is not only unusual and useless; it invites unnecessary
problems and confusions and blurs real problems. Finally and
most important, this strange use of "truth" is insidious because
it leads people to disparage correctness almost as if it were a
synonym of shallowness.

Many correct propositions are admittedly unprofound. To
look down on correctness for that reason is easy and not at all
profound. Of course, we prefer the Parthenon or a Beethoven
quartet to a high-school primer of mathematics, but such
works of art depend on many correct measurements, albeit on
much more than that. Plato would have been a greater philosopher than J. S. Mill, even if Mill should have penned more
correct propositions; and the reason for that is implicit in the
Gide quotation cited once before: "the importance of . . . a
new explanation of certain phenomena is not gauged only by
its accuracy, but also, and above all, by the impetus it gives to
the mind . . . by the new vistas it opens. . . ." To command
our respect, however, what is offered must be prompted,
among other things, by the desire for correctness, by a pas-

sionate impatience with the incorrectness of what went before.
If such an honest and determined effort culminates in explanations which, in turn, are not entirely correct, that only proves
how difficult correctness is to reach.

Nowhere is the disproportion between effort and result
more aggravating than in the pursuit of truth: you may plow
through documents or make untold experiments or think and
think and think, forgo food, comfort, and distractions, lie
awake nights and eat out your heart—and in the end you know
what can be memorized by any idiot.

What is the alternative? To suffer the tyranny of arbitrary
falsehood and deception. Many truths cease to seem trite as
soon as one views them as triumphs over prejudice, indifference, and dishonesty. To teach a truth without giving others
some experience of the quest, the passion, and the heartbreak
is a crime; for it makes men prey to that callow contempt for
correctness which is the bait of error.

An exciting and profound truth is one that affects a great
deal of the knowledge we once thought we had. Those who
spurn accuracy, like Heidegger and Toynbee, find it easy to
upset all previous knowledge. Revolutionary truths are difficult to attain, but few things are more exciting and confer a
greater sense of power—thus keeping men from seeking excitement and power in more obnoxious ways.

It is not as if the quest of revolutionary truths were in no
way antisocial or aggressive: it is an attack on society as it is,
a blow against custom, an attempt to destroy convention—but
inevitably establishes a new convention. It is comparable to
the strictures of the Hebrew prophets: a constructive criticism
which is not self-seeking or oracular. The false prophets of
truth, who disparage correctness, are self-seeking and oracular.
Incapable of finding revolutionary truths, they hide their incapacity in a fog.

25. TRUTH AND MEANING, OR: HOW TO READ A PHILOSOPHER.
Even if we equate truth with correctness, the truth of many
propositions is exceedingly difficult to determine. This is so es-

pecially in the case of philosophic propositions, as will be seen as soon as we consider a few famous ones. "The true is the bacchanalian reeling in which no member is not drunken; and because every one, if separated, is immediately dissolved, it is also transparent and simple repose," says Hegel. There are twelve categories, says Kant. According to Plato, justice is each performing his proper function, and there is a Form of justice. Whether a proposition is true, we cannot tell until we know what it means, and that is not always obvious.

What does Plato mean when he speaks of "Forms"? What is a Kantian "category"? What is Berkeley's conception of an "idea"? On such questions commentators differ, and there is often a vast literature. The outsider may say: if philosophers would only define their terms, this difficulty would disappear. Spinoza began his *Ethics* by offering six definitions, of which this is the first: "By cause of itself, I understand that whose essence involves existence; or that whose nature cannot be conceived unless existing." But what is the meaning of "cause" and "essence" and "existence"? What does the phrase mean "cannot be conceived unless existing"?

Hegel recognized these difficulties when he argued in the Preface to his first book that truth could be offered only in the form of a system. Philosophic propositions are not self-explanatory: they point beyond themselves and must be evaluated in context. Even a whole paragraph or chapter points beyond itself to a larger context. Reverence for single propositions gives away the nonphilosophic reader. He repeats statements out of context and often substitutes supposed synonyms for carefully chosen technical terms.

Philosophic propositions mean more than they say, and the reader who reverences the proposition is always in danger of missing its meaning. The philosophic reader realizes the inadequacy of all propositions, their fragmentary character—and nevertheless takes them seriously as clues to the author's meaning. *The esoteric meaning of philosophic propositions is revealed by their context.* The unit of greatness in philosophy is never a proposition: rarely, it is a proof; a little more often, a refutation; usually, a book.

There are degrees of understanding. To understand a philosophic book at all well—which in many cases is admittedly not worth the trouble—most men must read it more than once; for the later parts usually throw unexpected light on what has gone before; and the total design is relevant, too.

Sometimes this design becomes clearer as we read some of the author's other books, and some knowledge of his predecessors is often essential, too. Knowledge of his successors is apt to mislead as much as help; for they have usually indulged in partial readings and bent his ideas to their own designs. And no historical perspective can ever take the place of a close reading of the text which alone supplies the necessary cross-illumination.

All this does not rule out the possibility that a proposition has some *prima facie* faults which are in no way mitigated by further investigation; that relevant facts are misrepresented; that arguments are fallacious or confusion rank. All this is common indeed, even in philosophic classics. There is no need either to adopt the hypercritical attitude of positivism which does not see the wood for the imperfections of the trees in it, or the hyperhistorical attitude which denies that we can study the wood short of going into paleontology.

It is legitimate to consider a philosophy as a whole in relation to its antecedents, and no less legitimate to concentrate with critical intent on single arguments, propositions, or concepts. Both approaches can supplement each other.

We do not take a philosopher seriously enough if we are satisfied with the mere feel of his philosophy: if his propositions, taken at their face value, are false or contradict each other, if he relies on equivocations and his arguments are invalid, all that is worth pointing out, though insufficient. The question remains whether his propositions are *meant* to be taken at their face value.

Some readers fasten on a single exoteric interpretation; others, more sophisticated, make a catalogue of possible exoteric meanings; still others seek an esoteric meaning reserved for initiates—and all three types of readers ignore the context.

Few philosophers place confidence in any of their own

propositions. The poor student and the eclectic fasten on the proposition to champion it; the positivist, to refute it. The reader for whom one writes goes beyond the proposition to see what is meant.

Propositions can be *multivocal* without being equivocal: to the perceptive they speak with many voices, signify many things, and mean a great deal.

First, a proposition functions not only in an immediate context on the page where it occurs but also in a larger systematic context, in the author's over-all attempt at the time of writing. Secondly, there is the chronological context—the place of the proposition in the author's development. This is especially important if the statement does not formulate his considered opinion but only a passing fancy or a provisional stage of his thought. We must ask what the author meant by the terms he used, and whether he used these terms in the same sense in his early and his late works, or even throughout the work at hand.

All this will seem a matter of course only to those who have never read much theology or philosophic criticism. To give a single example: almost the entire Nietzsche literature flouts these rules.

Besides the systematic and the developmental meaning there are the many symptomatic meanings. The proposition may be symptomatic psychologically: the author's choice, and especially his abuse, of words, his imagery and his examples, his style and attitude, may invite psychological study. A proposition may also be symptomatic historically and reveal something about an era.

After we have asked about these three kinds of meaning —systematic, developmental, and symptomatic—yet another question remains which in some cases may be most important of all: What did the author see? The answers to such questions as, for example, what concrete instances he had in mind and against what view he aimed his proposition, do not necessarily solve this central problem, though they are relevant and important. Nor is the difference between what an author saw and said necessarily reducible to the difference between what *he* meant and what his proposition means. What he meant to say may well have been as wrong as his proposition, and nevertheless he may have seen something important.

At this level we must go behind not only what he said, but even what he meant, to recapture his vision. We use untenable propositions as clues in our search for truth. Even as it is the fascination of a detective story that the truth is finally discovered on the basis of a great many accounts of which not one is free of grievous untruths—even as it is sometimes given to the historian to reconstruct the actual sequence of events out of a great many reports which are shot through with lies and errors—those who study philosophers in the way here suggested use a lot of unauthentic pictures to draw a true map.

A philosopher may claim, for example, that A influenced B, and this may be disproved; but perhaps he noted a similarity which leads to the discovery of a common source or to a better understanding of A and B. Some of Nietzsche's and Freud's suggestions are open to conclusive objections; yet both men called attention to things which are much more important than their errors. To cite Nietzsche: "The errors of great men . . . are more fruitful than the truths of little men" (30).

Hegel's statement that truth can be offered only in a system is a case in point. He overstated the case for the system, but recognized the inadequacy of any proposition and saw the need for an interlocking web of propositions; he understood the principle of cross-illumination and the essential circularity of truth; he knew that, as T. S. Eliot has put it since, "in my beginning is my end" and "every phrase and every sentence is an end and a beginning."

To communicate truth, a larger unit than a proposition is required; but that unit need not be a system, let alone, as Hegel thought, an all-inclusive system. Hegel still thought that he himself was able to offer such an "encyclopaedia," but he had to rely on a great deal of erroneous information.

Today the polymath is almost the last man from whom we should expect the truth: we may turn to Toynbee to be titillated, but if we want the truth we turn to men without a system.

26. THEORIES OF TRUTH.   The difference between what is seen
and said may be illustrated with the major theories of truth.
The so-called correspondence and coherence theories of truth
certainly see something of the truth, and so does the pragmatic
theory. But if each said faithfully what it saw, they would not
contradict each other as in fact they do.

True is what is trustworthy and truth always involves a correspondence of appearance and reality or of expectation and
fulfillment. True is what does not deceive, what is not false,
what keeps its promise. All correspondence, however, is known
through coherence: we have no second sight to see whether
appearance and reality correspond, and if we would know
whether a proposition is true we must see whether it is consistent with what else we know, with our other experiences.

Even as correspondence is not known intuitively, coherence
here is not a matter of consistency with a fixed number of
other propositions, which is clearly not enough. Even if a system is internally consistent—as many a famous system, including Toynbee's, is not—that is no guarantee of its truth. Instead
of calling all the non-Euclidean geometries, as well as Euclid's,
true, and instead of dignifying only one with this epithet, we
should call them internally consistent systems which are useful for different purposes. In the case of equally simple rival
hypotheses which are equally compatible with everything else
we know, we also have no right to call one of them, let alone
all of them, true, although there may be reasons for preferring
one. In some cases a new discovery or crucial experiment may
eventually bring a decision.

As rival theories which would exclude each other, both
theories go beyond what they have seen: one notes that truth
involves correspondence, while the other one notes the importance of coherence—and both state their insights in a manner that necessitates objection. Moreover, both want to capture truth in a moment and lock it up, although in fact neither
correspondence nor coherence is given in a moment as a closed
fact. Truth—even that of the Biblical God—is experienced by
man only in time as a series of events, of promises fulfilled.
This temporal and open character of truth has been stressed

by the pragmatic theory, which, however, has not only been misunderstood in many quarters but has also frequently misstated its own insights.

Oddly, the phrase so often singled out for scorn by the religious critics of pragmatism, "true is what works," is very close to the Biblical conception of truth—close to it, not identical with it. The Hebrew *emeth*, which means firmness, reliability, and trustworthiness, and is sometimes rendered as *aletheia* in the Septuagint, has been explained by such scholars as Bultmann, Gogarten, and Hans von Soden as essentially not a static quality but something that manifests itself in time in the fulfillment of expectations and the justification of claims. The truth of God is inseparable from the works of God. Truth is the correspondence of promise and performance, a consistency that is not established once and for all but continuing and open toward the future. True is what proves itself continually.

Where less than this is meant by the slogan "true is what works," the word "true" is used rather lightly. That is a sin on which the adherents of this slogan do not have any monopoly. If William James was so generous with the word "truth" that he sometimes prostituted it, it is questionable whether this was due to his pragmatism or to his desire to defend religion —or rather private enterprise in religion. This is overlooked by those religious critics who would convict all pragmatists of guilt by association with William James.

Resignation in the face of the follies of mankind is the price of wisdom. And true wisdom wonders whether wisdom is not folly, too. But to blur the line between what we know and do not know, between the folly of knowledge and the folly of ignorance, and to curry favor with the mass of men by abandoning "truth" to them without requiring any effort on their part, that is not wisdom but contempt of truth, whether it be cynicism or romanticism.

Even if there should be something ultimately arbitrary about our truths, even if in some ultimate sense they profit us not, there is a deep difference between an honest piece of research and a fraud or sloppy piece of work. Even if neither of two accounts should be completely true, they are not necessarily equally true: there are degrees of truth.

The proposition that every proposition is either true or false is itself but a fragment of the truth. Whether a proposition is to be judged true or false depends on its meaning and hence on its interpretation, which must take into account the context. Are such propositions as the following true or false? "Truth means correspondence." "Truth means coherence." "True is what works." "There is no truth." Instead of simply judging them to be either true or false, we must exert ourselves to find out what, if any, truth there is in them—in other words, how true they are. Or, if that sounds too tolerant, how false they are.

That a belief "worked" on a few occasions in the sense that we did not suffer shipwreck with it, and some modest expectations which we based on it were actually fulfilled—that is clearly insufficient to establish its truth. True is what survives all tests and trials.

That is what the true God, according to the Bible, has in common with a true friend, a true Titian, and a true proposition. There are degrees of being a true friend as there are degrees of the truth of propositions, and a Titian may turn out to have been painted jointly by Titian and Giorgione, while a Rubens may have been completed by his pupils. In these cases truth is not apprehended in a moment, at a glance. What has interested philosophers rather more than the question of degrees of truth is the problem whether it is not possible in some cases to apprehend the truth in a moment without any regard for tests and trials.

Suppose, I see Picasso paint a picture: do I not perceive immediately that it is a true Picasso? Is the truth in such a case not given as a closed fact which is not in any sense open toward the future? We need only imagine that my testimony is contested: how can you be sure that this picture here is the one you saw him paint and not a skillful copy? How did you know that the man you saw was really Picasso? The truth of many propositions represents a closed case for us, but it can always be reopened in the light of new evidence or under the shadow of a reasonable doubt.

That statements which are true by definition, such as "a circle is round," are in a class by themselves has often been noted, and many attempts have been made to define other classes of exceptions, notably including historical statements, statements about our immediate sense impressions, about dreams and afterimages, and about emotions.

That historical propositions are not closed forever, but can be reopened not only in view of archaeological discoveries but also after a careful, critical re-examination of the documents long available to our predecessors, no historian today would deny. Nor would anyone who has some experience with accounts of dreams deny that an account of a dream can also be reopened, supplemented, and revised. Still, it may be questioned whether in this case there can be any tests. In principle, there can be. Of course, we must not expect the sort of test appropriate to mathematics; the case is closer to historical research. The criterion of coherence is applicable in at least two ways. In the first place, we can cross-examine the subject and at the very least ask him to relate his dream a second time, in which case new material is quite apt to come to light, and small discrepancies may turn out to be valuable clues for subsequent discoveries. Secondly, our knowledge of the person who relates the dream—of his other dreams, his problems, his experiences on the day preceding the dream, his plans, his character—may prompt more or less specific questions about details of the dream. And if we know of some external stimuli which may have been at work during the time of the dream, we can ask such leading questions as: Wasn't there a big noise at one point?

The last consideration applies no less to afterimages and immediate sense impressions. We can question propositions about such phenomena: Surely, you saw a six-pointed star, not a pentagram? Or: Didn't you fail to notice that the image appeared to you to be reversed?

There is no need here to go into the fine points of the epistemology of afterimages and sense impressions. Far more important, at least for those who would advance the study of religion or poetry, are attempts to cope linguistically with emotions.

27. WORDS AND EXPERIENCE.   Imagine a walk in the jungle and a tiger leaping at your companion. The word "tiger" tears the beast out of its original surroundings, transposes it into the environment of other similar animals, makes it a helpless object of comparisons, and exposes it to endless criticisms.

"Circle" and "tiger" differ insofar as no object of sense experience is really a circle, while some are really tigers. But every general concept is a norm. When I call an object a table, I no longer accept it without question; I propose a standard of criticism. When I call an object a table or a tiger, this is not like calling my son "Jehoshaphat" or my daughter "darling"; it is rather as if I set myself up as a judge and classified the case before me: it is as a table that I propose to judge you.

Words are not the names of objects of experience. Plato, supposing that nouns must be the names of objects but unable to find such objects in experience, posited another world beyond experience and peopled it with these indescribable objects. As long as "real" is an honorific term reserved for that which neither perishes nor changes, Plato was right to deny that the objects of sense experience are real, and we can understand why he sought reality in another world.

A noun is not the name of a thing but an attack on a thing: a noun tears a thing out of its environment, strips it of its defenses, and hales it into court for an indictment.

Beginning with Impressionism, modern art is a revolt against the noun—an attempt to experience the world ungrammatically, whether more reverently or more cynically.

Nouns, verbs, adjectives, and adverbs are all implicit comparisons and potential criticisms: they represent a thrust beyond the present, a violation of the given, a forcible removal of a thing, activity, or quality into a critical environment.

A pronoun is like the suit one gives a prisoner after he has been stripped of his identity.

A conjunction is the luxurious device of a jubilant reason which, no longer content to create another world, insists on finding its sovereign pleasure in the manipulation of its creatures.

The world of reason is poor compared to the world of sense —until *or, but, if, because, when, and, unless* populate it with endless possibilities.

Words are the works of art that make possible science.

Words are the abstractions that make possible poetry.

Words signify man's refusal to accept the world as it is.

With words man has been able to create a world, and it is fitting that the author of Genesis should have proposed that the world of sense experience, too, was created with words.

28. LANGUAGE AND EMOTION.   I do not know what I feel. The more deeply and intensely I feel, the less I know what I feel. If I have words for it, adequate words, the feeling is not deep and intense; if I have no words for it, I myself do not know what I feel.

Philosophers ask: Do I ever know that you are angry? The meaning and use of "angry" being what it is, I do. But do I ever know that I am angry? If I know that I am angry, am I really angry?

We know the behavior, the facial expression, the stereotype. We know some norm, vaguely perhaps, which a man's appearance must approximate more or less to make a term applicable. Do we know our own feelings? Again we have some vague notion of a norm which we name, and this name serves us as a label for feelings which come within a certain, not clearly definable, radius of the norm. Practically, this is adequate. Precision in describing emotions violates good form. When one is asked, "How d'you feel?" one is supposed to answer, "I'm feeling fine; how are you?" or possibly, "Not so hot." Even among the minority whose vocabulary is larger, accurate accounts of one's feelings are held to be in poor taste. One speaks of one's real feelings only after one has had too much to drink for accuracy.

For the most part, one is simply not interested in the shades of other people's inner life; anything beyond a rough suggestion is boring. Those who are interested often lack feeling for feelings: they operate with a fuller, but highly stereotyped, vocabulary which serves them as a clinical file cabinet. Practically—whether I want to play a game or try to give professional advice—this may be entirely adequate and even facilitate therapeutical success in some cases. But when it comes to giving an accurate account of feelings, few psychologists equal Faulkner at his best.

Faulkner concedes in effect that there are no adequate words for deep and intense emotions, and he does not create a new vocabulary, new stereotypes, new norms. Instead he misuses words, ravishes syntax, and outrages grammar. His prose represents a revolt against all stereotypes and, at its rare best, against all mere approximations, against imprecision. It is for this reason that he does not even try to say what a character feels: he tells us what the man thinks, of what he is aware—a smell, a sound, a memory, some associations. Often the characters are subintellectual, and their disorderly thoughts are interrupted by sense impressions which are not immediately classified. A wealth of impressions and associations takes the place of verbal pigeonholing, and a mood is built up without being named. Nor is there any adequate name for it. The atmosphere, for example, which Faulkner builds up on the opening pages of *Sanctuary* is as inadequately described by such a phrase as "dumb terror" as it would be conveyed by a cover showing a scantily clad blonde with her mouth suddenly covered from behind.

Suppose we followed the example of the scientists and named the mood after the man who described it; suppose I told you: "I had the most dreadful experience; I was simply faulknered." This would add another drawer to the clinical file cabinet. An expanded vocabulary of this sort is a great help in classifying emotions, but it cannot bear the burden of adequate description. It substitutes one approximation for another, invites judgment in the light of a new norm, and leaves out of account what is individual.

Is there any serious difference between calling an emotive state "being faulknered" and calling an animal a tiger or an object a table? In all these cases we leave out of account what is individual. But objects can be measured, not only classified, and the constellation of a great number of exact measurements may pin down an individual—like a butterfly in a glass box, lifeless, reduced to a piece of matter. Any uniqueness that may remain is accidental and on the level of a quantitative record, not of individuality: a wingspread exceeding by one-tenth of a millimeter that of any other known specimen—until another one like it is measured the next day which, however, has a barely smaller dot on the left wing. Individuality cannot be measured; individuality is never given in a moment; individuality requires time and appears fully only in a whole life. If I want a copy of the *Times*, I do not care about the history or individuality of the copy I get. In the case of an old book, I might care and prefer a copy once owned by Kant and later by Hegel. Individuality is apprehended through the history of an individual.

When we deal with our experience of an object rather than the object as it may be apart from our experience, the situation is the same as when we deal with an emotion. Not only the attempt to evoke the same experience in others but the accurate description of the experience presents a problem. If I want to describe my experience of this particular tiger, for example, measurement may be beside the point, even if the experience is not fraught with any deep emotion.

If I want to know what I feel, I must follow the example of the artist and set down my thoughts, impressions, associations, and memories as they occur to me. If a psychoanalyst wants to know what I feel, he must ask me to do this for him, as Freud discovered. The lover who wants to know what he feels, or wants his beloved to know it, also follows the artist's example, and finds that all his thoughts, impressions, memories, and associations revolve around her. Art, not psychology, is the language of the emotions.

In his books, Freud generally did not try to give an accurate account of feelings; he tried to classify a few typical complexes.

Psychoanalysis may sometimes help those who have lost the
ability to feel deeply and intensely. Those who do feel deeply
and intensely will instinctively turn to art, both for food for
their emotions and to express them. And anyone who wants
to describe an emotion, or any experience as it actually feels,
must also turn to art.

29. "LOVE." Love and some other so-called emotions do not
exist in a moment but only over a period of time. "Love" and
other similar terms are names not of single impressions but of
complex configurations of sensations, feelings, thoughts, and
actions. The similarity between some such configurations,
even those experienced by different people in different ages,
is sufficient to make it extremely useful to employ a single
word for anything that approximates certain public paradigms.
These models are generally neither definitions nor the experiences of any individual. Often they are found in works of art.

That the paradigms must be public is plain: the applicability of a public word to a merely private experience could
never be taught or learned directly. Nor can the paradigm be
found merely in the overt behavior of parents or other adults
from whom a child learns the language: there must be something more public than that to insure wide uniformity. Until
recently these public models were often found in literature—
especially in a few works which were widely known. Chief
among these for most Western peoples was the Bible, but depending on the culture, Homer and Dante, Shakespeare and
Goethe, performed a similar service.

One does not so much define wisdom as one gleans its
meaning from the tale of Solomon and the two women. And
love is the feeling of Jacob for Rachel, and then for Joseph
and Benjamin, and the feeling of Romeo and Juliet, and
Gretchen's for Faust, Dante's for Beatrice, God's for his "children," Isolde's for Tristan, and Leander's for Hero. These are
some of the paradigms, and our own experience and behavior,
and that of our contemporaries, are accorded the label when
it comes sufficiently close to one or another of these.

Today world literature with its infinite variety is being supplanted more and more by the relatively few, unsubtle stereotypes of Hollywood, the radio, and television; and millions of
young people get their notions of love and valor, dread and
wrath, from the undifferentiated, indifferent performances of
ephemeral idols whose body measurements are widely considered more important than their patent lack of any talent to
portray emotions.

The funnies and the most popular magazines do not counteract these tendencies, and one sometimes wonders whether
differentiated emotions will soon become extinct. But good
writers have by no means died out, and richly differentiated
emotions have always been the forte of the few. If Faulkner is
today read by a large audience more or less by mistake, only
for the sake of the sensational, the bulk of Shakespeare's audience went to his plays by mistake, too.

The emotions of Romeo and Isolde are much more complex
than any single impression or what Gilbert Ryle of Oxford
calls feelings, when he says in his *Concept of Mind:* "By 'feelings' I refer to the sorts of things which people often describe
as thrills, twinges, pangs, throbs, wrenches, itches, prickings,
chills, glows, loads, qualms, hankerings, curdlings, sinkings,
tensions, gnawings and shocks." (83 f.)

Some such sensations may form some small part of the experience of love or jealousy, but not in any specifiable con-
figuration which could be used as a definition. Moreover, they
appear conjoined with memories and associations, images and
thoughts, and usually also visual and auditory sensations.
What is experienced is a mass of details which it would be
almost impossible to describe fully—Faulkner sometimes captures its chaotic nature—and a word like "love" does not name
a sensation: it represents a triumph of abstraction.

The level of abstraction here achieved appears yet more
clearly when we turn to psychological reflection. In the first
place, even love between the sexes, not to speak of other love,
is experienced very differently in different cultures: we need
only compare the ancient Greeks and Hindus, Russians and
Spaniards, Elizabethans and Puritans.

Secondly, to quote the words of Robert Briffault, the anthropologist, "sexual love is spoken of as if it were a simple and irreducible emotion or impulse, whereas it is in reality the most composite and complex of sentiments. As Herbert Spencer pointed out, in addition to the sexual impulse and mating affection, which are quite distinct, it is made up of an almost boundless aggregate of feelings and sentiments." To give an idea of this aggregate, Briffault enumerates the following among others: "Love of approbation . . . hence love is irresistibly bred by love. . . . The aesthetic feelings which are themselves highly complex products of culture, and which not only imply an 'ideal of feminine beauty,' but also of charm, of character, of elegance and taste. . . . Sympathetic participation, mostly imaginary, in common tastes; the release of conventions in the freedom of intimacy, the gratification of proprietary feelings and of vanity must be added." Each of these component feelings in turn is not a simple atomistic impression like the basic data of Hume's psychology, nor on the level of Ryle's wrenches, itches, and prickings; each represents an abstraction from a chaotic stream of sensations and ideas. It is rarely recognized how crucial ideas are in this stream: what we ordinarily call moods, feelings, and emotions are, at least in many of us, nine-tenths thoughts. It may be physiological processes that predispose us toward certain kinds of thoughts, but moods and emotions are, to a large extent, complexes of thoughts.

The level of abstraction represented by a word like "love" far surpasses anything suggested either by a reference to cultural differences in the experience of love between the sexes or by Briffault's enumeration of some of its components; for "love" is, of course, by no means limited to love between the sexes. The same word designates the feeling of fathers and mothers for their sons and for their daughters, of sons and daughters for fathers and mothers, of boys for their sisters, girls for their brothers, grandparents for grandchildren, grandchildren for grandparents, nuns for Christ, some men for God, few for their neighbors, seventeen-year-olds for seventeen-year-olds, seventy-year-olds for seventy-year-olds, seventy-year-olds for seventeen-year-olds, men for their country, women for the fatherland, both for Beethoven, girls for pink, boys for a bow, girls for a beau, readers for some books, writers for their work, and not quite everybody for himself.

If I want to know what I feel, "love" is not a very precise answer. While few, if any, other labels for so-called emotions rival the abstractness, imprecision, and vagueness of "love," the over-all adequacy of language for the description of experience represents a problem.

30. WORDS AS CATEGORIES.   Words are categories not only insofar as "tiger" and "table" denote classes of objects but also in the more important sense that we understand the world in terms of words.

According to Kant, all human experience involves some degree of understanding, and man's mind understands in terms of twelve categories. For example, we understand all events in terms of cause and effect, unity and plurality, and substances. We may make mistakes and think that there is one thing where in fact there are two, and we may suppose that a drought was caused by a witch. Such mistakes can be corrected, but, according to Kant, we cannot help thinking in terms of the twelve categories which will furnish the mold for any correction, too.

Kant combines insights of true genius with a deliberate resolve not to be empirical and offers, here as elsewhere, an essentially unempirical psychology. He assumes without argument that the human mind does not differ in essentials in different ages and areas, and that his analyses are valid once and for all. The possibility does not occur to Kant that the moral consciousness he analyzes might be peculiarly that of a pietist who has lost his traditional faith, or that the conception of causality which he posits as a category of the human understanding might be peculiarly that of Newton. His analyses are far too penetrating to be of merely historical interest: he sees through a particular historical phenomenon to something more abiding. The morality he analyzes is not only that of an eighteenth-century Prussian, though it is certainly very different from that of Aristotle, for example; and the categorical structure of the understanding is not merely Newtonian, though Kant's conception of the category of cause and effect comes close to being just that. Could there not be a state of mind which assumes that most events have a cause in the Newtonian and Kantian sense, but that a few don't? Might there not have been an age in which people understood events not in terms of blind, mechanical efficient causes, but in terms of teleological final causes? Confronted with a total eclipse of the sun, is man indeed compelled by the very structure of his mind to ask: What immediately preceding events in adjoining places caused this phenomenon? Or does the structure of man's mind permit him to ask instead: What is the purpose of this calamity? Or perhaps: What does it portend? Or, more vaguely: What does it signify?

It is not difficult to imagine a civilization for which it is axiomatic that every event must have—not a cause but a purpose. Or a culture for which understanding something means understanding its significance. Since Kant's time we must also ask, as he did not: Can the categories of the human understanding be changed by evolution? Or by history? Are they perhaps different from culture to culture? Might they be revised by an act of will?

A language reflects what those who fashioned it considered important. Tenses, for example, are not the same in all languages, and the exact relations in time of complex events cannot be expressed in some languages. It may be possible to think of these events in the right order nevertheless; but what is possible and difficult in some languages, and requires a lengthy narrative in which a mistake, once made, cannot be corrected without starting all over again, is readily taken care of by the tenses and vocabulary of another. Similarly, a highly complex sequence of experiences which it would be exceedingly difficult to communicate in one language may be named by a single word, like "love" or "war," in another.

Words increase the range of experience—but sometimes at the cost of depth. They allow us to understand a lot of things with a minimum of effort and concentration: our attention need not linger on that part of the room there; we see at a glance that there is a wall lined with books that have all sorts of different colors, and there are two pictures, a rug, an armchair, and a lamp. What was in the pictures? We do not recall that, but we know that there were two pictures. What color were the books on the top shelf? We do not remember; we saw a wall lined with books. Able to classify things at a glance, the mind is free to give its attention to other matters. We generalize about rooms and libraries, about love and war; we think about different kinds of shelving for books, compare the backgrounds of various wars, and list or analyze typical components of love between the sexes. What is gone is the sense of mystery which distinguished childhood when we did not have a word for everything. Then we could not communicate in a single sentence that there was a wall lined with books, and that there were two pictures, a rug, an armchair, and a lamp; but we took in details that escape us now, and our lengthy circumstantial account of what we saw caught something of the experience of a child in a strange room.

That mere naming can reduce the uncanny and mysterious to the level of another object that can be discussed without feeling was known even in ancient times. Early, the Hebrews resolved that God must not be named, or that the name must be pronounced only once a year on a most awesome occasion. Eventually, the very pronunciation of the name was forgotten. Nor does the Christian God have a name.

Conversely, the scholar who writes "Yahweh" tries to strip the God of the Old Testament of all his mystery, to cut him down to manageable size and make of him an object for manipulation. A good blasphemy should be deliberate and individual; but this modern scholar's usage is an instance of the insolence of office: an impersonal and bureaucratic disrespect for mystery, ex officio. (Cf. § 89.)

The name rings out and undresses the person named—dresses him down: it informs him that he is now to be considered as if devoid of individuality. "Omega Brown!" How he wishes he had no name! How he wishes that one might have

to get to know him before being able to decide about him.
"Omega Brown!" He is done for.

A name makes possible manipulation without understanding; it allows us to label and classify without opening ourselves
to a new experience. A name is the tombstone of an individual
who will soon be resurrected as an abbreviation or a serial
number—perhaps even a mere digit.

But it is not so when Lear cries out: "Cordelia! Cordelia!"
Words can reduce experience emotionally. Words can mark
the triumph of the intellect at the expense of feeling. But it
would be folly to argue that a large vocabulary is incompatible
with the profound experience and superlative expression of
emotions. Shakespeare had a huge vocabulary, as did Goethe.
The question is how we use language—to vivisect experience,
killing it for the sake of generalized knowledge, or to capture
experience alive.

The scientist does the former, the poet the latter, and the
philosopher must often try to do both and capture the experience before analyzing it. At its best, philosophy does not live
in the shadow of either science or poetry: it offers something
compared to which both science and poetry are restricted in
scope.

That some philosophic writing is poor science and a lot of
the rest is poor poetry does not at all refute these claims:
among the great philosophers we also find some of the very
greatest scientists and writers, including first-rate mathematicians of great literary distinction, like Descartes and Leibniz,
and first-rate poets with rapierlike intellects, like Nietzsche.
And Plato, who wrote poetically even of mathematics, and
Spinoza, who wrote *more geometrico* even of the love of God,
need not fear comparison with any man. Here the partiality
of language is overcome: it becomes neither the slave of experience nor an absentee landlord.

It may seem at times as if the trouble were not that we
have so few words and expressions for our feelings but that
we have even these. For I can say, even if only to myself,
"the weather feels nice" or "I am in love" or "I am disappointed"—and feel almost nothing. But it is not the fault of

these expressions if I stoop to satisfaction with them. There are words enough to serve me if I should insist on a more accurate account.

When I do not insist and rest content with clichés, am I dishonest? Do I really feel a great many things that I disregard because they fail to fit my preconceptions? Or am I conscious only of what fits my preconceptions, while a dozen details remain on the fringes of consciousness? Or are they aggressively banished into unconsciousness because they would not fit? Surely, all these things happen at times. But to understand the situation better, we must take into account one further fact.

Language is a social phenomenon, and its primary function is to communicate what is of social importance: language is practical. Distinctions between things and shapes and sizes are likely to have practical consequences; hence we have a large vocabulary for them. Differences of taste and smell, except for a very few striking discrepancies, matter far less socially, and we have few words for them. It is similar with feelings and emotions: what words we have are dictated by practical significance. Anger, love, sadness, resentment, lust, and jealousy are emotions that make a great difference socially, and so we have words to distinguish them. But how precisely I feel during any period of five minutes, that is practically unimportant.

Language is adapted to what is public and practical—not to the subtle shades of difference between my feelings and yours. If our emotional experiences are sufficiently alike to result in similar behavior, language generally does not register the differences. When I say how I feel, I usually do not describe my feelings: I classify them in a way which informs others what they may expect of me and what they should not expect of me.

Are there feelings beyond what is contained in such reports, or are these practically minded accounts after all essentially complete? Our feelings are configurations of many ideas, impressions, memories, associations, and the like; and an adequate description differs from mere labeling by recounting the components and communicating them not singly but in the pattern in which they are actually experienced. A proposition like "I am disappointed" or "I am desperate" does not so much falsify an emotion as it distracts attention from the thoughts and impressions that constitute the emotion. In that sense, "I am desperate" is comparable to "I have been at the zoo."

An emotion is not some one thing that eludes all words or is destroyed by propositions: it is a conglomerate. Naming it suggests that the conglomerate is sufficiently similar to certain other conglomerates—perhaps especially to some paradigms in literature—to warrant a particular classification. Describing it, on the other hand, involves an account of the components. A scientific description will generally concentrate on typical elements which are often encountered, while a literary description is likely to aim at concrete and personal detail. The first will usually be more useful from a practical point of view, while the second will be truer to an individual's actual experience.

Everyday language does not readily lend itself to the poet's purpose. He must use language differently to communicate what is not practically useful: he does not wish to be useful to us, he wants to change us by radically altering, or at least extending, our experience. This is no defense of a so-called poetic style which has clichés of its own and is likely to be worse than ordinary usage. To do his job properly, the writer cannot adhere to poetic conventions any more than to the conventions of ordinary usage: he must rise above convention.

It does not follow that all who differ from convention are good writers; but it does follow that the mere fact that one differs from ordinary usage does not constitute an objection: rather it should prompt the question in what way, if any, the novelty is functional. Similarly, philosophers are not necessarily misled by their unusual expressions, as some "ordinary language" philosophers have taken for granted: the question is worth asking whether a philosopher has employed unusual expressions to describe and communicate what *is* unusual and not dreamed of in the philosophy of ordinary language.

Emotions and unusual experiences are often understood in terms of words—whether in terms of the names we give to the

emotions or in terms of the succession of internally spoken
words that make up the emotion. But are words constitutive
elements of *all* experience? Clearly not. Nor, for that matter,
are Kant's categories. An experience may consist, for example,
of a succession of nonverbal images or a sequence of nonverbal
sounds. We may listen to a symphony, in which case Kant's
category of causality is not necessarily a constitutive element
of the experience either, even if we try to "understand" the
music.

There are nonverbal experiences and even nonverbal orien-
tations toward the world. Words are categories in the sense
that we generally understand even nonverbal experiences in
terms of words. Yet nonverbal understanding is possible, too.
I may understand how you feel without any recourse to verbal
thinking, and I may show my understanding by my nonverbal
behavior. Words are categories, but not the only categories.

31. WORKS OF ART AS CATEGORIES.   Works of art can communicate experiences. They do not necessarily do this. Even a
building that evokes a powerful response can hardly be said in
all cases to communicate it. The emotion it arouses in me may
never have occurred to any of the builders or the architects
who successively changed the design. My response may depend on a perspective made possible only by the recent col-
lapse of other surrounding buildings or, as in the case of ruins,
on the disappearance of most of the building itself. In its original colors, crowded by other buildings, the Parthenon cannot
have moved the old Greeks in the same way in which it now
stirs our hearts.

Whether a work of art "communicates" an experience or
not, it frequently becomes inseparable in our minds from some
experience. Consider Michelangelo's slaves, struggling out of
the marble. We do not seek any specific causes to understand
their various postures. Each seems representative of one way
of experiencing the human condition. Several attitudes toward
life have here become stone. Did anyone before the artist
have precisely these attitudes? Similar attitudes must have

abounded. But the artist does not so much imitate nature as nature subsequently imitates him: he molds the attitudes and behavior of posterity. He creates a new category.

Henceforth we can think in terms of this category without first translating into words what is intended. It may appear that a verbal translation would insure greater precision; but in fact, as we have seen, a word—"love," for example—often covers up the crucial differences between a number of artistic paradigms. When we use works of art as categories of the understanding we may increase precision.

This increase in precision tells at most half the story. Mephistopheles is not just one subspecies of devil any more than *Liebestod* is merely an expression of one kind of love. What makes these creations categories and not merely welcome illustrations is that before Wagner this kind of love, with all its sublimity and bathos, had not been experienced; and Mephistopheles means a new conception of the devil. The great artist is a creator of categories in terms of which posterity understands its own experiences, reinterprets the past, and fashions the future. We may well doubt, Spengler notwithstanding, whether there were Faustian men before Goethe wrote his play. We can hardly doubt that there have been would-be Fausts in abundance ever since. The artist does not predict the future; he helps to make it. But he might turn over in his grave if he could see it.

The artist's intention may have differed considerably, for better or for worse, from the effect produced. Goethe's Faust, constantly the butt of Mephistopheles' mockery, but taken every bit as seriously as he takes himself by generations of German readers, is a case in point; Greek statues that have lost their paint, their arms, even their heads, furnish another instance; some of Rembrandt's pictures, like the so-called *Night Watch*, muddied by the lapse of time, a third. What makes a work of art a category is not the artist's primary intent but posterity: what is decisive is that later generations should come to understand their own experiences in terms of the artist's creation. In this sense the love of *Romeo and Juliet* is a category, Faust is a category, Mephistopheles is a category,

and the Bible is fuller of categories than any other book in all
the world.

32. COMMON SENSE. Philosophy and art, religion and science, represent a revolt against common sense. They are all
prompted in large measure by the aspiration to crack convention and to rise above the two dimensions of everyday life.

Today science is often justified by its practical usefulness.
Its remoteness from common sense, however, is closely related
to the immediate satisfaction science gives. The Greeks have
often been given credit for having been the first to develop
science in a disinterested manner. "Disinterested" here means
"unmotivated by practical uses." Being disinterested in this
way, one is more interested than any practical advantage
would ever warrant.

Scientific abstraction liberates us from the slavery of facts.
In mathematics we experience a taste of freedom: the bondage
of accidents is broken; the body is no longer the prison of the
soul; man is as a god. Pythagoras and Plato had this experience. But did the Egyptians and Babylonians really foresee the
practical uses of their calculations when they first began? And
why did generation after generation contain men who felt attracted to such abstract thinking? Surely, the same aspiration
was at work among these people as among the Greeks.

It has sometimes been said that magic is primitive science,
and the shaman a proto-doctor. There may be rather more
truth in the converse statement: the motivation of the modern
scientist is not altogether different from that of the shaman,
and science is founded in part on the same aspiration which
found expression in primitive magic. But the desire for the
unconventional and the drive for power are gradually disciplined into the aspiration for truth.

Soon science, like art and religion, and magic, too, establishes traditions of its own; and what began as a revolt against
convention terminates as another convention. There comes into
being an elaborate convention for those who wish to be unconventional.

The sculptor indulges in abstraction of a sort, leaves out, eliminates to heighten feeling, to celebrate an unprecedented experience—and establishes a style. The revolutionary becomes the fountainhead of a conservative tradition, even if not a dictator.

This process is most obvious in the case of morality. What could be more at odds with common sense than mankind's moral codes? And yet each of them soon becomes a convention and common sense itself for those who accept it—without ceasing to seem outlandish to those who do not.

Religion tells much the same story. The stiff-necked generation that is only too aware of the novelty of what is demanded of it gives way to the strict orthodoxy of generations to come. And the foolishness and the stumbling blocks of the first generation are accepted as unquestioned common sense in time to come, without ceasing to look foolish to nonbelievers. Today's individualist is canonized tomorrow.

No great philosophic book has ever been written by a member of a school or coterie; each bears the stamp of an individuality. Yet now and then one becomes the Bible of a clique. Coteries are based either on common emotions, which must be faint or vague to be held in common, or on common tenets which are neither questioned nor transcended. In short, coteries are incompatible with intellectual passion, while their heroes were dominated by it. The great philosopher defies convention; his followers derive from him a convention for being unconventional. He rebels against common sense; they need a rival common sense.

In his *Tractatus*, Wittgenstein attacked traditional philosophy, but was struck by the inadequacy of his prose when it came to suggesting his own philosophic flight. So he concluded his work: "Of that of which one cannot speak, one must remain silent." Many of his followers have accepted this dictum and ever since have spoken only of that of which one *can* speak. Only John Wisdom has gone to the opposite extreme, saying: "Philosophers should be continually trying to say what cannot be said" (50).

Because many great philosophers have tried to speak of that

of which one cannot speak—not easily, scarcely at all—they have coined words, used metaphor and paradox, and sometimes seemed to contradict themselves. When a philosopher has used a word in an odd way, one must ask whether he saw something odd to which he tried to call attention.

The notion that philosophers should study idiomatic expressions, while systematically ignoring experiences that are not reflected by a British idiom, elevates parochialism into a principle. As John Passmore has said: "It might be amusing, perhaps even instructive, to compare Ryle on ordinary language with W. D. Ross on *prima facie* duties. There is a close resemblance between Oxford deontology and Oxford linguisticism, not least in the assumption that duties, like verbal habits, are 'learnt in the nursery' [Ryle's phrase], and that what nurse has told us goes for the rest of the world, too" (62). Ryle's essay on "Ordinary Language" deserved this criticism; but his practice is superior to his preaching. His major work, *The Concept of Mind*, is a critique of the common-sense conception of mind as a "ghost in the machine" of the human body, though Ryle, characteristically, does not blame common sense but a philosopher—Descartes. John Wisdom goes too far in the opposite direction: he always seems willing to give metaphysical and religious statements the benefit of the doubt, as if there simply must be something to every one of them—even when he cannot say precisely what. (Cf. § 20.)

The point to note is that *"common sense" can mean two things,* and that philosophers must attack common sense—and at the same time appeal to common sense. They must criticize common *beliefs*—and appeal to reason, not to some private intuition or to prejudice.

If it means acceptance or even rationalization of common *beliefs*, "common-sense philosophy" is a contradiction in terms, no less than common-sense art or common-sense science. In that sense, common sense is what has trickled down from the science, philosophy, art, and religion of yesterday to the level of common misunderstanding. As Hamlet says: "Ay, madam, it is common."

Such common sense is opposed to all penetrating percep-

tion and emasculates even intense experiences: they gain ad-
mittance, clipped by stereotyped expectations, and are "understood" before they have been fully felt. We overpower them
lest we feel their power, and remember them almost before
we have had them. Even mystical experiences are similarly
molded by the common sense of some denomination. (Cf.
§§ 72 ff.)

At its best, philosophy wants to be more honest than common sense. This noble intention does not make it immune
against all criticism, but a mere appeal to common beliefs
won't do. On the other hand, the student who seeks refuge in
a philosopher's jargon, refusing to restate his points in plain
language, has not understood him; and if the points *cannot*
be made in plain language—albeit much less elegantly—we are
confronted with bad philosophy.

"Philosophy" and "art" are labels that cover two extremes.
A work of art is simply an artifact: a chest, a table, a rug.
Some such objects are distinguished by striking decorations or
unusual design, but we cannot stipulate at what point artifacts
become works of art: they are all works of art. The same is
true of buildings and of paintings commissioned for an altar or
as portraits.

When a man asks of a Mondrian, "Is that art?" he intends a
comparison with, say, Michelangelo. But while there is little in
the Museum of Modern Art that brooks comparison with
Michelangelo, that is also true of the National Gallery. There
is much more "great art" in the latter, because it makes a
difference whether you have many centuries to choose from or
a few decades. Most paintings are at best decorative and interesting and perhaps also exploratory: attempts to study the
relations between lines, colors, or shapes. But few artists—and
few philosophers—have much to say; few see anything that is
at all distinctive; and very few have a vision that fundamentally alters our experience.

There is a vast border area which includes many a sculp-
tured head on a cathedral as well as some relatively undis-
tinguished works by Rembrandt and most of the works of
quite a number of artists and philosophers. But the extremes

are so far apart that one must recall these intermediate creations to understand why the same label is used for both extremes.

The same disparity strikes us not only in philosophy but also
in religion. The religion of a superstitious Buddhist peasant is
far more similar to that of a superstitious Hindu or Catholic
peasant than it is to the Buddha's.

Most religion and morality involve and even stress conformity and compliance; and the study of science and philosophy
often consists in the appropriation of a tradition. But the heroes
of the tradition were rebels who revolted against the traditions
and the common sense of their time. The history of philosophy
is a history of heresy.

To understand the great philosophers one must recapture
the dissatisfaction with common sense and with their predecessors which motivated them. To understand their perplexity we
can begin with paradoxes and antinomies to demonstrate the
limitations of common sense; but such didactic devices as well
as the search for a method that would enable others to follow
and the accumulation of illustrations, footnotes, and bibliog-
raphies may all be afterthoughts: the philosophic flight may
have been prompted by scant provocation. Parmenides took
his chariot ride first, and Zeno devised his paradoxes a generation later. But if he offers no strong arguments at all, a man is
clearly no philosopher, though he may be a visionary and,
rarely, a fine poet.

Most philosophers have come to realize that no single point
of view is adequate, and that there is no hope of attaining
some new view which will supersede all previous views. Heidegger still talks as if such a new view were about to appear,
though he does not think it will be vouchsafed to our generation, which, nevertheless, should set out on the way and follow
him; but while he is leading his followers into the desert there
is not the slightest reason for believing that he will behold the
promised view, let alone that two of his disciples will enter the
promised land.

There is no need for self-pity. We are no disinherited generation. It is because there can be no definitive philosophy that

philosophy has a future. There is no definitive art or science either. These enterprises are their own reward.

The aspiration for truth and the love of philosophy can represent escapes into remote abstractions or into the study of the thoughts of others about the thoughts of others. In its inception, however, philosophy is a way of life and, as the Greek word suggests, a kind of love and devotion. It is the life of reflective passion—penetrating experience, unimpeded by accepted formulas, thought about. That was what philosophy meant to Socrates, and if we want to bring philosophy down to earth again, it can mean nothing less than that to us.

The opposition to common sense need not open the way for an oracular philosophy. What is wanted is responsible originality. A departure from common sense may be dictated by honesty.

Berkeley furnishes a fine example of responsible originality, and Plato and Nietzsche have recaptured in their prose the life of passionate reflection. Their common motto, for all their vast differences, was the motto of Socrates' Apology: "The unexamined life is not worth living."

Those who rave at random can be shown up without invoking the authority of common sense. To have a claim on our respect, a philosopher must submit to some kind of discipline which makes it possible for others to raise relevant objections. If myths or etymologies are introduced, a critic must be allowed to do likewise, pitting myth against myth, etymology against etymology.

The final question is never whether a philosopher has made mistakes. Antiseptic thinking is a virtue to impress on students most of whom are quite incapable of ever learning more, if that; but it is a virtue seldom found conjoined with passion and prolific penetration. The writings of the most worth-while philosophers are full of blunders which it is good to have students analyze to train their minds, but which it would be stupid to employ as an excuse for not learning from the texts.

The most crucial question to be asked about any philosopher—even more important than the question "What did he mean?"—is: What has he seen?

If he has seen something new that modifies our previous views in many ways, he should be forgiven a great many blunders. But if he has seen little or nothing and tries to hide a paucity of insight behind a façade of verbiage, his errors scarcely deserve detailed criticism. Philosophy walks the ridge between common sense and fantasy.

IV. RELIGION, FAITH, AND EVIDENCE

33. DEFINITIONS OF RELIGION. In discussions of philosophy it is usually—and quite rightly—taken for granted that there is no need of beginning with a definition. Philosophy is that branch of literature represented by Plato and Aristotle, Descartes and Spinoza, Hobbes and Locke, Berkeley and Hume, Leibniz and Kant, Hegel and Nietzsche, to name a few prominent exponents. Discussions of religion, on the other hand, begin typically with definitions. But not one of these definitions has won wide acceptance, nor is it likely that any ever will. Nevertheless, a quick look at some definitions may serve to warn us against common pitfalls and teach something positive, too.

Two kinds of definitions can be discounted at the outset as mere pseudo-definitions. First, figurative definitions: they do not really refer to religion but have in mind a figurative use of the word. Two examples will show this at a glance. H. Bosanquet said, a man's religion is what "he would die for rather than abandon," and Renan wrote, "My religion is now as ever the progress of reason; in other words, the progress of science" (Leuba, 353, 356). Renan means that he rejects all religions and instead puts his faith in the progress of science. And Bosanquet means that if a man would die for his possessions, his children, or the tenets of his party rather than abandon them, then we might say that *these* are his religion. But few people would die for their religion rather than abandon it, and many more would die for other things.

The second kind of pseudo-definition may be called propagandist, e.g., "all that is fine in man" or "the opiate of the people." One tries to enlist our sympathies for it, the other against it, but neither does justice to the phenomenon at hand.

The attempts at serious definitions are so vast in number that it helps to divide them into three kinds; and this subdivision shows at once how they have failed. The three kinds, long distinguished by Leuba, are: intellectualistic, affectivistic, and voluntaristic or practical definitions.

The first type, understandably most popular among philosophers, defines religion as a kind of knowledge or identifies it with a body of propositions. The central shortcoming of these definitions is that they are one-sided and ignore the importance of emotion and of practices, both ritual and moral. Specific examples are open to further objections: most authors elevate their pet belief into the essence of religion.

Recent writers, for example, have occasionally found the essence of religion in the faith that our universe is governed by a purpose, though in ancient Buddhism and Hinduism this belief was rejected. Max Müller, who translated the major Upanishads into English, found the essence of religion in a faith "which, independent of, nay in spite of, sense and reason, enables man to apprehend the Infinite." Must the object of faith really be infinite? And what is meant by infinite? "In spite of sense" is patently suggested by his field of study and less applicable to other religions, especially to so-called primitive religions. Herbert Spencer, finally, thought that the essence of religion is the belief "that all things are manifestations of a Power that transcends our knowledge." "A Power" limits religion to monotheism which is immediately watered down to Spencer's own agnosticism. There is no need for a catalogue of such definitions. Almost all of them have these two faults: they make the one belief that the author of the definition has retained the essence of religion, and they underplay the nonintellectual aspects of religion.

The second type, affectivistic, includes one attempt that has

gained prominence above all other definitions: Schleiermacher's famous dictum, "The essence of religion consists in the
feeling of an absolute dependence." Here, too, the author's
own religion is projected: the feeling of an absolute dependence is more prominent in Lutheranism than in most other religions. But this feeling is also encountered in the other Christian denominations, in Judaism and Islam, in Hinduism and
in "primitive" religions—though, to put it mildly, it is not especially characteristic of the Buddhist's piety.

The most telling objection to this definition is found in Section VI of Freud's *The Future of an Illusion:* "It is not this
feeling that constitutes the essence of religiousness, but only
the next step, the reaction to it, which seeks a remedy against
this feeling. He who goes no further, he who humbly resigns
himself to the insignificant part man plays in the universe, is,
on the contrary, irreligious in the truest sense of the word."
The feeling Schleiermacher isolates is shared by religious and
irreligious people. There are legions in both camps who lack
this feeling and legions who have it. Clearly, then, it cannot
be the essence of religion.

What Freud calls "the next step" and "the remedy against
this feeling" usually involves action of some sort: practices. And
attempts to find the essence of religion in a practice have been
common, too, and especially popular with anthropologists.
Specific definitions of this sort are open to particular objections. Lord Raglan, for example, says: "Religion is the quest
of life by means of symbols" (117). He is thinking of the Christian sacraments and what they have in common with the rit-
uals encountered in a great many other religions. But his
definition is inapplicable to the religion of the Hebrew prophets
or the Buddha, the Upanishads or the Bhagavadgita. There
are religions in which symbolism has no place and religions in
which "life" is not sought—rather a release from life.

Nor will it do to stress some practice quite apart from all
belief and feeling, as Lord Raglan does. A visiting anthropologist from some South Sea island might consider eating bread
and drinking wine the essence of Christianity. In fact, no practice as such is at all religious: it is only religious in the context

of certain beliefs and emotions. The anthropologist who sees
the ritual is apt to think that it is a mere practice void of all
emotion. He is wrong. Conversely, for the religious man every
practice may well be religious because for him it is suffused
with feelings and beliefs which in most cases he would find
it hard to describe to an anthropologist.

The chief lesson of a survey of attempted definitions of religion is that, in religion, practice, feeling, and belief are inter-
twined, and every definition that would see the essence of religion in just one of these three facets is too partial. Even
Matthew Arnold's famed attempt to fuse two of these elements will never do: "Religion is morality tinged with emotion." You can have morality tinged with emotion without
having religion.

The term "religion" has come into use as a label for referring
all at once to Judaism, Christianity, Islam, Buddhism, Hinduism, Taoism, and Confucianism, as well as a great many other
siblings, some of whom have proper names and some of whom
do not, but all of whom are taken to be sufficiently similar to
the seven mentioned here to make it useful to lump them together. Religion is a collective name, and what we say of religion should be true of the various members of the family. If
it is not, then our statements are wrong, though perhaps they
could be made right by substituting for "religion" some particular religion or religions.

If by "philosophy" we mean primarily the thought of Plato,
Aristotle, and their many heirs, it stands to reason that it is
much easier to generalize about philosophy than it is to generalize about religion; for the world's religions are not descended from the writings of a single author nor developed
from a clearly circumscribed tradition in a single tongue.

In the following pages, "religion" means primarily Christianity, Judaism, and Buddhism. Some remarks will be applicable
to Christianity more than to the others, and yet not to Christianity alone but also to the others. Occasionally, reference will
be made to individual religions, and later on there will be separate discussions of Buddhism, Judaism, and Christianity in an
attempt to do justice to important differences.

34. RELIGION AT THE BAR. Religion is not concerned with truths alone: feelings and practices are central in religion, too. Yet no religion is exhausted by rites or emotions or a fusion of the two: all religions are concerned with truth, too; and on this depends not only their occasional conflict with science—nowhere more in evidence than in the history of Christianity —but also much of their interest to philosophers. The present critique will concentrate almost entirely on the relation of religion and truth, though keeping in mind, and introducing where they are relevant, the nonintellectualistic aspects of religion.

It is often held that religious truth is basically different from other kinds of truth. It will not be possible to settle this crucial question at the outset, but it should prove helpful if we could show what a distinction between different types of truth involves in at least one field other than religion—and why it breaks down. We can then approach religion without the presumption that there are different types of truth.

One type of truth, if not the only type, has been discussed in detail: we have considered the aspiration for truth, the relation of truth and correctness, of truth and meaning, and, finally, different theories of truth. We have also given some attention to the difficulty of making true statements about our emotions.

The kind of truth we have discussed is a property of propositions. Asked whether a statement is true, we consider it as a hypothesis which is subject to investigation and must eventually be judged in the light of the relevant evidence. It is by no means immoral for a scientist, historian, or philosopher to hope that some proposition may be proved true, or to feel strongly about it. But it is considered immoral for him to be partial to the point of suppressing relevant evidence, and it is a sign of incompetence, if not a violation of professional ethics, if he fails to undertake a relevant investigation for fear that its results might be fatal for a belief he cherishes.

The attitude of religious people toward religious propositions is quite different from all this. If a man accepts a religious proposition as true, it is hardly ever after having first considered it as a hypothesis and found compelling evidence through an impartial inquiry. Few religious people have studied comparative religion, and hardly any have attained their beliefs as a result of such a study: yet this would be *de rigeur* if the religious person's attitude toward the religious propositions he believes were at all similar to the historian's or the scientist's attitude toward the propositions with which they concern themselves.

The fact that the religious person frequently considers his religious propositions ever so much more important only aggravates the problem. *The more important the issue at hand, the more it demands careful scrutiny.* This is a simple but important point which most religious people overlook.

Is there, then, another type of truth—or at least another legitimate attitude toward truth? An attitude often encountered among religious people and exemplified professionally by a great many preachers and theologians is that of the counsel for the defense. Here is an attitude toward truth quite different from the scientist's or the historian's, but no less methodical and disciplined and moral. Only it is governed by a different morality.

In many countries the counsel for the defense is expected to use all his ingenuity as well as passionate appeals to the emotions to gain credence for a predetermined conclusion—namely, that his client is innocent. He may ignore some of the evidence if he can get away with it, and he is under no obligation to carry out investigations which are likely to discredit his conclusion. If, after all that, he cannot convince the jury of the truth of his position, he will saddle his opponent with the burden of disproof; and if necessary he will rest content with a reasonable doubt that his position *might* be true.

Common though this attitude is toward religion, it is indefensible outside the courtroom, and it does not indicate a second type of truth.

In the first place, some unusual conditions obtain in the courts where this attitude is legitimate. The very fact of the indictment creates some presumption, psychologically, that the accused is guilty. Then, the prosecutor is an official of the gov-

ernment and aided by its vast resources, ranging all the way
from its prestige to its police. Against such formidable odds
the defense requires a handicap; and that is one reason why
it is conceded the liberties that have been mentioned. In the
case of religion, the situation is more nearly the opposite. Its
advocates are aided by the government's prestige and by volu-
ble testimony from officeholders and would-be officeholders;
and the case for all kinds of religious propositions is proclaimed
not only from the pulpits but in our most popular magazines,
too, and in the press, and over radio and television, while the
case against these propositions never gets a comparable hearing. If the courtroom analogy could be extended to the case
of religion, the prerogatives mentioned should be granted to
its critics to redress the balance.

Secondly, a jury is not asked to come up with the most likely
story or even the most likely culprit. The jury is confronted
with a single suspect, and truth is not the highest consideration. Better let two guilty men go free than punish one who is
innocent.

Suppose that the major philosophic positions were haled into
court, one at a time, each defended by a brilliant advocate.
Surely, these attorneys—it could even be the same lawyer every time—would succeed time and again in raising a reasonable
doubt in the mind of the jury that the position might be true.
The attorney might not even have to try very hard if the prose-
cution were under pressure to pull its punches, as it is in the
case of religion. Position after position would be acquitted. But
such acquittal of a philosophy or a religion creates no presumption whatsoever that the position is probably true. In the end,
those who care for a considered choice would still have the
whole field to choose from.

We have here two different attitudes toward truth, but not
two different types of truth. The second attitude, unlike the
first, subordinates questions of truth to other questions of a
moral kind. In fact, it might be argued that the verdict of
the jury, "We find the accused not guilty," is not so much a
determination of fact as it is a deceptively phrased recommendation for action. In line with this, the records show that when

juries know that a finding of "guilty" makes the death penalty mandatory they will find the accused guilty much less often.

There is no need here to distinguish legal truth from other kinds of truth: such a distinction only prompts confusion. Consider a case that happens occasionally: some of the evidence against the accused has been obtained illegally or was not legally admissible in court, and the judge therefore directs the jury to find the accused not guilty. There is no point whatsoever here in introducing any conflict between types of truth. Clearly, the truth is in this case subordinated to respect for civil rights. And the situation can be explained perfectly in terms of the one and only kind of truth we have encountered so far.

"Guilty" and "not guilty" are, in the mouth of a jury, elliptical expressions which are only apparently identical with these phrases in other contexts. In a verdict they mean "proved guilty (or not proved guilty) in accordance with the special rules of evidence and argument that govern court procedure." Thus the accused may well be guilty in the ordinary sense but not guilty in this more restricted sense.

A jury operates under unusual conditions and is not expected to decide more than the special question whether the accused has been proved guilty in accordance with a certain set of rules. Neither the jury's attitude nor that of the counsel for the defense is at all appropriate when we are asked if a religious proposition is true or not true. (Cf. also § 24.)

35. "SUBJECTIVE" TRUTH. Some people think that in addition to "objective" truth with which we deal in science we should recognize "subjective" truth which is allegedly legitimate in other contexts. "Subjective" truth means that something is "true for me." "Subjective" truth is a fond nickname for self-deception.

If this should not be evident at first glance, let us see what people mean when they are speaking of "subjective" truth. They may mean one or more of several things.

First, what they mean may be no more than subjective certainty. In that case, nothing is gained by speaking of subjective truth: "certainty" is much clearer and avoids misunderstandings. Instead of saying that a proposition can be subjectively true for a man regardless of its objective untruth, it is less misleading to say that a man may feel certain that something is true even when, in fact, it happens to be false.

Secondly, what is meant may be sincerity. Again, there is no point in speaking of two kinds of truth: a man can be sincere and wrong, and he can be right but a hypocrite. And in some contexts his sincerity is more important than the question whether he is right.

Third, what is meant may be that some belief makes you happy. In that case, face the facts and say: it may be false, but I wish it were true; indeed, if it is false, I do not want to know it, for the belief gives me happiness. That would be clearer than to say that "it is true for me."

Kierkegaard confused all three points—and not only these three—when he argued in the *Concluding Unscientific Postscript* that "truth is subjectivity." (See the Kierkegaard chapter of my *From Shakespeare to Existentialism*.) Apologists for him have sometimes claimed that what he meant was not the truth of propositions: a dubious defense in any case but, more important, quite at variance with his arguments and examples. Again and again he speaks of propositions, and he is guilty of a multiple confusion. We can believe something sincerely and with certainty, and it may make us happy—and be false.

Talk of "subjective" truth suggests that "objective" truth is, after all, not everything; and that is true enough. But it is all the truth there is.

36. KNOWLEDGE, BELIEF, AND FAITH. One distinction between types of truth is almost as old as philosophy itself: ever since the time of Parmenides and Plato, philosophers have distinguished knowledge and belief; and originally it was supposed that these differed in their objects. Knowledge was held to be the apprehension of what is eternal and immutable, while belief was identified with apprehension of the changing objects

of our sense experience. This distinction was accompanied by the conviction that belief is inferior to knowledge because knowledge is certain while belief is not.

Christianity inverted this position. The Christian holds that knowledge is apprehension of changing sense objects, while belief alone can grasp what is eternal and immutable; and belief is held to be superior because it alone is certain.

"I will destroy the wisdom of the wise," Paul writes to the Corinthians. "God has chosen the foolish things of the world to confound the wise." The "knowledge" of the Greeks is toppled from its height: "the Greeks seek after wisdom," Paul says scornfully; and our faith is "to the Greeks foolishness." While the god of Plato's *Timaeus* had been a mathematician, the Christians soon came to think of God as flouting mathematics, when they developed the conception of the Trinity.

It is not necessary in the present context to consider in detail the influence of Platonism on some of the early fathers of the church, or to distinguish Plato's *doxa* from the Christian *pistis*. The point is that in our time an effort to distinguish knowledge and belief is complicated by the presence of these two different traditions. Clearly, the customary notion that belief, unlike knowledge, always implies uncertainty is untenable. In the religious usage, and in other usages that have been influenced by this, belief is quite compatible with certainty and may even imply it.

What distinguishes knowledge is not certainty but evidence. When I say truthfully, "I know this proposition to be true," I assert, first, that I think that it is true, and, secondly, that my opinion is backed up by evidence sufficient to compel the concurrence of every reasonable person. When both conditions are in fact met, and I am, moreover, right, I really do know; but if the second condition is not met, then, even if the proposition happens to be true, I did not *know*. The mere fact that I feel certain and happen to be right does not mean I know.

This crucial connection of knowledge with evidence has been appreciated insufficiently even in what may well be the most suggestive discussion of knowledge in recent years: the essay on "Other Minds" by Professor J. L. Austin of Oxford.

He stresses the analogy between "to promise" and "to know" and writes: "If I have said I know or I promise, you insult me in a special way by refusing to accept it." "Where someone has said to me 'I know,' I am entitled to say *I* know too, at second hand. The right to say 'I know' is transmissible, in the sort of way that other authority is transmissible. Hence, if I say it lightly, I may be *responsible* for getting *you* into trouble."

We understand immediately what Austin means, and yet we should not dream of saying, "*I* know too, at second hand" merely because some other person has declared that *he* "knew," unless he was a quite uncommon person. When a politician or a preacher or one of my students says, "I know," I certainly am not entitled to say, "I know, too, at second hand"; and if I do say it I cannot claim in self-defense that he has been responsible for getting me into trouble: I am responsible myself. Before I make up my mind whether I am to accept a statement that is introduced "I know that," I must ask myself about the speaker's notion of evidence.

Austin's point that knowing is not an activity like reading is well taken: you could not answer the question "What are you doing?" by saying, "Oh, I am just knowing." He is also right that "I know" sometimes means "You can rely on it, and you won't get into trouble if you take my word for it." But even when it does mean that, this is not all that is meant. Else, to begin with a linguistic point, it would be possible to know "firmly" even as one may promise, believe, or rely firmly. And secondly, if this account were right, the question could never arise whether somebody *really* knows, except in the sense in which one might ask whether somebody really believes or promises something. When I say advisedly, "I know," I say something about the evidence corroborating what I claim. And if you take my word for it and don't get into trouble, but in fact there was not evidence sufficient to compel concurrence by all reasonable persons, then I did not in fact know.

I should even go a step further and say, contravening all the customary accounts from Plato to Austin, that it does make sense to say, "I know" and then, without retracting this, in answer to a further question: "Of course, I could conceivably be wrong." From Plato to Austin, philosophers have argued that "I believe" countenances the sad possibility that I might be mistaken, while "I know" does not. On the contrary: "I believe" is sometimes meant to rule out this contingency, especially in a religious context, while "I know" does not always involve such overconfidence.

If I told you that Nietzsche was born in 1844, and you asked me whether I merely thought so or knew it, I might well reply, "I know." I should mean that my assertion was not based on doubtful recollection or conjecture but on evidence sufficient to compel assent by every reasonable person. All the books by friend and foe agree on this point and I see no reason whatsoever for suspicion. Nothing indicates why someone should have cared to give a false date to begin with; and if someone had, I think it would have been found out by now. Should I admit an outside possibility in spite of this that after all I could conceivably be wrong? Of course.

If I were to be found mistaken, then I did not in fact know and I should no longer say "I knew," though my initial use of "know" was honest and responsible. Morally, it is as if I had said "I shall be there at 12," but subsequently did not come because I had a heart attack.

This may be a subtle point, but "I know" is not like "I promise": it is much less akin to a ritual word like that, or to "performative" words, to use Austin's influential term, then it is to assertions like "I shall be there at 12." If I have said this and then failed, I was mistaken. If I promised and failed, I still did promise. But if I have said, "I know it is 12" and it was not 12, then I was mistaken and did not really know. Therefore a purist might well argue that I should never say, "I know"—and that I should never say, "I shall do this" either, because I might not live to do it. But only a pedant will always add "God willing," and an agnostic pedant could not even say that. And "to the best of my knowledge I know" is a barbarism.

Knowledge and belief, like most interesting terms, have many correct uses, and no distinction is likely to do perfect justice to all correct uses. At best, it can illuminate most. If it meets that test, then it is no very serious argument against it if an unenlightened application or an overliteral persistence leads to blunders.

Belief has a wider sense in which it includes knowledge and a narrower sense in which it is contrasted with knowledge. In the wider sense, I believe that something is true if, and only if, I think it is true; and if I know that 2 plus 2 is 4, then I believe it, too. When I am asked whether I really believe something, the question is whether I really think it is true: I am asked whether I am in earnest.

When I say that I *know* that a proposition is true, I say that I think that it is true; that in fact it is true; and that there is evidence sufficient to compel the assent of every reasonable person. When I am asked whether I really know, the question does not concern myself alone (my earnestness or my sincerity) but also the evidence. If I think there is sufficient evidence to prove the proposition, I am apt to say that I know it is true; but if, in fact, the evidence is insufficient, then I did not know even if, by sheer good luck, it happened to be true.

In the absence of any universally acknowledged rules of evidence, the determination whether the evidence is sufficient to prove a proposition involves judgment—personal discretion. It is at this point, and at this point only, that, in Austin's words, "I give others my authority" when I say that I know. I am telling them that I judge the evidence sufficient for any reasonable person. Whether I really have this authority or not, that you must judge in terms of what you know of my qualifications to judge the evidence that is relevant.

The close connection between knowledge and evidence becomes particularly clear when we move from one field to another in which different standards of evidence obtain. A man may say that he knows something to be true; but if informed that his assertion, if repeated under oath, would send another person to the gallows, he might say that on second thought he did not know. The other way around, we should consider a man rather strange if, asked whether he knew that it rained in New York yesterday, he should apply the rules of evidence employed in the preceding case and say he did not know, because his belief was based on hearsay and on circumstantial evidence.

Belief in the narrow sense, in which it is contrasted with knowledge, is distinguished by the lack of evidence sufficient to compel the assent of every reasonable person.

It may seem that the introduction of "every reasonable person" is a screen for some kind of circular argument. This is sometimes true in ethics where some writers deem "unreasonable" all who disagree with their own moral judgments. In the present context, no such difficulty is encountered. The person who believes in the narrower sense of that word may well reserve some special epithets for those who do not share his own beliefs, but he will not insist that the cleft between those who do and don't believe will coincide with that between the reasonable and unreasonable. He may say that many reasonable people are predestined for damnation, perhaps also that, to cite the words of Paul once more, "God has chosen the foolish"; but he will not claim that the unregenerate are *eo ipso* the unreasonable. He will grant, in other words, that his belief is not supported by evidence sufficient to compel the assent of every reasonable person.

Faith is belief—usually belief in the narrow sense—that is held intensely, with some emotional involvement; and almost all statements that begin "I have faith that . . ." fulfill one further condition: one would be disappointed if one should be wrong.

One can say: "I have faith I shall recover." One cannot say, without doing violence to language: "I have faith that I have cancer." The degree of emotional involvement may differ greatly, and the disappointment if I should be wrong may range from brief regret, forgotten the next day, to a total breakdown. The word faith is by no means reserved for the last contingency, nor is it a good recommendation that it ought to be: it is too difficult to predict how a person will react if he is disappointed.

The conditions specified here explicate no more than certain minimal characteristics of all kinds of faith, ranging from

relatively trivial instances to a profound commitment. What
matters at the moment is that faith, being an intense and
confident belief, is not necessarily closer to knowledge than any
other belief. If you say, "I have faith that our team will win,"
I know that you think it will win; that you feel strongly about
this; and that you would be disappointed if it lost. But for
those engaged in an impartial investigation, a man's faith
creates no presumption whatsoever of a higher probability; on
the contrary, it is more suspicious than a less emotional belief. It raises the question whether there is considerable, albeit not compelling, evidence, or whether "faith" is out a
noble word for wishful thinking.

37. FAITH, EVIDENCE, AND JAMES.   That faith is usually not
supported by sufficient evidence to prove the truth of that
which is believed to every reasonable person, has been admitted frequently by many prominent religious writers. St.
Thomas conceded calmly that the crucial articles of faith were
not based on evidence sufficient to compel the assent of every
reasonable person. (Cf. § 45.) Some other Christian writers
have made this concession with an air of bold defiance if not
truculence. Paul boasted that what he believed was "to the
Greeks foolishness"; Tertullian, that it was "impossible";
Luther, that it contradicted reason; Kierkegaard, that it was
utterly absurd. The impression given is sometimes, in contemporary discussions, too, that there is a virtue in believing
without evidence as such. But this would open the floodgates
to every superstition, prejudice, and madness.

Proponents of religious faith sometimes define it as belief
which rests on no evidence whatever. This may be a clever
strategem, but the claim is manifestly false. There is something that moves a man to accept a religious proposition as
true: the testimony of a book perhaps, or of hundreds of books;
the testimony of some people whom he trusts; or the agreement of millions of people—to mention only a few possibilities. Such evidence is insufficient to compel assent by every
reasonable person; it would not stand up in court. And it is to

anticipate this discovery that it is said: faith rests on no evidence whatsoever.

In the two opposed papers on the question "Are Religious Dogmas Cognitive and Meaningful?" which were debated at the meeting of the Eastern Division of the American Philosophical Association in 1953 and published in advance, Professor Demos of Harvard claimed that faith rests on no evidence at all, and his opponent, Professor Ducasse, granted this, clearly because he thought that this admission was most damaging. So the gambit worked and withdrew attention from such crucial questions as: What kind of evidence is required for various beliefs? and in the absence of what kind of evidence would a belief become unreasonable? Demos' suggestion that the scientist has "faith" in the uniformity of nature and the reliability of memory without any evidence whatever blurs these all-important issues.

To be sure, Hume pointed out that any argument intended to prove that regularities in nature noted in the past will obtain in the future, too, is bound to be circular: what is said is usually that *in the past* the regularities observed in past events have recurred in the future; but we cannot claim that what has been characteristic of the past will be characteristic of the future, too, without begging the question. Still—Demos notwithstanding—we can readily conceive of negative evidence that would lead us to modify or renounce our belief. Again, we must concede that any argument for the reliability of memory is bound to invoke, at least implicitly, the reliability of memory. But does this establish that we may quite generally entertain beliefs without all evidence whatever? Does anything go, then?

At this point, Professor Demos harks back to another Harvard philosopher who blurred the same issues more than half a century before him: William James, in his slipshod but celebrated essay on "The Will to Believe." Instead of admitting that some traditional beliefs are comforting, James argued that "the risk of being in error is a very small matter when compared with the blessing of real knowledge," and implied that those who did not accept religious beliefs were cowards, afraid of risking anything: "It is like a general informing his soldiers that it is better to keep out of battle forever than to risk a single wound" (Section VII).

James' appeal depends entirely on blurring the distinction between those who hold out for 100 per cent proof in a matter in which any reasonable person rests content with, let us say, 90 per cent, and those who refuse to indulge in a belief which is supported only by the argument that after all it could conceivably be true.

Unlike Demos, James made an attempt to define "the permissible cases" in which it is intellectually reputable to believe in the absence of "sufficient" evidence—but his attempt failed utterly. The belief must, he argued, fulfill three criteria (Section I).

It must represent a "live" option. But one man's live option is another man's dead option: Roman Catholicism does not represent a live option for James ("to us Protestants these means of salvation seem such foregone impossibilities"), but for millions it is a living issue. This first criterion can be rephrased in all fairness: the belief must tempt us.

The second criterion is no less unhelpful: the option must be "forced." Consider his own illustration. If I say, " 'Either call my theory true or call it false,' your option is avoidable. . . . You may decline to offer any judgment as to my theory. But if I say, 'Either accept this truth or go without it,' I put on you a forced option, for there is no standing place outside of the alternative." To satisfy criterion two, all I need is a little skill in phrasing.

Finally, the option must be "momentous." If it is live, forced, and momentous, James calls the option "genuine" and claims that we have "the right to believe" without "sufficient" evidence. What else is this but an invitation to wishful thinking, provided only we are tempted very much?

James makes a virtue of wishful thinking: courage, to be specific. If a belief seems pleasing to you and matters to you, ask yourself: "Am I to accept it or go without it?" Only a coward will hesitate. In James' own words: "Our errors are surely not such awfully solemn things. In a world where we are so certain to incur them in spite of all our caution, a certain lightness of heart seems healthier than this excessive nervousness on their behalf" (VII).

To be sure, we must constantly act in the absence of complete certainty; we have to make decisions on the basis of partial evidence; and we are bound to make mistakes frequently. Challenged why we decide the way we do, we should cite the evidence we had in mind. There is no need at all for striking back: "Either accept this truth or go without it." There is no need for the faith that we surely must be right. We need believe no more than that, given our present information, this or that appears to be most probable.

It is a widespread fallacy that the alternative to the firm faith that we possess the truth must be weak indecision. It is quite possible to act with vigor, realizing that one might be wrong; especially, if one is sustained by the assurance that one's decision was conscientiously arrived at and that one is acting with integrity, though not infallibility.

It is not even true, though James shared this belief with most Americans of his time and our own, that to succeed one must believe one will succeed. If you should try to jump across a ditch which all but passes your capacity, what is decisive is not that you believe you will succeed but that you should give it all you have. If you have faith but do not try as hard as possible, you will not succeed. If you should think that it is most unlikely that you will succeed, but nevertheless you try as hard as you can, you may succeed. What matters is not faith but effort; and that effort without faith that we shall succeed is either psychologically impossible or doomed to failure, while faith spells success, that is a myth which most Americans believe—without sufficient evidence. They do not bother to distinguish between hope and faith and are impervious to the glory of the hero who lacks both. But where success is esteemed higher than integrity, there can be no understanding of tragedy.

James' essay reaches its nadir when near the end he formulates *"the religious hypothesis"* which confronts him—and his audience, he hopes—with a live, forced, momentous option.

Here are his own words: "Religion says essentially two things. First, she says that the best things are the more eternal things, the overlapping things, the things in the universe that throw the last stone, so to speak, and say the final word. 'Perfection is eternal,'—this phrase of Charles Secretan seems a good way of putting this first affirmation of religion, an affirmation which obviously cannot yet be verified scientifically at all. The second affirmation of religion is that we are better off even now if we believe her first affirmation to be true." If we suspend judgment, "although we do avoid error in that way *if religion be untrue,* we lose the good, *if it be true,* just as certainly as if we positively chose to disbelieve."

Surely, no religion really says what James here claims "religion says." But if it did, what exactly would it be saying? What does it mean to say that "the best things are the more eternal things"? "Best" is vague, and "more eternal" comes close to being nonsense: either something is eternal or it is not. To add that the best things are "the overlapping things" and "throw the last stone, so to speak" only adds further mystification. Is James referring to God but embarrassed to say so? And what are we to make of his concession that this affirmation "cannot *yet* be verified scientifically"? He writes as if "the religious hypothesis" were a more or less scientific hypothesis for which no crucial experiment had been devised as yet: one almost gets the feeling that a colleague is working on it even now in the next room, that verification is around the corner, and that we should be stupid if we did not take a chance on it without delay.

In Section IV of his essay, James had argued that "our passional nature not only lawfully may, but must, decide an option between propositions, whenever it is a genuine option that cannot by its nature be decided on intellectual grounds"—and even used italics for these lines. But in the last section he maintains "*in abstracto,* that we have the right to believe at our own risk any hypothesis that is live enough to tempt our will," and adds: "*In concreto,* the freedom to believe can only cover living options which the intellect of the individual cannot by itself resolve; and living options never seem absurdities to him

who has them to consider." And he adds further that it would
be queer and fantastic to suspend belief "till such a time as
our intellect and senses working together may have raked in
evidence enough." We are no longer limited to cases which are
by their nature undecidable—and about which we should
surely have to ask what the proposition that tempts us means
—but may believe in all cases where decision is difficult, even
if it is only difficult for *us*.

Perhaps Santayana was right when he said in his amusing
essay on James: "He did not really believe; he merely believed
in the right of believing that you might be right if you believed." Certainly, James did not believe in the Christian God.
And in a later work, *A Pluralistic Universe,* where James
proclaims, "I hold to the finite God" (111), he still ends up
by furnishing a "faith ladder" which leads up from "It *might*
be true" to "It shall be *held for true,* you decide; it *shall be*
as if true, for *you*" (328 f.)—no higher. The locution "true
for me" has been discussed in Section 35.

Surely, James himself had "the will to believe" and Santayana was wrong when he explained James' motivation: "he
wished the intellectual cripples and hunchbacks not to be
jeered at." But Santayana's central criticism may be safely accepted: "If the argument is rather that these beliefs, whether
true or false, make life better in this world, the thing is simply false. To be boosted by an illusion is not to live better than
to live in harmony with the truth; it is not nearly so safe, not
nearly so sweet, and not nearly so fruitful. These refusals to
part with a decayed illusion are really an infection to the mind.
Believe, certainly; we cannot help believing; but believe rationally, holding what seems certain for certain, what seems
probable for probable, what seems desirable for desirable, and
what seems false for false."

James' essay on "The Will to Believe" is an unwitting compendium of common fallacies and a manual of self-deception.
Two errors remain to be noted. First, he blurs the distinction
between facts which my belief could at least conceivably help
to bring about—e.g., that a girl reciprocates my love—and facts
which no belief could help to bring about if they were not

facts to begin with—e.g., that God exists or that Jesus was resurrected on the third day.

Secondly, he assumes without argument that religion in general offers us some kind of a hypothesis, which he himself calls, using italics, "the religious hypothesis." In fact, religion in general is an abstraction while there really are a number of historical religions which are characterized among other things by many utterly heterogeneous beliefs which cannot by any means be dealt with in like fashion. Individual religious affirmations are much more like a great many nonreligious affirmations than they are like scores of other religious affirmations of a different type.

The answer to the question "Are religious dogmas cognitive and meaningful?" might well be that some are and some are not. The affirmation that Jesus is of one substance with the Father poses problems utterly different from the affirmation that he rose on the third day or that he was crucified under Pontius Pilate, and suffered, and was buried. Certainly, it is not true that all these statements rest on no evidence whatever or that they are all of a kind with the statement that the future will resemble the past.

Suppose a man wrote a paper maintaining that Lincoln was never shot, or that there is a star between earth and moon, or that there are eight devils: it would never do for him to retort when challenged for the evidence, "What evidence have you got for the uniformity of nature or the reliability of memory?" Different kinds of propositions require different kinds and quantities of evidence. Confronted with the affirmations to which different religions attach great importance, we cannot simply assume without examination that all such propositions are in the same class with the assertion of the uniformity of nature. Religious statements differ widely.

38. THREE TYPES OF RELIGIOUS PROPOSITIONS. There are more types, but a brief glance at three should suffice to illustrate the heterogeneity of religious propositions. In all three

cases, evidence is relevant, but the procedures of evaluation differ.

First, there are historical statements. We know what kind of evidence is required to substantiate such propositions as "Lincoln was shot in 1865" or "Lincoln himself said, 'with malice toward none.'" There are eyewitness accounts and newspaper accounts the following morning, if not the same day, which agree in essentials; and in the second case we might even find the manuscript of the speech in Lincoln's handwriting. If there were any reason for suspicion, we know what evidence would support a charge of forgery or falsification of the records; and if need be, we are quite prepared to consider the motives of our witnesses, the possibility of a conspiracy among them, the chance that all of them had been deceived, and so forth.

Taken literally, such statements as "Jesus rose from the dead the third day" or "Jesus himself said, 'no man comes to the Father, but by me'" are in the same category: they are historical statements. They are supported by some evidence which, however, does not compare with that for the above two statements about Lincoln. There are no eyewitness accounts but only documents written decades after the events which they discuss, by men who were demonstrably influenced by the needs and violent polemics of a later age and often disagree on vital points. Nor did the writers have the regard for historical accuracy which is common in some quarters today.

It is further relevant when Matthew tells us, for example, that when Christ died, "the graves were opened; and many bodies of the saints which slept arose, and came out of the graves after his resurrection, and went into the holy city, and appeared to many." Evidently, the resurrection did not seem to Matthew as extraordinary as it does to our contemporaries: it was to his mind, and his audience's, unusual—a little more so than the earthquake he reports in the preceding verse—but by no means unique.

Many a claim that is a stumbling block to the contemporary Christian was a powerful aid to belief when it was first presented: if Jesus had been the Messiah, then he must have fulfilled certain prophecies by way of satisfying the criteria for messiahship, or, to use the semi-Greek term, Christhood.

It is now a commonplace among Protestants no less than Jews and has even found its way into the Revised Standard Version of the Bible that the verse in Isaiah of which Matthew thought that it demanded a virgin birth as one of the criteria of Christhood had been mistranslated in the Greek Bible. And for thousands in the Hellenistic world, anybody who was anybody at all simply had to be the child of deity and virgin.

Paul's recital of the historical evidence for his central claim that Jesus "was raised on the third day in accordance with the scriptures" (I Cor. 15) persuaded the Corinthians but is a stumbling block to many modern Protestants who want to interpret the resurrection less literally.

Ascriptions of qualities to a historical figure are also historical statements, provided that the quality is defined independently of the ascription; e.g., "Lincoln had a sense of humor" or "Jesus was more vituperative than the Buddha" or "Jesus was perfect."

The point regarding all such statements that is too often forgotten is that there *is* evidence supporting them, and in some instances also evidence against them, and all this evidence has to be evaluated. This evaluation involves such questions as these: How close are the accounts which support a belief to the events which they describe, both spatially and temporally? How consistent is each account taken by itself, and how consistent with each other are the different accounts we have? What else has a bearing on the credibility of these accounts? What can we say about the biases of each? about its motivation? and the history of the texts?

If Paul, whose Epistles antedate the Gospels, never refers to the virgin birth, which would have been of the greatest interest to his audience, this must count as evidence against the virgin birth, though certainly not as conclusive evidence against it; while if Paul did not refer to Jesus' childhood in Nazareth, a name that would have meant little or nothing to his audience, that would not count against the belief that Jesus spent his childhood there.

Again, the childhood in Nazareth and the birth in Bethlehem are by no means equally probable: the latter was believed to be required by tradition—"for thus it is written by the prophet" (Matt. 2.5)—and there is no agreement on it in the Gospels. The birth in Bethlehem is known only to Luke and Matthew, who give conflicting accounts of it. Moreover, each couples it with a different historic claim which seems false in the light of our independent knowledge of that period: the census in Luke and Herod's massacre in Matthew, which recalls the birth story of Moses, as does the flight to Egypt. Both of these claims also raise problems of internal consistency. Thus there is considerable reason for doubting the claim that Jesus was born in Bethlehem. (Cf. Major 231 ff., 266 ff.)

Inherently less likely claims must be supported by stronger evidence to win our credence. To believe that Jesus literally rose from the dead the third day, I require stronger evidence than to believe that he was born in Bethlehem.

The second category of religious propositions can be dealt with much more briefly: generalizations: "Only Etonians are brave under fire" and "The Christian faith begets charity" belong in the same category, and the procedure for verifying or falsifying such statements is sufficiently familiar to require no discussion. Yet there is an extraordinary reluctance to admit that religious generalizations must be treated like any others, which is the less reasonable because such statements are unmistakably meant literally and not symbolically or any other way.

To illustrate this reluctance, take the refrain "You can't have guts without [belief in] God" which so endeared the yarns of a Canadian to the editors of *Reader's Digest*—until his stories were proved a complete hoax. As soon as we look for negative instances, this generalization is seen to be preposterous. Did Leonidas and his Spartans lack "guts"? Or Mutius Scaevola? (Cf. § 61.) Or Stalin?

By persistently encouraging and even inculcating such false generalizations—some relatively trivial, like "There are no atheists in foxholes"; others like those concerning the relation between faith and works, as essential doctrine—the Christian churches have been, and still are, fountainheads of anti-intellectualism and opposition to critical thinking. Nor is it an extenuating circumstance that religious sophisticates occasionally fall back on nonliteral interpretations (which will be considered later) or redefine some of the terms to make such statements tautological; for the impact of these statements depends on their literal meaning. And to rely on this when speaking from the pulpit, while resorting to qualifications in discussions with philosophers, does not spread a regard for intellectual integrity.

The third category of religious statements consists of speculative propositions, e.g., "The center of the earth is fiery, and some of the dead are frying there" or "Consciousness survives death." Such propositions require corroboration or refutation of a kind different from that appropriate for generalizations or historic statements. Obviously, the procedure will differ significantly even for different speculative statements, as is evident from the two examples just given.

In sum, the propositions to which a religion attaches decisive significance and in terms of which it defines itself do not constitute a category by themselves but are utterly heterogeneous. Confronted with a religious statement, we must determine in which category it is, and this in turn will tell us what kind of evidence is relevant for deciding whether the proposition is true, probably true, probably false, or certainly false.

39. RECOURSE TO REVELATION OR MIRACLES.   Some religious people think there is one kind of evidence which proves conclusively the truth of their beliefs: revelation.

Are we to believe that God exists because a book asserting his existence was revealed by him and therefore must be right? Or that Jesus was God because Jesus said he was, and if he was God he could not be wrong? After all, when Father Divine makes the same claim, most of us do not believe him. Even if we assume that Jesus made this claim—which is highly doubt-ful in view of the evidence—why should we believe him, unless it were because we think he really was God, which begs the question.

Even if we grant, for the sake of the present argument, that God exists and sometimes reveals propositions to mankind, the two questions remain which John Locke noted long ago: How do we know in any given instance whether what confronts us is a true revelation? and how do we know that we understand it right? The first of these two questions asks about criteria by which we can recognize trustworthy revelations and has never been answered at all adequately.

Those who have tried to answer it have adduced five criteria which are quite inadequate, both separately and taken in con-junction. The first of these is subjective certainty, which would sanction every fanaticism. That this is not a *sufficient* criterion of revelation will be readily acknowledged. But is it even a necessary condition? Some of the Christian mystics felt any-thing but sure that it was God who spoke to them, and even searched their souls in fear that it might possibly have been the devil.

The second criterion, supposed widely to be a safeguard against reprehensible fanaticism, is that the "fruits" of the alleged revelation must be good. This suggestion overlooks that an evaluation of the "fruits" involves a value standard. Are we to suppose that we know what is good and evil, and then judge the "fruits" according to our lights? Clearly, this would leave room for wide disagreement. More important still, what is allegedly revealed is in most cases that some things are good and should be done. If a man claims to have had a revelation telling him to kill all infidels and sets about to do this, by what standard should we judge the "fruits"? More-over, the word "fruits" is vague. Are we to think primarily of the effects of the alleged revelation on the life of the man who has had it? In many cases, it is far from obvious what these effects have been. Are we to charge his conduct to his strange experience or to the weakness of his character or to some other causes? Or should we think not so much of the fruits in his life as those in history? What, then, are the fruits of the mystic experiences of Francis of Assisi? Do they include those developments in his order which conflicted with his own intentions and grieved him? Do they include the prominent participation of his order in the Inquisition? And how should we evaluate the fruits of Luther's inspiration? of Mohammed's? or of Jesus'?

The third criterion, indispensable for any church, is that the revelation, to be genuine, must not conflict with an accepted body of tradition. This tradition, however, is in almost all cases sufficiently ambiguous to permit the great religious figures to cite tradition against tradition. Surely, this is what all the great religious figures have done: they were always opposed to much tradition. If this third criterion were applied with rigor, it would restrict the name of revelation to convenient corroborations of what we have known for ages, and it would bar novelty. In any case, this criterion is no help in the most crucial cases: in the case of Moses, Jesus, and Mohammed it quite fails us.

The fourth criterion is championed by some authors, including St. Thomas and, to name a Protestant, Paul Tillich, but rejected by a host of others: to be genuine, a revelation must not oppose reason, though it may add to our rational knowledge. Presumably, this would rule out alleged revelations that ten times ten is ninety, which is hardly very helpful; but it leaves room for a multitude of sins. The meaning of "reason" in this context must, moreover, be quite narrow to allow for the doctrine of the Trinity, to give a single instance: if that is not ruled out it is hard to see what claim that a religious person might make would be ruled out by this fourth criterion.

There remains a fifth one: that the experience must not be explainable in wholly naturalistic terms. The first point to note here is that it is debatable whether ordinary vision and hearing and dreams, or any process involving some form of consciousness, is *fully* explainable naturalistically. Secondly, it is not clear why experiences which are as explicable as others should be sweepingly ruled out as possible revelations: certainly, the Bible thought that dreams could be used by God to reveal things to man; and would the claim that St. Paul was an epileptic necessarily rule out the claim that he had a revelation on the road to Damascus? Thirdly, there does not seem to be any significant correlation between experiences that are particularly hard, if not impossible, to account for and those which are alleged to have been revelations. As Pratt says in a highly sympathetic account of mysticism, "certainly the facts of mysticism are not such as to drive us out of the realm of all possible scientific knowledge." And a few sentences later he adds: "The Absolute may explain *everything;* it cannot explain anything in particular" (446). *The Personality of Man,* a Pelican Book by G. N. M. Tyrrell, contains brief accounts of vast numbers of experiences which are far harder to explain in contemporary scientific terms than most alleged revelations, and the annals of the Society for Psychical Research, on which Tyrrell draws, contain hundreds more; yet few people would claim that such experiences are revelations.

It is highly doubtful, then, if any of the above five criteria could be said to be necessary conditions of revelation; and it is clear that none of them is a sufficient condition. The possibility remains that in conjunction these five might be sufficient. If a man has an experience which seems to defy naturalistic explanation and he derives some firm belief from this, if this belief is not contrary to reason nor at variance with what we have believed all along, and if his conduct after this experience is agreeable or even admirable, would this prove that he had a revelation? Those who believe in revelation would be among the first to say that it would not.

When we come to the claims that certain books are revealed scriptures, these five criteria are even more obviously inadequate. Clearly, the bare fact that some people feel certain that a book has been revealed by God is insufficient; and the people in question generally feel no less certain that the certainty of their rivals is no proof at all. The "fruits" of a book cannot be judged for the reasons mentioned above. Conformity with a tradition is not applicable; that the book should not contradict "reason" is no help at all; and those who do not accept the claims of some specific scripture find it none too difficult to account for the writing of the book without invoking any supernatural event.

There is no need, therefore, to examine in detail the difficulties raised by John Locke's second question: Confronted with a revelation, how should we know that we understood it right? It will suffice to call attention to the fact that those who do accept a certain scripture as the revelation of the Lord are generally very far indeed from agreeing how it should be understood. This is true to some extent of Jews and Muslims but especially of Christians, who entertain the most divergent interpretations not only of the Old Testament but also, and above all, of the New Testament.

The present account falls far short of an exhaustive study of revelation and is designed mainly to show why no belief can be established by recourse to revelation—unless, of course, there is prior agreement not only that we are confronted with a revelation but also on a lot of other things, including principles of exegesis.

Occasionally, miracles are cited as a royal road to confirmation of beliefs. The main point regarding miracles has long been made by David Hume: if a miracle is by definition utterly improbable, then it is far more probable that our senses have deceived us or that those whose testimony leads us to believe the miracle either deceived us or were deceived themselves by other witnesses or by their senses.

Moreover, no miracle in the New Testament, Old Testament, or Koran is attested half as well as lots of alleged miracles at Lourdes and other Catholic shrines; and yet these "Catholic miracles" do not persuade Jews, Protestants, or Muslims. Similarly, Catholics are not swayed by miracles ascribed to some Hassidic rabbis. And members of all three religions are agreed in discounting the miracles performed before our eyes by magicians, witch doctors, mediums, and Yogis.

A miracle, in other words, is not a brute fact, and the word is not coterminous with "wonderful event." Some such events are classified as miracles by certain people who at the same time refuse to classify in the same way a host of others.

A miracle requires faith: to those who lack faith it is not a miracle. Appeal to miracles as evidence to prove beliefs is therefore circular.

Some may feel like adding that we cannot have recourse to miracles and revelations to establish a belief "as an objective truth," but that belief *can* be established in this manner as "subjective" truth, as "true for him" who had the revelation or accepts the miracle. "Subjective" truth, however, has already been considered in Section 35.

If what is meant is merely that an experience which one takes for a revelation or a miracle can induce firm conviction, nobody would dream of disagreeing. But the same is true of dreams and of hallucinations, of deception and of self-deception.

40. FAITH AND ITS CAUSES: CONTRA JAMES.   The causes of a man's belief are usually introduced as negative evidence: a belief is held to be discredited once we know why it is held.

The classical objection to this procedure has been advanced by William James. Before he introduces his "empiricist criterion: By their fruits ye shall know them, not by their roots," he argues, early in *The Varieties of Religious Experience:* "The medical materialists are therefore only so many belated dogmatists, neatly turning the tables on their predecessors by using the criterion of origin in a destructive instead of an accreditive way." One can see what James means and still show that he goes much too far.

Unquestionably, there are cases in which this genealogical approach is hardly pertinent. Consider the philosophy of Bishop Berkeley who, writing in the early eighteenth century, denied the existence of matter as a substratum in which the qualities that we experience inhere. A British author of repute, John Oulton Wisdom, comes along and writes a book on *The Unconscious Origin of Berkeley's Philosophy*. He tries to show how the philosopher's denial of matter was rooted in his childhood experiences and especially his toilet training, but relies on speculative inferences rather than independent evidence. He writes: "God, as pure creator who commanded unsullied power and possessed a pure cement in the form of good faeces for building the world, is a substitute for the father Berkeley valued; and the mathematicians and deists, creators of Matter and bad faeces, godlike enemies of God, were substitutes for the father Berkeley hated because of withholding from his son his faeces and great power of defecation" (182). After quoting this passage, the sober *Times Literary Supplement* of London commented in part: "Whose faeces and power of defecation are in question is a matter best left, perhaps, in the cloacal darkness appropriate to it."

One need not be a Philistine to sympathize with this harsh comment. But if we met a man who denied the existence of matter just as stubbornly as Berkeley did, though, unlike Berkeley, he was quite unable to produce reasons for this strange denial, we should feel justified in asking what had caused his strange belief. Or if the man produced a reason and we were able to convince him that his argument was patently fallacious, and he then adduced another argument as faulty as the first, and this procedure was repeated again and again till finally he said, "Even if all possible arguments for my position should be quite untenable, I should not budge from my belief," no doubt, we should feel free to seek the roots of his belief.

What distinguishes Berkeley and has made him famous is that he was able to support his position with arguments so good that most philosophers, beginning with David Hume, have found them quite irrefutable. If a man supports his beliefs with arguments, then we must begin by considering these arguments, whether it is Berkeley or Zeno, Nietzsche or Freud, St. Thomas or St. Paul. What is wrong with psychological analyses of men like these is that so often they are substituted for philosophical analysis. Psychological analysis cannot take the place of other kinds of criticism; but as one approach among others it is not only justifiable but often of considerable importance.

James' apology for eccentric beliefs on the ground that after all they might conceivably be right, strikes at the roots of all intellectual discipline and the foundations of our civilization. When it came to his beloved "right to believe," he failed to grasp the distinction between a legal right and an intellectual right. Legally, I have the right to believe not only without sufficient evidence but even what is demonstrably false; and many of us are prepared to defend this right. But intellectually I have no such right; intellectually it is not reputable: indeed, it is proof of my irrationality. And while a great deal can be said for tolerance of irrationality by the state, no less can be said against tolerance of irrationality by philosophers.

People who have false beliefs and are irrational about them may be very kind. It may even be the case, more rarely, that their kindness is connected with their false beliefs in such a way that we might vaguely call this kindness a "fruit" of their false beliefs. Surely, this does not entitle us to speak of an "empiricist criterion: By their fruits ye shall know them." When we want to know if a man's beliefs are true or false, his kindness is irrelevant, although in other contexts we may be more interested in his kindness than in the truth or untruth of his beliefs.

There are beliefs which can be tested by employing them as "working hypotheses" by way of seeing whether predictions based on these beliefs are fulfilled. But this is possible only where we can formulate predictions which would be fulfilled if, and only if—or at least almost only if—the belief should be true. I may formulate the hypothesis that A influenced B and then proceed to stipulate conditions which would have to be fulfilled if this were true. That two or three or even dozens should in fact be fulfilled would still be inconclusive if all the facts discovered could be accounted for, too, if A did not influence B but, for example, A was influenced by B.

James applies no stern tests to the beliefs he considers, and his pious references to Jesus' dictum "By their fruits ye shall know them" is a crude piece of apologetics. So is his opposition to all questions about roots.

There is a principle of parsimony which must be invoked at

this point. Beliefs are legion, and we cannot give equal consideration to all. If a belief is based on badly insufficient evidence or faulty arguments or both, then we are generous indeed if we still stop to ask: What causes those who maintain this belief to cling to it? Heuristically, this question is worth while in many cases: we may discover sufficient evidence for a belief a little different from the one maintained. But if we find instead that a belief backed by flimsy evidence and poor reasoning can be readily accounted for when we look at the causes that have led to its adoption, then we need not fear the outside chance that after all it could conceivably be true. Of course, it could be. But if we are worried about that, then we deserve the stricture that James would apply unjustly to those who insist on evidence: we are guilty of "excessive nervousness."

If you prefer propositions which could be true only by coincidence to propositions which are based on evidence, and you make decisions on the basis of horoscopes and palmistry because the advice you get could, after all, be right, while you withhold attention from relevant evidence, then you are irrational, unreasonable, and irresponsible, even if you should be lovable in spite of that.

41. SEVEN CAUSES.   If we ask why a belief, whether religious or not, is held, a great many answers are possible, of which seven may be detailed briefly. The first is in a different category from the others.

First, a belief may be accepted because arguments have been adduced in its support. In that case, a critique will involve an examination of the validity of these arguments, and of their presuppositions, and of the evidence cited. If these credentials are all in good order, a philosopher may feel small inclination to go further. If one finds a few faults, some constructive criticism may be possible. But continued acceptance of invalid arguments and insufficient regard for the evidence will invite further inquiry into the causes of belief.

The following six causes are not mutually exclusive, and in

many cases all of them will be found to have contributed to the acceptance of a belief.

Secondly, a proposition may be believed simply because it was encountered, whether orally or in a book or even in a newspaper, and nothing spoke against it. For any understanding of the genealogy of beliefs it is fundamental to realize that *statements are believed if nothing militates against them.* When one of our trivial beliefs is challenged, we all recall occasionally that we believed it simply because we read or heard it somewhere. When the belief is not trivial, it may hurt our pride to make the same admission; but the situation often is the same. To be sure, we do not believe everything we read in the paper, and perhaps next to nothing we read in some papers, which we therefore generally do not read; but in such cases something does speak against acceptance of a statement: our opinion of the editors, for example.

Third, a belief may not be traceable to any one source. It may be common in a man's environment and be accepted by osmosis.

Fourth, a belief may be accepted because it fits in well with our prior beliefs. In one of those many experiments whose outcome might have been predicted without the experiment it was found that, presented with a lot of material about General Franco, those who liked him tended to remember what placed him in a favorable light while those who disliked him tended to recall what placed him in a bad light. Higher education seeks to counteract this tendency to some extent, but even as highly educated a man as Toynbee accepts, often quite uncritically, what fits in with his prior beliefs while he forgets, ignores, or does not accept what does not.

Fifth, there may be penalties for not accepting a belief. Capital punishment, torture, and concentration camps have been employed to implement acceptance of beliefs, but there are also many less drastic penalties, ranging all the way from social ostracism and nonadmittance to certain positions or organizations to making Mother very unhappy or deeply disappointing Father.

Sixth, there may be positive rewards for accepting a belief.

And seventh—there is no need here for a longer list—a belief may be accepted because it gratifies us or answers a psychological need.

42. FREUD AND WISHFUL THINKING.   From this brief survey of seven causes three conclusions emerge. First, a widespread consensus does not prove that a belief is probably true. Many people suppose that if a belief is widely accepted, there must be something to it: where there is smoke, there must have been a fire. But it may have been fire and sword or the stake.

Secondly, a widespread consensus does not establish any presumption that the millions sharing a belief must have a deep need for it. Most people would readily concede this point, no less than the preceding one, regarding the beliefs accepted in totalitarian countries. The same considerations apply to religious beliefs.

Finally, it is inherently unlikely that all, or even most, religious beliefs should be prompted by any single psychological motive, as Freud contended in *The Future of an Illusion*. Wishful thinking is indeed characteristic of the diluted religion of William James and many others, but much less so of the religion of Jeremiah or the Buddha. And even the faith of James can be illuminated by the first principle of all genealogy of beliefs, that statements are believed if nothing speaks against them. His belief is not created out of nothing by his wishful thinking; it is what remains of the religion of his fathers after he has eliminated everything against which too much seemed to him to speak.

Neither contemporary believers nor the founders of those religions and denominations which had founders have made up their beliefs out of whole cloth. The founders of religions have either codified or modified traditions that preceded them.

The historic evidence does not bear out the claim that all, or even most, of these modifications were inspired by a single motive such as wishful thinking. Nor is there good evidence that all religions go back to a single founder who was motivated in this way or that all of the complex traditions which the founders codified and modified were born of wishful thinking.

Freud did not do justice to man's creative impulses when he ascribed the symbolism of our dreams to censorship and self-deception, when he described art in terms of substitute gratifications, and when he proposed to find the root of all religious beliefs in wishful thinking: "We call a belief an illusion when wish fulfillment is a prominent factor in its motivation, and we disregard its relation to reality, even as the illusion itself does. If after this survey we turn again to religious doctrines, we may reiterate: they are all illusions" (Chapter VI). Our conclusion, on the contrary, is that wish fulfillment is not a prominent factor in the motivation of all religious doctrines, although faith, secular or religious, is by nature close to wishful thinking.

Religious doctrines are of many different kinds and origins. Many are fanciful and show no great regard for common-sense reality; it does not follow that all doctrines that are fanciful are the product of wishful thinking. And belief in doctrines that originally were the product of wishful thinking need not be prompted by wishful thinking. The origin of the idea of hell need not coincide with John Doe's motive for accepting it.

According to a poll, the vast majority of people in the United States believe in hell, but very few indeed have ever entertained the thought that they might go there. Surely, millions rather like the thought of hell; they would be disappointed if a Hitler and a Stalin should have got away with all their crimes against humanity; they wish there were a place where men like these are punished. It neither follows that everybody who believes in hell is prompted by wishful thinking nor does it follow that belief in hell originated in this way.

Freud heeds these distinctions insufficiently, to put it mildly; but the point is so important for the genealogy of beliefs that it deserves to be stated clearly—as it was by Nietzsche in 1887 in his *Genealogy of Morals:* "For every kind of historiography there is no more important proposition than this, which has been discovered with so much effort, but now also ought to be discovered once and for all: the cause of the origin of a thing and its eventual usefulness, actual employment, and incorporation into a system of aims lie worlds apart." (452) This is true of beliefs, too.

Freud's confusion was due in part to two reasons which have not yet been mentioned in this context. A man might gradually evolve a complex theory without being guided by wishful thinking; he might write it up and submit it to a scientific journal. From that moment on, if not before, he has a stake in the truth of his construction and is almost bound to wish that it were true. If it were now shown to him that he has been mistaken, he would certainly be disappointed.

The situation is essentially the same with religious beliefs. Many such beliefs are accepted in the manner outlined in the preceding section—I refer to causes two through six—without wishful thinking entering the picture. Whether beliefs are forced on people in their childhood or perhaps in adult life with dire threats by a dictator and his henchmen, what is crucial is that at some point a man begins to feel committed to what he believes and wishes it were right. It would hurt his pride to have believed something that was quite wrong. This attachment is not necessarily a function of the contents of his faith: it may be a function of the man's commitment.

This was probably the major reason for Freud's supposition that all religious doctrines were motivated by wishful thinking. Some other reasons for his confusion have been pointed out as well. But one reason remains. Freud was not thinking so much of the beliefs considered in the present chapter. He was thinking above all of the belief in gods or God. For this belief, he thought, there was no evidence to speak of. This belief, he argued, was begotten by a wish. This assertion is tainted by the confusions examined here. Even so it may serve to remind us that our reflections on faith have stopped short of God. The time has come to remedy this insufficiency.

V. THE GOD
OF THE PHILOSOPHERS

43. GODLESS RELIGIONS. To many people religion means the worship of God, and religious belief means belief in God. We have seen that there are a great many religious beliefs which contain no overt reference to God, including historical affirmations, generalizations, and speculative propositions; and we may now add that there are whole religions without any god.

In some discussions of religion it is taken for a mark of some sophistication to admit that there is one religion which is atheistic. Hinayana Buddhism. This is considered an exception, if not a freak. One feels broad-minded if one's definition of religions leaves some room for Hinayana Buddhism, but one concentrates on the more normal members of the genus. The remark that in addition to the Hinayana there is Jainism places an author under the suspicion that he tries to show his learning. Yet the Hinayana is not an exception, and neither the religion of the Buddha nor that of the Jina is a freak.

The following picture is much closer to the facts. There are three kinds of religions. The first of these believes in many gods. Examples may be found in ancient Egypt, ancient Greece, and ancient India.

The second type believes in one god only. Whether there are prehistoric forerunners of this kind of religion is sometimes debated, but the four examples known in history are younger than belief in many gods, which all four attacked. The first two monotheisms in history are that of the Hebrews and that of Ikhnaton, the fourteenth-century pharaoh—their profound differences will be noted in Section 83—and Christianity and Islam accepted their belief in one god from the Jews.

The third type of religion does not believe in any god. Again, it is a matter for debate if this religion has prehistorical precursors. The allegation that it is confined to two men in northern India in the sixth century B.C. is in any case quite false. Unlike monotheism, it did not spread from a single point. In India it antedates the Buddha and the Jina and is found in the Upanishads; in China it was codified by Confucius while a different version was laid down by Lao-tze in his haunting *Tao-Teh-Ching*. There are, then, at the very least five godless religions, and their founders and chief exponents include some of the most profound and impressive men of all time. At least some of these religions were developed in deliberate opposition to polytheism, and in this sense, too, one may consider godless religion as an alternative to monotheism.

After the age of the Upanishads and the Buddha, the Jina, Lao-tze, and Confucius, the masses reverted to older forms of worship and did not retain the godlessness and the freedom from superstition that had been so characteristic of their teachers. Certainly, this is no argument for theism—polytheism, to be specific—any more than it is evidence for the truth of the many superstitions found among these people.

While the atheism of the Buddha and the Jina is admitted frequently, Lao-tze's is usually passed over in silence, and the teachings of the Upanishads are glossed over as pantheism. This label is too unclear to be false, but it is certainly misleading. It distracts attention from the radical rejection not only of the many gods in whom the people even then believed but of any superhuman being whatsoever who might help man, and of any prayer, worship, or service. This is not "theism" of any kind at all: any *theos,* any god, is decisively rejected.

The issue between theism and godlessness is not reducible to that between religion and lack of religion. Yajnavalkya and the other sages of the Upanishads, Lao-tze, and the Buddha were not less religious than their superstitious followers in later ages, nor is Suzuki, a Zen Buddhist of our time, less religious than contemporaries who pray or sacrifice.

It is a corollary of these observations that most statements about natural belief are simply false empirically; and that includes the allegations Rudolf Otto makes in his discussion of "The Holy as an *a priori* Category" in his important book on *The Idea of the Holy.* It is false that the belief that the world was created by a god, or the belief in God's omniscience and omnipotence, is inscribed in the heart of every man; and this claim remains false even if we add, as Otto does, "if he show any susceptibility for religious feeling"—unless this addition is meant to make this statement a tautology, which plainly is not Otto's purpose. It is the absence of natural belief that has led to the attempt to "prove" beliefs.

44. PLATO'S PROOF THAT GODS EXIST.   The first philosopher who tried to prove the existence of gods was Plato—in the tenth book of his last work, which he wrote at eighty, the *Laws.* Since he introduces his attempt with a rejection of two proofs which he does not consider valid but which he considers old and venerable, it is clear that Plato was not the first man to essay such a demonstration; but it also seems clear that the two proofs he repudiates were not the work of a philosopher but arguments encountered in popular discussion. Plato dismissed them without argument as obviously insufficient. The first tries to establish the existence of gods from the consensus of all peoples and would obviously be invalid even if there were such a consensus, which in fact there is not. The second is the argument from design, which will be considered in the next section.

The context of Plato's attempt at a proof is crucial. He begins: "No one who in obedience to the laws believed that there were gods, ever intentionally did any unholy act, or uttered any unlawful word; but he who did must have supposed one of three things: either that they did not exist, which is the first possibility; or secondly that, if they did, they took no care of man; or thirdly that they were easily appeased and turned aside from their purpose by sacrifices and prayers." And a little further on Plato concludes expressly: "The duty of the legislator is and always will be to teach you the truth in these matters."

What we find here are a number of conceptions which are quite remote from the spirit of the Hebrew scriptures but have left a lasting imprint on Christianity. Plato proposes legislation about men's beliefs; he formulates the beliefs which he would demand; and he insists that those who have these right beliefs will be immune against all immorality. Indeed, it is this last point which makes it incumbent on the legislator to enforce acceptance of these saving beliefs and to prosecute all those who do not hold to even one of them. What matters is not the affront of public blasphemy but the lack of belief.

In his enormously sympathetic book on *Plato,* which is widely accepted as a classic, A. E. Taylor comments on the tenth book of the *Laws:* "Plato appears as at once the creator of natural theology and the first thinker to propose that false theological belief—as distinguished from insults to an established worship—should be treated as a crime against the State and repressed by the civil magistrate. He is convinced that there are certain truths about God [Taylor's use of the singular illustrates his tendency to make an Anglican of Plato] which can be strictly demonstrated, and that the denial of these leads directly to practical bad living."

It should be added that, according to Plato, the affirmation of these beliefs results of necessity in moral conduct. Thus he formulated, centuries before Augustine and other Christians who were influenced by him, the false doctrine that faith begets good works and that without faith good works are impossible; and moreover he set a precedent by making quite clear that he did not mean faith in some vague, elusive sense: he furnished clear-cut formulations of the propositions which must be believed and thus created the concept of dogma—and its counterpart, the concept of heresy.

It may be a measure of Plato's humanity that, confronted with a heretic, he wants to reason first of all. Even so, he was realistic enough to realize that his attempts at proofs were quite inadequate to stamp out heresy. To do that, Plato in the tenth book of the *Laws* demands stiff prison sentences for heretics—the least penalty is five years—and for those convicted a second time, death is mandatory.

Plato's arguments for the existence of the gods and for what he takes to be their nature have the virtue of simplicity. His "proof" of the existence of the gods is an argument from motion. There are, as he sees it, ten kinds of motion: motion on an axis, locomotion, a combination of these, separation, composition, growth, decay, destruction, external motion, and spontaneous motion. The last of these, "the motion which is able to move itself, is ten thousand times superior to all the others." More important, it must have come first and be "the origin of all motions."

Next, "the motion which can move itself" is identified with the soul. If both of these steps are accepted, we have indeed "the proof that the soul is the first origin and moving power of all that is." Plato specifically rules out the possibility that the first origin of all there is could be traced back to a single soul: "we must not suppose that there are less than two—one the author of good, and the other of evil." Neither here nor elsewhere, however, does Plato suggest that in fact there are only two such souls: what he insists on is that there could not be only one because in that case evil could not be accounted for. Plato proceeds apace to say that the soul of the sun "ought by every man to be deemed a god"; and he adds: "And of the stars, too, and of the moon, and . . . all things are full of gods." With that, he feels that he has "said enough . . . to those who deny that there are gods."

If we analyze this argument, we are immediately faced with a hidden premise; namely, that rest alone is natural while motion is in some sense unnatural and must be traced back, as it were, to some disturbance, to some force which started it. Many writers, including some of the best, feel that it is unfair to question any such presuppositions, and that the historian should make them explicit only to enable us to feel our way back into the spirit of the age. This, we are told, is how men used to think; in those days they could not think otherwise.

But in the case at hand, and in the case of all the proofs of God's existence, this claim is manifestly false.

Plato's older contemporary Democritus, who was perhaps the greatest thinker of his time, next to Socrates and Plato, although Plato never deigns to mention him, had been quite able to dispense with Plato's premise in this instance and in fact had denied it explicitly. He had held that all things consist of atoms, and that these atoms are naturally in motion and have always been in motion. He had expressly denied the need for any separate principle of motion and had thus differed from his predecessors who had introduced a number of such principles. He was a younger contemporary of Socrates, and his philosophy must have been known to Plato and his audience.

Even if we grant Plato the hidden premise which he needs, his argument is not compelling. He leaps to the conclusion that what moves itself must be a soul, and from the soul to god. His introduction of the soul is highly questionable, and his claim that all these souls are gods lacks even plausibility—unless you happen to believe in gods before the argument begins.

The introduction of the word "gods" is crucial not only because the existence of the gods was the thing to be demonstrated by this proof but also because it is this term that leads Plato to say immediately—although this neither has been proved nor is even consistent with what he himself has said a few lines back—that the gods are, of course, "perfectly good" and "hear and see and know all things" and hence must care about men's actions and, moreover, being just, cannot allow themselves to be bribed by either sacrifice or prayer. And thus all of Plato's dogmas have been "proved."

Even if all motion could be traced back to self-propelled souls, not one of Plato's dogmas would follow. Giving these souls the title "gods" may look like a mere matter of courtesy or terminology; but this is not the case. As long as we call them souls, they might well be fellow sufferers, as Eastern wisdom has it; some might be evil, as Plato himself says at one point; or at the very least they might not deserve worship.

Plato's proofs fail, but it is interesting that even the great Plato should have incurred such a mass of errors; the more so

because the very same mistakes are found in his successors.
Indeed, the very argument that Plato used to prove that there
are many gods was used by later writers to establish the existence of the one and only God. Some did not even bother to
adapt it.

45. ST. THOMAS AQUINAS

To build! Not like a child that moulds the sand
and lays his little will before the waves—
no, not for pleasure, heedless of the morrow!
Nor like a man who makes himself a mansion,
the mirror of his mind that some admire:
some spend their youth in it, and some old age,
one adds a wing and one tears down some part,
and in the end it is a striking ruin
in the museum of the human mind.

To build the spirit's fortress for mankind,
using the columns left us by the Greeks
and, as the Normans do in Sicily,
link them with walls and Arab vaults, providing
new columns where required to support
the Biblical mosaics of the ceiling.

To build—not a small chapel for myself,
using what stones my native land provides,
but, drawing on the best the world can give,
the wisdom of the Greeks, the subtle learning
of Jews and Arabs, and the Holy Scriptures,
construct the universal church of man.

Too many readers—and writers!—see St. Thomas either as
the man who with relentless logic provided a rational base for
the Inquisition or—and this is more fashionable today—as a
man who was right about everything, or at least almost everything. Étienne Gilson, having written on Thomism and medieval philosophy for a generation now, says in the Foreword to
his latest study of *The Christian Philosophy of St. Thomas*

Aquinas: "Personally, I do not say of Thomas that he was right, but that he *is* right." But in Gilson's many studies there is hardly a mention of hell or the Inquisition. Yet when Gilson deals with Hegel, for example, he is quick to try to discredit him by pointing to his political philosophy. Indeed, he relies on Scribner's *Hegel Selections* and quotes as "Hegel's own words" an English mistranslation of a phrase due to one of Hegel's pupils (*The Unity of Philosophical Experience,* 246). What would Gilson say of a scholar whose critique of Thomas had a comparable foundation? Throughout the work of Gilson and Maritain one can hardly fail to be struck by the vast difference between their treatment of Thomas and their often very cavalier criticisms of other philosophers. In that way, surely, Thomas' superiority cannot possibly be established.

The grandeur of Aquinas' *Summa Theologica* is undeniable. One could easily spend one's life studying it, without ever ceasing to be amazed both by the wealth of detail and by the intricate planning which finds a suitable place for this sentence from Aristotle and that verse from Scripture, and for so much from the Pseudo-Dionysius, from Averroës, and from Maimonides.

It is easy to underestimate the originality of St. Thomas because he seems to synthesize Scripture and Aristotle, making ample use of all the labors of his predecessors. But as Gilson says in *Christian Philosophy in the Middle Ages* (365), St. Thomas made "Aristotle say so many things he never said"; and Gilson might well have added that St. Thomas also made Scripture say what it never had said. "In order to metamorphose the doctrine of Aristotle, Thomas has ascribed a new meaning to the principles of Aristotle"; and in order to transform the religion of the Bible, he ascribed a different meaning to God.

Partly because he was unable to read either Scripture or Aristotle in the original, partly because he falsely imputed to Aristotle some books which had in fact been written by other men, much later, St. Thomas was never fully aware of the extent of his originality. He was humble, gave credit where it was not due, and became a saint.

To understand him and his work, we must first of all understand how his contemporaries viewed Aristotle. The Greek had long been known as a logician, but now, suddenly, beginning a little before Aquinas' birth, Aristotle's other works were translated into Latin, partly from the original Greek, partly from Arabic versions. The impact was tremendous. Aristotelianism became the intellectual fashion of the age, and a terrible threat to Christianity. A new spiritual continent had been discovered, an alternative to the Christian world.

In 1215, ten years before Thomas was born, Aristotle's works on metaphysics and natural philosophy were banned at the University of Paris, where Thomas was to teach later. "In 1229 the professors of Toulouse, in order to attract students, issued a notice saying that lectures could be heard there on the works of Aristotle. . . . An attempt was made in 1245," when Thomas was twenty, "to extend the prohibition to Toulouse also, though by that date it had become impossible to check the spread of Aristotelianism" (Copleston, 60).

St. Thomas went forth, but did not slay the dragon. He pulled its fangs and made it subservient to the church. That was a major part of his accomplishment but by no means all of it. After all, most theologians meet the philosophic fashions of the day, from Plato down to Heidegger, by trying to show that their religion has taught all along what now appears in a secular garb; and in the process of their demonstration they show that they have not really fully understood the philosophy with which they deal, and, more important, they transform their religion.

Aquinas differed from other theologians in several important respects. First, it was his good fortune that the rival in his time was no less a philosophy than Aristotle's. That alone made his attempt much more significant than the efforts of some contemporary theologians to assimilate Heidegger.

Secondly, even Aristotle himself was not a sufficient opponent for Aquinas. As he saw it, the dragon was reason itself; and the contest he tried to settle once and for all was the competition of reason and faith. He attempted nothing less than to pull the fangs of reason and to make it subservient to the church.

Luther, 300 years later, exhorted men to blind their reason, and to kill it. (Cf. §§ 55, 65, and 69 below.) Aquinas realized no less than Luther that reason posed a great threat to the Christian faith, but he also saw that it could be employed in the service of faith, which he proposed to do.

Like the old Plato, Aquinas realized that reason could not be held in check merely by his determination to use it in support of faith. Thomas was much more conscious than many of his modern admirers of the problematic nature of his demonstrations. In his discussion of faith in the Second Part of the Second Part of his *Summa Theologica,* he repeats again and again that it is "impossible for one and the same thing to be an object of science and of belief for the same person" (Question 1, Article 5), and "in one and the same man, about the same object, and in the same respect, science is incompatible with either opinion or faith," for "the object of science is something seen, whereas the object of faith is the unseen" (Reply 4).

Aquinas does not agree with those who argue that "sacred writers employ arguments to inculcate things that are of faith; therefore such things can be an object of science." To this objection (2) he replies: "The arguments employed by holy men to prove things that are of faith are not demonstrations; they are either persuasive arguments showing that what is proposed to our faith is not impossible, or else they are proofs drawn from the principles of faith, i.e. from the authority of Holy Scripture, as Dionysius declares. Whatever is based on these principles is as well proved in the eyes of the faithful as a conclusion drawn from self-evident principles is in the eyes of all. Hence, again, theology is a science"—but a science which presupposes faith, not a system of arguments that can induce faith.

Now it may be objected that "certain matters of faith have been demonstrated by the philosophers, such as the existence and unity of God, and so forth. Therefore things that are of faith can be an object of science." To this objection (3) Aquinas replies that "Things which can be proved by demonstration [without recourse to Scripture and without presupposing faith] are reckoned among what is of faith . . . because they are necessary presuppositions of matters of faith." For example, "one may know by demonstration the unity of God, and believe that there are three Persons in God" (Reply 4).

Emphatically, Thomas did not believe that one could rely on reason to prove the articles of faith. Indeed, "It is necessary for man to receive by faith not only things which are above reason, but also those which can be known by reason; and this for three motives. First, in order that men may arrive more quickly at the knowledge of divine truth." If they had to rely on reason, "it would be far along in life that man would arrive at the knowledge of God"; and if he died before this lucky event, he might be damned in all eternity. "The second reason is, in order that the knowledge of God may be more widespread." Thomas thinks of faith as much more widespread than reason, since in his world millions had the right faith, but few could follow his theology. But the third reason is the most interesting: "The third reason is for the sake of certitude. For human reason is very deficient in things concerning God. A sign of this is that philosophers, [even] in their inquiry into human affairs by natural investigation, have fallen into many errors, and have disagreed among themselves." Hence the need for faith to establish certainty (Question 2, Article 4).

We are always prone to forget how contentious the climate of opinion was in which Thomas lived. Debates were the order of the day, reasons were pitted against reasons, and a seemingly good argument might easily be set aside by a still better argument in favor of a slightly different conclusion. Also, Thomas knew that his arguments never cut much ice with the Franciscans, though his Franciscan opponents in his own time are less famous today than their successors, Duns Scotus and William of Ockham. Finally, it is worth recalling that "in 1277, three years after Aquinas' death, Robert Kilwardby, the Dominican archbishop of Canterbury," a member of Aquinas' own order, "followed the example of the bishop of Paris in censuring a number of propositions which included a few that had been held by Aquinas." It should be added, though, that "the Parisian censures of 1277 were withdrawn, as far as they affected Aquinas," after Aquinas was canonized in 1323 (Copleston, 235).

Seeing that Aquinas says expressly that we "ought to believe matters of faith, not because of human reasoning, but because of the divine authority," why did he exert himself to construct his vast *Summa Theologica?* "When a man has a will ready to believe, he loves the truth he believes, he thinks out and takes to heart whatever reasons he can find in support thereof." It is only when faith is primary and we are finding reasons for what we already believe that "human reasoning does not exclude the merit of faith, but is a sign of greater merit" (Article 10).

Without the aid of Scripture, without building on a prior faith, reason can prove very little, according to Thomas—not nearly as much as we must believe in order to be saved. "The reasons which are brought forward in support of the authority of faith are not demonstrations which can bring intellectual vision to the human intellect; and so the unseen is not removed . . . and hence such reasons do not diminish the merit or measure of faith. On the other hand, though demonstrative reasons in support of the preambles of faith, but not of the articles of faith [which depend on revelation], diminish the measure of faith, since they make the thing believed to be seen; yet they do not diminish the measure of charity, which makes the will ready to believe them, even if they were unseen. And so the measure of merit is not diminished" (Article 10, Reply 2).

Thomas did not consider his own philosophy either essential or sufficient for true faith and for salvation. A non-Thomistic Franciscan might well be saved, while a non-Catholic, confronted with both Thomism and another philosophy, might not be persuaded by Thomas and die without the true faith.

One cannot rely on reason alone to conquer reason that attacks faith. And although the magnificent two-volume edition of *Basic Writings of Saint Thomas Aquinas*, which is designed to introduce the saint to a large public, breaks off soon after the passages cited here, with Question 7, and although Gilson and Copleston, who try to win friends for the saint, also omit what follows, Question 11, Articles 3 and 4, constitute an integral part of Thomas' system: heretics must be "shut off from the world by death."

There is nothing vengeful in Thomas' treatment of this question; he does not raise his voice when he gives reasons to justify the practice of the church in his day. But it would be a grave mistake to suppose that his argument in support of the Inquisition was an incidental all-too-human shortcoming which the saint shared with his age. Not only is it presented in exactly the same logical form as everything that has gone before, but what has gone before cannot be fully understood apart from the question "Whether Heretics Should Be Tolerated?" The reader might suppose mistakenly that Thomas considered his many arguments self-sufficient, when in fact he realized that Aristotle and even Scripture could also be cited by way of proving very different conclusions from his own. He was not as naïve as one might suppose he was when one reads some of the books written by his admirers.

Linking Greek columns with walls to construct a church is, no doubt, an impressive feat, and Biblical mosaics can be stunning; but there are those who would still prefer the ruins of the unfinished Greek temple at Segesta, forsaken on a hill, with the wind blowing between the unfluted columns and the sun shining on grass, flowers, and life. Some of us might prefer to linger in the unfinished, open structure of Plato's thought, which certainly does not equal the grandiose single-mindedness of Thomas, rather than live in Aquinas' church. One might even cherish the open vistas of one's own thought. Thomas knows that in that case his arguments do not avail.

"With regard to heretics, two considerations are to be kept in mind: (1) on their side, (2) on the side of the Church. (1) There is the sin, whereby they deserve not only to be separated from the Church by excommunication, but also to be shut off from the world by death. For it is a much more serious matter to corrupt faith, through which comes the soul's life, than to forge money, through which temporal life is supported. Hence if forgers of money or other malefactors are straightway justly put to death by secular princes, with much more justice can heretics, immediately upon conviction, be not only excommunicated but also put to death. (2) But on the side of the Church there is mercy, with a view to the conversion of them that are in error; and therefore the Church does not straightway condemn, but after a first and second admonition, as the Apostle teaches [Epistle of Paul to Titus, 3.10]. After that, if he be found still stubborn, the Church gives up hope of his conversion and takes thought for the safety of others, by separating him from the Church by sentence of excommunication; and, further, leaves him to the secular court, to be exterminated from the world by death."

The similarity with the tenth book of Plato's *Laws* is staggering; but what was there the musing of an old man without authority has here become the accepted practice of an enormously powerful church which rules over the lives and thoughts of millions. Thomas' greatness was not the greatness of Amos or Isaiah, who defied the religious institutions of their day, pitting their moral convictions against the age and attacking the conscience of the time like a storm that breaks down walls and exalts life and spirit above convention and belief. Aquinas gave all to his church, fortified its conscience, built imposing walls to protect it against storms, and was canonized.

There remains yet another feature which distinguished Thomas from all other theologians: the vastness of the edifice he built. You look at his five ways of proving God's existence, in Part One of the *Summa*, Question 2, and suppose perhaps that they are on a par with other proofs, like Plato's, for example. Pleased, you notice how small they are, how little space they take: less than two pages for the five of them. They are not padded with persuasion like so much contemporary literature, and they are not inflated with so many illustrations that you lose the thread. There they stand, small, separate, and quite distinct, like five fine figures over a cathedral portal.

Perhaps you become absorbed in *the first proof*, which Thomas himself calls "more manifest." Its first premise could not be simpler: "It is certain and evident to our senses, that in the world some things are in motion." Already you are half prepared to assent to the conclusion. It is all so straightforward. The second premise seems hardly less simple: "Whatever is moved is moved by another." Just before you accept that, too, you recall that Plato in *his* proof of gods arrived at just the opposite conclusion: there were souls that moved themselves, and they turned out to be the gods whose existence Plato tried to demonstrate. Is Thomas trying to put something over on us? Far from it, he immediately produces a subsidiary argument to prove his second premise by way of reflections on potentiality and actuality. We become involved in Thomas' metaphysics, in his adaptation of Aristotle. Should we still go along? Suppose we do, tentatively, just to see what lies ahead. Having shown, or tried to show, that "whatever is moved must be moved by another," Thomas continues: "this cannot go on to infinity, because then there would be no first mover, and, consequently, no other mover, seeing that subsequent movers move only inasmuch as they are moved by the first mover." And he concludes: "Therefore it is necessary to arrive at a first mover, moved by no other; and this everyone understands to be God."

The last seven words recur with only minor variations at the end of all five arguments. At first it seems that with these words logical argument has been forsaken and Aquinas merely states what is at best a historic fact. You feel, Aquinas might have added: and if anyone does not understand this to be God, we burn him.

There are many difficulties here. On the face of it, the conclusion seems to contradict the second premise: have we not after all arrived at a being that moves itself, like Plato's gods? As you read on in the *Summa*, you find what you may have suspected on the basis of your knowledge of Aristotle: there is no contradiction. Aquinas' God, like Aristotle's first movers, is unmoved. But Aristotle used this argument in his *Metaphysics*, from which Thomas has derived it, to infer the existence of over forty unmoved movers. Is not Thomas arbitrary in supposing that there is but one? Later in the

Summa, he tries to show why there can be only one god. But
why call this one god "God"? From a Christian point of view
even Aristotle's *god* is not at all godlike: unmoved, he contemplates his own thoughts, unmindful of the world which he
did not create, moving the things in the world by attraction,
"as the beloved" moves the lover. Aristotle's god does not love.
He is utterly unmoved, like a statue of a Buddha lost in contemplation that moves us to contemplate him. But in the following pages of the *Summa,* Aquinas, bit by bit, tries to prove
that the unmoved mover of his first proof has the qualities
which the church associates with the Christian God.

Most of the objections to this first proof are thus discussed
elsewhere; and, to see if they have really been taken care of,
you have to scrutinize other parts of the system: the apparently so short, clear, and distinct proof that seemed self-
sufficient turns out to be part of a vast structure, like a plant
with deep roots that spread through the surrounding soil.

Can you not believe in an infinite regress instead of a first
mover? Thomas is willing to grant temporarily, for the sake
of the argument, that the world was not created but is eternal.
Even then, when you do not postulate any beginning in time
and are willing to go back endlessly horizontally, there must
yet be, as Thomas sees it, a first mover that, vertically, as it
were, underlies the whole series of movements.

What at first seemed to be a simple proof is in fact a world
view in miniature, an image of the world projected onto half
a page. Is it a proof of God's existence which, taken by itself,
compels assent, quite independent of what we may think of
Thomas' metaphysics or the remainder of his system? Definitely not. Did Thomas think it was?

He says emphatically before he begins: "The existence of
God can be proved in five ways." And shortly before that,
he says the same thing several times. He also rejects St. Anselm's so-called ontological argument. So it seems that he considers his own proofs compelling.

Thomas assumed not only that where Aristotle, as interpreted by him, agreed with Scripture, as interpreted by him,
Aristotle must be right, but also that in such cases human rea-

son, unaided by revelation, could evidently demonstrate the truth. But even if it were the case that Aristotle was right in all such instances, while Democritus and Lucretius, Spinoza, Hume, and Kant were wrong, it is assuredly not the case that on purely rational grounds we must accept Aristotle's metaphysics—either in its original form or in its Thomistic version. At most, Aristotle's metaphysics, as interpreted by Aquinas, presents one possible alternative for us; and at worst, this metaphysics has been refuted on a number of points by later philosophers.

The Angelic Doctor does not only give reasons for believing in God; he also demonstrates the existence of angels, for example. As Gilson says in his latest book on Aquinas, "Some historians pass over in complete silence this part of St. Thomas's work or at best dismiss it with a few allusions." But the belief in angels is no more excrescence on the body of the system: "Angels are creatures whose existence can be demonstrated. In certain exceptional cases they have even been seen. To disregard them destroys the balance of the universe considered as a whole"—or at least of Thomas' conception of the universe. "The nature and operation of inferior creatures, men for example, can only be well understood by comparison and contrast with angels." In other words, Thomas' conception of man depends on his belief in angels, and we cannot "omit the consideration of one whole order of creatures without upsetting the equilibrium of the system" (160).

Clearly, it is also possible to give reasons for *not* believing, either by criticizing Thomas or by constructing a rival system without God or angels, or perhaps, as C. D. Broad comes close to doing in *Religion, Philosophy and Psychical Research*, without God but with angels. Confronted with Broad's searching criticisms of "The Validity of Belief in a Personal God" and of "Arguments for the Existence of God" no less than with Thomas' demonstrations, our faith might be corrupted. Hence the need for exterminating heretics and imposing censorship. Thomas believes that his own reasons are good and that his own beliefs are true, but the human reason alone, unaided by censorship and threats, may not see that Thomas' reasons are better than those of heretics and that his beliefs are true while theirs are not.

What has here been said of the first proof applies in a general way to the other four as well. *The second one* closely parallels the first but is centered in the concept of cause rather than motion. "In the world of sensible things we find there is an order of efficient causes." The conclusion is that there must be "a first efficient cause, to which everyone gives the name of God."

Here an analysis of the concept of causation, possibly along the lines suggested by Hume or Kant, could cause grave difficulties. Clearly, Aquinas would have burned both Hume and Kant, as well as most other modern philosophers; and he could have adduced—and his followers have adduced—further reasons for accepting his metaphysics rather than Hume's or Kant's philosophy. But for the unaided reason, these arguments are of no avail.

Whether taken by itself or in conjunction with the first proof, the second way no less than the first says in essence that the universe cannot be understood without postulating at least one occult entity. This is not necessarily true for other conceptions of the world; and the conclusion of these two proofs is religiously uninteresting apart from Thomas' attempt in the subsequent pages of the *Summa* to clothe this occult entity with the attributes of God.

The third proof contains, on the face of it, a fallacy. The first premise is: "We find in nature things that are possible to be and not to be, since they are found to be generated, and to be corrupted." The second premise is that "it is impossible for these always to exist, for that which can not-be, at some time is not." From this second premise, about which one may well have one's doubts, Thomas infers—fallaciously, it would seem—"Therefore, if everything can not-be, then at one time there was nothing in existence." This inference, to which we shall return shortly, is crucial for his proof.

He proceeds: "if at one time nothing was in existence, it would have been impossible for anything to have begun to exist." This second inference requires an unstated premise which most readers would willingly grant: namely, that from nothing, nothing issues; or, to put it positively, that there must be a sufficient reason for all things. To be sure, Thomas held that God created the world out of nothing; but there was at least God in whom there may have been a sufficient reason. Seeing, then, that there are things in existence now, there cannot be contingent things only, "but there must exist something the existence of which is necessary." The ultimate conclusion is: "Therefore we cannot but admit the existence of some being having of itself its own necessity, and not receiving it from another, but rather causing in others their necessity. This all men speak of as God."

Now one might not only question the second premise: even if we grant that premise, it does not follow that if everything is contingent, "then at one time there was nothing in existence." No U.S. senator is elected for more than six years at a time, but it does not follow that at one and the same time all senators are up for re-election: they have staggered terms. Similarly, contingent things might well have staggered terms in such a way that at no time there was nothing in existence. If we accept a naïve, common-sense notion of time and suppose that by now an infinite time has elapsed, we must conclude, if we embrace this alternative hypothesis to Thomas, that there must have been an infinite number of contingent things; but that, of course, is not at all absurd and actually easier to imagine than Aquinas' God. On this alternative his proof seems to be shipwrecked.

Neither Copleston nor Gilson deals with this objection, but Copleston says that many modern Thomists consider this third proof especially fundamental (122 f.). What both Gilson and Copleston do in effect is to assimilate this argument to the first two until no very significant distinction remains. Again, the infinite series is granted more or less explicitly, but it is claimed that, as it were, vertically, a necessary being must underlie the whole series.

Since the conclusion in all three arguments does not follow from simple premises which are altogether overt and understandable in themselves, it is hard to say whether these proofs are valid as far as they go or not. To yield the desired conclusion, the premises must be interpreted as containing a great deal of Aquinas' metaphysics in a nutshell; and if you accept that metaphysics, you will indeed find that it requires something in addition to contingent beings, namely, at least one necessary being. But what is a "necessary being"?

A "necessary being" is comparable to a "valid being" and to a "necessary triangle" and a "neurotic triangle." We understand the adjective and the noun, but their conjunction is illicit. As Kant noted in his *Critique of Pure Reason* (B 620 ff.), the adjective "necessary" has no applicability to beings: "One has at all times spoken of an *absolutely necessary* being, without exerting oneself to understand whether and how one could even think of such a thing. . . . All examples are, without exception, taken only from *judgments*, not from *things* and their existence. But the unconditional necessity of judgments is not to be confused with the absolute necessity of things. For the absolute necessity of a judgment is only a conditional necessity of the thing or the predicate in the judgment. The previously cited proposition does not assert that three angles are altogether necessary but rather that, assuming the condition that a triangle exists (is given), three angles also exist necessarily (in it)."

A "necessary triangle" is obviously in the same category with a "neurotic triangle." But "being" is such a general term that it is less obvious that "necessary being" is in the same category, too. Yet there are predicates that cannot be ascribed to beings. "Valid being," for example, and "cogent being" are as illicit as "necessary being."

Nor will it do to substitute for "necessary being" some such phrase as "a being that necessarily exists." Even as "valid" has meaning only in relation to some logical or legal framework, "necessary" has meaning only in relation to presupposed conditions. It makes sense to say that, if A and B exist, C must necessarily exist. But taken by themselves, the last four words do not make sense.

To get around this last objection, one might rephrase

Thomas' argument, which he took from Maimonides' *Guide for the Perplexed,* Book II, Chapter 1, while Maimonides had taken it over from the Arabic philosophers, and speak of eternal and ephemeral beings instead of necessary and contingent beings; but this variant proof would be invalidated by fallaciously ruling out staggered terms.

The fourth proof, unlike the first three, seems to have some religious significance, but it depends more obviously than any of the others on Aquinas' metaphysics and his weird Neoplatonic notions about nature. I shall quote it in full:

"The fourth way is taken from the gradation to be found in things. Among beings there are some more and some less good, true, noble, and the like. But *more* or *less* are predicated of different things according as they resemble in their different ways something which is the maximum, as a thing is said to be hotter according as it more nearly resembles that which is hottest; so that there is something which is truest, something best, something noblest, and, consequently, something which is most being, for those things that are greatest in truth are greatest in being, as is written in [Aristotle's] *Metaphysics.* Now the maximum in any genus is the cause of all in that genus, as fire, which is the maximum of heat, is the cause of all hot things, as is said in the same book. Therefore there must also be something which is to all beings the cause of their being, goodness, and every other perfection; and this we call God."

The first premise, that things really are more or less good or noble instead of merely being esteemed more or less, involves a good deal of metaphysics but might be acceptable to many non-Thomists. The second premise will recommend itself to few readers indeed. In spite of its noble ancestry, we should not admit that "the maximum in any genus is the cause of all in that genus," as if there must be something hottest that is the cause of all heat and something most purple that is the cause of purple in all purple things.

The number of difficulties that arises in connection with this so-called proof is stupendous. It will suffice here to comment on one only. Thomas argues that one single being is the cause of all perfections in all things, and also the maximum in each perfection. Do these perfections not exclude each other? Is not Thomas' conception of God as self-contradictory as the idea of something that is completely red and completely green all over? He himself deals with this objection in Question 4, Article 2. The second objection there taken up is that "opposites cannot coexist. Now the perfections of things are opposed to each other," and therefore "it seems that the perfections of all things are not in God." Against this, Thomas asserts that since "God is the first producing cause of things, the perfections of all things must [!] pre-exist in God in a more eminent way. Dionysius touches upon this argument by saying of God: It is not that He is this and not that, but that He is all, as the cause of all." So there.

When Thomas comes to his specific replies to the objections soon after, he again quotes Dionysius as having said that the sun, "while remaining one and shining uniformly, contains within itself first and uniformly the substances of sensible things, and many and diverse qualities; a fortiori should all things in a kind of natural unity pre-exist in the cause of all things"—and St. Thomas merely adds: "and thus things diverse and in themselves opposed to each other pre-exist in God as one, without injury to His simplicity. This suffices for the Reply to the Second Objection." Does it? And was Dionysius right about the sun?

It is easier to understand historically what has happened here than to be moved by the force of the argument. The ancient Greeks believed that there must be a god or goddess of love, wisdom, war, and so forth. They believed in many gods but supposed that one of them, Zeus, was *primus inter pares*. From Homer we gain the impression that this was a projection of the situation among the Greek tribes: each had a king, but one of the kings, Agamemnon, was *primus inter pares*.

Later, Xenophanes lampooned the anthropomorphism of the Homeric religion: if oxen and asses believed in gods, they, too, would picture the gods like themselves. Plato sought to meet such criticisms, and particularly moral objections to the behavior of the gods, by expurgating Homer in his *Republic;*

and soon after, in the same dialogue, he proposed his theory of Forms, which is very nonanthropomorphic indeed but salvages the old idea that there must be a perfect embodiment—or rather an unembodied quintessence—of justice and wisdom and beauty; and again there emerges one Form that is *primum inter pares,* the Form of the Good. In the myth of the two horses in the *Phaedrus* the old theological background of this theory comes through in an image as we behold the Form of beauty "once again enthroned by the side of temperance upon her holy seat" (254).

When St. Thomas takes over these ancient Greek ideas, he encounters two difficulties. First, he must perform the leap of Plato in the tenth book of the *Laws* to re-endow his desiccated gods with the attributes of divinity; and then there is the further leap to fuse these questionable maxima into a single maximum, his God. Thomas takes these two hurdles in the opposite sequence. First he claims, without argument, that there is only one God; then he endows this one God with all the attributes of divinity, one by one; and then he proves that there can be only one such God. The Greek idea that there might be many gods, of whom not one has *all* the attributes Thomas ascribes to God, is ignored. So are other rival systems.

"*The fifth way* is taken from the governance of the world." It is a variation on the argument from design which Plato already knew and repudiated. Thomas has transformed it by infusing it from the start with his own world picture: "we see that things which lack knowledge, such as natural bodies, act for an end, and this is evident from their acting always, or nearly always, in the same way, so as to obtain the best result." If we "see" that, we are, no doubt, ready to "see" God, too. But if we tone down this premise as it usually has been presented by other writers, by way of making it acceptable, then we are very far from the desired conclusion.

If we say, as the popular version of this proof has it, that the world resembles a human artifact, and that every artifact has been made by an intelligent designer—if, in other words, we merely see that things which lack knowledge behave *as if* they acted for an end, and in truth we cannot "see" more than that—then our proof is based on an analogy, and our conclusion is at best probable: "Therefore some intelligent being exists by whom all natural things are directed to their end; and this being we call God."

How probable this inference is depends on how close the analogy is: if it is very close, the argument gains in probability; but if the analogy is weak, the argument has little force. Philo in Hume's *Dialogues Concerning Natural Religion* argues persuasively that the analogy between the universe and a human artifact is not close, and he suggests some other analogies which seem to him at least as close, if not closer. One compares the universe to an organism, another to plants. Each of these two analogies would suggest a different kind of origin, seeing how animals and plants are begotten. Moreover, there is instinct as an alternative to intelligence. Beyond that, one may question the propriety of inferring that the whole universe came into being in the same manner as any part of it whatever: after all, we could not infer the manner in which a human being is begotten from the way in which a human hair grows. The fact is that we have never witnessed the construction of anything very much like the universe, and all our analogies are weak. But if our analogies are weak, then our argument has little or no force.

If we ignore our first objection and admit, if only to be nice about it, that this argument is based on a close analogy, then, on this analogy, "many worlds might have been botched and bungled ere this one was arrived at." Alas, this one might well be one of the botched ones. Perhaps—all these suggestions are still Hume's—our world was made by an apprentice deity who ever since has been the laughingstock of all the other gods. Perhaps it is the product of a superannuated deity whose powers failed him. Perhaps he has even died meanwhile.

If we press the analogy, it leads to impious conclusions; and if we recoil in horror and admit that the analogy is not close and hence does not warrant these conclusions, our argument disintegrates.

On the less sensational side, this argument—once we grant

the analogy on which it rests—suggests three conclusions which were palatable to the Greeks, among whom it appears to have originated, but which are irreconcilably at odds with Christianity, Judaism, and Islam.

First, this argument—if we agree to overlook its fatal weaknesses—leads to the conclusion that the world was made even as things are made by human beings.

Secondly, this analogy, if pressed, is an argument for polytheism. In the first place, our experience tells us that the greater and the more complex an artifact is, the more beings have been involved both in the design and the execution. In the second place, there is abundant evidence of what on this analogy we should have to call cross-purposes.

Finally, this analogy would justify us in ascribing imperfections to the author of so many imperfections. If it should be argued that what looks like imperfection to us is not really imperfect, then what to us appears to be design might well not be design.

Among the things that seem imperfect from the human point of view, Hume in various places mentions want, fear, anguish, impotence, oppression, and injustice; violence, war, disease, and idiocy; famine, gout, toothaches, and rheumatism. Those who want a longer list may turn to Schopenhauer. Those who prefer a brief but poignant description of a couple of imperfections will find them in Ivan Karamazov's argument with his brother Alyosha. And those few who have an adequate moral imagination will be amply served with no more than the daily *New York Times;* or let them read the *Times'* annual sketches of "The Hundred Neediest Cases."

One can, like Job, trust in the Lord in spite of all this suffering; but in that case one will have to heed the implications of God's challenge to Job: "Where wast thou when I laid the foundations of the earth?"

Clearly, the God of Aquinas' theology is not the God of Job, Moses, or Jesus. Gilson, to be sure, tries to persuade us in book after book that Aquinas' God *is* the God of the Bible. In the third chapter of his Gifford Lectures on *The Spirit of Medie-*

val Philosophy (51 ff., 433 f.) and in his Powell Lectures on
God and Philosophy (40 ff.), he insists that God's answer to
Moses in Exodus 3, "I AM WHO AM," says *in ovo* what
Aquinas developed in detail. In his *History of Christian Philosophy in the Middle Ages,* we are startled to encounter suddenly among hundreds of more conventional names in the "Index of Authors" an entry: "I AM WHO AM (HE WHO IS)."
But in *The Christian Philosophy of St. Thomas Aquinas,* Gilson admits in effect that the God of Aquinas' books was not
the Biblical God: "To appreciate the importance of what is at
stake we have only to compare St. Thomas' interpretation of
the text with St. Augustine's. When St. Augustine read the
name of God, he understood 'I am he who never changes.' St.
Thomas reading the same words understood them to mean 'I
am the pure act-of-being'" (93). What Moses understood will
be considered in Section 89.

The God of Aquinas' *books* was not the God of the Bible,
and it is of course with his books that most theologians keep
dealing. But three months before his death, in December,
1273, Thomas had a religious experience while saying Mass;
and after that he gave up his work on the third part of his
Summa and resisted all persuasion to continue writing because, he said, "all I have written seems to me like so much
straw compared with what I have seen" (Copleston, 10; Chesterton, 143). One shudders to imagine his estimate of his
prolific admirers.

His confession before his death—so his confessor is said to
have whispered—was that of a child of five. Before his confession, as he lay on his deathbed, he asked to be read to. Not
Aristotle. Not theology. "He asked to have The Song of Solomon read through to him from beginning to end" (Chesterton, 143 f.; cf. Vaughan, last chapter).

46. PERFECTION AND THE ONTOLOGICAL ARGUMENT.   The one
major argument for God's existence which St. Thomas did not
consider valid has been used in various forms by many other
thinkers since his time. It is usually called the ontological ar-

gument and tries to establish God's existence not from his effects in the world, like all of Aquinas' "five ways," but from God's essence. What is claimed is that God must exist by definition.

It is customary to credit St. Anselm of Canterbury with the invention of this argument, but for two reasons it seems better not to concentrate on his version of it. First, he did not bring the key notion of God's perfection out into the open but spoke of that *quo nihil maius cogitari potest*—that than which nothing greater can be thought. "Greater" is such a vague word—and Anselm makes no effort to define it—that his argument can scarcely be called a proof. Secondly, it is offered in his *Proslogion* in the context of a prayer: "I do not try, Lord, to penetrate thy depth . . . but a little I want to understand thy truth which my heart believes and loves. Nor do I wish to understand in order that I may believe, but I believe in order that I may understand [*credo ut intelligam*]."

Anselm wants to understand what he believes, and what follows is less an attempt at a proof than an attempt to spell out in conceptual terms what he believes about the God of whom his heart is full and to whom he speaks. Anselm's words are so charged with emotion, the mood of the whole passage taken in context is so poetic, and the key term of his so-called proof is so utterly vague that it seems somehow besides the point to single out his version for criticism. Characteristically, his proof does not end like Aquinas' proofs, "and this everyone understands to be God," but rather: "And that art thou, Lord, our God. Thus thou, Lord, my God, art so real that thy not-being cannot even be thought."

The most common form of this proof is reducible to these two premises: God is, by definition, perfect. And perfection entails existence. Therefore, God, by definition, must exist.

Critics have generally granted the first premise, which, in fact, need not be granted. The idea of a perfect being is based on a confusion. Perhaps there can be a perfect sledgehammer or a perfect tackhammer; certainly, it makes no sense to speak of a perfect hammer. Nor does it make sense to speak of a perfect nail. One meaning of perfection is complete adequacy to some purpose. In this sense, perfection involves limitation to a function: it makes sense to speak of a perfect horse if, and only if, it is assumed that horses have a certain function, or exist to serve a purpose, which the individual horse can serve more or less adequately.

If someone says, "This is a perfect day," we may accept this statement as expressing an emotional response about which only fools would argue. But if an argument were asked for, one would have to ask: perfect for what? And then a disagreement might be taken care of by explaining that the day is perfect for one purpose but bad for another. For the needs of a certain community, a particular church may be perfect; but it makes no sense to speak of a perfect building.

The greater the level of generality is, the less sense does it make to speak of perfection; and being is probably the most general term we have. It is for similar reasons that Martin Foss says in his illuminating little book on *The Idea of Perfection in the Western World* (26): "A perfect God . . . is an irreligious concept."

Now there is another meaning of "perfect." Looking at the white marble torso of the Aphrodite from Cyrene in Rome, or at a Greek temple, one might say that it was perfect, without thinking of adequacy to any purpose. In addition to the instrumental perfection discussed above, one might therefore speak of inherent perfection. Whether this, or any phrase containing the word perfection, is a good term for what is meant is debatable; but the experience in question is important, and apart from it one cannot do justice to the ascription of perfection to God.

What is meant where perfection is used in this second sense is not the absence of flaws which might interfere with the fulfillment of some special purpose, but rather the absence of flaws which generally characterize human beings. It is difficult to be precise about this, but what is ascribed is a triumph over some inadequacy which weighs us down. This is best understood in connection with man's aspirations. (Cf. §§ 23, 81, and 97 ff.)

It is only in this second sense that we can grant the first

premise of the ontological argument; namely, that God is, by definition, perfect. Even this is not true of all conceptions of God. (Cf. e.g., §§ 54 f.)

We are ready for the second premise: perfection entails existence. This usually means: perfection is the sum of all good predicates, and existence is one of these. To this, Kant objected that "existence is evidently no real predicate, i.e., a concept of anything that could be added to the concept of a thing." Instead of arguing whether existence is a predicate or not, let us attempt a slightly different approach.

First of all, this second premise rests on the assumption that existence is, to put it crudely, a good thing. A Hindu or a Buddhist might well question this. At the end of the first chapter of Genesis we are told that "God saw every thing that he had made, and, behold, it was very good." From this, some theologians and philosophers infer that to exist is good, and that to lack existence is an imperfection. Hence they argue that perfection must entail existence.

Now we have already seen that perfection, if it means the sum of all good predicates, is self-contradictory no less than the idea of a being that is completely red and green all over. But if we mean perfection in the second sense we have considered—a triumph over flaws that weigh us down—does this entail existence?

The phrase "entails existence" is equivocal. There is a sense in which subjunctives and a point do not take up space, while pink elephants do. Nevertheless, the following syllogism is fallacious because it depends on equivocation: pink elephants take up space; whatever takes up space exists; therefore pink elephants exist. "Take up space" in this syllogism is as equivocal as "entails existence" in the ontological argument.

There is a difference between a perfect being—whatever may be meant by that—thought of as existing (rather than as dead or as a mere chimera) and a perfect being which in fact exists. From the definition of God we can only learn how he is to be thought of, not whether he exists.

It might be a possible definition of God that he is the incarnate triumph over man's inadequacies, thought of as existing, that he is the embodiment of that state of being after which all men—or most men—aspire, thought of not as a logical possibility but as existing. From this definition, however, we could not infer that God actually exists.

47. KANT'S POSTULATE. Further objections to the ontological argument may be found in Gaunilo's reply to Anselm "On Behalf of the Fool" (to which Anselm, in turn, replied), in Kant's *Critique of Pure Reason* (2nd ed., 620–630), and in Schopenhauer's essay on *The Fourfold Root of the Principle of Sufficient Reason* (Chapter 2, Section 7). We all think in the context of a tradition and are deeply indebted to our predecessors, even if we do not consider their essays as final. What is definitive, if anything, is an occasional refutation. But even those who offer conclusive refutations usually get involved in errors of their own. And nowhere are such errors more frequent than in the passages in which philosophers speak of God.

Having shown in his own way that the ontological argument for God's existence is invalid no less than the argument from design, which he called teleological, and the argument for a necessary being, which he called cosmological; and having shown further that the cosmological and telelogical arguments fall back on the ontological argument if they infer that a necessary being must *eo ipso* be a perfect being—having thus smashed natural theology—Kant proceeded to compose his *Critique of Practical Reason* in which he offered his own postulate of God's existence. He claimed that reason demanded free will, the immortality of the soul, and the existence of God, although reason could not prove them and we could never know whether what reason demands is in fact the case.

Unlike his celebrated refutations, Kant's postulate of God's existence has been almost entirely without influence—unless it should have helped to persuade thousands of people, contrary to all the facts, that belief in God's existence, in an afterlife, and in free will is the quintessence of religion. The Buddha was by no means the only great religious figure without belief

in any god (cf. § 43), the Hebrew prophets did not believe
in an afterlife, and many outstanding Christians have denied
free will.

The highest good, or *summum bonum,* says Kant, consists
in the conjunction of perfect virtue and perfect happiness; and
reason demands that we should bend our efforts to the reali-
zation of this highest good—and that the goal for which it is
our duty to strive must be attainable. Perfect virtue or holiness, however, cannot be attained in a finite period of time.
Hence reason demands the immortality of the soul no less than
free will as the necessary conditions of perfect virtue.

Further, we do not find in this world a proportionate conjunction of virtue and happiness, nor any agency that might
bring about such a conjunction in the long run. Hence reason
demands, thirdly, as a necessary condition of this conjunction,
that there be such an agency outside this world of experience.
And this agent certainly comes closer to what most Christians
and Jews mean by God than any First Cause.

Kant admits emphatically that we do not know that reality
conforms to these three postulates, and he even argues that
such knowledge would undermine disinterested morality. But
he does claim that reason demands that the will be free, that
the soul be immortal, and that there be a God.

On the face of it, it is plainly false that reason demands all
this. The catch is, of course, that it is supposedly the *practical*
reason that makes these demands. Kant's notion of practical
reason, however, has been repudiated in effect by almost all
philosophers since his time, and any detailed critique would
therefore be of purely historical interest. It would be "academic."

Even the greatest thinkers, not to speak of minor men, begin to stumble and fumble when they try to deal with God;
but Kant does not lose his greatness altogether even here where
he is weakest. His fame rests above all on his *Critique of Pure
Reason* and, next to that, on his *Critique of Judgment* and his
Foundation for the Metaphysic of Morals; but his postulate
of God's existence is in some ways comparable to these major
works. With a fundamental candor he spells out the workings

of his own mind and of hosts of others like his: he offers a
painstaking analysis of his own moral consciousness which he
shares with many of his contemporaries and thousands who
came before and after him; and his postulate of God's existence shows a deep insight into a religious consciousness which,
while certainly not common to all men by virtue of their reason, as Kant thought, was certainly not merely Kant's own
idiosyncrasy. This kind of religious consciousness facilitated
the acceptance of belief in an afterlife among the Jews at the
end of the Old Testament period, at a time when they suc-
cessfully resisted many other Persian and Hellenistic notions.

The religious consciousness which Kant portrays can be understood historically. But it does not provide strong evidence
for God's existence.

48. CAN ONE PROVE GOD'S EXISTENCE?   The major arguments
for God's existence fail to prove their point. Even if we grant
their premises and overlook fallacious reasoning, most of them
are arguments for occult powers and establish an overwhelming presumption in favor of the existence of a great many such
powers, of which not one resembles the God of Moses, Jesus,
or Mohammed. The ontological argument tries to prove the
existence of a perfect God but is fallacious. Kant, whose God
is similar to that of Judaism and Christianity, does not succeed
in showing that reason demands his existence. The question
remains: Can one prove God's existence?

Yes, but this does not mean that God exists. The classical
syllogism is: All men are mortal; Socrates is a man; therefore
Socrates is mortal. It provides the recipe for proving with
equal elegance that Socrates is immortal: All men are immortal; Socrates is a man; therefore Socrates is immortal.

By the same token, we can construct an indefinite number
of proofs of God's existence. If Jesus was trustworthy, God
exists; Jesus was trustworthy; therefore God exists. The construction of premises from which the existence of God will
follow as a valid conclusion is a mere matter of ingenuity:
valid proofs of God's existence are not hard to find. The crux

is whether any such proof can be based on plausible premises. In that respect, the proof just offered is superior to the proofs of Thomas: millions would consent that both premises are plausible.

All valid proofs are if-then propositions: if the premises are true, then the conclusion must be true. When the argument is valid, those reluctant to admit the truth of the conclusion need only question the premises. Even where there are no other grounds for doubting the trustworthiness of any witness, the fact that he advocates a dubious belief is sufficient ground for asking whether he could not have been mistaken at least once.

In the case of Jesus, moreover, Albert Schweitzer and other New Testament scholars have long argued that he was mistaken about one of the most central tenets of his message; namely, that the world would come to an end before some of those who heard him would taste death. Schweitzer even argues that Jesus' ethic was designed only for the short interim before the end of our world and hence not only is inapplicable today but never was applicable.

Proofs which are based on *ad hoc* premises, made to measure for the conclusion, are even weaker. To give a crude example: If there is life, God must exist; there is life; therefore, God exists. Whoever is reluctant to accept the conclusion will question the major premise.

In the examples given so far, God appears in one of the premises. Can we prove God's existence with a valid argument in which God does not appear in any of the premises? Clearly, if God does not appear in any of the premises, he will not appear in the conclusion either: if he did, the argument would have to be invalid. But could we prove the existence of a being which has all of God's characteristics so that in effect we could prove God's existence, only without using the term "God"?

This question must be answered in the negative. The God of Judaism and Christianity is not one of a class of beings with a set of specifiable characteristics. Whatever can be proved to exist by means of arguments in which God does not figure in one of the premises is, from the Biblical point of view, a false

god. Hypothetical functionaries can be proved like that, not
God.

A functionary whose existence is implied not by *ad hoc*
presuppositions, but by a scientific theory or by a metaphysic
which did not assume this functionary to begin with, is a stopgap, likely to be dated by a future theory, and presumably not
required even now by rival theories. But the God of Moses
and of Jesus is no stopgap.

49. PASCAL'S WAGER. Pascal, mathematician, physicist, po-
lemicist, and mystic, sewed into the lining of his coat a piece
of parchment dating from the day of his great mystical experience, to remind himself that the God of Abraham, Isaac, and
Jacob is not the God of the philosophers and theologians. He
saw the weaknesses of the old proofs of God's existence and
had some intimations that faith is related somehow to commitment. His attempt to spell out this commitment in his
posthumously published *Pensées* is, however, weirder still than
any of the proofs of the philosophers and theologians.

"Either God exists, or he does not exist," argues Pascal; and
neither proposition can be proved. So we must wager: this
strange word is Pascal's own; and with a desperate concern,
he proceeds to figure out the odds. If we wager that God exists
and we are right, we win everything; if we are wrong we lose
nothing. If you passed this up, "you would be imprudent."
What more could you ask?

Pascal stops with these two possibilities; but we might as
well complete the picture and spell out all four possibilities.

	God Does Exist	*God Does Not Exist*
We wager, God ex-ists:	We win everything; we hit the jackpot; up we go.	We lose nothing.
We wager, He does not:	We lose everything; we have had it; down we go.	We win nothing.

Clearly, this is the opportunity of a lifetime. Anybody who is not out of his mind will bet that God exists. This looks much better than the proofs of Anselm and Aquinas. Or has Pascal, too, overlooked something?

The first objection of which people usually think is ill advised. They say that we cannot induce belief merely by representing to ourselves the great advantage of belief. But it is Pascal's *logic* that is at fault, not his psychology.

"Follow the way by which they began; by acting as if they believe, taking the holy water, having masses said, etc. Even this will naturally make you believe, and deaden your acuteness." Pascal's psychology is corroborated by millions of examples in totalitarian countries: once people realize the dreadful risks of nonbelief and the rewards for the acceptance of beliefs, it takes most men at most a few years to believe quite firmly. First, one makes believe that one believes, and soon one does believe.

That is the origin of most religious faith: the child begins by acting like the grownups who believe, and soon believes himself. The proofs come later, if at all. *Religious belief generally starts as make-believe.*

What Pascal overlooked was the hair-raising possibility that God might out-Luther Luther. A special area in hell might be reserved for those who go to mass. Or God might punish those whose faith is prompted by prudence. Perhaps God prefers the abstinent to those who whore around with some denomination he despises. Perhaps he reserves special rewards for those who deny themselves the comfort of belief. Perhaps the intellectual ascetic will win all while those who compromised their intellectual integrity lose everything.

There are many other possibilities. There might be many gods, including one who favors people like Pascal; but the other gods might overpower or outvote him, a la Homer. Nietzsche might well have applied to Pascal his cutting remark about Kant: when he wagered on God, the great mathematician "became an idiot" (578).

Even an astounding competence in mathematics provides no safeguard against pathetic pitfalls when it comes to arguments about religion. Some people think that the existence of some scientists, especially atomic physicists, who hold traditional beliefs creates a strong presumption that these beliefs must be true. Clearly, it does not.

Arguments based on the realities of this world can prove at best the existence of such morally revolting functionaries as Kafka portrays in his two great novels, and the God of Pascal's wager who saves those who shun imprudent risks is not the God of Abraham. When God said to Abraham, "Go from your land, and from your kindred, and from your father's house to the land that I will show you," Abraham could not have wagered that he stood to win all without risking anything. The God of Abraham, Isaac, and Jacob asks men to risk everything.

VI. GOD, AMBIGUITY,
AND THEOLOGY

50. GOD AND AMBIGUITY. Propositions about God pose an important problem which is often overlooked: What do they mean? What does "God" mean?

The meaning of the word "God" is learned in large measure from the Bible, as is the meaning of "Methuselah" or "Moses" —or "paradise" or, to a lesser extent, "holy" or even "love." (See § 29.) We do not only permanently associate some words with particular Biblical sentences, passages, or stories, but the Bible is the world in which many of us—and many of our elders and hundreds of the writers whose works have formed our imagination and vocabulary—first encountered certain words, conceptions, and experiences.

Initially, we encounter God as a proper name. He is an individual whose character is manifested in his words and deeds. The character is complex, and as soon as we start abstracting traits from the many things he says and does we are in grave danger of falling into contradictions.

Even when we consider "God" as a proper name, certain differences between "God" and "Methuselah" or "Moses" are obvious. First, "God" occurs in so many more different contexts, in almost every book of the Bible, that the resulting complexity is many times, though not literally infinitely, greater than in the case of "Moses," not to speak of "Methuselah." Secondly, this appearance in widely different contexts and this relevance to radically divergent situations—to everything, in fact—becomes an essential feature of God.

Moreover, the character of God is not made manifest solely by what he says and does. He also appears, much more frequently and characteristically than anyone else, as the subject of direct address, as one to whom sacrifices are made or thanks given, and as the object of visions, love, or awe. To give an example: "hallelujah"—literally, "praise Yah (the Lord)"—is for most of us not so much a way of giving praise to someone whose existence is known independently as it is a shout of joy. We may associate it with the music of Handel or perhaps with the voice of Marian Anderson singing a spiritual. For some of us it may be nothing less than the ultimate expression of joyous emotion, of a triumph over sorrow, of release from care. Though we do not take it literally as meaning "praise the Lord," it enters into what "God" means to us.

Some emotions are intimately associated with, and most readily expressed in, phrases in which "God" appears in one way or another. The Bible and various hymns and benedictions inspired by it have given classical expression to any number of experiences—and raised our sights to all kinds of experiences which otherwise we might not know at all.

"God-fearing" denotes an attitude not fully conveyed by any paraphrase, and certainly not by any such literal rendering as "afraid of the deity." Or consider the priestly blessing: "The Lord bless thee and keep thee; the Lord make his face shine upon thee and be gracious unto thee; the Lord turn his face toward thee and give thee peace." What is meant is not that there is a character named God who has a face which, like the sun, he can let shine upon us. Indeed, it is not at all easy to say with precision what is meant, but again these words help to inform the meaning of "God."

We read Isaiah's account of the experience of his calling. He sees God on a throne surrounded by seraphim—probably, fiery serpents, not angels—with six wings. Is the Lord here still a character or, like the six-winged seraphim, part of a vision—the central element in an overpowering experience which can be represented only by using the most majestic terms: throne, holy, the whole earth, glory—and the Lord of hosts? We need not believe that one of the seraphim literally touched Isaiah's

lips with a live coal, or that the Lord sat upon a throne surrounded by six-winged seraphim: surely, the writer had no
such intention, but his vision has left a permanent mark on
subsequent thought and feeling and the meaning of "God."

We may not know what to make of Isaiah's vision or the
priestly blessing or the first chapter of Genesis, but our notion
of God, whether we believe in him or not, is nourished by
these sources; and when we read that a Hollywood star has
said that God is "just a livin' doll" we hardly trust our eyes.

Now if we asked seriously whether this proposition about
God is true or false, two kinds of answers could be given without broaching the problem of God's existence. In the first
place, we can construe this statement precisely like a statement about Moses: we can ask whether it is in accordance
with our literary reports. Asked whether Odysseus was phenomenally stupid, we could say No without committing ourselves regarding his historical existence.

Secondly, we can say that statements about God belong to
a universe of discourse which has its own characteristic conventions—for example, the Jewish or the Christian religion—
and we can then ask whether the proposition is in accordance
with these conventions.

The two approaches, though they lead to the same verdict
in the case at hand, are different: the conventions are not always in complete accord with the Bible. Pascal's familiar distinction between the God of Abraham, Isaac, and Jacob and
the God of the philosophers needs to be supplemented with a
similar distinction between the God of Scripture and the God
of the creeds, the dogmas, and the theologians.

Asked if it is true that God loves man, one might say on the
basis of Scripture, "Yes, but . . ." But if the universe of discourse is defined by the conventions of the Christian faith, the
answer would be simply Yes, seeing that the proposition to be
judged is itself one of these conventions. To judge whether a
proposition about God is true or false, we must know to what
universe of discourse it belongs. "A bishop can move diagonally
only" is true if the universe of discourse happens to be chess;
not otherwise.

Much discourse about God is therefore meaningful and even verifiable in an important sense without implying that God does in fact exist. In some kinds of discourse statements about God are legitimately verified by references to the Bible, or found false because they are in conflict either with express assertions or with implications of some passages in Scripture. In other kinds of discourse statements about God are found to be true or false by referring back to the traditions of a religious community or a denomination. In both cases, disagreement may be frequent: in the case of Scripture, because different passages say different things and seem to have divergent implications; in the case of the traditions of denominations, because these traditions are not necessarily consistent and because different denominations disagree. For all that, there is an area of agreement, and some propositions about God would be considered true by almost everyone brought up against the background of the Bible, others false. All this is independent of the question whether God exists.

The question whether God exists is of a different nature. First of all, it is ambiguous in the sense that this question, too, might be asked without all reference to the question whether God *really* exists. What may be meant may be whether, according to the Bible or according to the traditions of some particular community, God exists. Answer: the Baalim and Ashtaroth do not exist, the Lord does.

In this context there is a legitimate sense in saying that God exists by definition. Without committing oneself to a scholastic metaphysic one might even say that in the Bible God is the most real being: this would be a trope, not altogether different from such colloquialisms as "Boy, does he ever exist!" Or "if he doesn't, who does?"

Interpreted at this level, the question whether God exists is comparable to the question whether Odysseus was cunning: what is asked about is an essential part of the conception. If the universe of discourse is Scripture, Judaism, or Christianity, "God exists" is true.

If we are asked whether Moses ever killed a man, the answer according to Exodus, and according to the denominations which accept this book as part of their canon of Scriptures, is: he did. But one could also ask whether Moses *really* killed a man. In that case, it would be assumed that there really was a historical character named Moses who in other respects was sufficiently similar to the character described in the Bible to warrant our identification of the two, and the question would be whether this particular incident, related in the second chapter of Exodus, was historically true or not. Asked whether Moses ever really existed, we could clearly say he did, if we were sure that all the statements made about him in Exodus, Leviticus, Numbers, and Deuteronomy were true. But if some of them were true and others were not true, the question might be difficult, if not impossible, to answer in one word. If there was a man who did all the deeds and said all the things ascribed to Moses, but his name was not Moses; or if there were two men, one who led his people out of Egypt and another who gave them their laws; or possibly many more than two, who during a period of two centuries had done some of the major deeds ascribed to Moses, while still other feats were done centuries later; then it would be impossible to say whether Moses ever really existed, unless we analyzed the question into several component queries.

The question whether God *really* exists offers the same difficulties as the question whether Moses really existed, but to a much higher degree. In the case of Moses, there is the name to hang on to: if a man by that name either led the Jews from Egypt or gave them at least some of their laws, we could say: yes, he did exist, but he did not do everything ascribed to him. And if a man named Moses performed both these feats— which is extremely probable (cf., e.g., Albright's essays)—we should have no hesitation whatever in affirming the historic existence of Moses even if some statements made about him in the Bible should be false. In the case of God, we have no name to hang on to, and he is credited with so much more than even Moses that *the question whether God really exists has no clear meaning.*

Furthermore, the word "exists" raises problems of its own.

If it is meant in the same sense in which Moses might have existed, the sense in which chickens and chairs exist, most people would say that God does not "exist." The assertion of such spatial existence would immediately raise the question where, in what particular location, God could be found.

Those asserting God's existence have therefore often maintained that there are different modes of existence. This is a doubtful doctrine. It is said that not only material entities exist but also, as Plato claimed, mathematical objects, such as points, triangles, and numbers, as well as justice, love, and beauty. It is highly dubious whether anything is gained by speaking unidiomatically of the "existence" of such entities.

Even if it were legitimate to speak of different modes of existence, what could be meant by asking whether God "exists"? Saying that God exists in the same sense in which mathematical points exist would be hardly less atheistic than saying that his existence is comparable to that of unicorns. Those asserting the existence of God have sometimes recognized this difficulty and contended that God's mode of existence is unique, that he does not exist in the same sense in which anything else exists but in a sense peculiar to himself. Logically, however, this is no different from saying that God does *not* "exist."

One of the outstanding Protestant theologians of our time, Paul Tillich, admits as much when he says in an essay on "The Concept of God" that "the very term 'existence of God' is almost blasphemous" and that "every true theistic statement must be contradicted by an atheistic statement." And in the first volume of his *Systematic Theology* (237) Tillich writes: "It is as atheistic to affirm the existence of God as it is to deny it."

In spite of our ordinary way of speaking, which makes theism positive and atheism negative, the theist cannot say what he affirms; he can only deny the atheist's contention. The theist is not the man who affirms God's existence—on reflection, he admits that God does *not* "exist"—but the theist denies that God "exists" in the same sense in which unicorns exist.

It may seem that this extraordinary conclusion is incompatible with the way in which Tillich follows up the sentence quoted from his *Systematic Theology*: "God is being-itself, not *a* being." Tillich's affirmation suggests that theists affirm something after all, and that this affirmation is denied by atheists. But no atheist would deny the affirmation that "God is being-itself"; he would only say that in that case we might as well dispense with all reference to God and—like Heidegger, for example, to whom Tillich is exceedingly close—speak of "being." If Tillich really meant that "God is being-itself," he would not significantly disagree with atheists, except insofar as he was reluctant to give up the name of God and liked to use it redundantly for something for which we already have a perfectly good word. But Tillich, of course, does not really mean what he says here. Remember that "every true theistic statement must be contradicted by an atheistic statement." According to Tillich, "God is being-itself" is a true theistic statement; so we must add immediately that, of course, God is not really being-itself. Or perhaps we need not add it *immediately*.

In sum, terms applied to God do not mean what they generally mean. Those who say that God exists do not really mean that he "exists" in the same sense in which anything else exists. Those who say that God is being-itself, or a spirit, or love, do not mean these terms in any ordinary sense. But if terms applied to God do not mean what they generally mean, if they have a unique meaning when applied to God, then all such talk about God is conducted in a peculiar language with rules of its own.

In chess, "king" and "bishop" do not mean what they usually mean, but every term has a precise meaning, and the game would not be changed if we substituted "fool" for "bishop," as the French do, or "devil" for "king." But assertions about God depend entirely on their ambiguity: it is their apparent meaning, their surface sense, that counts 99 per cent of the time, and it is only under questioning that this is modified, and only under persistent attack is it withdrawn to the point where frequently no sense at all remains.

This is true not only of assertions about God. A world-famous Thomist says to an undergraduate who asks about the meaning of the new dogma about the assumption of the Virgin Mary: there has been an unfortunate movement in recent Catholicism that has depreciated the body, and by declaring that the Virgin's body was taken up to heaven we counter this ascetic tendency. A colleague asks: but if the body in the dogma is the physical body which asceticism depreciates, then it must take up space. Is heaven then to be understood spatially, and must a location in space be assigned to the body of the Virgin Mary? The Thomist replies: oh, no, there are all kinds of bodies, and the body of the Virgin that was assumed in heaven was not a spatial body.

To understand such peculiarities of theology, one must remember that theology, and indeed any systematic discussion of God, was born as a defensive maneuver. It is the product of a distinctive historic situation. Claims of a less sophisticated age have been exposed to rationalistic attack when theology appears to salvage the tradition. The word theology is encountered for the first time in Plato—at the point where he proposes to expurgate Homer's epics to rescue belief in the gods from the cynicism of the Greek enlightenment (*Republic*, 379). The theologian defends his religious heritage by sacrificing its plain exoteric meaning. He says to the atheist: you are quite right to deny what you deny, but I deny it, too; what you repudiate is indeed superstitious and wrong—but you are wrong, too.

The situation would be simple if the theologian rebuked the atheist for taking literally what ought to be read as poetry. But in that case the infidel might well reply: we are agreed; I like to read the Scriptures, too. The difference arises over the theologians' determined attempt to make univocal translations of essentially ambiguous propositions.

"God" is not a univocal term. The deeds and words of God; the visions, phrases, and relations into which God enters; and the thoughts and feelings about Him which are recorded in the Hebrew Scriptures add up to a conception overcharged with meaning. The God of Abraham, Isaac, and Jacob is not simply "being-itself." And now there have been added to this overrich conception of the Hebrew Scriptures the sayings of

Jesus and the stories of the Gospels, the theologies of the fourth evangelist and Paul, the ideas of the other authors of New Testament Epistles, the visions of the Revelation of St. John the Divine, and the vast lore, if not of the Talmud, Midrash, and the Jewish mystics, of the church fathers and the Christian mystics, the scholastics, and innumerable theologians and philosophers.

Seeing that "God" is so far from being a univocal term and that the terms applied to him by theologians are admittedly not intended to mean what they generally mean, it is no exaggeration if we conclude that *most statements about God are essentially ambiguous.* They cannot be called true or false. Interpretations of them which are true are usually ingenious or trivial or heretical—and often all three. The propositions themselves defy translation.

51. THE AMBIGUITY OF DOGMA. Speaking of dogma, I mean definitively formulated propositions of which a religious institution says authoritatively that salvation depends on belief in them. Not all religions are religions of salvation: the Hebrew prophets, for example, did not believe in any afterlife, and their religion was not a religion of salvation. The religion of the Old Testament was a religion without dogmas. Later Judaism, also a religion without dogmas, will be considered in some detail in Chapter VIII.

Buddhism was a religion of salvation from the start, and the Buddha himself seems to have considered acceptance of four propositions essential for salvation. His Four Noble Truths (see § 62) were clearly meant to be unambiguous.

The Christian dogmas, however, were defined gradually as one controversy after another made it necessary to draw a line to guard against excessive disagreement. These dogmas must be understood with reference to the conflicts of opinion they were meant to settle.

When it is asked what a particular Christian dogma means, the word "means" is capable of different interpretations. Two deserve special attention. First, it may be asked what construc-

tion of the dogma is most profound, most edifying: what is
wanted is a homily. Secondly, the question may be what the
people meant who framed the dogma: what is wanted is historical information. In both cases, many different meanings
can be specified. Of homilies, of course, there is no end. (The
explanation of the dogma of the assumption, cited in the previous section, is presumably a homily.) And the historical question leads to a wide variety of answers, too.

Those who originally agreed on the dogma may have accepted it as a compromise formula which may even have been
expressly designed to permit a number of different interpretations, lest preference be given to one faction. Moreover, different interpretations are bound to have developed later and—
a further complication—some of these are likely to have been
condemned specifically by some denominations but not by
others. No one familiar with the history of dogma will speak
deliberately of *the* meaning of a dogma, except in a sermon.

Most of the Christian dogmas as well as most propositions
about God are essentially ambiguous. A univocal translation
may serve some special purpose admirably, but it must always
be rejected in the long run as a mistranslation; for it is more
dispensable than the vast multiplicity of associations, the inexhaustibility, the unfathomability of the original statement.
The history of the development of Christian dogma is a continual fight for the abundance of mystery and not for rationalistic clarification.

Are religious dogmas cognitive and meaningful? The Four
Noble Truths are both. The Christian dogmas, however, communicate a profusion of knowledge and suffer from an excess
of meaning no less than most propositions about God and the
immortal stories of the Book of Genesis. The good preacher
extracts the insights and teaches the wisdom without ever ex-
hausting the endless possibilities of his material. No sermon,
however profound, would be an acceptable substitute for the
original text. A very partial translation of a dogma, or of one
of the stories of Genesis, might be true or false; the texts themselves, though perhaps literally untrue, are fountainheads of
wisdom and of superstition, beyond true and false. Or rather

they belong to a deeper stratum at which the question of true and false has not yet occurred. Or to put it much more simply: they are through and through ambiguous.

52. ANALOGY. The attempt to salvage religious propositions by admitting their literal falseness while maintaining their truth, provided only that they are interpreted as analogous or symbolic, must fail. It ignores the essential ambiguity of the propositions it would salvage.

To begin with analogy, this means a partial resemblance between two entities, attributes, or activities. When it is argued that analogy is the key to propositions about God, what is meant is that the attributes and activities ascribed to God do not have literally the same meaning they have in discourse about human beings, but are similar in meaning. God's love and justice are held to have something in common with human love and justice—enough to make these words appropriate—but they are somehow more perfect. The body of the Virgin Mary that was assumed in heaven is similar enough to a human body to warrant the use of the word "body" but dissimilar in not being spatial.

The attempt to interpret such propositions by means of analogy breaks down when we ask what the nonspatial body has in common with a human body, and when we realize that all the other key terms of the proposition are also used in a nonliteral sense. Heaven is somehow like the sky, but is not really the sky but also nonspatial. The "assumption" of a nonspatial body in a nonspatial place is not an assumption in any ordinary sense. The word "virgin" poses problems of its own. What we have here is not one analogy but a proposition that is ambiguous through and through.

The statement that God loves man cannot be explained either by saying simply that "love" is here employed analogously. Nor does it really help to say that the kind of love meant has been specified to some extent: it is said to be like a father's love for his children. At other times it is compared to a man's love for his unfaithful wife (in Hosea, for example),

like a man's love for the beloved of his youth, like a man's love
for his bride—but not one of these metaphors can bear the
strain of consistent interpretation as an analogy.

Nor is it true that love has a precise meaning, and that we
apply the word to God more or less as an afterthought. We
glean the meaning of love not from any clear-cut definition,
but from sentences some of which speak of God's love. (Cf.
§ 29.) Still more important: the contention that these statements are analogous overlooks the essential ambiguity of
"God."

If "God" were the name of an individual who is known
independently of such statements as, for example, that he loves
man, or if God could be defined as some kind of a stopgap or a
hypothetical functionary, the case would be far simpler than
it is in fact. It is a besetting fault of most discussions about
the nature of God that it is simply assumed at the outset that
everybody knows what "God" means, as if the issue were
merely whether "He" is this or does that along with what else
is already known about "Him."

Of course, people have often thought of God in terms of all
kinds of analogies, and one of these has been considered in
some detail in the section on Aquinas: the analogy between
God and an architect or artificer. But under scrutiny these
analogies break down as the argument from design breaks
down. We return to the text which says, "In the beginning
God created the heaven and the earth," and this proposition
is thoroughly ambiguous and lends itself to endless exegeses.
Insistence on any one analogy can only lead to superstition
and is likely to be repudiated in the end as heresy or as sim-
plistic.

In discourse about God analogies are tenable only as passing tropes, as groping metaphors. As soon as an analogy hard-
ens into assurance it must be rejected by Christianity and Judaism themselves.

The analogy between the God of popular Roman Catholicism and a cruel Caesar is striking: one must serve Him in
every way and praise Him all but continually; those who dis-
please Him are given over to eternal torture; He cannot be

approached directly even with petitions; the best procedure is to ask somebody who has found favor—a saint, and a particular one depending on the nature of one's case—to intercede with the mother of His son, in the hope that she may take up the matter with her son, and the son with the father.

Today the bare mention of such an analogy sounds like a critique, at least in democratic countries, but the analogy was central in the imagination of believers for well over a thousand years. At one time the earthly hierarchy was thought to be sanctioned by the supposed analogy to the heavenly hierachy; today, when the terrestrial version is widely repudiated, the celestial picture is less apt to seem a prototype than a projection. Any tenacious insistence on this analogy is not ultimately acceptable from the religious point of view because it leads to superstition and gross misunderstanding; and the conception of analogy must be renounced in favor of thoroughgoing ambiguity.

It would be foolish to suppose that considerations of this sort had altogether escaped Aquinas. He realized clearly that any ascription of qualities to God stood in grave danger of being equivocal. In Question 13 of Part One of his *Summa Theologica,* where he discusses "The Names of God," he considers the argument that "no name belongs to God in the same sense that it belongs to creatures" and that "Therefore whatever is said of God and of creatures is predicated equivocally." St. Thomas admits more than once that "univocal predication is impossible between God and creatures"; but he adds: "Neither, on the other hand, are names applied to God and creatures in a purely equivocal sense, as some have said" (Article 5). Professor Pegis informs us in a footnote that Thomas here refers to Maimonides' *Guide for the Perplexed,* Book I, Chapter 59.

Maimonides retells a well-known story from the Talmud (Berachoth 33b): Once one of the rabbis heard a man praying, "God that is great, powerful, awesome, strong, forceful, feared, firm, courageous, reliable, and revered." After he had finished, the rabbi told him a parable. Suppose that a king of flesh and blood owned a thousand myriads of gold coins, and someone were to praise him for owning some silver coins: would not that be a slight? Maimonides argues that it is not even seemly to employ in prayers all of the attributes ascribed to God in the Bible. We may read them in context as we come to them, but it is unseemly to use them to talk about God. "You know what a great sin it is to speak of God in an unseemly manner, and it is in no way necessary for you to enter into positive assertions about God in order to glorify God according to your lights." The attributes encountered in the Bible may be understood either as characterizations of God's works or as negations. "But the most remarkable expression along these lines is that of king David in the Psalm: Thou art praised in silence." And Maimonides also cites Psalm 4: "Ponder it in your heart upon your bed and be silent."

St. Thomas replies that "Such a view is against the Philosopher, who proves many things about God, and also against what the Apostle says: The invisible things of God are clearly seen, being understood by the things that are made (Rom. 1.20). Therefore it must be said that these names are said of God and creatures in an *analogous* sense."

Since Aristotle, *"the* Philosopher," proved many things about God and St. Paul can be cited in a similar vein, St. Thomas considers himself justified in filling literally hundreds of pages answering precise questions about the nature of God with the utmost precision; and he rests his case on the concept of analogy.

Still in Article 5, he explains: "whatever is said of God and creatures is said according as there is some relation of the creature to God as to its principle and cause, wherein all the perfections of things pre-exist excellently. Now this mode of community is a mean between pure equivocation and simple univocation. For in analogies the idea is not, as it is in univocals, one and the same; yet it is not totally diverse as in equivocals."

The crucial assumption of Aquinas is that "all the perfections of things pre-exist excellently" in God; or to cite Article 3, the "perfections are in God in a more eminent way than in creatures"; or to cite, finally, Article 2: "it was shown above that God prepossesses in Himself all the perfections of creatures, being Himself absolutely and universally perfect."

Where "above" was this shown? As Professor Pegis points out in a footnote, it was "shown" in Question 4, Article 2—which has already been discussed in Section 45 in connection with Aquinas' fourth proof of God's existence. It is precisely the least plausible of his five proofs, the one most embedded in a quasi-Platonic metaphysics, that must bear the burden of St. Thomas' theory of analogy. In fact, the theory of analogy depends not only on this proof but also on the specific arguments of Question 4, Article 2, which we have already discussed and found wanting.

It will be recalled that Thomas considered the objection that "opposites cannot coexist. Now the perfections of things are opposed to each other" and therefore "it seems that the perfections of all things are not in God." Against this objection, Aquinas cited Dionysius—or rather that early medieval writer who claimed to be the first-century Dionysius—as having said that the sun, "while remaining one and shining uniformly, contains within itself first and uniformly the substances of sensible things, and many and diverse qualities; a fortiori should all things in a kind of natural unity pre-exist in the cause of all things"; and Aquinas simply added: "and thus things diverse and in themselves opposed to each other pre-exist in God as one, without injury to His simplicity. This suffices for the Reply." But does it?

Eventually, St. Thomas misquotes Exodus as saying: "the Lord answered him: Thus shalt thou say to them, HE WHO IS hath sent me to you (Exod. iii. 13, 14). Therefore this name, HE WHO IS, is the most proper name of God." St. Thomas, unable to read the verse in the original, did not realize that it neither contained any reference to "the Lord" nor, alas, the words which Thomas considered "the most proper name of God." (Cf. §§ 45 and 89.) But for all that, Thomas succeeded in fusing dubious Bible quotations, the pseudo-science of a late fifth-century writer whom Thomas believed when he claimed that he had been converted by St. Paul and present

at the death of the Blessed Virgin Mary, and a strange mixture of Aristotelianism and Neoplatonism into a vast system.
By its sheer vastness and intricacy it reduces potential critics
to that respectful silence which Maimonides, but not Aquinas,
considered fitting before the Lord.

Maimonides' quotations from Scripture, like those of the
rabbis before him, are highly questionable, too. But Maimonides, though certainly a theologian of sorts, retained far more
feeling for Scripture than Aquinas—partly because he was intimately familiar with the Hebrew Scriptures in the original,
instead of having to rely on a Latin translation that transposed
them into an utterly alien sensibility. Hence any idea of describing God as he is in himself—as an object of reason—was
expressly ruled out by Maimonides. We can say only what
God is *not;* and the predicates encountered in Scripture must
be interpreted as descriptions of God's activity in relation to
man.

Aquinas, too, says at the beginning of Question 3 that "we
cannot know what God is, but rather what He is not"; and
Aquinas even repeats this occasionally. But by the beginning
of Question 12, after he has ascribed a great many predicates
to God, Aquinas tells us: "hitherto we have considered God as
He is in Himself [*secundum seipsum*]."

Instead of summing up Aquinas' view myself, I shall turn
to Frederick Copleston, S.J., Professor at Heythrop College,
Oxford, and at the Gregorian University in Rome. In his volume on *Medieval Philosophy: Augustine to Scotus,* he devotes
all of four pages to a chapter on "Jewish Philosophy," and
exactly two pages to Maimonides, compared to 130 on Aquinas. In these two pages he says among other things: "But if
Maimonides anticipated most of the types of proof given later
by St. Thomas [who had read Maimonides], he [Maimoni-
des] was more insistent than the latter on the inapplicability
of positive predicates to God." And again: "But Maimonides
was rather more insistent on the *via negativa*" (240). Thus
Copleston finds Aquinas' originality in his partial deviation
from Maimonides' insistence that God cannot be described as
he is in himself—and those who feel that one cannot be too

insistent on this point, and that even Maimonides went too far, will hardly admire St. Thomas for proceeding as far as he did in objectifying God.

To be sure, Thomas was able to cite in his behalf not only Aristotle and the Pseudo-Dionysius but also Romans 1.20, which evidences the influence of Greek philosophy on St. Paul; but he might have pondered the Book of Job, and especially the words cited once before, and ascribed to the Lord himself: "Where wast thou when I laid the foundations of the earth" (38.4)? What Thomas describes is clearly not the God of Job, nor the God of Abraham, Isaac, and Jacob, though it may be the god of the man who claimed falsely that he had been present at the death of the Blessed Virgin Mary; the man who so boldly, if implausibly, explained the workings of the sun; the man on whose queer notions about the sun Aquinas based his claim that we can after all ascribe predicates to God.

A final, most important, objection to the claim that all human perfections "are in God in a more eminent way" will be adduced in Section 54. To anticipate: the whole theory of analogy, even if otherwise free of holes, would still be shipwrecked on the Christian conception of hell.

53. SYMBOLS: CONTRA TILLICH. Some people think that the conception of "symbols" which is fashionable in our day can do the job that "analogy" has failed to do. It is argued, for example by Professor Stace of Princeton, that religious propositions which are literally false are true when understood symbolically.

The first point to note here is that *there is no nonsense whatever which may not be said to be symbolically true*, especially if its symbolic meaning is not stated. To show that religious propositions are true when understood symbolically, one must do three things: specify what each proposition symbolizes; show that the meaning one finds in it is not arbitrary but warranted by the proposition; and show that other interpretations are not just as plausible.

If the last specification is not satisfied—and it never is—it is admitted in effect that the proposition is essentially ambiguous. If that is what is meant by calling religious propositions symbolic, this is a misleading way of saying what is meant.

Regarding the second requirement—that it should be shown how the symbolic meaning claimed for a proposition is not arbitrary but warranted by the proposition—Stace, for example, in his discussion of religious truth in *Religion and the Modern Mind* fails at this point. He says sweepingly of "religious doctrines and dogmas" that "none of them is *literally* true"—a generalization which is surely literally false—and then attempts a large-scale salvage operation by construing all creeds, doctrines, and dogmas as symbols of the same truth.

Neither in *Religion and the Modern Mind* nor in *Time and Eternity*, in which he defends the same thesis at greater length, does Stace discuss in any detail the dogmas of Christianity, the Four Noble Truths, the teachings of the prophets, or the revelations of Mohammed: he shows neither that they are literally false nor that they all symbolize the same truth.

That there are certain ways of life which most of the best-known religious teachers of mankind condemned is true. There are also ways of life which all the great philosophers have repudiated; but that does not prove that all philosophies symbolize the same truth. Areas of agreement deserve study, but we should also face the fact that the great religious teachers have recommended widely different ways of life. Social justice, which meant almost everything to Amos and some of the other prophets, meant little to Jesus and Paul, to the sages of the Upanishads and to the Buddha. The faith in Christ which appeared essential to Paul and Luther had no place at all in the great religions of India and China. The gospel of radical detachment which the Buddha preached is different from the ethos of Christianity and Judaism. One cannot salvage the dogmas of Christianity by claiming that they are all symbols of the truth which the Buddha and the Bhagavadgita taught, too.

Some religious propositions are clearly meant to be taken literally, for example, the Four Noble Truths and some of the historical assertions made by Jews and Christians. Others, like the verses constituting the first chapter of Genesis, are not meant to be taken literally, and any single interpretation in terms of analogy is bound to be much less impressive than the original text; and even if the exegesis is profound, we should be greatly impoverished if we accepted it as definitive, instead of insisting on the essential ambiguity of the original. Still other propositions, like some of the Christian dogmas, were meant to be taken literally by some of those who helped to formulate them while others who contributed to their crystallization did not mean them literally; and most of these propositions are of such a nature that it simply makes no sense to speak of any literal interpretation. What, for example, is the literal meaning of "God"? Or "Holy Spirit"? Or "hell"? Nor are such key terms as these, or propositions about them, symbols in the same sense in which the fish or the lamb were in early Christianity symbols of Christ; the ship, a symbol of the church; the phoenix, of resurrection; or the serpent, of Satan.

Some writers would distinguish between mere signs and true symbols; for example, Tillich (cf. § 50), whose attempt to construe discourse about God as symbolically true has had very wide influence. With his radiant lack of resentment, he has no liking for personal polemics and would rather emphasize significant agreement; and it would be easy to enlist him as an ally even concerning some of the central motifs of this book. But he is first and foremost a Christian theologian; and it won't do to ignore that. Moreover, the question of the symbolic interpretation of religious propositions is so acute today, and Tillich's position is so regularly cited in this connection, that a critical discussion of his view can hardly be side-stepped. But remember: if the claim that religious propositions are symbolical means that they are richly ambiguous, it is true—but put very misleadingly.

"The statement that God is being-itself is a non-symbolic statement," Tillich says in his *Systematic Theology*. "However, after this has been said, nothing else can be said about God as God which is not symbolic." Then Tillich reminds us of "the insight that symbol and sign are different; that, while the sign bears no necessary relation to that to which it points, the symbol participates in the reality of that for which it stands. The sign can be changed arbitrarily according to the demands of expediency, but the symbol grows and dies according to the correlation between that which is symbolized and the persons who receive it as a symbol" (238 f.).

What Tillich here calls an insight is no more than a perfectly legitimate stipulation. But is it fruitful or illuminating? Does a proposition about God really "participate in the reality of that for which it stands"? This suggestion is extremely unclear. It sounds profound, but a moment's reflection will show that such "participation" is very common and not in the least mysterious—nor particularly relevant to discourse about God.

First, a relatively minor point: Tillich's distinction between sign and symbol has no foundation in our language. In mathematics it would make no sense; and when Churchill said in his message to the people of Europe, July 20, 1941, "The V sign is the symbol of the unconquerable will of the occupied territories," he used "symbol" quite correctly, though not in Tillich's sense. A little more important: "signs" often participate in the reality for which they stand. In *Much Ado About Nothing* (III.2), Shakespeare writes: "If he be not in love with some woman, there is no believing old signs. He brushes his hat o' mornings; what shall that bode?" And here is a similar example from Byron's "The Giaour":

> *If changing cheek and scorching vein,*
> *Lips taught to writhe but not complain,*
> *If bursting heart and madd'ning brain . . .*
> *Betoken love—that love was mine,*
> *And shown by many a bitter sign.*

In a similar vein, the Bible speaks of "the signs of the times" (Matt. 16.3); and so does Reinhold Niebuhr in the title of one of his books.

In his "Reply" at the end of the co-operative volume on *The Theology of Paul Tillich*, he writes: "May I add here something which I repeat again and again in my classes. He who says 'only a symbol' has completely misunderstood the meaning of symbol; he confuses symbol with sign, and ignores that a genuine symbol participates in the reality of that which it symbolizes." In fact, he who says "only a symbol" has at most refused to make a distinction which Tillich would like to see established generally.

But it is to be hoped that Tillich's usage—apparently suggested to him at least in part by the work of C. G. Jung—will not become established. Ernst Cassirer's almost diametrically opposite suggestion is much more in accordance with our language; it does not involve the somewhat occult notions of the growth and death of symbols; and, most important, it does not distract attention, as does Tillich's distinction, from the crux of the matter.

Cassirer also insists that "we must carefully distinguish between *signs* and *symbols*," but goes on to point out that "we find rather complex systems of signs and signals in animal behavior" and that domesticated animals "are extremely susceptible to signs" (50). Now the sign to which an animal responds usually "participates in the reality of that for which it stands," to cite Tillich's definition of symbols; but nobody would speak of a symbol when a dog understands his master's reach for hat and cane as a "sign" that he will go out.

Symbols, according to Cassirer, are of a higher order than signs not because they grow and die but because they are "not only universal but extremely variable" (56). To explain the first point, Cassirer says: "Universal applicability, owing to the fact that everything has a name, is one of the greatest prerogatives of human symbolism." But it is the variability of symbols that plainly points in the opposite direction from Tillich's suggestion.

"A sign or signal is related to the thing to which it refers in a fixed and unique way. . . . A genuine human symbol is characterized not by its uniformity but by its versatility. . . . In primitive mentality . . . the symbol is still regarded as a property of the thing. . . . In mythical thought the name of a god is an integral part of the nature of the god. . . . The same holds good for symbolic actions. A religious rite, a sacrifice, must always be performed in the same invariable way

and in the same order if it is to have its effect. Children . . .
tend to think that a thing 'is' what it is called. But . . . every
normal child will learn very soon that it can use various symbols to express the same wish or thought. For this variability
and mobility there is apparently no parallel in the animal
world" (56 f.).

Tillich's distinction between sign and symbol is not only
arbitrary; in Cassirer's phrases, it would make "mythical
thought" and the "primitive mentality" of undeveloped peoples and children the norm for all of us.

Tillich holds that too many Protestants "are unaware of the
numinous power inherent in genuine symbols, words, acts, persons, things" (*The Protestant Era,* xxiii). But this emotional
impact and sense of mystery have surely nothing to do with
any genuine participation in the reality for which the symbol
stands. The Catholic theologian Gustave Weigel, S.J., is clearly
right when he says, without any reference to Tillich: "Actions
which once were meaningful from their immediate physical
circumstances are retained though the circumstances are completely changed. Since the old meaning can no longer explain,
a symbolism is found to justify something originally quite unsymbolic" (288). And we may add: at that point they *become*
mysterious and sometimes even numinous.

The crucial distinction from which Tillich's discussion of
signs and symbols distracts attention is this: as these words are
generally used, both in ordinary language and by the most
judicious writers, symbols no less than signs, and *Symbole* no
less than *Zeichen,* stand for something specific, while propositions about God are essentially ambiguous.

The lamb, as a sacrificial animal, is not an arbitrary sign for
Jesus Christ, and some of the associations with lambs which
antedate the birth of Christianity and which made the adoption of this symbol appropriate are presumably the sort of
thing people mean when they say that symbols are not made
but grow. The same applies to the bread and wine where these
are viewed as symbols of Christ's flesh and blood. But in all
these cases the symbol stands for something that can be specified. It is not ambiguous although it has many connotations

in addition to its denotation. We can state with precision what each symbol symbolizes. But the verses of Genesis 1, most of the Christian dogmas, and most other religious propositions which are allegedly literally false but symbolically true are not symbols of some specifiable truth. They are ambiguous.

Tillich admits that if the term "God" remained ambiguous, this would invalidate his whole approach to propositions about God. In his "Reply" he writes: "An early criticism by Professor Urban of Yale forced me to acknowledge that in order to speak of symbolic knowledge one must delimit the symbolic realm by an unsymbolic statement. I was grateful for this criticism, and under its impact I became suspicious of any attempts to make the concept of symbol all-embracing and therefore meaningless. The unsymbolic statement which implies the necessity of religious symbolism is that God is being itself. . . ." And a page later, Tillich argues against Professor Randall of Columbia who "wants to include in symbolism the statement which I call the only nonsymbolic one, namely, that God is being-itself." But this is surely neither a symbolic statement nor a nonsymbolic statement: it is no statement at all, it is a definition—and as it happens, a definition utterly at odds with the meaning of "God" in probably more than 95 per cent of our religious tradition.

In Section II of *Civilization and Its Discontents*, Freud remarked: "One feels like taking one's stand in the ranks of the believers to confront the philosophers who think that they are saving the God of religion by substituting for him an impersonal, shadowy principle, with the admonition: Thou shalt not take the name of the Lord in vain." What Freud failed to note was only that the theologians are much more inveterate offenders than the philosophers.

Tillich's "being-itself" is neither the God of Abraham, Isaac, and Jacob nor the God of Jesus and Paul, of Matthew and Luke, of the martyrs and Reformers, or of the vast majority of religious people today. Tillich's appeal depends on the ambiguity of "God": he talks about being-itself, and his audience thinks of whatever they mean by "God." Some think of the God of Job and some of the God of Paul, some of the God of Calvin and some of their own idol, and many more think of nothing in particular but feel edified.

In short, Tillich's propositions about God are through and through ambiguous. And taken literally as statements about being itself, they are for the most part false. They depend entirely on their ambiguity.

In his *Systematic Theology*, Tillich says: "Many confusions in the doctrine of God and many apologetic weaknesses could be avoided if God were understood first of all as being-itself or as the ground of being" (235). He assumes that "God is the ground of being"—a phrase that recurs often in his works —is a "nonsymbolic statement" no less than "God is being-itself." But "ground of being" is even more transparently ambiguous than "being-itself." It does not even permit any literal interpretation.

Tillich's surface clarity and precision are misleading no less than the clarity and precision of Kafka's style in *The Castle* or in his myth "Before the Law." His apparently so simple and straightforward diction hides unfathomable ambiguity.

Kafka once stopped to make this point himself, right after telling his brief myth in *The Trial;* and in an artist such ambiguity would not be objectionable even if he had not called attention to it himself. Tillich and other theologians, on the other hand, have and give the impression that their prose is *not* ambiguous; and the very title *Systematic Theology* suggests a mode of thought almost at the opposite pole from Kafka's myths, and from myth generally.

That the stories of Genesis are an inexhaustible fount of interpretations is no objection: it is this very quality that repays every return to the text. But if this rich ambiguity is irreducible and reappears covertly in theology, then the validity and worth-whileness of theology become questionable. We might prefer overt myths.

54. DEMYTHOLOGIZING AND VALUATIONS. The problem that Rudolf Bultmann, Protestant theologian and outstanding New Testament scholar at Marburg, posed with his famous attempt

to "demythologize" the New Testament is by no means of merely parochial interest. Whether a theologian likes Bultmann's term or resents it as a barbarism, he demythologizes when he uses the texts to point a moral or to construct an avowedly nonmythical conception of God, creation, or resurrection which goes beyond a mere retelling of the Bible stories in an attempt to spell out their meaning.

Any critique of Bultmann should begin by recognizing that demythologizing is not his private project but common to all theologians, and not only theologians. Even so, Bultmann's conception of the problem and his specific suggestions are open to serious criticisms. But before going into that, it may be well to consider a form of demythologizing which is relatively uncontroversial.

There is a story to which Mahayana Buddhists attach considerable importance: that the Buddha was tempted by Mara to enter Nirvana immediately after his enlightenment under the bodhi tree, but refused because he wanted to proclaim his insights to other men. Instead of grasping the chance of immediate salvation, he decided to live on to help others. Mahayana Buddhists add that the bodhisattvas—their saints—permit themselves to be reborn again and again in order to help suffering mankind.

That there is scant evidence for these claims is certainly worth pointing out, but it would be stupid to dismiss them as almost certainly false hypotheses. Their moral intent is unmistakable. In a very important sense of the word, though not in Bultmann's sense, we demythologize these claims. We say: they are myths and their moral can be restated in nonmythological form. Any such restatement is less impressive, less vivid, and less beautiful than the original myths. But the fact remains that *these* myths *can* be demythologized.

This is also true of some Biblical stories, for example, that of Jonah. The "big fish" in that story which most readers take for a whale, although we are told explicitly that it was a fish, is certainly a red herring. It distracts attention from the point of the book.

Jonah was sent to Nineveh, the capital of Assyria, the arch-

enemy of his people, to cry out against its "wickedness." He
fled on a ship but was ultimately brought back in the belly
of the great fish and told again to go to Nineveh. He went and
cried out "Yet forty days, and Nineveh shall be overthrown."
Then the people repented and returned from their evil ways,
"and God repented of the evil which he had said he would
do to them, and did it not." This "displeased Jonah exceedingly, and he was very angry." He felt that he had been right
in the first place: "Therefore I fled to Tarshish: for I knew
that thou art a gracious God, and merciful." Now Jonah did
not want to return to Nineveh and retract his prophecy. He
went away and sulked, sitting down where he might be able
to see what would become of Nineveh. And God let a *kikayon*
grow up quickly, so Jonah could sit in the shade and enjoy
his sulk. But then God dispatched a worm, and the *kikayon*
withered. When the sun came up, Jonah was wretched. God
asked him whether he was angry about the *kikayon*, and Jonah
replied that he could not be angrier. "Then the Lord said:
you pity the *kikayon* for which you did not labor . . . which
came up in a night and perished in a night; and should not
I spare Nineveh, that great city . . . ?"

The lesson of this story is surely that God can and does
freely forgive the repentant sinner without requiring any cir-
cumcision, baptism, or other ritual, let alone conversion to another religion or acceptance of dogmas. This is one of the central ideas of the Old Testament and of Judaism. In the Jewish
liturgy, the Book of Jonah is read in the early afternoon of
the highest holiday, the Yom Kippur or Day of Atonement, to
remind every Jew that the two central commandments for the
sinner are to repent and to return—no more, no less.

Two quotations from the Babylonian Talmud show how the
same point was made in later Judaism. According to Berachoth
12b, "Rav said: Whoever commits a transgression and is filled
with shame thereby, all his sins are forgiven him." And according to Sabbath 31a, "When a man appears before the
throne of judgment, the first question he is asked is not: Have
you believed in God? or: Have you prayed and observed the
ritual? He is asked: Have you dealt honorably and faithfully

in all your dealings with your fellow men?" Again, it would be perverse to dismiss such dicta as highly unlikely conjectures. The point is not speculative but moral.

Such sayings and stories cry out to be demythologized. Trying to identify the "great fish" or the *kikayon* is like asking for the evidence that the Buddha was really tempted by Mara. In the prophetic books such fish stories are unusual, and perhaps the great fish and the *kikayon* are specifically designed to tell us that Jonah was not a historic figure like Isaiah and Jeremiah.

In some cases, then, it would be stupid to stop short after an examination of the evidence for a saying or a story: we must also consider the valuations implicit in it. Those who feel that they are in secure possession of a set of true values will judge these implicit valuations by their own standards. Many, for example, will approve of the moral content of the Book of Jonah and of the unselfishness preached by Mahayana Buddhism. But the crucial point is that we do not fully understand these stories and beliefs until we also grasp the lessons they teach.

Even if we postpone judgment and admit humbly that our values are deeply influenced by stories of this sort, the fact remains that some stories can be demythologized at least in part and that we have been demythologizing them ever since we were first exposed to them. The common belief in man's supranatural dignity, for which it is not easy to find good reasons, is in part begotten by the first chapter of Genesis: perhaps nothing in world literature equals the majesty of this portrayal of God, the Creator; and after the full impact of this has been felt in the creation of the heaven and the earth, we are told emphatically that man was made by God in his own image. An interpretation will be attempted in Section 83.

Explications of the moral import of beliefs and stories have been prominent in Christianity, too, from the start. The fourth evangelist particularly emphasized the valuations implicit in the central Christian belief: "For God so loved the world that he gave his only begotten son, that whoever believes in him should not perish, but have eternal life. For God sent his Son into the world, not to condemn the world, but that the world might be saved through him. He who believes in him is not condemned: but he who does not believe is condemned already, because he has not believed in the name of the only begotten Son of God" (3.16 ff.). And again: "This is my commandment, that you love one another as I have loved you. Greater love has no man than this, that a man lay down his life for his friends. You are my friends, if you do whatever I command you" (15.12 ff.).

The valuations implicit in the Christian conception of Christ's atonement which are here spelled out by the evangelist are not, however, those which some readers have found here. Although there can be no doubt whatever that the high value of love is extolled here—to say that God loves man means, at least in part, that love of man is divine—a supreme valuation of love is expressed far more clearly and unequivocally in the Mahayana stories which have been mentioned and in the Book of Jonah. In the Gospel according to John it is immediately added that those who do not believe are damned. And anyone who recalls the Sermon on the Mount will wonder about John's affirmation, "Greater love has no man than this, that a man lay down his life for his friends." Might not a man lay down his life for his enemies—or at least for men who do not do whatever he commands them? Might not the bodhisattva's love be greater when he allows himself to be reborn again and again, stretched out "upon the rack of this tough world"—not for a few hours only but for generation after generation, and not for his friends only but for all creatures?

Why should God have so ordered the world that all men were headed for everlasting damnation and that he was unable to help them except by begetting a son with a woman betrothed to Joseph, and by then having this son betrayed and crucified and resurrected, by having him fetch Abraham and a few of the damned out of hell while leaving the rest to their lot, and by saving only that small minority among men who first heard this story and then believed it? Surely, such a God is not an unequivocal symbol of love. Indeed, if human terms are to be applied to this God analogously, he would appear to be at least as interested in bizarre effects, shrouded in an air of mystery, and in dire vengeance on all who fail to believe what is exceedingly difficult to believe, as he could possibly be said to be concerned with demonstrating the significance of love.

As long as we cling to the conception of hell, God is not love in any human sense—and least of all, love in the human sense raised to the highest potency of perfection. And if we renounce the belief in hell, then the notion that God gave his son to save those who believe in the incarnation and resurrection loses meaning. The significance of salvation depends on an alternative, and in traditional Christianity this alternative is eternal torment.

Mahayana Buddhism is also a religion of salvation, and here, too, there is an alternative. In the first place, however, the suffering from which the Noble Eightfold Path brings salvation is not eternal: everybody is to be saved, and nobody is, as in the Westminster Confession of Faith, which is the basic document of Presbyterianism, "foreordained to everlasting death." Or, to cite the same document: "The rest of mankind God was pleased . . . to pass by and to ordain them to dishonor and wrath." Or, to cite the seventeenth-century Baptist Confessions of Faith: "God hath, before the foundation of the world, foreordained some men to eternal life through Jesus Christ, to the praise and glory of His grace: leaving the rest in their sin, to their just condemnation, to the praise of His justice." Or, to cite Aquinas, who devotes the whole of Question 23 (*Summa, I*) to predestination: divine "reprobation includes the will to permit a person to fall into sin, and to impose the punishment of [eternal] damnation because of that sin" (Article 3).

In the second place, Buddhism does not preach the existence of an omnipotent God who is both in some sense responsible for the suffering in this world and supremely deserving of worship. The most venerable being for the Buddhist is the Buddha who cannot in any way be charged with cruelty but who is the embodiment of insight and a peculiarly detached compassion.

That Christianity demythologized does not yield the values which most liberal Protestants would like to find in it does not necessarily constitute any criticism of traditional Christianity. The liberal Protestants might have the wrong values. But without applying to traditional Christianity any external, arbitrary standards, one should note that its moral valuations are deeply equivocal.

Christianity preaches that love is divine and points to Jesus as the incarnation of love; but a Buddhist, and not only a Buddhist, might well say that the sacrifice of a few hours' crucifixion followed by everlasting bliss at the right hand of God in heaven, while millions are suffering eternal tortures in hell, is hardly the best possible symbol of love and self-sacrifice. The boss's son who works briefly at lower jobs before he joins his father at the head of the company would hardly reconcile the workers to their fate if they should be tormented bitterly without relief. Of course, some Christians have felt this strongly and it has troubled them deeply, but the dominant note in the New Testament and ever since has been one of astounding callousness.

When the Christ of all three Synoptic Gospels speaks the following words to his apostles as he sends them on their mission, his dire threat seems clearly meant to comfort them: "And if any one will not receive you or listen to your words, shake off the dust from your feet as you leave that house or town. Truly, I say to you, it shall be more tolerable on the day of judgment for the land of Sodom and Gomorrha than for that town" (Matt. 10.14 f.). Mark's version agrees with this almost literally, except that he writes "shake off the dust that is on your feet for a testimony against them" (6.11). And in Luke we even find the substance of this saying twice, both in Chapters 9 and 10.

Suzuki, the best-known Zen Buddhist of our time, has said, if he believed in heaven and hell he would certainly refuse to go to heaven and insist on going to hell to share the sufferings of the damned. Here he speaks as the heir of Mahayana Buddhism, while in Christianity the valuation of love is equivocal, and hell and damnation have traditionally been discussed without compassion. These conceptions have been far more prominent in the "Documents of the Christian Church," to cite the title of Henry Bettenson's fine collection, published by the Oxford University Press, than love of one's neighbor, not to speak of love of one's enemies. Indeed, this is a gross understatement.

These reflections throw some light on two topics previously considered. There is, first, Pascal's wager which has been criticized above for its fallacious reasoning (§ 49). It could also be criticized for the valuations implicit in it. Pascal assumes that the man who believes in order to save his neck, unequivocally prompted by self-seeking prudence, will be saved, while the man who denies himself the comfort of belief in the name of intellectual integrity will not be saved. What, then, does Pascal consider godlike?

Secondly, we have seen that the proposition that God loves man cannot be interpreted analogously because the conception of God is essentially ambiguous and because the word love is ambiguous, too. These objections are relatively academic compared to the objection which can now no longer be avoided.

Few Christians would be in doubt what to think of a father who tortured his children for forty-eight hours because they did not agree with him or did not obey him; and if he had a great many children and had given only a few of them a single chance while offering the vast majority no opportunity at all to know his will, most people would consider this the epitome of an inhuman lack of love and justice. The God of traditional Christianity, however, outdoes even this analogy by relegating the mass of mankind to eternal torment. Nor is this an esoteric doctrine which is not widely known. It is found in the basic dogmas and confessions and has been celebrated in the greatest Christian poem of all time by Dante. Indeed, the greatest Protestant epic also deals with Satan.

If this doctrine were all there is to the Christian religion, one would have to conclude that it deifies superhuman cruelty. But the fact is, of course, that Christianity also preaches love. Even so it is amazing how so many people today can say and think that Christianity, coming into the world over five centuries after the Buddha and the prophets, introduced into the world the high estimation of love and the recognition—to use Harnack's influential phrase—of "the infinite value of every human soul" (63 ff.). Harnack got this notion from Hegel, who said (*Encyclopaedia,* 3rd ed., 1830, § 482): "This idea came into the world through Christianity, according to which the individual *as such* has *infinite* value, being the object and end of God's love. . . ." In Hegel's time, one could plead extenuating circumstances for one's ignorance of other religions. But today no longer. In Judaism, Hinduism, and Buddhism, no soul is damned eternally.

When it is asked whether goodness, love, and justice are ascribed to God analogously or symbolically, it should not be forgotten altogether that these terms in anything at all resembling their usual sense, which they have when applied to human beings, simply cannot be applied at all to the God of traditional Christianity.

Consider the justice of the God of St. Augustine—and by no means only St. Augustine. All men deserve damnation, but God elects a few for salvation. They do not deserve this: the grace of God would not be *gratia* if it were not *gratis.* Yet the damned cannot complain that God is unjust, for no man receives a worse lot than he deserves, only some receive a better lot, and this shows God's infinite mercy.

No student would be in doubt for a moment what to think of the justice of a teacher who gave a test that everybody failed and then nevertheless gave a few of his students "excellent," justifying his procedure along the lines suggested by Augustine. This is precisely what we mean by injustice.

Love and justice cannot be ascribed to the traditional Christian God in the same sense in which these terms are applied to human beings. But the difference is not, as is usually suggested, that God possesses the same qualities in a higher degree: so much higher that the quantitative difference gives way to a qualitative one. Far from it, the difference is quite expressible in human terms.

At this point some historical perspective becomes necessary, in two ways. First, we must keep in mind that our own con-ʹeptions of love and justice are not the only ones. Plato considered it the essence of justice that everybody should perform his proper function; and with reference to some of the less appealing features of his ideal city, an unkind critic has pointed out that in practice this means that the ruler should rule and the slave, slave. To many of us today this seems the very essence of injustice. It is similar with Augustine's conception of justice. And the traditional Christian conception of divine love is the love of a God so jealous that he condemns to eternal torment all who have failed to love him as he wants to be loved, including those who, for one reason or another—and according to some denominations even in pursuance of his own express decree—never had any chance of loving him. This, too, is a conception of love. We may open our hearts to it and try to sympathize with it and learn whatever it may have to teach us; but many of us will be quite unable, after all is said and done, to consider such love ideal.

Historical perspective is also required because the beliefs of individuals must not be treated as if these beliefs had originated with them when in fact they have been accepted, usually at an early age, from a long and powerful tradition. An individual's differences with this tradition, however slight, may tell us more about his valuations than we could ever hope to learn if we examined his beliefs without all reference to this background. Even so, these differences do not entitle us to assume that a man has altogether rejected the traditional valuations when in fact he prides himself on the continuity. Loyalties, too, express valuations.

The attempt to spell out implicit valuations frequently demands a great deal of judiciousness; but short of this we cannot fully understand a belief or do justice to it. Confronted with the story of the Buddha's temptation or the Christian belief in the virgin birth, and with many propositions about God, at least a partial attempt at demythologization is imperative. One must become aware of the moral implications regarding, for example, the superlative importance of compassion or the high estimation of virginity and, conversely, the association of sex with sin.

Given the belief that man was created in the image of God, or that God will save all who go on crusades to kill infidels and to conquer the supposed sepulcher of Jesus; or that God will torment everlastingly all who reject one of the Christian dogmas and, as some of the great Christians taught, permit the saved to watch this spectacle eternally; or that charity alone is sufficient to ensure salvation—a heresy condemned by all the major Christian denominations—we must ask not only about the evidence for such beliefs, but also about their moral implications.

55. CONTRA BULTMANN.   What Bultmann means by demythologizing is not the attempt to spell out the moral implications of the text. Apparently, he associates this moral emphasis with liberalism and considers it dated by Heidegger.

In the essay which prompted the great controversy over demythologizing, Bultmann defined the task as .follows: "The real meaning of the myth is not to furnish an objective world picture; rather it expresses how man understands himself in his world: the myth wants to be interpreted not cosmologically but anthropologically—better, in existential terms" (23). The German word here, *existential*, is a technical term which refers to Heidegger's interpretation of human existence in *Sein und Zeit* and is sharply distinguished by Bultmann from *existentiell*, which is less technical. Even as *Sein und Zeit* culminated in the demand for resolution, Part One of Bultmann's essay concludes: "The question is whether the New Testament offers man an understanding of himself which confronts him with a genuine demand for a decision" (28). In his answer to Jaspers' polemic, Bultmann says similarly: "This—making visible what Christian faith is, making visible the question of decision—seems to me to be the only thing, but also the decisive thing, that the theologian has to do . . . He must make clear the question which God puts to man . . ." (61).

One may agree that if God put a question to man, it certainly needs clarification. But one may wonder whether the New Testament poses any single question. Bultmann's bland assumption that this question must be whether we accept *the* conception of human existence offered by the New Testament does not allay this doubt.

Jesus himself, though according to Matthew he taught "let your speech be Yea, yea; Nay, nay; anything more than this is evil," was a master of ambiguity, according to all of the Gospels, and his favorite modes of expression were hyperboles and parables. The history of Christianity bears witness that many of these are as ambiguous as Kafka's little parable "Before the Law": no single translation is convincing enough to reduce its many rivals to silence. Nor did all the writers whose books constitute the New Testament understand man in the same way. The great difference between James and Paul, which led Luther to call the Epistle of James "straw" (XIV, 105), is a commonplace; and so is the contrast between Matthew and John. Following Luther, Bultmann takes his cue from Paul and John—and he tends to select what he likes while ignoring what he does not like.

This last charge is readily illustrated from his *Theologie des Neuen Testaments*, which has been rendered into English in two volumes: it simply does not discuss eternal damnation, hell, unquenchable fire, wailing and gnashing of teeth, the place of torment, the lake of fire burning with brimstone, or "shall be tormented day and night for ever and ever," although Mark 3.29, 6.11, 9.43–48; Matthew 3.12, 5.22, 5.29 f., 8.12, 10.15, 11.20 ff., 13.40 ff., 13.50, 16.18, 18.8, 22.13, 23.33, 24.51, 25.30, 25.41, 25.46; Luke 3.17, 12.5, 13.27 f., 16.19–31; and the Revelation of St. John the Divine are all part of the New Testament.

It is not surprising, therefore, that few Protestant theologians—not to speak of non-Protestants—have accepted Bultmann's reading of "the message of the New Testament." What holds together Christendom and constitutes Christianity is the body of what Bultmann calls myths. Christians interpret these myths differently: most Christians believe them, some do not, but all revere them. What Bultmann offers when he demythologizes is essentially a sermon, as he comes close to admitting when he says of Jaspers, who has criticized him: "He is as convinced as I am that a corpse cannot come back to life and rise from his tomb. . . . What, then, am I to do when as a pastor, preaching or teaching, I must explain texts . . . ? Or when, as a scientific theologian, I must give guidance to pastors with my interpretation" (62)? Readers who fail to grasp the full import of these lines should transpose the familiar Christian accents into Marxese.

Bultmann sometimes speaks of what he calls a *Vorverständnis*, a preunderstanding, and this conception has been criticized by Karl Barth. Much more crucial, however, is his *Vorentscheidung*, his predecision. He makes every effort to devise sublime interpretations; and when he is unable to do this, he does not renounce his predecision but skips. His imposing scholarship is placed in the service of apologetics, and his attitude toward the New Testament is quite different from that with which he reads other books, not to speak of his approach to rabbinical Judaism. He does not heed the words of the Fifth Book of Moses, 25.14: "Thou shalt not have in thine house divers measures, a great and a small."

So much for Bultmann's approach. Now consider his results: first, a specific exegesis, and then his over-all interpretation of "the message of the New Testament." Let us begin with Mark 9.43: "And if your hand causes you to sin, cut it off; it is better for you to enter life maimed than with two hands to go to hell, to the unquenchable fire." (Bultmann omits the last four words.)

Origen, the great church father who castrated himself after reading this verse, or the parallel passage in the Sermon on the Mount, Matthew 5.27 ff., may have taken these words too literally, though the primary reference to sexual desire is plain in Matthew: "But I say to you that everyone who looks at a woman lustfully has already committed adultery with her in his heart. If your right eye causes you to sin, pluck it out and throw it away; it is better that you lose one of your members [the eye is no member, no μέλος] than that your whole

body be cast into hell." T. W. Manson, the great British exegete, comments: "The point is the same as in I Cor. 9.27: 'I
buffet my body, and bring it into bondage: lest by any means,
after that I have preached to others, I myself should be rejected'" (449).

If a wider interpretation seems called for, there are Luther's
dicta: "Whoever wants to be a Christian should tear the eyes
out of his reason" (V, 425) and "you must part with reason
and not know anything of it and even kill it; else one will not
get into the kingdom of heaven" (VII, 985 f.).

Making allowance for some ambiguity, we can agree with
The Interpreter's Bible that this "is Oriental hyperbole and
teaches that one must, at all cost, remove from one's life anything which will lead to sin." Or, to put it negatively, this is
the opposite of an ethic of self-realization or sublimation.

Bultmann's exegesis of Mark 9.43, which he quotes in his
Theologie, comprises two sentences: "This renunciation of the
world, this 'de-worldlization,' is not by any means asceticism
but the simple readiness for God's demand. For what corresponds positively to this renunciation and what constitutes the
readiness for God's kingdom is the fulfillment of God's will
as Jesus explains it in his fight against Jewish legalism" (9).
The immediately following discussion of this "fight" (§ 2)
will be discussed in Section 57. For the moment, consider
what Bultmann says on the immediately preceding page:
"Now is *the time for decision* and Jesus' call is *the call for
decision.* . . . *He in his person signifies the demand for a decision.* . . . Now it is either/or! Now the question is whether
a man really wants God and his kingdom or the world and its
goods; and the decision must be made radically." Then, leading up to the quotation from Mark, Bultmann cites Jesus' demand that one leave one's family and all earthly goods; and
throughout he associates Jesus' novelty and superiority over
the Judaism of his time with this radicalism.

Many Americans feel that the man who wrote all this
should have welcomed the time for decision a few years earlier
when Hitler gave him a rare opportunity to show that he really
wanted God and his kingdom and was not inhibited by any

regard for his family or his life. Seeing that he did not become a martyr, they charge this to the weakness of the flesh and either denounce him, more or less self-righteously, or find it rudely insensitive that anybody should touch on such a personal matter. But Bultmann was no coward and what is at stake is not his character, which need not fear comparison with that of his critics, but his interpretation of Scripture.

First, Bultmann's exegesis of the verse from Mark is much less convincing than many a rival interpretation. Secondly, the decision of which he makes so much remains vacuous. Protestants in the American North who are under the impression that the amendments to the Constitution come straight out of the New Testament, Luther, and Calvin readily read their own political convictions into Bultmann's rhapsodies about decision and then blame him for not living up to principles which he never professed—and which Luther and Calvin, Jesus and Paul, never professed either. It is at least arguable that Bultmann is closer to the Reformers and to Paul than are the Christian socialists, Niebuhr, Tillich, and other Protestants concerned about social justice.

In spite of his occasional effusions about the teachings of Jesus, Bultmann's conception of "the message of the New Testament" comes out of Paul's First Epistle to the Corinthians, Chapter 7, and out of Heidegger's *Sein und Zeit*. In his controversial essay, Bultmann freely owned his debt to Heidegger, but added: "Martin Heidegger's existential analysis of man's being appears merely as a profane philosophical version of the [*sic*] New Testament view of man's being" (35). Paul already taught that "care" dominates human life and that only a resolute decision can liberate man. The required decision consists in the "de-worldlization" or emancipation from this world to which Bultmann refers in his comments on Mark 9.43, but which is explained better in his earlier essay. In Heideggerian terminology, which is prominent throughout that part of the essay, Bultmann defines it, in italics, as *Gelöstheit von allem weltlich Verfügbaren*, which means cutting all ties to earthly things. *"Freedom"* is expressly defined as *"de-worldlization"* in this sense.

"This *de-worldlization* is emphatically not asceticism but a distance from the world: all participation in worldly matters is conducted in the stance of the 'as if not' ὡς μή, (I Cor. 7.29–31). . . . The believer can rejoice with them that rejoice, and weep with them that weep (Rom. 12.15), but he is no longer subject to any power in this world (I Cor. 7.17–24). For him, everything in this world has been relegated to the indifference of that which is meaningless in itself" (31). The whole of I Corinthians 7 should be read in this connection, but these lines sum up much of the rest: "Every one should remain in the state in which he was called. Were you a slave when called? Never mind. . . . For the form of this world is passing away. I want you to be free from cares."

What is surprising is not that Bultmann and most of the other, at least equally Lutheran and Pauline, members of the defiant Confessing Church did not say and do more during the Hitler years; what is astonishing is rather that they should have done as much as they did. What is surprising is that, in his *Theologie des Neuen Testaments,* Bultmann ignores Romans 13.1 f.: "Let every person be subject to the governing authorities. For there is no authority except from God, and those that exist have been instituted by God. Therefore he who resists the authorities resists what God has appointed, and those that resist will incur judgment." Verses like these and Paul's "as if not," which comes close to being the core of the New Testament for Bultmann, might well have been taken to justify a complete quietism.

In sum: all important decisions come before interpretation, and the selection and exegesis of the texts is dictated by the prior convictions of the exegete. This is as true of Bultmann's life as it is of his theology, as three illustrations may show.

First, in an essay on Harnack, Bultmann says: "it is characteristic of him that the Pauline 'as though not' (I Cor. 7.29–31) played no role in his thought" (xi). Bultmann versus Harnack: one selection versus another.

Secondly, the courageous stand which Bultmann and other members of the Confessing Church took concerning "all those among the Jews who believe in Christ" without extending it in the same measure to those who did "not recognize God's Christ in Jesus" (Jannasch, 13, 80) can be explained only in terms of conscience. The New Testament could have been cited easily to demand complete acquiescence or, on the contrary, the stance of the Good Samaritan.

Thirdly, though he simply ignores Luke 16 and similar passages in his *Theologie,* Bultmann says, at least privately, that he should not care to go to heaven if there were—as he is certain there is not—a hell.

To vary Bradley's dictum about metaphysics: theology is the finding of dubious reasons for what the theologian has believed all along; and when the chips are down, he consults his conscience and, if necessary, forgets his theology. Sometimes this means a decided improvement.

This is as true of most other theologians as it is of Bultmann. He has been singled out here for his qualities rather than his defects. Among Protestant theologians today, he is probably the outstanding New Testament scholar, and he has raised more interesting questions than most of his colleagues: in particular the question of demythologization. In this connection one further objection remains to be developed at some length because it raises issues of the greatest importance for any critique of religion.

The "mythical world picture" of the New Testament, which, according to Bultmann's controversial essay, is dated and cannot be revived, need not have been accepted by the early Christians either. Their age was almost as syncretistic as our own, and even in the New Testament we encounter the Sadducees, who did not accept belief in any afterlife. Obviously, one did not *have* to believe in eternal damnation. Bultmann avoids the crucial question whether the writers of the New Testament always made the best possible choices among the ideas current in their time; whether parts of their "mythical world picture" were not downright superstitious even then; and whether in their valuations, too, they did not sometimes inspire anything but confidence.

The many fascinating parallels between the New Testament

and the Dead Sea Scrolls do not dispose of these questions. The same charges might be pressed against the Dead Sea sect.

A special problem is posed by Jesus' world picture. In his *Theologie* (4 f.) Bultmann writes: "Thus Jesus does take over the apocalyptic picture of the future, but with a decided reduction. What is new and singular, however, is the assurance with which he says: *'Now the time has come! The kingdom of God is breaking in! The end is at hand!'*" Yet Bultmann himself says in *Das Urchristentum:* "It is not necessary to mention that *Jesus was deluded in his expectation of the proximity of the end of the world*" (102; italics in the original, though not in the English version).

It is hard to see why it should not be necessary to mention that "what is new and singular" in Jesus' world picture is a delusion. Of course, Bultmann does mention it more than once, but almost by way of a footnote and only after his glowing account of what is new and singular has done its work of making us feel Jesus' tremendous superiority over the thought of his time.

The seriousness of this problem can hardly be stressed sufficiently. If first-rate scholars like Rudolf Bultmann and Albert Schweitzer are right that Jesus was mistaken about the central tenet and premise of his message, why should not this undermine our confidence in his authority? Yet hardly any Christian seems to be greatly concerned about this: almost everybody shrugs it off as something that "it is not necessary to mention."

Schweitzer is an exception. In his important but neglected essay on "The Idea of the Kingdom of God," he writes: "All attempts to escape the admission that Jesus had a conception of the kingdom of God and its impending arrival which remained unfulfilled and cannot be taken over by us mean trespasses against truthfulness" (19). Among Jesus' ideas are some "which we can no longer experience as truth or accept. Why is Christianity condemned to this? Is not this a wound for which there is no balm? Should it be impossible to maintain Jesus' freedom from error in religious matters? Doesn't he cease then to be an authority for us? . . . I have suffered deeply from having to maintain out of truthfulness something which must give offense to the Christian faith" (18). What is astounding is how little offense it has given.

Bultmann is surely right that the world picture of Jesus and the early Christians should be viewed against the background of what other men in the same environment believed in those days. But he stacks the cards with his caricature of rabbinical Judaism which is a hangover from Harnack and Hegel and much less excusable after the labors of Baeck, Billerbeck, Herford, and G. F. Moore.

Consider the belief in eternal damnation in this perspective. Professor G. G. Coulton, one of the greatest historians of the Middle Ages, has dealt with this belief in considerable detail, especially in the first volume of his *Five Centuries of Religion,* which contains chapters on "The Lord of Darkness" and "Hell and Purgatory" as well as an Appendix on "The Medieval Hell" with special sections on "The blessed rejoice in the sight of the damned" and "Infant perdition" and "The chances of hell."

He remarks: "It was from the New Testament that Augustine's exegesis, pitilessly and anachronistically literal, insisted on the mathematical accuracy of that word *eternal;* and he and his fellows laid almost equal emphasis on that sentence which added terror to terror: 'Many are called, but few are chosen'" (68).

Anyone who takes the trouble to read Book XXI of Augustine's *City of God* will have to accept Coulton's summary: "To Augustine, it was 'very absurd' that Christians, from sentimentality, should hope for any end to the agonies of the damned, so long as they believed in the eternal happiness of the blessed" and "The saints do not pray for the damned, since these are not the saints' enemies but the enemies of God; nor can we believe that Christ, when he spoke of '*eternal* fire,' was threatening what he did not mean" (27 f.).

One can hardly recommend Coulton's work too highly as a supplement to the works of Gilson, Maritain, and Copleston; and to those who prefer to read a Catholic's report on some of the outstanding saints, one may commend Malcolm Hay's enormously exciting book, *The Foot of Pride: The Pressure of*

Christendom on the People of Israel for 1900 Years. What is
questionable about the sentences quoted from Coulton is
merely the manner in which he exempts the New Testament
from his strictures.

When Jesus said in Matthew 25, which Augustine quoted,
"Depart from me, you cursed, into eternal fire" and again
"these shall go away into eternal punishment," did not he—or
if not he himself, then the evangelist—offer an "exegesis, pitilessly and anachronistically literal," of two isolated verses in
the Old Testament, namely, Isaiah 66.24 and Daniel 12.2?
And was not this far stranger than what Augustine did, seeing
that in the New Testament this idea had become central?

The greatest among the Pharisees were not so "pitilessly and
anachronistically literal" about Isaiah 66.24. Rabbi Akiba
taught: "The punishment of the wicked in Gehinnom lasts
twelve months; for it is written [Isaiah 66.23]: It will be from
month to [the same] month." And this dictum, based on very
bold and nonliteral exegesis, was accepted in the Mishnah
(Eduyyoth 2.10) and is assumed elsewhere in the Talmud, too
(e.g., Sabbath 33b and 152b). Beyond this, Akiba taught
that Isaiah 5.14 meant that the underworld had opened its
mouth "for lack of an observance"; and on the basis of that he
argued: "It does not say for the lack of observances, but of an
observance; only those who possess no good deeds at all will
descend into the netherworld" (Finkelstein, 186; cf. Makkoth
24a and Sanhedrin 81a).

The Talmud of Jerusalem (Haggigah 77a) also ascribes to
Akiba the dictum in the Mishnah (Haggigah 2.1): "He that
ponders four things—what is above, what is below, what is
before, and what is after—it were better for him if he had never
been born. He that has no consideration for the honor of his
Creator—it were better for him if he had not been born." A
similar sentiment finds expression in a passage that is cited
twice in the Talmud (Berachoth 34b and Sanhedrin 99a):
"All the prophets prophesied only concerning the messianic
days; but as for the future world: Apart from thee, O God, no
eye has seen it [Isaiah 64.3]."

This blend of a reverent agnosticism with charity contrasts

sharply with the evangelists and the Revelation of St. John the Divine. No less sharp is the contrast between the development of this rabbinical attitude by Maimonides and the bold and pitiless speculations of Aquinas and Dante. "Jewish imagination did not indulge itself in inventing retaliatory modes of torment in hell, such as flourished in the Orphic and other Greek sects and in India," says George Foot Moore (II, 392); and he might well have added the Christians to the Greeks and the Indians.

Bultmann and others have tried to present the New Testament in a somewhat different light by contrasting it not with the Pharisees and Sadducees but with a couple of intertestamentary Jewish apocalypses—without mentioning that these books were never accepted as canonical or normative by the Jews and have survived only in Christian translations. If it were not for the esteem in which the early Christians held these fantastic visions, they would have been lost altogether.

Again and again, the Jews accorded the highest honor to men like Hillel, Akiba, and Maimonides, while the Christians have consistently condemned the relatively humane teachings of Origen regarding hell, of Arius concerning Christ, and of Pelagius against original sin. The church persecuted those who championed these views, and it canonized St. Athanasius and St. Augustine. Calvin still burnt Servetus, the Unitarian.

Of what great Christian could the following story have been told which a later age wove around Akiba? Certainly not of Augustine or Aquinas, of Luther or Calvin. Of St. Francis? He fully accepted the authority of the church, of its teachings, of its hierarchy, of its decisions. Of that ardent Franciscan mystic, St. Bonaventura? "St. Bonaventura actually contends that the damned have merited even more pain than they suffer in fact" (Coulton, 72).

That this story obviously did not really happen makes the valuations implicit in it only still more poignant. Indeed, this fact is a tribute not only to the humanity and charity of Akiba which inspired this story but also to those who made up and told and retold this wonderful legend, which has come down to us in many versions.

It is said that Akiba once walked through a graveyard and
saw a charcoal burner who was running around like a frantic
beast of burden, carrying wood. Akiba said to him: "My son,
why such heavy toil? If you are a bondsman, and your master
imposes such a yoke upon you, I shall redeem you and set
you free. If you are poor, let me help you." The man, however,
replied: "I am of the dead: day after day I am fated to gather
wood and to be burnt." Akiba asked him what he had done.
"I was a tax-collector, and I favored the rich and was a scourge
to the poor. I even seduced an affianced virgin on the Day of
Atonement [when even marital intercourse is forbidden]."
Akiba asked him if there was no remedy for him. At first the
man replied that there was none, but then added on second
thought: "I did hear them say that my punishment would be
relaxed if I had a son who could stand up in the congregation
and proclaim publicly: Bless ye the Lord who is worthy to be
blessed. But I had no son. Yet on my death I left my wife with
child, but whether she bore a boy or girl I do not know. And
if she did bear a son, who would teach him?" Akiba asked his
name and his wife's, and then traveled from town to town
asking for her. One day he came to a village where the wife
was known. The people remembered her husband with horror,
and the boy, it turned out, had not been circumcised. Akiba
fasted for forty days, and a heavenly voice was heard: "Because of this boy you fast?" Akiba replied: "Yes." And he
taught the boy the alphabet, and he taught the boy Scripture,
and he taught him to stand up in the congregation to say:
"Bless ye the Lord who is worthy to be blessed." Then the
charcoal burner appeared to Akiba in a dream and told him
that he had been rescued from hell, and Akiba replied by citing a Psalm: "O Lord, thy Name is for ever; thy memorial, O
Lord, for all generations" (Montefiore, 591 f.).

Obviously, not all Jews have been like Akiba, and hatred
and superstition can be documented from Jewish literature, too.
But we can hardly escape two questions. First, whether there
is not a certain consistency among the men whom the Jewish
people have regarded for centuries as their greatest teachers;
and whether there is not also a certain consistency among the

men whom the Christians have regarded for centuries as *their* greatest teachers? We should compare Hillel and Akiba with the writers of the New Testament books, and Aquinas with Maimonides.

Secondly, this Jewish lore reminds us that world pictures are not as inevitable a feature of an epoch as Bultmann implies. The writers of the New Testament might have agreed either with the Sadducees, who denied any life after death, or with Akiba, instead of accepting the ideas they did in fact espouse; and a later age could still have availed itself of the humane teachings of Origen, Arius, and Pelagius. But when we consider the beginnings of a great religion, we ought to raise our sights still higher and consider the very greatest religious figures of all time.

If we view Moses or Lao-tze, Amos or the Buddha, in their historic context and ask how they measure up when we compare their world pictures to those of their contemporaries, we are struck by their immense stature. We see them living in superstitious ages, surrounded by all sorts of fantastic beliefs and cults, by moral callousness and deep indifference to the sufferings of others; we find that they had every excuse for being just like their contemporaries, for sharing endless faults of which it might be said that they were fated by the age; yet they were not, to cite Paul's famous words (I Cor. 9.22) "all things to all men": they *defied* their age.

The Egyptians had the most elaborate concern with the afterlife ever known to man; Moses had none. The Egyptians had a profusion of gods, some half human and half animal; Moses accepted nothing of all this. The Egyptians had a caste of highly educated priests, but otherwise Egypt was, not only for the Hebrews, a "house of bondage." Moses said to his people: "Ye shall be unto me a kingdom of priests" and "Ye shall be holy"—not merely some but all; everyone is called to make something of himself. Perhaps this was the most revolutionary idea of world history.

As strangers, the children of Israel had been oppressed in Egypt, but in one of the most astounding revaluations of all values Moses bade them again and again: "The stranger that dwells with you shall be to you as one born among you, and thou shalt love him as thyself; for you were strangers in the land of Egypt." Moses flew in the face of the superstitions and moral ideas of his time, as Elijah did after him, and Amos, and Micah and Isaiah, who proclaimed: "nation shall not lift up sword against nation, neither shall they learn war any more."

The Buddha, confronted by the rival world pictures of the Upanishads and Jainism, of various philosophic systems and of popular superstition, dismissed them all with a sovereign contempt. Like Moses and the prophets, he had some things in common with his age, some of its wisdom and some of its limitations. Nevertheless, all these men stand out as titans against the background of their times. If the men of the New Testament do not, is this a matter which it is not necessary to mention?

56. GERRYMANDERING. This is a political term, but unfortunately, politicians have no monopoly on dividing districts in an unnatural and unfair way to give one party an advantage over its opponent. Many theologians are masters of this art. Out of the New Testament they pick appropriate verses and connect them to fashion an intellectual and moral self-portrait which they solemnly call "the message of the New Testament" or "the Christian view"; and out of other Scriptures they carve all kinds of inferior straw men.

Theologians do not just do this incidentally: this is theology. Doing theology is like doing a jigsaw puzzle in which the verses of Scripture are the pieces: the finished picture is prescribed by each denomination, with a certain latitude allowed. What makes the game so pointless is that you do not have to use all the pieces, and that pieces which do not fit may be reshaped after pronouncing the words "this means." That is called exegesis.

In fashioning straw men to represent other religions, theologians do not always find it necessary to use the pieces provided by rival Scriptures. Protestant theologians frequently rely on what Luther said about Catholicism, and both Protestants and

Catholics get the major pieces for their portraits of Judaism from the New Testament. Those with scholarly pretensions go on to seek some corroboration from the primary sources. But obviously

> *Quotations can be slander*
> *if you gerrymander.*

That quotations *must* be unfair, does not follow. (Cf. §§ 5, 6, 10.)

What about the present book? The quotations from Aquinas, Tillich, Bultmann, and—later on (§ 68)—Niebuhr are plainly not compromising obiter dicta but represent central claims. Nor are these men picked for their shortcomings; on the contrary, they are, according to common consent, among the very best and foremost Christian theologians. Any critique of theology that would ignore them would certainly be accused of fighting a straw man.

Still, this *Critique* emphasizes in some instances what has been systematically ignored. But instead of presenting its own arbitrary selections, it goes out of its way to consider the received images before pointing out where they have gone wrong. Also, it returns occasionally to the same landscapes to criticize different distortions: Fromm's "humanistic" gerrymandering of Judaism, for example (§ 77). Nor is it the avowed aim of this book to offer a comparative history of religion; but rather to show the utter inadequacy of the popular pictures, to see the familiar in new perspectives, to make suggestions for a new map—and to stimulate thought.

Of course, this *Critique* is exceptionally vulnerable to slander by quotation and critics cursed with short breath, structure blindness, and myopia will be all but bound to gerrymander it. Would rereading a few sections in Chapter I help to restore perspective?

57. THEOLOGY. The long association of philosophy and theology in American colleges and the great reputation of men like Niebuhr and Tillich have obscured the basic differences

of philosophy and theology and the important limitations of the latter. First, theology is of necessity denominational. Second, theology is essentially a defensive maneuver. Third, it is almost always time-bound and dated quickly.

Theology is the systematic attempt to pour the newest wine into the old skins of a denomination.

In his *Theology of the New Testament*, Bultmann says that Jesus represented "a great *protest against Jewish legalism,* i.e., against a piety which finds the will of God in a written law and in the tradition which interprets it." Among the bad consequences of any such piety Bultmann enumerates "that a host of legal rules which have lost the meaning they had in dated conditions of life remain in force and have to be bent to fit the present by means of artificial interpretations"; and that a host of things come "to overshadow in many ways the essential demands for goodness" (10).

This is a very dubious interpretation of Jesus' preaching, however dear it may be to many Protestants today. Bultmann himself has to admit that "There is not the slightest trace in Jesus' words of any polemic against the *temple cult*" (16). And in an earlier work on the Synoptic Gospels, Bultmann makes another concession: "In Mark 2.18–19; 2.23–26; and 7.1–8, it is related that the disciples did not fast, that they plucked ears of grain on the Sabbath, and that they did not observe the ritual of washing their hands before meals. How are we to explain the fact that all this is related of the disciples only and not of Jesus himself? . . . These stories originated in the Christian community and must be understood in terms of its situation. The 'disciples' who have broken with these customs are the primitive Christian community . . ." (23).

The protest against the law which Bultmann and other Protestants ascribe to Jesus is at best highly equivocal in the Synoptic Gospels, while it is found emphatically and unequivocally in the prophets. And even as legalism developed in Judaism in spite of the prophets, Protestant theology, in spite of this very doubtful interpretation of Jesus, approximates the very attitude which it condemns. The theologian's piety finds the will of God in a written text "and in the tradition which interprets it"; and a host of ideas and formulations "which have lost the meaning they had in dated conditions of life remain in force and have to be bent to fit the present by means of artificial interpretations" which come "to overshadow in many ways the essential demands for goodness." We could hardly ask for a better description of theology.

Bultmann's demythologizing represents an attempt to minimize these tendencies; but it could also be said that he goes particularly far in bending old ideas and formulations by means of artificial interpretations until they seem to him to fit the present. To his critics it seems that by a tour de force of exegesis he finally discovers Heidegger's early philosophy in the New Testament, and that Bultmann's theology was dated at birth since by that time Heidegger had proceeded from *Being and Time* to his so-called second phase.

Tillich's similarity to Heidegger extends even further. He attacks theism and, like the later Heidegger, speaks profoundly of Being. Often he seems to leave theology altogether, but after a section on "Theism Transcended" he winds up in the church even in *The Courage to Be:* he discovers "The God above God" and concludes as an apologist for "the Church under the Cross which alone can" give men "a courage which takes doubt and meaninglessness into itself" (188). At the last moment he slams the door in the face of Heidegger, Nietzsche, agnosticism, and the Old Testament—but one almost feels he did not mean to. His praise of Nietzsche, Freud, and Marx and his opposition to theism are at least as plausible as he is in championing the church "without sacrificing its concrete symbols" (188).

In *The Protestant Era,* he denounces Protestantism in the name of "the Protestant principle" of constant protest and criticism, and one gathers that the Hebrew prophets were probably the best Protestants of all time, and that Marx, Nietzsche, and Freud were the most genuine Protestants since 1800—but before "the power of the New Being that is manifest in Jesus as the Christ . . . the Protestant protest comes to an end. Here is the bedrock on which it stands and which is not subjected to its criticism. Here is the sacramental foundation of Protestantism, of the Protestant principle, and of the Protestant reality. It is not by chance that a chapter on sacramental thinking appears in this book" (xxii f.). In sum: Tillich wants to have his Nietzsche and eat his bread at communion, too.

That Tillich's theology is utterly arbitrary in curbing critical thinking at the points he specifies—no less arbitrary than Bultmann's theology has been shown to be in Section 55—should be obvious. Catholic theologians strike bedrock much earlier.

Tillich baptizes Heidegger's *Entschlossenheit* and christens it "The Courage to Be." The vacuity of Heidegger's "resolution" and Bultmann's "decision" (cf. § 55) seems overcome: the question "resolved for what?" is answered "to be." But on reflection "the courage to be" is as empty as "resolution"; and the claim that Christianity alone teaches "the courage to be" hardly makes sense. The phrase is actually a little more evocative in connection with Judaism; but it certainly does not deserve the philosophic status which Tillich would give it. He has merely poured the newest, but hardly the best, wine into the old skins of Christianity.

When we turn to the two outstanding theologians of the nineteenth century, or indeed of the whole period from the French Revolution to the First World War, the picture is much the same. During the heyday of romanticism, Schleiermacher tried to show that one could be a romantic and a Christian, too. Nothing could be more romantic than Christianity: it was true, genuine, original romanticism. This theology ceased to be interesting when romanticism ceased to be the fashion. In the days of liberalism, Harnack tried to show that one could be a liberal and a Christian, too. Indeed, nothing could be more liberal than true Christianity: Jesus was the greatest liberal of all time.

Something of Harnack still lingers in Bultmann's thought and colors his image of Jesus. But on the whole, Bultmann and Tillich try to show that one can be an existentialist and a Protestant, too, and that nothing could be more existentialist than true Protestantism. Meanwhile, Maritain argues that nothing could be more existentialist than Thomism.

Some theologians do not go all out for one "ism" and yet fit the same account. Reinhold Niebuhr has shown how we can denounce liberalism, capitalism, and everything bourgeois with as much vehemence as any Marxist, while picturing Marxism as a secularized version of Christianity. We can take up Freud and at the same time regret his secularization of the doctrine of original sin. And so forth.

It is not as if all these theologians were completely wrong. Far from it. Of course, romanticism has roots in the Gospels and Pauline Epistles—and Leo Baeck actually called Christianity *the* "Romantic Religion," to cite the title of his most stimulating polemic. Existentialism, too, has roots in the New Testament, and liberalism and Marxism have certainly taken some of their fire from the prophets—much less, if at all, from Jesus and Paul. But it usually takes secular movements to remind the theologians of their religious heritage, which they then develop in accordance with the fashions of the day.

The famous theologians come after the great original thinkers and try to defend their religious heritage against the competition of the latest developments. As soon as another great philosopher or a new intellectual fashion comes along, a theology is usually dated.

Theology is a timely interpretation of timeless myths. Its most characteristic error is to consider itself timeless.

The chief trick-in-trade of modern theologians is the loaded alternative. They write and talk as if the alternative to Christianity must be materialism, and as if the denial of an inane optimism forced us to accept belief in original sin and the writings of Paul and Augustine.

The orginal sin, or moral error, of the theologians is that they use material which was meant to give offense in an attempt to be ingratiating. Most theologians are priests who make a point of scorning priests and praising prophets.

The theologian ministers to the temper of the times. The prophets attacked the temper of their time: they did not speak or write "to be read in churches" or "as living literature," or to edify, and least of all to give preachers guidance or—to cite Tillich's definition of the purpose of his *Systematic Theology* —to provide "a help in answering questions" (viii).

This contrast between Scripture and theology must be qualified by the admission that theology begins in the New Testament. In an important sense, the Old Testament is untheologi-
cal. And one book of the Old Testament, one of the few that in
its final form is post-Greek, is violently antitheological: Job.
It represents an inspired derision of theology which is denounced in the end by the Lord himself.

In different ways, the sacred books of the East are no less
antitheological. In his little book of five thousand characters,
Lao-tze rules out any attempt to reason about the Tao and
speaks of his subject matter in poetic ambiguities. In some of
the Upanishads the central message is still more emphatically
antitheological, and for the Buddha even the Upanishads were
still too theological. Among sacred scriptures, the New Testament is exceptional in that it contains so much theology.

In the New Testament, theology begins with the writers'
acceptance of the Hebrew scriptures and their use of scores of
verses from them which to quote from Bultmann's characterization of Jewish legalism once more—"have to be bent to fit
the present by means of artificial interpretations." The Gospels
and Epistles are full of instances on almost every page. But
the theology of the New Testament does not stop there: it
culminates in the attempt to turn the God of Abraham, Isaac,
and Jacob into a naturalized Greek, and Jesus of Nazareth into
the *Logos*. Almost immediately these interpretations—to cite
Bultmann's critique of Judaism once more—come "to overshadow in many ways the essential demands for goodness."

Paul and John try to assimilate their religion to the fashion
of the day, to the Hellenistic mode of thought, to the philosophy of their age. Unlike Amos and Hosea, they write to be
read in churches, to edify, to give preachers guidance, and to
provide a help in answering questions. Paul, more than John,
still retains something of the old prophetic fervor and even
speaks of giving offense, but he exerts all his powers to make
this offense ingratiating by providing timely arguments.

It would be an understatement to say merely that Paul and
John became part of the Christian canon. Scholars agree that
the Pauline Epistles were written earlier than any of the Gos-

pels. Christianity defined itself in terms of its theology. To speak of a pretheological original Christianity which was unfortunately Hellenized at an early date is downright wrong. Before Paul there was only another Jewish sect and no Christian religion. Nor was Christianity rejected by the Jews. Christianity was born as a separate religion when Paul developed a theology and rejected Judaism.

Judaism certainly has had its theologians, too. Philo, a little before Jesus' time, was a theologian of sorts; and so was Maimonides, a little before Aquinas' time. Judaism, however, had established its identity and even closed its canon before the theologians came along, and so theology remained a peripheral phenomenon. It was similar with Islam. Christianity alone is a theological religion.

It is often supposed that Luther represents a break with this theological tradition and a return to original Christianity. Indeed, he did try to go back to original Christianity—and took his clue, as he himself insisted, from Paul and John. He did not only call John "a master above all other evangelists" (VII, 2008); he said that "one might even call him alone an evangelist" (XI, 1462). And Luther's closest associate in the Reformation, Philip Schwarzert, who Hellenized his name into "Melanchthon," was no mean theologian. That he is not read widely any more is merely another illustration of the proposition that theologies are generally dated quickly.

The fact that Christianity contains so much theology in its very core and canon, which cannot be dismissed as dated because Christianity has defined itself in terms of this, creates unique problems for Christianity today, quite different from those which confront other religions.

Confronted with Scriptures of which some are richly ambiguous while others make unequivocal, but often unacceptable, demands, the theologian accepts all of them and attempts to give a univocal interpretation of all at once. If his theology is really univocal it represents a vast impoverishment and is at best a good sermon which needs to be supplemented with an indefinite number of other such sermons; if it covertly retains the rich ambiguity of the Scriptures, we should prefer the overt ambiguity of the Scriptures; and in no case can a theology really do justice to the Scriptures because it refuses to take into account their heterogeneity and their deep differences.

It does not take the devil to cite Scripture against any one theology: practically all the other theologies do that. But to consider the case against theology in general a little further, one could do worse than turn to Satan. A dialogue will permit concentration on some of the problems rather than a set of specific answers.

VII. SATANIC INTERLUDE
or
HOW TO GO TO HELL

Satan: I just had an argument with a man who tried to re-habilitate metaphysics as a kind of poetry.

Theologian: How ridiculous! Judged as poetry, Spinoza's *Ethics* and Hegel's *Logic* would be worse than ever.

Satan: Of course. And in poetry inconsistency is permissible, while in metaphysics, once you commit yourself to what is sometimes called a root metaphor, you have to stick to it. The whole point of the game is to see how far you can get with it.

Theologian: But it is not *meant* to be a metaphor.

Satan: How true! The metaphysician claims that his meta-phors are no metaphors—or at the very least that his meta-phors are the only ones in terms of which everything that is at all understandable can be understood. Hegel and Spinoza are not proposing one way among many others: each claims that his own metaphysic is the most rational yet. Homer, Shakespeare, and Goethe made no comparable claims for their creations.

Theologian: Still, one can see why people might compare metaphysics and poetry.

Satan: Sure. Metaphysics is a kind of lyrical chess—a game in which a man's feelings about the world are expressed in quasi-mathematical fashion. But the metaphysician wastes

his life playing a single game without ever realizing that
it is a mere game. And when he sees another man playing a
similar game he is sure that the other fellow is wrong. He
mistakes his own tactic for the truth.

Theologian: Are you in earnest? A metaphysic is not an epi-
sode begun at pleasure. Metaphysics is an epic, and the
metaphysician is a bard who wants to correct mistakes made
by his predecessors. It is against them that he pits his skill
in an effort to hear the true melody. And chess and other
such games are metaphysics deprived of dimension, meaning, and consequence. They are pale substitutes for man's
proper vocation, which they reduce to the level of pleasure
without profit and rivalry without risk. No wonder that
these petty games can never satisfy and that the quest of
satisfaction leads from game to game in an endless but
futile search for what really can be found only on a different plane: in metaphysics—or eventually in theology.

Satan: I don't like the twist you have given to my line. But I
can afford to lose an argument about metaphysics, which,
after all, interests me only as a snare for theologians and
others who, but for its fatal lure, would probably have gone
to heaven. But losing an argument about theology might
cost me my job.

Theologian: Do you consider theology a game, too?

Satan: Would you deny its playfulness?

Theologian: What could be more serious?

Satan: That, my friend, is a spurious alternative. Play and
seriousness do not preclude each other. Think of *King Lear.*

Theologian: Are you punning on the word "play"?

Satan: No. There is something playful about a play, even
about a tragedy: it gives free play to the imagination and
yet follows certain rules; it has its life in a world of its own,
a world of leisure and fancy; it is its own reward and requires no justification in terms of expediency; it offers suspense and is yet repeatable, and the suspense does not
evaporate with repetition.

Theologian: I remember having read something similar in

Huizinga's little book, *Homo Ludens;* but he did not extend these ideas to theology.

Satan: Yet he shows how they are applicable to philosophy. He points to the play element in the performance of the Sophists; he emphasizes the origin of Greek philosophy in leisure and the similarity of philosophic puzzles to non-philosophic puzzles; and he cites Plato in his own behalf.

Theologian: The Sophists, of course, were playing; but Socrates and Plato were not. Plato was as serious a thinker as ever lived, and Socrates even paid for his ideas with his life.

Satan: Your spurious alternative again! Of course, they were serious; but unlike most theologians they had a sense of humor: they realized that they were playing a game of sorts. And Socrates' childlike delight in his own clever moves and his frank laughter at the clumsiness of his opponents infuriated his fellow Athenians. One by one he challenged them to engage in a contest with him, and one by one they lost, not in the privacy of a study but in the market place where other men of leisure came to watch the game and see the greatest reputations bested by the witty Socrates with his inimitable irony.

Theologian: Well, if that is what you mean when speaking of a game and playfulness, I suppose you find a contest of sorts in the dialogues of Plato, too. Certainly, the *Greater Hippias* and *Protagoras* are playful in a way, and the *Symposion* is cast in the form of a contest.

Satan: The whole form of the dialogue is playful. The dialogue is a kind of a play—certainly serious, but no more so than *King Lear.* The trouble with most later philosophers was that they accepted the same false alternative which you have urged against me: being serious, they thought that they could not be playful, and soon little laughter was heard among philosophers.

Theologian: I suppose the time has come for *me* to say that I can afford to lose an argument about metaphysics, while losing an argument about theology might cost me my job. You are quite right: the philosophers are merely playing around with petty puzzles, trying to best each other and to win an argument. But theology is very different.

Satan: Was Abelard a theologian?

Theologian: One of the greatest.

Satan: You will remember that he started out as a philosopher. Do you also recall why he first turned to the exegesis of the Bible?

Theologian: To win a bet. You are coming back to Huizinga. Yes, Abelard admitted that he liked the arms of dialectic better than the arms of war, and he enjoyed triumph after triumph till at last he encamped his school upon a hill to "besiege" his rival who held the chair in Paris. And Huizinga says that the same mixture of rhetoric, war, and play can be duplicated in Muslim scholasticism.

Satan: All right, if you admit that, we can forget Huizinga. Just let me quote him once: "In the whole development of scholasticism and universities the agonal element is as crucial as possible. The long popularity of the problem of universals as the central topic of philosophic discussion, and the division into realists and nominalists is certainly connected with the primary need to form parties over some issue." Surely, Huizinga is right that there is a playful element in polemics. And with that I am quite willing to leave him.

Theologian: Are you admitting no difference at all between theology and philosophy?

Satan: In theology the stakes are higher—and people used to get burned on them. Not only that: one was threatened with eternal damnation. The game had a Roman touch and for centuries never quite lost the odor of the arena. And the forcible disputes with rabbis in the Middle Ages were not altogether unlike a bullfight.

Theologian: Let bygones be bygones! The modern theologian does not participate in contests or besiege his adversaries.

Satan: He composes monologues, alas! And most of them are quite unreadable.

Theologian: I suppose *you* prefer to read Gibbon and Voltaire, Nietzsche and Freud. But surely that is quite beside the point. What matters is that the modern theologian is a highly serious person, much more similar to a professor of history or science than to a Sophist or a gladiator.

Satan: Surely, more similar to a Sophist!

Theologian: I wish you would be serious for once. Some theologians are fine historians.

Satan: You mean that "theology" is often very loosely used to embrace any study of religion. Indeed, according to one of the definitions in Webster's—"the critical, historical, and psychological study of religion and religious ideas"—*The Decline and Fall* and *The Future of an Illusion* would be classics of theology, and Gibbon, Nietzsche, and Freud would qualify as theologians. But that is surely ridiculous. Nor should we call every scholar who happens to be teaching at a seminary a theologian. Or would you insist on calling atheistic church historians theologians?

Theologian: Of course not. But some outstanding theologians have been, and are, good historians.

Satan: A theologian who is also a candid historian is like the author of *Alice in Wonderland* who was also a mathematician—and even more like Penelope who unraveled at night what she had woven by day.

Theologian: Let us forget about theologians and discuss theology.

Satan: Theology is a contradiction in terms: there can be no "science of God," comparable to geology, biology, or physiology. A god who could be studied scientifically would be no god.

Theologian: Theology is the queen of the sciences and older than they are.

Satan: Theology was founded by Plato and Aristotle, who eulogized their highest principles by calling them divine. Theology is an impertinence perpetrated by a couple of philosophers.

Theologian: How preposterous! There are good scholarly books on the theology of the pre-Socratics and of the Old Testament.

Satan: Their titles are glaringly anachronistic. To be sure, the pre-Socratics spoke of "gods"; but they did not pretend to speak of them scientifically. Heraclitus spoke of the divine in veiled aphorisms; Parmenides, in poetry. Nor can you find in them the least trace of apologetics for traditional religion. They have only one thing in common with theologians.

Theologian: What is that?

Satan: They often used the word "god" in the strangest ways.

Theologian: And what of the Old Testament?

Satan: That certainly did not purport to offer nonpoetic discourse about God.

Theologian: What, then, do you make of the Book of Job?

Satan: I have mixed feelings about it. I like it because it is one of the very few places in the Old Testament in which I am mentioned. What I don't like is that I am given such a pitifully small part. It never even occurs to anyone that the problem of evil might be explained by giving me some credit. And that goes for the author as well as the characters.

Theologian: That only shows the profundity of the book. The author wisely realized that crediting you would not solve the problem. The next question would have been: And why did God allow you to have your will? But what I meant with my question was whether the Book of Job was not theological?

Satan: In the first place, it is poetic and not scientific discourse; in the second place, the book probably owes its final form to Hellenistic times; and in the third place, it is the most antitheological treatise ever written.

Theologian: You take too narrow a view of theology.

Satan: It is in Plato that we first encounter the word; but that of which he and Aristotle furnished a science, or a pseudoscience was not God.

Theologian: You mean that it was not the Christian God?

Satan: It was neither the God of Abraham and Job nor the God of Jesus; it was not the Brahma of the Upanishads and not the Tao of Lao-tze.

Theologian: Of course not. Who said they wrote about Brahma or the Tao? You are being ridiculous.

Satan: About the God of Abraham, Job, and Jesus there can be no connected nonpoetic discourse any more than about the Brahma or the Tao; and the God of Job says so outright. In Athens, Socrates had been sentenced to death for not believing in the gods and for corrupting the youth of Athens. Plato and Aristotle did not believe in the old gods either, but they called their own highest principles divine and escaped the fate of Socrates. Even so, Aristotle had to flee in old age, "lest the Athenians sin twice against philosophy."

Theologian: What you insinuate about their motivation is ridiculous.

Satan: Their motivation does not matter. The road to my home is paved with splendid motivations. What is important is that "theology" was a fantastic misnomer from the beginning. Plato and Aristotle were most generous with the epithet of divinity and freely accorded it to principles and to physical objects like the stars. Aristotle wrote a *Physics* and a *Metaphysics* but spoke freely of "God" and "theology." And the early Christians failed to see this.

Theologian: That is a stupid point! You are just peeved because Plato no sooner mentions that there must also be an evil soul or god than he forgets about it. But you must not take things so personally. You see, the early Christians were not at all interested in Aristotle.

Satan: My point is that the early Christians conceived of God in terms of the Greek or Hellenistic *Logos.* Right in the New Testament, too. That is the beginning of Christian theology. It was a fantastic misunderstanding, the worst mismarriage on record. At first the theologians tried to wed the God of Abraham and Jesus to *Hellenistic* philosophy; then, in Augustine's time, to Plato's; still later to Aristotle's; and finally Luther went back to the Hellenism of the Fourth Gospel and of Paul. To think that the God of Job could be identified with Aristotle's magnetlike attractive god!

Theologian: In the first place, the New Testament was not Hellenistic but profoundly Jewish, as W. D. Davies and David Daube have shown, and as the Dead Sea Scrolls prove beyond a doubt. And in the second place, there was a profound humility in the admission that the Hebrew Scriptures did not contain all the wisdom of which man was capable: the men you deride were modest enough to be willing to learn from the Greek philosophers.

Satan: First, it was not Greek, and secondly it was! Both your points are untenable. The first depends on a fallacious alternative which you wrongly attribute to your authorities. It is neatly exposed by two brief quotations from Albright: "Greek ways of thinking undoubtedly affected Ecclesiastes about 300 B.C. or a little later" (20) and "The New Testament arose in a Jewish environment which had been enriched by Hellenic and Iranian elements" (23). And as for your second point: only today I read a reference to "the Apostle Paul, the man who became Christianity's greatest salesman."

Theologian: What has that to do with my point?

Satan: Did he really learn humbly, or was he trying to sell a bill of goods to the Gentiles? He simply found that he could not sell it unless he dressed it up in accordance with the latest fashions of Hellenistic thought. "If I do this thing willingly, I have a reward," he frankly tells the Corinthians (I.9); and then he explains his strategy: "To the Jews I became as a Jew, that I might gain the Jews; to those under the law, as under the law . . . to those outside the law, as outside the law . . . that I might gain those outside the law. To the weak I became as weak, that I might gain the weak." And Paul himself sums up his approach: the point is to be "all things to all men." Surely, Amos and Jeremiah had not been "all things to all men." They had defied all men. But John, the Evangelist, went even further than Paul. Before long they had thrown in a good dose of gnosticism as well as the sacraments of the Greek mysteries and some talk of the *Logos.* Others added a story how Jesus was begotten in the manner made popular by Zeus; Matthew copied some details from the birth of Moses; and Luke added a few sentimental touches. No effort was spared, and their exertions were crowned with success. They offered al-

most everything that any other religion offered—and heaven,
too. What you call humility was really unprecedented brass.

Theologian: I refuse to engage in debate on that level. The
early Christians surrendered the haughty exclusiveness of
the Jews and——

Satan: Followed the example of less exclusive Jews, like Philo,
who had spoken of the *Logos* in a similar vein a few generations before John.

Theologian: Have it your way: a few of the Jews already had
been willing to learn from the Greeks, and the early Christians followed their example rather than the isolationism
of the Pharisees. They were willing to concede that the
ideas implicit in the poetry of Scripture could be clarified
by the wisdom of the Greeks.

Satan: They were merely trying to ingratiate themselves with
their audience. Look at John! He writes at a time when the
Jews were proscribed by the Romans, and so he goes to absurd extremes to dissociate his religion from that of the
Jews by denouncing them on every turn while he fawns on
the Romans and turns the hardy Pontius Pilate, who in fact
crucified Jews by the hundreds, into the incarnate milk of
human kindness.

Theologian: Surely, your facts are questionable.

Satan: Bultmann, who doubts that Jesus ever considered himself the Messiah, concedes that "the movement he sparked
among the Jewish people may and must be designated as a
messianic movement, for it was inspired by the faith that
the messianic expectations would now be fulfilled, and that
the kingdom of God was at hand. . . . The Roman procu-
rators resorted to bloody suppression of such movements,
and Jesus, too, fell victim to the intervention of the procurator Pilate. When he entered Jerusalem with his followers,
his bearing evidently struck the procurator as politically
dangerous. . . . In no case may one suppose that Jesus'
ethical teaching so infuriated the Pharisees and scribes that
he finally fell victim to their hostility. The constant opposition of the Pharisees and scribes rests upon the sche-
matic imagination of the later Christians" (34 f.). But I

admit that Bultmann and his colleagues hesitate to draw the inescapable conclusion about the motivation and the moral character of the evangelists and the early Christians.

Theologian: I don't want to argue about people's motives. Do you or do you not admit the humility of the early Christians toward Greek thought?

Satan: You can hardly blame me for being fascinated by people's motives. That is part of my business, you know. But as for your question, the answer is an emphatic No. The attitude of the Book of Job, in which I am mentioned and, as you may recall, make a great point of motivation—that attitude is humble. It humbly admits the impossibility of all theology. But the pontifical dogmatizing of the Christian theologians from Paul and John down to the present is anything but humble. It is arrogant to the point of being ridiculous.

Theologian: You seem to feel that the Old Testament was enough——

Satan: After all, it invented *me*.

Theologian: The Jews took you over from the Persians; so by the same token you could stop with Zoroastrianism, which also assigns you a far bigger role than the Old Testament ever did.

Satan: But the Old Testament gave me my name. And the Zoroastrian Ahriman had to fight all the time against the god of light. You should not confuse him with me, really. I am much more civilized. I do not like to fight. I like to talk.

Theologian: What I meant to ask you was this: Do you think that the early Christians could not learn anything at all from the Greek philosophers?

Satan: They could have learned a lot, but they learned the wrong things. They might have learned critical thinking; and there was humor in Greek philosophy, too. But there is little of either in the New Testament.

Theologian: You should not complain: it makes a great deal more of you than the Old Testament.

Satan: In the Old Testament I have a small role, but I like it. In the New Testament I play a big role, but I am the subject of endless calumny, and my home is represented as if it were all fire and brimstone and howling and gnashing of teeth.

Theologian: You have a genius for getting away from the subject. I don't want to talk about you, I want to talk about myself—or rather about theology. Your objections depend on understanding theology too narrowly as a kind of science.

Satan: First, you objected that I called it a game when it really was a science; and now you object that I call it a science. What is it?

Theologian: Theology is the *Logos* of God, the word concerning God.

Satan: The word concerning God is poetry and may be found in the *Tao-Teh-Ching* and the Upanishads, in Genesis and Job. *Theology is a misguided attempt to make poetry scientific, and the result is neither science nor poetry.*

Theologian: Theology is a noble attempt to understand and give a systematic exposition.

Satan: To understand poetry one does not give a systematic exposition of it. That is precisely your mistake. You should study the poetry in its historical context, give attention to its form and to the weight of the words, and in the end re-experience it. That is the most important thing: everything else is merely preliminary.

Theologian: How do you re-experience poetry?

Satan: You try to get at the experience which has found its way into the poem.

Theologian: What do you mean? In the case of the Old Testament alone that would mean hundreds of experiences.

Satan: To get the most out of the Old Testament, you can't do less. And anyone who has not recaptured these experiences and tries to explain the whole book by writing a theology of it is an impostor.

Theologian: Might there not be a few basic or central experiences, and one experience above all, the experience of God?

Satan: Perhaps what you call the experience of God was really a host of very different experiences all of which have been lumped together under this one label. But be that as it may, you cannot lead people to recapture an experience by giving a systematic exposition of what you take to have been its contents, let alone by threatening with damnation all who disagree.

Theologian: You said that if you lost an argument about theology, that might cost you your job. Now it would seem that if you win your argument you face the same prospect.

Satan: Would I be Satan if I were prudent? or egotistical? What could be more satanic than to bite the hand that feeds me, regardless of the consequence to me? Is not that how I became the Lord of Hell? Let the pious be prudent! What else is their piety, in nine cases out of ten, but enlightened selfishness? What is satanic is not egoism but the love of truth at the expense of happiness—to find one's happiness in truth, to oppose illusion, to value integrity above God, and character above salvation.

Theologian: But isn't Satan a materialist?

Satan: The materialists who want to go to heaven say materialism is the devil, and the egoists who want to go to heaven say that egoism is satanic. But can you imagine a materialist or egoist who would not want to go to heaven?

Theologian: Heaven is for those who love God above riches, and their neighbor as themselves, if not more.

Satan: At most—and even this is rare—they renounce small sums for huge gains, which is hardly renunciation, and they give their neighbors what they themselves have come to feel is not worth having, which is hardly love. They distribute unto the poor what moth and rust corrupt to gain treasure in heaven where neither moth nor rust corrupt.

Theologian: That is a complete perversion of Christianity.

Satan: What, then, are the words in Luke 18.22 that follow upon "sell all that you have and distribute to the poor"? What are the very next words?

Theologian: "And you will have treasure in heaven." But surely that is not the spirit of the Sermon on the Mount.

Satan: Oh, isn't it? That is just one of the favorite fables of the theologians. How they rhapsodize about unselfishness, obedient love, and all the rest, as if the Sermon on the Mount were not constructed around the theme of enlightened selfishness. Surely, this morality is not centered in the neighbor but in salvation. It is an otherworldly *Lohnmoral*.

Theologian: Not only theologians know how wrong you are: everybody knows it.

Satan: What everybody knows is often untenable. Need I tell *you* that? The Sermon on the Mount opens with the so-called beatitudes, and each of the nine promises a reward, culminating in the conclusion: "For great is your reward in heaven." In the Sermon that follows, promises of great rewards and threats of dire punishments alternate continually: "shall be called great in the kingdom of heaven"; "shall in no case enter the kingdom of heaven"; "judgment"; "hell fire"; "your whole body should be cast into hell"; "for if you love those who love you, what reward have you?"; "otherwise you will have no reward"; "will reward you openly"; "your heavenly Father will also forgive you"; "neither will your Father forgive your trespasses"; "lay up for yourselves treasures in heaven, where neither moth nor rust corrupt"; "all these things shall be yours as well"; "that you be not judged"; "and the measure you give, shall be the measure you get." And in the end—the conclusion should not be ignored—the moral is stated quite explicitly; those who do not do what Jesus commands "will be like a foolish man," while those who do as they are bidden are likened to "a wise man." St. Thomas was quite right in agreeing with Aristotle that prudence was a virtue from the Christian point of view, too. He forgot to add that it was the Christian virtue par excellence. You Protestant theologians are trying to assimilate to Kant what is basically anti-Kantian. You are embarrassed by any talk of prudence in ethics.

Theologian: You completely misunderstand Aquinas' conception of prudence, and you forget that Calvin came centuries before Kant. Certainly, Calvin's ethic was not prudential. And was Luther's? Worst of all, you talk as if charity had no place at all in Christian ethics. Yet Christianity preached love and changed the morals of untold barbarians by inculcating a supreme regard for love.

Satan: A supremely hypocritical regard for love. Charlemagne sought to convert the Saxons to Christianity by threatening with death all who refused to become his loving subjects. You should read the article on slavery in the *Encyclopaedia of Religion and Ethics,* written by one of your friends, not by a foe of Christianity. You will find that the captives taken by Charlemagne after his defeat of the Saxons "and by Henry the Fowler and his successors after the defeat of the Slavs were sold as slaves." Most of the Saxons, of course, had preferred death and were butchered.

Theologian: Didn't Christianity abolish slavery? Surely, you are falsifying the facts.

Satan: Read that article, my friend. Your apologist there admits that "the abolitionist could point to no one text in the Gospels in defence of his position"; and also that the church tended, "owing to its excessive care for the rights of the masters, even to perpetuate what would otherwise have passed away." Face the facts: "Legislation forbade Christian slaves to be sold to pagans or Jews, but otherwise tended to recognize slavery as a normal institution." And again: "The general tone of this legislation can hardly be said to favor the slave." And did you really not know that the church itself "was a slave-owner"?

Theologian: You don't expect me to stand up for the Catholic Church, do you? In the Reformation love became central.

Satan: Surely, you do not suppose that Luther was against slavery any more than the Catholic Church? Do I have to quote Luther to you? "There is to be no bondage because Christ has freed us all? What is all this? This would make Christian freedom fleshly! . . . Read St. Paul and see what he teaches about bondsmen. . . . This claim, therefore, goes straight against the Gospel and is criminal in that each robs his master of his body which is his master's property. For a bondsman can be a Christian and have Christian freedom, even as a prisoner and a sick man can be Christians, even though they are not free. This claim aims to make all men equal and to make a worldly, external kingdom of the spiritual kingdom of Christ. And this is impossible. For a worldly kingdom cannot exist unless there is inequality among men, so that some are free and others captive" (581).

Theologian: That is the late Luther, counseling the Swabian peasants to keep the peace. That was written under the stress of extraordinary events that were endangering the whole Reformation. If he had supported the peasants, he would have lost the crucial support of the princes.

Satan: The late Luther? In 1525, four years after the Diet at Worms! You admire Luther for breaking with Catholicism, but cease to admire him the moment he broke with it.

Theologian: There is nothing inconsistent in that.

Satan: But there is, assuming you agree with Luther that the right faith begets good works; and that without the right faith good works are impossible. For you believe that he did the right things as long as he clung to the wrong faith, and that he began to do wrong as soon as his faith became entirely right. You amuse me, but your conception of the "late" Luther won't stand scrutiny. It hinges on the ridiculous assumption that the young Luther was a democrat, and that he later betrayed principles for the mere sake of expediency. But he never was a democrat, nor did he betray his principles any more than Paul whom he was following. Luther gave very similar advice to Christian prisoners of war who had been made slaves by infidel Turks: "You are robbing and stealing your body from your master, your body that he has bought or acquired in some other way, so that it be no longer yours, but his property, like cattle or other goods" (581 f.).

Theologian: You are getting away from the subject. We were talking about love.

Satan: You mean to say that this has nothing to do with love? But actually it was you who changed the subject by introducing love. What I was talking about was prudence. Even when it stares you in the face, you simply ignore it. Yet Jesus himself concludes the Sermon on the Mount, which he began by harping on the theme of reward and which he continued with promises and threats, by saying expressly that anybody who does not obey is a fool while those who do obey are "wise." Now if Satan were an egoist, as you suppose, he would not be at all satanic. There would not be a drop of wickedness left in him; he would simply be a wretched fool. Every pious soul would be much shrewder.

Theologian: What troubles me is precisely that you are *not* wicked. Wrong as you are in many ways, you seem full of decent, even noble, feelings; scholarly and gentle; and in places I feel closer to you than to many theologians.

Satan: If I had come to you with horns and tail, speaking of the delights of wine and sex, should I have got this far with you? Would I be Satan if I had no eye for my audience? After all, I am speaking to a decent, even noble, person, scholarly and gentle——

Theologian: False flatterer! Now I know you.

Satan: I do not worship numbers. Let the theologians learn from me, give up theology, and go to heaven. There are too many of them in hell as it is. For centuries they have been sending each other to me. What I want is less of the blind leading the blind and more who choose hell with open eyes.

59. DIALOGUE BETWEEN SATAN AND A CHRISTIAN

Satan: God is not a person but a panacea, like love. This invalidates all the psychological theories that would explain belief in God in terms of one or two needs. God gratifies man's self-respect in easily a dozen ways and allows man to feel humble, too; he gives strength and permits weakness; he is the great symbol of hope and yet justifies despair; he signifies the reality of all that one could wish for, and yet allows the outcry: what is man? He is someone to address when one is utterly alone, someone to praise, thank, implore, complain to, and accuse. He explains everything, even *why* one can explain things, and why one cannot. He backs up law and morals, guarantees the existing social order, listens to the oppressed, is the safety valve for the slave's resentment, leads revolutions (rarely), gives man a surpassing sense of power, can be thanked for victories, and sends defeat as a long-deserved punishment. He can be blamed for man's inadequacy—not necessarily outright—and as long as he figures in the drama, a man's sordid condition is at least not despicable: "I amount to nothing not because I am abject but because Adam defied God." Is any further explanation needed why men cling to him?

Christian: But God exists.

Satan: What does that mean? What does "God" mean? and what "exist"? Surely you do not believe that there is an old man with a long white beard up in the sky?

Christian: God is love.

Satan: When you say that God exists, are you merely asserting that there is love in the world?

Christian: I assert that the world was fashioned by infinite love.

Satan: Infinite but impotent?

Christian: Infinite and omnipotent.

Satan: Why does a god who is omnipotent and loving permit men to suffer? Could it be that eternity is so frightfully long? Could it be boredom? Surely, he must have some weaknesses if he saves only those who eat his son.

Christian: Atheist!

Satan: Am I then unanswerable?

Christian: God is perfect. He has no weaknesses.

Satan: The problem of evil has occupied your best minds for two thousand years; and it depends on your claim that God is perfect. But in other contexts you do not hesitate to ascribe to God what in human beings would be called not merely imperfections but downright perversions.

Christian: Impious villain! What do you mean?

Satan: He metes out eternal punishments, damns the unbaptized, and could save men from the hell that he created only by sending his son to be crucified, by persecuting for thousands of years the descendants of those who did not

believe all the words of his son (and who today believes all
the words of his son?), and he saves only those who eat and
drink on regular occasions what they themselves consider
his son's flesh and blood.

Christian: That is a caricature of Christianity.

Satan: Are you denying that this is what Christians have believed for nearly two thousand years?

Christian: You must not judge a religion by its worst adherents.

Satan: Is not that exactly how you have always judged every
religion except your own? But this is not what I have done:
I have taken my clue from St. Paul and St. Augustine, from
St. Thomas, Luther, and Calvin, from the dogmas and
the sacraments which almost all denominations have in
common.

Christian: The God in whom I believe is not like the god you
impugn.

Satan: The God I impugn, I understand; indeed, he resembles the popular misconception of me. But what does the
god do in whom you believe?

Christian: He has made you and me.

Satan: Why did he make me?

Christian: He created you as an angel, but you rebelled and
fell.

Satan: When your children rebel, do you punish them
eternally?

Christian: You were an angel and should have known better.

Satan: But apparently I did not know better, and it was, you
say, God that created me. Tell me, do you really believe
in angels?

Christian: No.

Satan: But there are angels in your Scripture.

Christian: I do not take them literally.

Satan: Do you take me literally?

Christian: No.

Satan: I am glad; so I can be blunt. Do you take God literally?

Christian: What do you mean?

Satan: You believe in God, and you believe that atheists are very wrong. What exactly is it that you believe and they deny? What exactly are you saying when you say that God exists?

Christian: God exists—that means: life is bearable, the reality of everyday life is not the only reality; our dreams are not mere dreams; our ideals, whatever they are, have authority; the passion for justice, however conceived, is no mere quixotism; reason is not a capricious quirk of evolution; I am made in the image of one who is infinite and eternal and perfect, who fashioned the heavens, the stars, suns without number, planets and plants, whales, tigers, snakes, and whatever is frightening—it was all made by him in whose image I was created; I that seem small am greater than anything else in the universe; beware oppressors: my avenger lives; he sees my enemies even now; he hears me if no one else does; he loves me if no one else does, and what I do has infinite significance.

God exists—that means: I that am made of dust am all that I say of God, only less so; I, worm that I am, shall judge the angels; I that am of no account and never shall be, am not what I seem, and the great are not what they seem: we are equal, and if they do not bow before me, I shall yet behold their damnation from heaven; the world has a purpose, and I am part of that purpose, exalted above the sun and the moon which stop in their tracks or are blackened on my account; and the center of the universe with its glittering milky ways is in my heart.

God exists—that means: I shall not want, I will fear no evil, the ocean and the mountains hold no terror for me, nor does man; for me the whole world is the footstool of God's glory; my enemies are his instruments, and he cares for me; I am in good hands; and though life be agony, I shall endure.

Satan: Is not that just what I said in the beginning, though you have, no doubt, said it more beautifully—or at least with more feeling?

Christian: I believe that God exists.

Satan: I can see that this statement means a great deal to you, and you have expressed very well what it means to you. But while I understand how you feel, I still do not understand what it is that, you think, exists, or in what way it exists. Does God take up space as you do?

Christian: Of course not.

Satan: Why, then, do you say that he exists?

Christian: Surely, many things exist that do not take up space.

Satan: Name three.

Christian: Does a dream take up space? Or a feeling? Or a thought?

Satan: Is God a dream, a feeling, or a thought?

Christian: Certainly not.

Satan: Try again.

Christian: What of justice?

Satan: What of justice indeed? Does it exist? Is it not an idea, or if you prefer, an ideal? Something toward which men aspire? Injustice exists, but justice is a name for what does not exist.

Christian: You admit that injustice exists. Does that take up space?

Satan: Injustice is a word that sums up a complex state of affairs together with the speaker's reaction to it. It is not an entity.

Christian: Love exists.

Satan: Love is another word that does not designate an entity but a highly complicated pattern of feeling, thought, and behavior.

Christian: I never said that God was an entity.

Satan: But when you speak of God, you do not mean a mere concept or a pattern of human feeling, thought, and behavior. And I do not know what exactly you do mean. And I think you don't know yourself.

Christian: If you do not know what I mean when I speak of God, read Scripture.

Satan: You know that I can cite Scripture to my purpose.

Christian: You must not take verses out of context——

Satan: Like preachers and theologians?

Christian: You must consider the over-all picture of God in the Bible.

Satan: Especially in the New Testament?

Christian: Yes.

Satan: Beginning with the Holy Ghost and the Virgin?

Christian: Read the words of Jesus.

Satan: Jesus himself said that he spoke in parables to ensure that, except for his twelve disciples, men should "not understand, lest at any time they should be converted and their sins should be forgiven them" (Mark 4.12). And at times the very same parables are understood differently by the evangelists, and Jülicher and Bultmann (25), among others, have argued that the evangelists themselves have often misinterpreted the parables. Certainly, you can read the whole New Testament, including all the letters, too, and still have no clear idea what you, my friend, might mean by "God." Believe me, I have read it many times and found all sorts of curious superstitions as well as all kinds of moral ideas, but I still do not know what you mean when you say that God exists.

Christian: Have you read our theologians and philosophers?

Satan: Read? I have talked with many of the best of them for centuries. They discuss the attributes of God as if they knew to begin with who it is that has these attributes. They argue whether he is in time, conscious, separate from the world, as if they knew whom they are discussing.

Christian: God is the Supreme Being.

Satan: Thank you. That is a great help. What do you mean by "supreme"?

Christian: Highest.

Satan: But he doesn't take up space?

Christian: The most powerful and perfect.

Satan: Oh, that again! We are back at your contradictory idea of a being who damns the unbaptized in all eternity, saves those——

Christian: Stop it! Leave out perfection for the moment. By "God" we mean the most powerful being.

Satan: Have you done research to find out which being is

most powerful? What is more powerful—a virus or an ele-
phant? That a most powerful being exists is as true as that
a smallest being exists, though, of course, in both cases there
might be several that are neck and neck. The contest would
turn on definitions: what you mean by "powerful" and what
is, and what is not, a being. And who else is admitted to the
class of beings that do not take up space?

Christian: Your facetiousness is insufferable. God is the Creator.

Satan: That's no help. As long as the assertion that there is
a Creator was held to exclude the truth of scientific theories
like Darwin's, for example, one had some idea what was
meant. But if you accept science, what are you saying when
you claim that the world has been created?

Christian: Never mind your subtleties. The point is: God exists.

Satan: "God exists" is not a statement but a shibboleth: those
who utter it, belong; those who refuse to, do not deny anything in particular but refuse to conform. The philosophers
who speak of God do not agree with each other or with the
man in the street: they make their obeisance to conformity.
They use a traditional term for untraditional ideas and make
the most of the fact that the word conveys no precise meaning.

Christian: Are you making excuses for atheists?

Satan: "Atheist" is a label that covers up more than it shows.
Atheism can be aggressive nonconformism, but in certain
countries it may be timid or unthinking conformism; it may
be the protest of the maladjusted or an expression of ultimate
serenity; it may be inspired by the desire to shock or hurt,
to be grown-up, enlightened, sophisticated, or honest. And
theism is equally protean. Let us not generalize about such
vague labels!

Christian: But theism is true, and atheism false.

Satan: No doubt, some atheists are very wrong, and so are
some theists. Theism is a language, a way of speaking, rather
than a claim of fact.

Christian: What do you mean?

Satan: Look at it this way. At the end of your prayers you
say: "This we ask through Jesus Christ, our Lord." Need

God be told? Must he be approached through proper chan-
nels? Protestants find fault with Catholicism on similar
grounds? What is the moral?

Christian: Christ's word concerning mote and beam.

Satan: Rather: Protestantism strikes agnostics just as Catholicism strikes Protestants. And an infidel is simply a man who
agrees with Catholics about Protestants and with Protestants
about Catholics. All religions look quaint from the outside
but are all things to the believer. That is true of atheism,
too: it looks impious from outside and honest from the
inside. And this is applicable to all religious rites and phrases:
viewed without sympathy, they all seem odd. Take even a
service of your own denomination: as soon as it is conducted
according to another tradition or in a different language, it
immediately becomes problematic and usually seems all
wrong.

Christian: There is some truth in that. People have that attitude confronted with translations of the Bible to which
they are not used. But what does that prove?

Satan: Religion can be a matter of habit, and it can be intense
through and through; but it is incompatible with detached
scrutiny.

Christian: Religion is like love: for him that experiences it,
nothing else matters so much.

Satan: For those who observe its manifestations without sympathy, it seems madness.

Christian: That is no objection to religion any more than it
constitutes a criticism of love. Religion, like love, has inspired generosity——

Satan: As well as wars——

Christian: It has inspired sacrifices——

Satan: Especially of others——

Christian: And works of art.

Satan: To be sure, religion has had good fruits as well as foul
ones; and where would I myself be without it? But all this
does not establish the truth of its claims. And it is in no
position to dispute the results of any of the sciences.

Christian: The quarrels of religion and science belong to history.

Satan: Nor is it clear what religious statements mean.

Christian: They remind us that a scientific attitude toward the world is not the only one.

Satan: Every artist knows that, and whoever loves art, and every lover.

Christian: Art and love are intimations of Christianity.

Satan: Christianity signifies the emasculation of love and art, the triumph of the fig leaf over classical beauty, the maculation of conception, and the vilification of love both between men and between men and women.

Christian: You are mistaking the prudery of certain ages for the doctrine of Christianity.

Satan: Is it not written in the New Testament: "It is good for a man not to touch a woman. Nevertheless, to avoid fornication, let every man have his own wife, and let every woman have her own husband." Is it not written: "Come together, that Satan tempt you not for your incontinency. But I speak this by permission, and not of commandment. For I wish all men were like myself." And Paul, whose words are as sacred to Protestants as they are to Catholics, concludes: "I say therefore to the unmarried and widows: It is good for them if they abide even as I. But if they cannot contain, let them marry: for it is better to marry than to burn."

Christian: Has not Christianity modified these words of the First Epistle to the Corinthians? Did it not survive by modifying them?

Satan: The teaching of the New Testament has remained authoritative. To avoid fornication, permission has been given for properly regulated conjugal love. But what is done to avoid fornication is no longer the consummation of love: it is an unclean bodily function, coupled with a sense of sin. Even at best, married love is only considered a lesser evil: "it is better to marry than to burn."

Christian: You stress those words too much.

Satan: The words of Paul are the clue to Catholicism as well as Protestantism. They permit us to understand the Catholic saints and the Catholics' veneration of the saints; they explain monasticism and the fear of hell.

Christian: Is there the least evidence that these words were taken as seriously as you suppose?

Satan: "St. Jerome's words are epoch-making and are passed from generation to generation of medieval writers as a classical commonplace: 'Marriage peoples the earth, but virginity peoples heaven'" (Coulton, 444).

Christian: That is a mere mot.

Satan: Here is another mot, my friend, a bon mot, also from St. Jerome. There was, he said, a place for matrimony no less than for virginity: *est crater ad bibendum, et matula ad secretiora naturae (ibid.)*.

Christian: Would you mind translating that?

Satan: Not at all: "There is a cup for drinking, and a chamber pot for the secretions of nature." Isn't that a lovely view of love between the sexes? A Christian view, perhaps? And Jerome was not fastidious. It was one of his maxims that "when a man has once been washed in Christ, there is no need that he should wash again" (Coulton, 554). And this precept was highly honored by medieval monks. You should contrast these attitudes with Jewish marital ethics and rules about bodily cleanliness and with republican Rome.

Christian: Surely, Jerome was an exception.

Satan: No doubt, he was. He was a great scholar and translated the Hebrew Scriptures into Latin. His achievements could not be copied widely, but the precepts I quoted were adopted by large masses of people. St. Bonaventura does not equal Jerome's erudition, but "St. Bonaventura decides that there is no *aureola* in heaven for married folk" (Coulton, 445).

Christian: I am sick of your medieval lore. Luther broke with monasticism and the saints.

Satan: Because he read Paul and concluded that "it is better to marry than to burn." He considered it sinful to try to please God by works. But far from considering love divine, as the Jews and the Greeks had done, Christianity considered it sinful; and being sinful, man must believe in Christ and

hope for salvation by grace. Today, of course, many Protestants agree with me, not with Luther.

Christian: Christianity is the religion of a higher love.

Satan: Christianity is the religion that made love a sin. But
how could it face the world without some subterfuge? It
could not openly declare war on man's noblest passion. So
one talked as if one were opposed to one kind of love only,
and as if there were another kind.

Christian: But there is: love of the neighbor, love of one's
enemies, charity.

Satan: What religion is less charitable than Christianity?
What other religion has as much as conceived of eternal
damnation? What other sacred book contains as much
venom as the New Testament? What great religious figure
breathes vengefulness like the Jesus of the Gospels? How
different is all this from the Upanishads and the Bhagavadgita, not to speak of the teachings of the Buddha!

Christian: You mistake prophetic wrath for vengefulness.

Satan: The threats of the Old Testament prophets are clearly
intended to change the hearts of those who are addressed;
and a whole book is given over to the instruction of a
prophet who is slow to understand this: Jonah. But even he
has no wish for revenge in the first place, though he is sent
into the very capital of the enemy, Nineveh. In the New
Testament a new note is struck: personal revenge and eternal
damnation.

Christian: But Christianity introduced a note of hope: glad
tidings.

Satan: Precisely. The glad tidings of the turning of the tables
in the world to come.

Christian: The glad tidings is salvation through Christ.

Satan: Precisely. The Christian jubilates that he will be saved—
in a world in which, unfortunately, the mass of mankind
will be damned. The idea of salvation was not new. The
idea of eternal damnation was.

Christian: You talk as if the Christians had invented these
notions. In fact, it was through Christianity that the truth
was revealed.

Satan: What truth?

Christian: The truth is that those who believe in Christ and partake of the sacraments may be saved, while those who don't are damned.

Satan: What exactly do you mean when you say "saved" and "damned"?

Christian: Those who are saved see God.

Satan: Is God visible? I thought you said he did not take up space.

Christian: He doesn't, and he is not visible.

Satan: Then those who are saved do not see him?

Christian: They are near him.

Satan: Near? But not in space?

Christian: You are being stupidly literal.

Satan: The fact is that I still don't understand what you mean by saying that some are saved. And I think you don't know yourself what you mean. *You are repeating words that once designated very understandable superstitions. Now you denounce these superstitions but cling to the same words and believe that you are still saying something.* And the less sure you feel of yourself, the more you want others to agree with you, and the more you resent or pity those who don't.

Christian: Those who are saved escape everlasting torture.

Satan: In hell?

Christian: Yes. But of course hell is no place; it is a name for alienation from God, for being far from him—but not in space.

Satan: I suppose, God is like a father, and the saved are those who after death feel secure in his love, while the damned feel excluded and labor, as it were, under a bad conscience.

Christian: Yes.

Satan: Any loving father would go out of his way to make his children feel that they have not been excluded from his love, and that he loves them no less because they have rebelled against him or disappointed him.

Christian: That is why God sent his son down to earth.

Satan: What would you think of a father who gave a few of his children a single chance, and the rest of them none at all?

Christian: You always harp on hell.

Satan: There is no place like home. And you might as well get used to the idea: haven't you been told that I enjoy the company of those who cannot answer me any better than you?

Christian: But I don't understand at all. Only hysterics think of going to hell themselves.

Satan: I know: good Christians consider hell a place for others. But don't you realize that if you are right about everything, you, and those like you, are undoubtedly headed for hell? Don't you see how immeasurably you stand to gain if Christianity is untenable? It is I that bring you glad tidings. Believe me and you are saved. That God exists, that is a ritual phrase, charged with emotion and a thousand connotations: some sheer superstition, some myths, some true, some false, and most of them vague. But here is the truth that shall make you free: I do not exist.

Christian: If Satan does not exist, I must have dreamed. So I might as well go on believing what I have always believed. But what exactly do I believe? That is the question.

60. DIALOGUE BETWEEN SATAN AND AN ATHEIST

Atheist: You look so content. Have you grilled another theologian for breakfast? Or did you heat up a Christian for your lunch?

Satan: Both, my friend.

Atheist: I have often wondered how you catch Buddhists. After all, they do not believe the sort of thing Christians believe, so you can't undermine their faith.

Satan: I get them to fall in love with the world.

Atheist: By dangling beautiful women in front of ascetics?

Satan: Not necessarily. Their aim is to fall out of love with the world. I try to show them that suffering is worth while.

Atheist: That's what I said: women.

Satan: That works only in the least interesting cases. The others I try to interest in some cause, some task, some mission. I may even persuade them to spread their knowledge to as many men as possible. As soon as I have kindled some ambition I generally do not find it too hard to involve men in all sorts of compromises. But there are other ways.

Atheist: Just name one more.

Satan: Sometimes I try to lead them from detachment into callousness and indifference to the sufferings of others. But that works only in the early stages. Once a Buddhist has developed his peculiarly detached compassion he represents one of the hardest cases that I know. A Christian theologian is child's play compared to that.

Atheist: Who else gives you trouble?

Satan: For a long time the Jews did. I took the wrong approach. I argued about Scripture with them and got nowhere. They knew the texts as well as I did, made connections from verse to verse across a hundred pages much more nimbly than I did, and were never, absolutely never, fazed by anything I said. I could not shock them. Usually they produced some rabbi who, more than a thousand years ago, had made my point and been given some classical answer. They considered the whole thing a game even more than I did: after all, for me it was business, too. For them, talking about Scripture was a sheer delight. It was their favorite pastime which allowed them to forget their business and all their troubles. Where a Christian might have blenched they laughed, told stories to refute me or make fun of me, and I wasted my time.

Atheist: But couldn't you show them that their interpretations were untenable?

Satan: I tell you, they considered the whole thing a game, and they played it according to special rules: by their rules, their arguments were tenable. They never claimed that Moses had meant all the things they put into his mouth. Of course not. But according to the rules of the game it could be argued that an interpretation of the words of Moses was correct in spite of that—even several conflicting ones. What mattered was that you played well; and compared to some of their rabbis I didn't.

Atheist: So what happened?

Satan: I tried to get them to speak irreverently about God. Sometimes they did, but then it turned out to have been humor, and so it did not count. Threats, on the other hand, stiffened their backs, and most of them would rather be martyred than blaspheme under pressure. As long as the Christians martyred so many of them, there was a real dearth of Jews and Buddhists in hell, and the place began to fill up with Christians and Muslims. It got terribly stuffy, and there began to be talk of discrimination. I was even accused of having adopted a quota system. But now things have changed.

Atheist: Did you change your policy of admission?

Satan: Not at all. But when the Christians stopped persecuting the Jews, I began to be phenomenally successful with a new approach. I told them that their way of life was dated, that their laws were not made for the modern world, that freedom was the big thing now, and that their ancient laws interfered with their freedom.

Atheist: Do you mean to say that all Jews who eat pork go to hell?

Satan: Of course not. But once they give up their laws, their old way of life goes by the board, and they no longer study Scripture as they used to. By now many of them know the Bible as little as Christian youths.

Atheist: And does everyone who doesn't know the Bible go to hell?

Satan: No, certainly not. But when they get to that point I ask them what right they have to call themselves Jews, religiously speaking. And that does make a dent. Then they begin to worry. And whether they worry or not, their religion has become a social affair for most of them, just as for the Christians.

Atheist: I am glad to hear that. More and more people are beginning to see the light. I have been joking with you, asking about people going to hell. I don't really believe in hell. So far as I am concerned religion is bunk.

Satan: Just what do you mean by saying that? Bunk?

Atheist: I mean, it is a lot of nonsense which isn't worth bothering about. There are sensible things like science, especially psychology and anthropology, which are much more profitable. Religion is a stupid waste of time.

Satan: Oh, I don't think so at all. There is nothing that interests me more. Religion is one of the most fascinating subjects in the world. I suppose you don't like poetry and art either.

Atheist: You are wrong. There are some painters and poets whom I like. Picasso, for example, and a lot of modern art. I like Tolstoy, too, before he became a Christian, or tried to become one. And Dostoevsky, in spite of his crazy religious ideas. I am interested in their psychology.

Satan: What about the Book of Genesis?

Atheist: I don't read stuff like that. Next you will ask me if I say Psalms. I must have been exposed to things like that as a child. But I have mercifully forgotten it.

Satan: Have you read no religious scriptures at all?

Atheist: I have only an amateur's interest in anthropology. I have read a bit about primitive religions. But I have never followed it up. There are all sorts of handy cheap editions now; perhaps I'll try some of them next time I travel by train. Usually I drive.

Satan: But these things were not written for a quick dip on the train between a crossword puzzle and a whisky sour.

Atheist: And why not? You would not want me to go to church to catch up with the Upanishads?

Satan: Of course not. You don't go to church to catch up, as you call it, with *Lear;* but at least you take off an evening for it and give it your whole attention and let it do something to you.

Atheist: And what should these scriptures do to me? At most I should want to fill a gap in my education. I don't want to be converted.

Satan: Well, these are not things merely to know about or to have handy for a dinner conversation. The Bible and the Buddha, the Upanishads and the Bhagavadgita, Lao-tze and the Tales of the Hassidim, these are not things about which one is informed or not informed: what matters is that they speak to you and in some way change you.

Atheist: Have you become a preacher, Satan?

Satan: I am merely shuddering at the prospect of having to spend an eternity with you. I should rather like to make a human being of you before you settle down in my place. I don't agree with the people who accept these scriptures, but I can talk with them and, to be frank, I rather enjoy talking with them. But you! I wish you'd go to heaven.

VIII. TRUTH
IN THREE RELIGIONS

61. RELIGION AND TRUTH.   It is often claimed that religion is above all else a way to truth and that the primary concern of the great religions is with truth. No doubt, the word truth can be given such a wide sense that this claim would be justified. Another generalization, however, is much more illuminating and does not involve any *ad hoc* redefinition of truth.

The Spartans valued resourcefulness, courage, and indifference to pain above honesty, and character above truth. Their education was not designed primarily to teach truths, or any one truth, but to build character. The boy who stole a fox and, surprised, hid it under his tunic to escape detection and gave no sign of pain as the fox bit deep into his abdomen became a hero for dying with calm self-control. That Leonidas and his three hundred men who stood off the armed might of the Persians at Thermopylae and died to the last man should have become public heroes is much less surprising to the modern mind, at least in the West; but the point to note is that honesty and truth-seeking had no place in the Spartan ideal.

Mutius Scaevola is the best symbol of the similar attitude of the ancient Romans. When the king of Etruria besieged Rome, Mutius disguised himself, found his way into the enemy camp and into the royal tent, but, mistaking the royal secretary for the king, stabbed the wrong man. Seized and questioned, he gave no answer except to admit he was a Roman. Then he put his right hand on an altar of burning coals and told the king, without a sign of pain, that 300 young Romans like himself had conspired against the king's life and had entered the camp, pledged to kill him or to die in the attempt. The king lifted the siege, made peace with Rome, and withdrew.

Does the history of Rome down to the end of the republic boast of an equally impressive display of honesty or dedication to truth? Is there a Spartan who has thrilled men more than Leonidas? At least as taught until quite recently, history has been the story of men like these: a vast record of intrigue, daring dishonesty, valor, and, at best, character.

Indeed, war has received far more attention than courage, and conquests have been chronicled and praised more than any trait of character. Ambition, strategic genius, and success have been glorified; and, more rarely, dedication to liberty and humane qualities. If it had not been for the pathetic gesture of Parson Weems' story about the little Washington, dedication to truth would have been out of the picture altogether.

Today most religious people, insofar as they are religious, prize kindness above candor, and goodness, whatever they may mean by that, above truth in any form. The primary concern of the great religions is not with truth, and least of all do they agree in teaching the same truths: they agree in considering truth secondary. Their ultimate concern is with something else, but the object of this ultimate concern is different in different religions. Before generalizing further about religion we should consider the divergent attitudes toward truth and the ultimate concerns of at least a few of the great religions.

62. BUDDHISM AND TRUTH. The core of the Buddha's own teaching is transmitted in the form of the Four Noble Truths which are held to be literally true and were clearly intended this way by the Buddha himself. All life involves suffering; all suffering is due to attachment and ultimately to ignorance; if we could abolish the cause, the effect, too, would disappear;

the discipline recommended in the Noble Eightfold Path will lead to this cessation. Understandably, Nietzsche called Buddhism the only positivistic religion in history (587).

Nevertheless, Buddhism does not by any means place a supreme value on truth, and it certainly does not extol the search for truths. The Buddha invites comparison with a physician who treats a single disease, knows how to treat it, and does not care to know anything else. His disparagement of metaphysical speculation resembles the apparently similar attitude of the positivist only superficially.

The Buddha considers such speculation frivolous because the world is burning and "the one thing needful" is salvation. His objection to metaphysics is that it is not required for salvation. In this one respect he resembles Kierkegaard.

The Buddha would have been no less opposed to positivism or analytic philosophy. His attitude was not so much antimetaphysical as it was antiphilosophical. He disparaged metaphysics because it dominated the religious thought of his time, still preserved in the Upanishads. His followers asked him questions about the world and the soul, and he told them that their questions did "not tend toward edification." There is no reason whatever to suppose that his answer would have been different if they had asked him instead whether the good is a simple and unanalyzable quality, or what he thought of sense data, or how I *know* that there is a goldfinch in the garden. The same goes for questions about history or mathematics, chemistry, philology, or physics.

The supreme concern of the Buddha was not truth but salvation: a state of being. Peace of soul comes closer to it than accumulation of knowledge. In a sense, this attitude is antiintellectual; but some cultivation of the intellect is considered indispensable for salvation, and the fool is therefore branded repeatedly as the most hopeless of men. Any glorification of the poor in spirit or the pure fool, in the manner of *Parsifal,* is so remote from the doctrine of the Buddha that in this sense one could call it intellectualistic. Some intellectual discipline and some knowledge are required to attain pervasive detachment, but their value is instrumental. Any hunger for truth that would keep a man awake at night and set his soul on fire would be a disease.

A conflict between this religion and science is conceivable on two levels. First, a psychologist could conceivably take issue with the Buddha's analysis, which, however, seems eminently sound. Secondly, the Buddha repudiates any pure science, if only by implication, not as impiety but as frivolity. And this attitude toward truth has molded the minds of millions.

63. ZEN BUDDHISM AND TRUTH. As Buddhism spread to China and Japan it came to be more and more remote from the Buddha's original teaching, and on the face of it Zen Buddhism seems to be based on an outright rejection of his doctrines. In *An Introduction to Zen Buddhism*, D. T. Suzuki, the outstanding interpreter of his religion, quotes from the sutra that "is daily recited in the Zen monasteries," both the first thing in the morning and before each meal: "There is no knowledge, no ignorance, no destruction of ignorance . . . there are no four truths, viz., there is no pain, no origin of pain, no stoppage of pain, and no path to the stoppage of pain" (50 f.).

Needless to say, the truth claims of other religions receive no kinder treatment: "The contemplations and prayers of St. Ignatius [Loyola] are, from the Zen point of view, merely so many fabrications of the imagination elaborately woven for the benefit of the piously minded" (42). With this, many positivists might agree. But Zen goes much further: it ridicules all propositional truth.

Empty-handed I go, and behold the spade is in my hands;
I walk on foot, and yet on the back of an ox I am riding;
When I pass over the bridge,
Lo, the water floweth not, but the bridge doth flow.

"This is the famous gatha of Jenye (Shan-hui, A.D. 497–569), who is commonly known as Fudaishi (Fu-tai-shih), and it summarily gives the point of view as entertained by the followers of Zen" (58).

The beginning of wisdom, according to Zen, is the recognition of the limitations, and indeed the futility, of all propositional truth, and above all of any dogma, any sacrosanct formulation, any rigid statement. A monk once asked a master: "All things are reducible to the One; where is this One to be reduced?" The master retorted: "When I was in Tsin district I had a monk's robe made that weighed seven *chin*." And "this is one of the most noted sayings ever uttered by a Zen master" (72).

It may be asked why the master did not rather answer like the Buddha that such questions "do not tend toward edification." Why did he refuse to give a reasonable answer? This question is reinforced by those many other tales in which the masters do not give serenely irrelevant answers but slap their students, often quite hard. One student even gets his nose twisted until it is "literally put out of joint" (94), while in another case "The master was furious, and finally taking hold of Hakuin gave him several slaps and pushed him off the porch. He fell several feet to the foot of a stone wall, where he remained for a while almost senseless" (128).

The most shocking story perhaps is that of the master who, when asked a question, liked to lift one of his fingers. "His little boy attendant imitated him, and whenever the boy was asked by strangers as to the teaching of the master he would lift his finger. Learning of this, the master one day called the boy in and cut off his finger. The boy tried to imitate the master, as was his wont, but the finger was no more there, and then suddenly the significance of it all dawned upon him" (72). One could do worse than associate this tale of the ninth century with Jesus' saying: "It is better for you to enter the kingdom of God with one eye." One finger may not have been an excessive price if "the significance of it all dawned upon him."

The question remains why the Zen masters give such oddly irrelevant answers and slap and hurt their students instead of explaining things to them. Clearly, they have little faith in verbal explanations and a real horror of repetition and imitation. They do not want to provide future theologians with say-

ings that lend themselves to quotation out of context or employment in a creed. They want to forestall the creation of
systematic theologies.

They want to get across that religion is not a matter of
words or truths. Forcibly, they want to push their students
back into reality, into substantial experience. A robe that
weighed seven *chin* is more substantial than all talk about the
One. The experience of a good hard slap is more substantial
than all speculation.

What is ultimately wanted, and after all was ultimately
wanted by the Buddha, too, is an experience and not the safe
possession of a formula. And if the Four Noble Truths become formulas which are taught and discussed, analyzed and
believed, then they become obstacles on the way to that experience which alone really matters. To argue the point would
lead to the creation of more and more obstacles. What is
needed is an altogether new approach. Not a more fantastic
approach with all kinds of bizarre beliefs, miracle stories,
legends, speculations, and a vast literature, as we find it in
Mahayana Buddhism, which also developed in China and Japan, but a royal road to enlightenment, a short cut compared
to which even the Buddha himself offered a detour: in one
word, Zen.

Zen masters have come to the conclusion that a slap in the
face may lead to a sudden awakening and that a provocatively
irrelevant answer, meditated upon, may lead to *satori*. "*Satori*
may be defined as intuitive looking-into, in contradistinction
to intellectual and logical understanding" (88). "If *satori* is
amenable to analysis in the sense that by so doing it becomes
perfectly clear to another who has never had it, that *satori*
will be no *satori*" (92). "Religiously, it is a new birth; intellectually, it is the acquiring of a new viewpoint" (95). Is
it something esoteric, reserved for initiates?

A Confucian poet and statesman asked a Zen master to
initiate him. He replied: "There is a passage in the text with
which you are perfectly familiar which fitly describes the
teaching of Zen. Did not Confucius declare: 'Do you think
I am hiding things from you, O my disciples? Indeed, I have

nothing to hide from you.'" Later they took a walk: "the wild laurel was in full bloom and the air was redolent with its scent. Asked the Zen master, 'Do you smell it?' When the Confucian answered affirmatively, Kwaido said, 'There, I have nothing to hide from you.' This reminder at once led Kozan-koku's mind to the opening of a *satori*" (92 f.).

Genuine esoteric wisdom cannot be learned from any book or by virtue of admission to a secret society or cult. It *is* restricted, it *is* only for the few, but to cite *Lear: "ripeness is all."*

When the mind is ready for it, there it is, not hidden but obvious like the scent in the air. But asked about this new wisdom, all you can produce are trite adages which you could have cited before your experience, too. Now, indeed, you find your hard-won wisdom in all sorts of places: you open a book, and there it is. It was there all along, but earlier you did not see it even when it stared you in the face. So the Zen master makes a point of not giving you old saws, of not telling you what is in the book, too. He tries to turn you away from books and saws and propositions of all kinds. He tries to push you back into experience.

To us the Zen masters seem too ready to slap and hurt their students. There is a cruelty in these tales that reminds the Western reader of Japanese motion pictures like *Rashomon, Ugetsu, Gate of Hell,* and *The Golden Demon.* In a general way, however, the Zen masters were surely right that it is only through suffering, through being hurt, that one can attain the sort of wisdom that is wanted: it cannot be induced by means of a textbook or a set of dogmas. In the Western world, no one has made this point better than Hermann Hesse in his great novels from *Siddharta* to *Das Glasperlenspiel* (translated as *Magister Ludi*).

Hesse's work poses the question whether this form of indirect communication cannot help one who is seeking, albeit only as a dim foreshadowing at the beginning of his way of that which he will have to find for himself much later. Hesse, of course, had learned a great deal from the Eastern religions and named his *Siddharta* after the Buddha. But Hesse goes

beyond the Eastern religions, beyond the ultimate concern of both the Buddha and the Zen masters. After the experience there still remains art. And art is not only a form of indirect communication which tries to be of some help to others and places a greater trust in words than Zen does; it is also a further experience for the artist himself. "Life," says Sartre in *The Flies*, "begins on the other side of despair." And one might add: great art and philosophy begin on the other side of ineffability.

For the philosopher, knowledge and understanding are no mere instruments for the attainment of an experience, as they were for the Buddha, nor does he repudiate them when he finds them unreliable guides. For the philosopher, every experience is a steppingstone to deeper understanding and a higher knowledge.

"Only great pain, that long, slow pain in which we are burned with green wood, as it were—pain which takes its time —only this forces us philosophers to descend into our ultimate depths. . . . One emerges as a different person, with a few *more* question marks—above all with the will to question more persistently, more deeply, severely, harshly, evilly, and quietly than has ever been questioned on this earth before. . . . The love of life is still possible—only, one loves differently. . . .

"What is strangest is this: afterward one has a different taste—a *second* taste. Out of such abysses, also out of the abyss of great suspicion, one returns newborn, having shed one's skin, more ticklish and sarcastic, with a more delicate taste for joy, with a more tender tongue for all good things, with gayer senses, with a second dangerous innocence in joy, more child-like and yet a hundred times more subtle than one has ever been before."

These reflections from the Epilogue of *Nietzsche contra Wagner* (681), the last work which Nietzsche completed, using passages from his earlier works, slightly revised, suggest the difference between the philosopher and the Zen master. Nietzsche's ultimate concern is with truth. The Buddhist's is not.

64. JUDAISM AND TRUTH.   Judaism, like Buddhism, is far less prone to come into conflict with specific scientific doctrines than Christianity. The main emphasis falls not on truth but on what Christians since St. Paul have usually, though very misleadingly, called "the Law." Before we attempt a more adequate translation of Torah, it may be helpful to quote Rhys Davids about India: "In India, indeed, the same word is used by followers of every school of thought for law and for religion—the word Dharma, etymologically equivalent to the Latin *forma* . . . 'good form' . . . not . . . legislation. It was rather custom, established precedent; and a sense of duty to the established order of things included and implied a reverential attitude toward the gods" (2).

The primary concern in Judaism is with a way of life. This way of life involves a strong sense of tradition and a determination to realize certain ideals. Both may well be stronger than in any other religion. This unique directedness from a historical past into a messianic future, from Mount Sinai to justice for orphan, widow, and stranger and the abolition of war, has saved Judaism from death by ice and death by fire, from freezing in awe of a rigid tradition and from evaporating into utopian reverie.

It was Scripture that defined this direction and, for more than two thousand years, nourished the thought and imagination of the Jews. It was Torah which in the wider sense is the whole of Scripture and in the narrow sense the Five Books of Moses, and in neither case merely *nomos*, "the Law," as Paul would have it. Surely, Genesis is not a compilation of laws, but it received at least as much loving attention as any other book. The Hebrew word *Torah* means not law but teaching.

One can teach an art as well as truths, a way of life no less than doctrines. What the Jews have traditionally sought in the Torah was not merely a way of life nor truths but—this is scarcely an exaggeration—everything. And their attitude toward truth was molded less by any particular teaching of Scripture than by their belief that almost everything could be found in it.

God is central in Judaism, but because the Jews never lost

their intimate awareness of the multifarious riches of their Scriptures no dogma could ever gain authority. Under the influence of Greek philosophy and Muslim theology, Maimonides attempted some definitive formulations, but Judaism never accepted them as sacrosanct nor allowed them or any other such attempts to come between itself and the inexhaustible texts. Hence one kind of tension between religion and the quest for truth is almost unknown in Judaism: no sacrifice of the intellect is demanded.

Indeed, in a very important sense it might be said that the search for truth was never esteemed more highly in any other religion nor even among the Greeks. Among the Jews, learning was not considered the province of men of leisure only. The traditional Jewish attitude toward learning is beautifully illustrated by a passage in the Babylonian Talmud (Yoma 35b).

"The Rabbanan taught: The poor man, the rich man, and the rake appear at the judgment. When the poor man is reproached for not having studied the Torah and he replies that he has been poor and burdened with work, he is answered: Have you been any poorer than Hillel? It is told of Hillel the Older that with his work he daily earned a few cents of which he gave half to the janitor of the school while using the other half to support himself and his family. One day he found no work, and the janitor of the school did not let him in; so he climbed up and sat down on the skylight to hear the words of the living God from the lips of Shmaya and Ptollion. It is told that it was on a Friday in the middle of the winter, and snow fell on him from the sky. As the dawn came, Shmaya said to Ptollion: Brother Ptollion, on every other day the room is light, but today it is dark; is the day really so cloudy? When they looked up and noticed the shape of a human being in the window, they climbed up and found him covered with nine feet of snow. They got him out, washed him and put salve on him, and seated him by the fire, saying that he deserved it that for his sake one desecrate the Sabbath." There follow two similar stories about the rich Rabbi Eleazar ben Harsom and the handsome Joseph.

This love of learning and scholarship has characterized
Judaism through the ages, leaving its mark on the Jews who
since the emancipation in the modern world have become estranged from their religion. But as long as the Jewish religion
defined the general atmosphere and the conditions of scholarship, the quest for truth differed decisively from that conception of free inquiry which comes to us from Socrates'
Apology. From a modern point of view one might say that
the search for truth in Scripture was not directed toward propositional truth, and that the very conception of propositional
truth was lacking. The most persistent intellectual energy and
the most prodigious analytic effort were devoted to the loving care of a tradition, to the continual contrivance of beautiful and profound interpretations, and to questions of morality
and ritual.

Since the Bible and quite especially the Five Books of
Moses were considered God-given, it might seem that the resulting fundamentalism must have led to conflicts with science. But this inference involves a common misconception:
those who consider the Bible God's revelation need not take
every sentence literally; indeed, they can hardly afford to do
this. Taken literally, many sentences in the Bible would contradict each other. Hence it was one of the first principles of
the rabbinical tradition—still very much in evidence in the
Epistles of Paul in the New Testament—that the sentences
and words of the Bible need not be taken literally, and truly
daring interpretations were common.

In the resulting climate of thought, the question whether
some specific statement is really poetic and only symbolically
true could not even arise: the essential ambiguity of Scripture was granted implicitly, and *every* verse could be interpreted poetically. There is a vast body of such exegesis of the
Hebrew Scriptures, not only in the Talmud and various com-
pilations of Midrash but also in the New Testament. When
it is Hebrew, it is usually called Haggadah.

It is customary to juxtapose Haggadah with Halachah,
which is the interpretation of laws as laws. In the field of Haggadah there is no one right or true view: there are at most

degrees of beauty and profundity, and two conflicting interpretations may both be highly respected. Even in the field of
Halachah the attitude of the Talmudic rabbis was not altogether different from this; witness the following story from
the Talmud:

"For three years the school of Shammai and the school of
Hillel argued: one said the halachah was to be decided according to it, the other said the halachah was to be decided
according to it. Then a heavenly voice was heard and said:
the one and the other are words of the living God, but the
halachah is to be decided according to the school of Hillel.—
But if the one and the other are words of the living God,
why was it granted to the school of Hillel that the halachah
was decided according to it?—Because it was peaceable and
modest and studied not only its own views but also those of
the school of Shammai; even more, it placed the words of the
school of Shammai before its own. . . . This teaches you that
when a man humbles himself, the Holy One, Blessed be He,
exalts him . . ." (Erubin 13b).

In this case the accepted rules of exegesis permitted more
than one interpretation of the text, but it evidently seemed
necessary to reach agreement on a point of law, and the decision was made on moral grounds. This tale also illustrates
the compatibility of playfulness with seriousness. This fusion
is one of the abiding characteristics of the Jewish religion and
even better illustrated by another, similar, tale on the same
page of the Talmud:

"The Rabbanan taught: For two and a half years the school
of Shammai and the school of Hillel argued: one said, it were
better for man not to have been created than to have been
created, and the other said, it was better for man that he
was created than that he should not have been created. Then
they took a vote and agreed that it would indeed have been
better for man not to have been created, but that, since he
has been created, he should ponder his [past] actions. Some
read: he should deliberate his [future] actions."

Huizinga's remarks on the long popularity of the problem
of universals and the agonal division into nominalists and

realists, which Satan quotes to the theologian (§ 58), are most
pertinent. Two teams are formed, and the contest proceeds
according to clearly defined rules. A grim view of life does not
keep these men from their playful debate; neither does their
playfulness veil their freedom from illusion.

These same points find even clearer expression in one of
the profoundest stories in the Talmud. It concerns Rabbi
Akiba and his interpretations of Scripture which were sometimes based on the use of the same word in two widely different places, as were those of his colleagues, and occasionally
even on a single letter, though never, it seems, on the way a
word was written, relying on as little as a tiny hook on one
of the letters. But even such small peculiarities were carefully
copied in every new scroll.

Akiba's interpretations were not always accepted, but they
were generally admired for their profundity. The men credited with having told the following story shared in the general love for Akiba, and anyone who would consider the tale
an inspiration of malice would miss its significance.

"Rabbi Yehudah said in the name of Rav: When Moses
climbed the mountain he found the Holy One, blessed be
He, sitting there and fashioning little crowns for the letters.
Then he said to Him: Lord of the world, for whose sake are
you doing that? He replied: there is a man who will come
to be after many generations, called Akiba ben Joseph; he will
one day present heaps and heaps of doctrines concerning every little hook. Then he said before Him: Lord of the world,
show him to me. He replied: turn around. Then he turned
around and sat down behind the eighth row, but he did not
understand their conversation and was dismayed. When Akiba
came to a point about which his students asked him how he
knew, he replied to them that this was a doctrine given to
Moses on Sinai. Then Moses was calmed; and he turned back
and stepped before the Holy One, blessed be He, and said before Him: Lord of the world, you have such a man and give
the Torah through me! He replied: Be still, that is how it
entered my mind. Then he said before Him: Lord of the
world, you have shown me his knowledge of the law; show

me his reward too. He said: turn around. Then he turned around and saw Akiba's flayed flesh weighed in a butcher's shop. Then he said before Him: Lord of the world, this is the Torah, and this its reward? He replied: Be still, that is how it entered my mind" (Menahoth 29b).

The rabbis did not presume that Moses himself had meant what the sentences which, according to tradition, he had written could be shown to mean by their methods of exegesis. They were trying to get not at Moses' meaning but at God's. And they were not doing it in the expectation of any material rewards. The study of the Torah was for them an end in itself. It was their way of life.

Their mode of interpretation and the structure of the Talmud may be illustrated with a final quotation which also explains Akiba's death. Let us begin with the Mishnah, which is the definitive codification of the so-called oral tradition, as determined and edited in the second century A.D., and quote a passage from the first treatise in the Talmud entitled "Blessings." In Section 9, paragraph 5, we find these words:

"Man must give praise for the bad no less than for the good, for it is written [Deut. 6.5]: Thou shalt love the Lord, thy God, with thy whole heart, etc. With thy whole heart: with both your impulses, with the good impulse and with the bad impulse. With thy whole soul: even when He takes your soul." The Mishnah was discussed for centuries until finally the discussions of the rabbis were written down. These discussions form the so-called Gemara which together with the Mishnah constitutes the Talmud.

From the Gemara for the passage cited we learn that it was Akiba who taught that the Biblical command to love God "with thy whole soul" meant "even when he takes away thy soul." His reason: there must be a special meaning to "whole soul" which adds something to "whole heart." After crediting this interpretation to Akiba, the Gemara proceeds:

"The Rabbanan taught: Once the infamous government had given an order that the Israelites should no longer concern themselves with the Torah. Then Papos ben Yehudah met Rabbi Akiba as he held public meetings and concerned

himself with the Torah. Then he said to him: Akiba, are you
not afraid of the infamous government? He replied: I shall
tell you a parable to which this is comparable. A fox once
walked along the bank of a river, and when he saw fish con-
gregating everywhere, he said to them: what are you fleeing?
They replied: the nets that men put out for us. Then he said
to them: Then may it please you to come on land, and we,
I and you, shall dwell together as my ancestors once dwelled
together with your ancestors. Then they replied to him: Is it
you that is reputed to be the cleverest animal? You are not
clever but stupid; if we are afraid even in the element in
which we have our life, how much more in the element in
which we die! Thus it is with us, too: if it has come to that
even now when we sit and study the Torah of which it is
written [Deut. 30.20], 'for it is thy life and the length of thy
days,' how much more if we go and withdraw from it!"

A very few days later, Akiba was apprehended. After a long
imprisonment, he was led to his execution at the time of day
when the liturgy calls for the reading of the so-called Shma:
"Hear, Israel, the Lord our God, the Lord is One. And thou
shalt love the Lord, thy God, with thy whole heart and with
thy whole soul . . ." This is how the Gemara relates his death:

"His flesh was ripped off with iron combs, but he took upon
himself the yoke of the kingdom of heaven. His students said
to him: Master, so far? He replied to them: My whole life
I have grieved over the verse in Scripture, with thy whole soul
—even when He takes your soul; for I thought, when shall this
opportunity be given to me, and I shall do it. And now that
it is given to me, I should not do it? He prolonged the word
'One' so long that his soul expired on 'One.' "

Like Socrates, Akiba would sooner die than cease searching
for truth in his own peculiar way. Like Socrates, he had a
sense of humor and realized that the search for truth was not
altogether unlike a game; but this game was his life. What he
died for was not some one particular truth but his concern
with truth, his determination to go on seeking truth—which
he did by way of interpreting Scripture. About particular
truths he was willing to argue and ready to be shown that he

was wrong, provided it was done according to the rules of the game. But the quest itself he would not give up: he would rather give up his life.

These important similarities between Akiba and Socrates should not obscure the important difference. Akiba's conception of the quest for truth involves an overriding loyalty to a written tradition and an oral tradition, to certain texts and principles of exegesis. This loyalty bars certain questions altogether—questions about the origin and the reasonableness of the texts and the rules of interpretation—and it does not encourage, to put it mildly, the study of other literatures, of history, or science.

The contemporary Jew faces no grim problems in connection with specific scientific statements. He need not choose between dogma and Darwin. Whatever dogmas various Jewish theologians may have thought up from time to time the contemporary Jew can repudiate and still be a pious Jew, even a so-called orthodox Jew. In the field of legal interpretation, of Halachah, there is also room for argument and different traditions; but, allowing a little leeway for exegesis, the 600-odd commandments and prohibitions of the Five Books of Moses are accepted as obligatory by traditional Judaism and go far toward defining the traditional Jewish way of life. The crucial problem for Judaism today is not the relation of religion and truth but rather this: what, if anything, remains of Judaism as a religion if the traditional commandments and prohibitions are no longer accepted as obligatory?

This question is not rhetorical, but it is hard to answer. Those who would like to answer it with some sort of affirmation must show that what they propose to call Judaism has sufficient continuity with historic Judaism to deserve the name; and if this is done, the question remains whether what is then called Judaism depends for its existence on the survival of historic Judaism in its more traditional form. It might be a mere way station through which successive generations pass on the way from religion to irreligion.

In principle, a Jewish religion without the traditional Halachah seems entirely possible because the canonical Scriptures of Judaism do not only contain so much that is not Halachah but also so much that may be interpreted as an impassioned plea against the identification of Judaism with Halachah, notably in the prophetic books.

Part of the difficulty arises from the fact that the nonlegal literature of the Old Testament as well as the morality of the prophets has become the common property of such a large part of mankind and has therefore in a sense ceased to be distinctively Jewish. But seeing that it has become common property on a level of such unprophetic shallowness, and seeing that the haggadic portions of the Old Testament, like Genesis and Jonah, and the poetry of Ecclesiastes and Job, are so widely appreciated with so little understanding there is a real possibility here for a revival of the Jewish religion without the traditional Halachah. Whether there are any signs of that today is another question.

What has doomed most such efforts in the past is their attempt to fuse what must be a genuine creation with an effort at assimilation. Even if they did not move their Sabbath to Sunday they still tried to turn the synagogue into a church, began to read the Bible in English in an adaptation of the King James Version, and increasingly lost hold of their traditional heritage and of whatever was distinctive in it.

The development of Jewish theology and the search for Jewish "beliefs" are on a level with the attempt to turn Hanukkah into an *Ersatz* Christmas. Yet Sukkoth, the Feast of Tabernacles, offers something that the Christian child is not offered: the chance to live in a hut for a week. And Judaism offers something the Christian is not offered: a religion without theology.

If some of the liberal Protestants were right in thinking that Jesus tried to establish a kind of Reform Judaism—and as a matter of historical fact they are probably wrong—then it would have to be said, and some of them have said, that Paul wrecked this early attempt with his effort at assimilation, with his fusion of this religion with the beliefs and practices then current in other religions. Paul used Haggadah to destroy Halachah; but he did not stop with that: having destroyed the

"Law" he put into its place an intricate theology as well as all kinds of new beliefs.

The attitude of Judaism toward truth may be summarized in terms of some reflections on the expulsion of Spinoza by the synagogue of Amsterdam. This expulsion may have been influenced in part by political considerations: it may have seemed imperative to dissociate oneself from his radical ideas. And personal jealousies played their part, too. But Spinoza did not merely take issue with specific doctrines or fail to base his propositions on the interpretation of Scriptures: he expressly denied the authority of the Bible in matters of truth. No major Western philosopher who knew Scripture had ever done this. He repudiated a whole way of living and thinking, and his offense in the eyes of those who expelled him was less untruth than disloyalty.

For all its traditional intellectualism, Judaism, too, has in a way set bounds for the inquiring intellect. At times—for example, in the nineteenth century in Eastern Europe, in an effort to stave off the threat of assimilation and the destruction of a traditional way of life—these bounds have been narrow and rigid: in such novels as *Judith Trachtenberg* and *Der Pojaz*, Karl Emil Franzos (1848–1904) created unforgettable pictures of this conflict. But even at other times the Jewish religion prescribed a mode of thought for the search for truth; and the intellectual virtues which it cultivated were subtlety and ingenuity in exegesis rather than the requirements of untrammeled inquiry.

Even at the time of the prophets, before the establishment of the exegetical mode of thought, free inquiry had no place in Judaism, and a Socrates would have been unthinkable in Biblical Jerusalem. Even those who feel that a further development of the Jewish religion is quite possible in which uninhibited inquiry will have its place—not the current way-station Judaism which certainly makes no attempt to inhibit inquiry of any kind whatever—will have to admit that historic Judaism has had its ultimate concern not with truth but with a way of life. In Micah's words:

"You have been told, man, what is good; and what does the

Lord demand of you but to do justice and love of mercy and to walk humbly with your God?"

65. JEWISH AND CHRISTIAN FAITH. In Christianity the problem of the relation of religion and truth is central as in no other major religion. This is a function of the Christian conception of faith. Christianity knows two kinds of faith: faith in and faith that. Although the word "belief" can be used in both senses, let us here use it to designate the second kind only, the faith that a proposition is true, and call the other kind of faith "trust."

Faith in Judaism, including the faith of Abraham which Christian thinkers from Paul to Kierkegaard have considered exemplary, is trust. It is an attitude rather than belief that anything is the case. The King James Bible has Job say, "Though he slay me, yet will I trust in him"—in a verse [3.15] which was more accurately rendered in the superb German translation of the Hebrew Scriptures by Harry Torczyner (now Tur-Sinai): "He will slay me? For that I hope. But my ways I will maintain to his face." (Cf. § 79 and the detailed discussion in *The Interpreter's Bible* where the King James Version is flatly rejected as "an impossibility," while the five "possible" translations agree in substance.) In the end, however, Job's attitude is close to that suggested in the "Authorized" mistranslation, though the Hebrew author resists even such a formulation. Clearly, there is no submission to dogma of any kind; no acceptance of any theodicy, however impressive; no belief that certain propositions are true. On the contrary, the whole compendium of propositions offered by Job's friends, and reiterated endlessly ever since, is rejected in favor of an attitude of trust.

Even trust is not the best word for the characteristically Jewish type of faith; there is another word that really goes to the heart of the matter: intimacy.

Sometimes Abraham's attitude toward God is indeed one of trust; at other times it is predominantly one of obedience and from the outside looks like blind obedience; but at still other times, most notably in his great argument with God in Genesis 18, neither "trust" nor "obedience" describes his attitude. The phrase (חלילה לך) in verse 25 which the King James Bible translates with its usual majesty, "That be far from thee to do after this manner," might also be rendered so as to stress the root of the word, which means desecration, profanation: "Shame on you if you act like that!" Elsewhere—for example, twice in Genesis 44—the King James Bible renders the same phrase "God forbid": it always precedes something that is considered shameful and disgraceful, as it does in Abraham's argument with God. And in the preceding chapter, after God has promised Abraham once more that Sarah shall yet give birth to a son—"I shall bless her that she become nations, and kings of people shall come from her"—the text continues: "Then Abraham fell on his face and laughed, and he said in his heart: Shall a child be born to one who is a hundred years old: And Sarah, should she at ninety still give birth?" The pervasive features of Abraham's piety is not trust, even less belief, but intimacy with God.

Jonah, in the second verse of the last chapter, expresses a very exalted conception of God, but as Michelangelo realized when he came to paint the prophet, placing his rebellious image over the pope's most holy altar, Jonah's attitude was scarcely one of trust. It came closer to Job's: "He will slay me? For that I hope. But my ways I will maintain to his face."

The same attitude of intimacy with God rather than trust in him is found in the most monumental of all the Psalms, the only one attributed to Moses himself, the 90th: "A Prayer of Moses, the man of God." Many other Psalms show the same lack of all illusion, but usually, as in Ecclesiastes, this is mitigated by a pious conclusion. But should we deny the name of piety to the 90th Psalm which may have been preserved from this fate by the unique prestige of Moses' name? Or to the rabbis who decided that it would have been better for man if he had not been created? This is an unusual sort of piety: a Jewish piety which consists above all else in intimacy with God. Of course, not all Jewish piety is, or has been, like this.

Although this notion of intimacy is one of the implicit

leitmotivs of the Hassidic lore which Martin Buber has presented to us, he equates the Jewish type with "trust" in *Two Types of Faith*. The central contrast in that book is encumbered with an elaborate attempt to prove that Jesus, of whom Buber says in his Preface that ever since his youth he has "experienced him as my big brother," had the Jewish kind of faith and not the Christian. This thesis and the large body of interpretations of New Testament passages is much more controversial than the central contrast need be from which it distracts attention. It will therefore be best to proceed here independently of Buber's book.

Paul, Luther, and Kierkegaard did not merely pay lip service to the Jewish kind of faith, insofar as it can be identified with trust: this was part of their faith, too. But Paul, and Christianity since his time, merged trust with belief and introduced a growing body of dogma. Assent to propositions is essential in Paul's religion; and this is crucial even though in Paul this assent is informed with an attitude of trust and supported by intense personal experience.

Mere belief that certain propositions are true, mere assent to dogma in the same spirit in which a boy accepts the truth of geometric theorems, falls far short of what Paul wants. Still, he also demands belief that certain propositions are true. And the same consideration applies to subsequent Christianity, whether Greek Orthodox or Roman Catholic, Lutheran or Calvinist.

That intimacy which had been so prominent in Jewish piety became wholly exceptional in Christianity—there are touches of it in Eckhart—and is lacking even in such fervent Christians as Kierkegaard, Calvin, and Aquinas. Eloquent confirmation of this may be found in the fact that most Christians would, no doubt, consider it highly inappropriate, if not blasphemous, if one added that these men lack all sense of humor in their relationship to God. Any contrast of Jewish and Christian faith that omitted this point would be incomplete and misleading.

Reinhold Niebuhr has devoted a whole essay to showing "why there is laughter in the vestibule of the temple, the echo of laughter in the temple itself, but only faith and prayer, and no laughter, in the holy of holies." This is the conclusion of his "sermon" on "Humour and Faith"—*Christian* faith. Clearly, he has either never read or does not understand Sholom Aleichem's immortal stories, such as *Tevye, the Dairyman.* For Niebuhr, laughter belongs in "the no-man's land between cynicism and contrition" (121). He knows neither the humor beyond faith nor the humor that informs faith—in the following story from the Talmud, for example; but also in several cited in Sections 64 and 77, and in the Talmudic dictum: "It is taught: if one dies laughing, it is a good sign for him" (Kethuboth 103b). Certainly, this deeply unchristian attitude toward death was not acceptable to all Jews, but the admission of laughter into the temple and the coloring of faith itself by humorous intimacy have been sufficiently prominent in the Jewish tradition to constitute part of the meaning of what is called "Jewish humor."

"Rabbi Kahana sold baskets, and once a housewife propositioned him. He said to her: I shall go to prepare myself. Then he climbed on the roof and jumped. Elijah appeared and caught him, but complained: I had to rush 400 miles for your sake. He replied: If it were not for my poverty, would I have got into this position? Then Elijah gave him a pot full of coins" (Kiddushin 40a).

For the traditional Christian a miracle is something to be believed; for the untraditional Christian it is, for the most part, an embarrassment—because he assumes that belief is essential. Tertullian believes what he considers impossible; Kierkegaard tries to believe what he considers absurd. Paul speaks triumphantly of the *skandalon* and jubilates that he is able to believe what to reason must seem foolishness; Luther exults: "Whoever wants to be a Christian should tear the eyes out of his reason" (V, 425). For the traditional Jew a miracle story is a significant story, and he knows several interpretations of its significance. He feels at ease with it, and his attitude toward the story does not preclude a touch of loving humor.

The story of Rabbi Kahana and Elijah makes no attempt to lampoon or deride miracle stories. Neither, however, is it told by way of demanding belief that the story is true. What we have here is not belief that something is the case nor, in any ordinary sense of the word, trust. Is the story, then, wholly unrelated to faith or piety? Certainly not. It is an illustration of intimacy.

"Faith!—There is none, I almost said. There is only—love. The coercion of the heart to consider this or that true, which is what one usually means by faith, makes no sense. . . . And you, as a Jewess, with so much of the most immediate experience of God, with such ancient awe of God in your blood, should not have to concern yourself with any 'faith' at all. . . .

"I have an indescribable confidence in those nations which came to God *not* by way of faith but who experienced God by means of their innermost national heritage. . . . For the others God is something derivative, something from which away or toward which they strive, essentially as strangers or estranged —and so they need the mediator ever again. . . . The achievement of *these* nations, to be sure, is 'faith': they must overcome and train themselves to consider true what for the God-rooted *is* something true, and therefore their religions slip off so easily onto the moral plane. . . . Religion is something infinitely simple. It is not knowledge, not a content of feeling . . . but . . . a direction of the heart."

The writer? Rilke, in a letter from Muzot, December 28, 1921. As in so many of his letters—and, alas, not only in his letters—there is a lack of complete candor; Rilke is posturing. But, as usual, enough remains to repay close reading. The note of falseness finds expression mainly in the diction, but also in the romantic glorification of that attitude which was more remote for the writer. Surely, this Jewish piety is more problematic than he admits.

Originally, this piety depends on a preintellectual climate of thought and feeling. The prophets could speak without self-consciousness, unembarrassed by questions of meaning. Their religious language was not criticized even by their opponents. All emotions—indignation as well as joy and even doubt and despair—found natural expression in a religious idiom in which "God" figured prominently. The price Israel paid for this was the absence of science and philosophy and, in Biblical times, the underdevelopment of the critical intellect. Indeed, one kind of intellectual conscience never came into being.

Any claim that in the Hebrew Scriptures truth was not valued, or that, while so many other things were expressly prohibited, lying was never forbidden, would be utterly false. The very same central chapter of Leviticus which contains the admonition "thou shalt love thy neighbor as thyself" and the express commandment to love the stranger, too, "as thyself; for ye were strangers in the land of Egypt," also explicitly forbids lying (19.11). The prophets are no less emphatic: one need only look up Micah 6.12, Jeremiah 9.3, Isaiah 59.4, and Zechariah 8.16. In the Psalms, too, this is a central motif; for example, in the 101st Psalm: "Ho who works deceit shall not dwell in my house: he who tells lies shall not tarry in my sight." The Proverbs make the same point again and again: "A righteous man hates lying" (13.5).

"The rabbinical literature of all periods abounds in similar sayings," says George Foot Moore in the second volume of his great work on *Judaism in the First Centuries of the Christian Era* (188), and he documents this judgment with a great many quotations and references, ranging from mottos like "The world stands fast on three things, on justice, on truth, and on peace" to the admonition that one should not promise a child something and not give it to him because that would teach the child falsehood. The school of Shammai even argued that the bride at a wedding must not be eulogized "beautiful and lovely bride" unless she really happens to be beautiful and lovely, seeing that the Torah says (Ex. 23.7): "From lying words stay far."

In spite of this, the Socratic conscience remained undeveloped. Although dishonesty was considered a major vice, one did not analyze the meaning of one's beliefs; and in Biblical times their justification was not made a matter of conscience either, while in post-Biblical times the citation of an appropriate verse from Scripture was considered sufficient justification.

As one came into contact with Hellenism at the time of the Maccabees, foreign beliefs no less than idolatrous practices were proscribed because they were foreign and pagan, and their adoption by a Jew was considered disloyal. At a time when foreign tyrants tried to impose paganism with the sword, it was understandable enough that those who succumbed should have been viewed as quislings. Nor has this situation ever changed completely: Antiochus Epiphanes of Syria was in time followed by Roman emperors and Christian popes, and eventually the Inquisition gave way to Christian anti-Semitism which in turn paved the way for social anti-Semitism.

The intimacy with God which has characterized so much Jewish piety through the centuries is, no doubt, wonderful in many ways; but even the Jews do not have it, Rilke's metaphor notwithstanding, in their blood. The Socratic conscience, once awakened, poses problems for this kind of piety and eventually dates it. When this has happened, one cannot go back to it. The intimacy still remains in the form of a humor which, but for its peculiar flavor, would be blasphemous; but this Jewish humor becomes more and more wistful as it reflects a glory lost forever.

Gershom Scholem concludes his *Major Trends of Jewish Mysticism* with a Hassidic tale which has come down to us in several versions. Buber, in *Die Chassidischen Bücher* (517), relates one of the variants. The tale begins with the founder of the Hassidic movement, the so-called Baal Shem, who died in 1760. As Scholem tells it, the master used to go to a certain place in the woods and light a fire and pray when he was faced with an especially difficult task—and it was done. His successor, the so-called great Maggid, followed his example and went to the same place but said: "The fire we can no longer light, but we can still say the prayer"—and what he asked was done, too. Another generation passed, and Rabbi Moshe Leib of Sassov went into the woods and said: "The fire we can no longer light, the prayer we no longer know; all we know is the place in the woods, and that will have to be enough." And it was enough. In the fourth generation, Rabbi Israel of Rishin stayed at home and said: "The fire we can no longer light, the prayer we no longer know, nor do we know the place. All we can do is tell the story." According to Agnon, the novelist from whom Scholem got the tale, and according to Buber, too, that proved sufficient.

They fail to add what the next generation said: "The fire we cannot light, the prayer we do not know, and the place we do not know. We can still tell the story, but we do not believe it. Indeed, a little research might recover the prayer and determine the place, but we do not think that knowing both would help. We do not think it ever did help. It is a beautiful story, full of significance, but it is only a story." And a yet later generation might add for good measure that the story illustrates the nature of Jewish piety as opposed to Christian piety.

Belief that anything is the case was not required at any point in this tale. But outright disbelief or even any express doubt whether the story is true, and how we can be sure, that does introduce something new and fatal. And once this Socratic doubt has appeared we cannot return to the precritical state of mind without becoming dishonest. We can be nostalgic or admire ourselves in the pose of extolling something which, when we are completely truthful, we cannot admire without reservation; or we can try to become as little children; but in that case we attempt that very "coercion of the heart" to which Rilke sought an alternative. But perhaps another possibility of piety remains?

66. INFIDEL PIETY. While refusing to permit himself the least ambiguity in matters of faith, a man may nevertheless find that some kind of religious language, both in its traditional form as we find it most notably in the Bible—for example, in the 90th Psalm—and in spontaneous outbursts, now blasphemous, now desperate, is emotionally more adequate for him, more of a relief for an overflowing heart, than any other idiom he commands. If he could compose a first-rate poem, that might be still more adequate; but he cannot, and in his present quandary he addresses God. He does not believe anything about God and accepts no dogma of any sort. He does not feel more tolerant of the theologians than before. He turns

to God as one might turn to a Shakespearean outcry or a Negro
spiritual or a walk up a mountain, without belief.

You may ask how this differs from reading *Lear,* or even
seeing and hearing *Lear,* without constantly reminding oneself
that one really does not believe the story. The difference parallels that between reading, seeing, and hearing on the one hand,
and crying on the other.

The dialogue without belief is not a matter of witnessing a
spectacle, however sympathetically. It is an explosion of the
heart, a bursting of its walls, a breakdown of inhibitions. One
does not relax one's honesty; on the contrary, one does not
permit one's beliefs or disbeliefs to get in the way of an honest
expression of one's inmost heart. And if, more rarely, one should
feel addressed, one listens first and asks questions later.

Surely, questions must be asked later on; else one invites
self-deception. We can keep questioning, making absolutely
everything subject to critical reflection, without necessarily
sacrificing our emotional life and becoming intellectual shadows. We need not choose between thinking and feeling. Nor is
it true that those who think most feel least. Men like Plato and
Sophocles, Goethe and Nietzsche, show how the most impassioned thought and emotion can grow together.

There are those who, without belief, find themselves address-
ing and addressed spontaneously, now often, now rarely, and
reflect on these experiences instead of arbitrarily limiting themselves to the more usual forms of sense experience. They are
not trying to use these experiences to bolster up a precon-
ceived system, but simply feel that in all honesty they must
seek to do justice to them.

Paul experienced the Christian faith as an overwhelming
liberation from Jewish piety. Today, when many are smarting
under the oppressive weight of the Christian faith, the very
possibility of an undogmatic piety, unencumbered by beliefs,
may be no less a relief; and this antitheological extension of
Jewish piety may spell liberation for a few.

But did not the Jews always believe that God *exists?* They
did not even have a word for existence. They had a magnificent
story like that of the creation in Genesis 1, and never extracted

from it any such definitive formulation as, for example, that God created the world from nothing, until they came under foreign theological influences in post-Biblical times. They had the story of the Garden of Eden and did not formulate propositions about original sin. Only late, first under Greek philosophic influence (Philo) and then also in response to the challenge of Christianity, they began to define all sorts of beliefs that this or that is the case. Even after the belief in an afterlife had been introduced from outside, one could be a good Jew and accept this belief like the Pharisees, or repudiate it like the Sadducees. Gradually, attempts were made to emulate other religions, and at the same time to define oneself against them, by defining one's beliefs; but owing to the lack of any central authority in such matters, these attempts were none too successful.

Even that God is *one* was originally less a formula that had to be believed than a summary rejection of all polytheistic objectifications of the divine. The one God was the crucial term of a common language, but no effort was made to define God, and the way was left open for a multitude of different ideas. The intolerance of the Old Testament concerned practices rather than beliefs.

This antitheological piety may well have a future. Today the many want theology and Socrates, too. Infidel piety is for the few whose beliefs are not dictated by their emotions and whose emotions are not shriveled by their unbelief. Later, others may fall in with it and make of it what the many have always made of every kind of piety: something that is either superstitious and possibly also fanatical or, more likely in this case, shallow and complacent.

67. LIBERAL PROTESTANTISM AND TRUTH. It was, no doubt, liberal Protestantism that Rilke had in mind when speaking of religions that "slip off so easily onto the moral plane." Why did he consider this a falling off? Obviously, he lamented the loss of what struck him as distinctively religious, the loss of dimen-

sion. In other words, he considered liberal Protestantism shallow and complacent.

Even before Rilke wrote his letter, Protestant theologians had developed the same protest much more elaborately, spearheaded by Karl Barth. Eventually, in the nineteen-thirties, Reinhold Niebuhr took up the same cry and popularized it in the United States. Whether the critics of liberal Protestantism spoke in the accents of Kierkegaard or Marx—or both, as Niebuhr did—the charge was always essentially the same: shallowness and complacency.

It is far from obvious, the early Niebuhr notwithstanding, that the shallowness and complacency of so many liberal Protestants derived from their liberalism. Certainly, one can repudiate orthodoxy, including belief in original sin, without subscribing to any shallow or complacent optimism. (Cf. § 77.)

The religion of the many has generally been shallow and complacent when it was not superstitious and fanatical, and neo-orthodoxy could avoid both pitfalls only as long as it was the protest of the few. Since it has become popular, it has lost the right to its high moral stance. Indeed, by the time Niebuhr took up the cause, radicalism was quite the fashion among secular intellectuals, too; and after World War II, when radicalism went out of fashion, Niebuhr, too, ceased to be radical.

The central shortcoming of liberal Protestantism lies in its attitude toward truth. Even if, unlike Niebuhr, we give it credit for having its heart in the right place, we should press the charge that it shows a radical disregard for history and philology. This is an explosive internal criticism, for liberal Protestants pride themselves on their broad-minded acceptance of the so-called Higher Bible Criticism. Initially, the liberals considered themselves as radical as the neo-orthodox did when they rebelled a generation later; but both rebellions were not half as courageous as they seemed to the leaders: both were in accord with the intellectual fashions of the day which they swallowed uncritically.

The Higher Bible Criticism is open to a host of nonfundamentalist objections (see Chapter X); and the liberals, though genuinely eager to do justice to science, and to history and philology in particular, swallowed a fashionable pseudo-science, compounded of popular Darwinism, gross materialism, a sprinkling of anti-Semitism, and a heavy dose of Christian apologetics.

In the case of the New Testament they ended up, as Reinhold Niebuhr did a generation later (cf. § 68), by reconstructing Jesus in their own image, in flat defiance of the texts and of all historic probability. By a curious twist of logic, this idealized self-portrait with the bold caption "Jesus" convinced the interpreters not only that Jesus was the most wonderful of men and a moral genius but also that their own ethic, seeing that it agreed with his, must be right.

The profound complacency of this approach is independent of whether the interpreter likes the social *status quo* or wants to change it: many of the liberals endorsed social change. What is complacent is the refusal to change *oneself* or even to admit any discrepancy between one's own ethic and that of Jesus. What is complacent is the failure to read the text with an open mind; the predecision that, of course, we are right, and Jesus is right, and we can keep our ethic and our religion, too. What is complacent is the easy assumption that truth is simply what one believes anyway and that autonomous sciences like history and philology must furnish us with a convenient proof of our prejudices.

The major objection to the liberal Protestants' reading of history can be stated briefly. From the days of Jesus' clashes with the Pharisees and Sadducees, his followers have been distinguished by certain beliefs about his person and not by the morality of Harry Emerson Fosdick. About moral and legal questions one could argue, and the rabbis did argue—if anything, too much. There is no evidence that Jesus differed more from them in this regard than they differed from each other. Matthew's comment on the Sermon on the Mount is relevant—and doubly pointed if we recall that scholars agree that no such sermon was ever delivered, and that it was the evangelist who collected Jesus' most striking sayings in this form while they are widely scattered over the Gospel according to Luke. Matthew concludes, "the people were astonished"—and we should certainly expect this after such a collection of the master's most radical dicta; but Matthew continues: "for he taught them as one having authority, and not as the scribes."

Again and again the Gospels bear testimony that it was Jesus' conception of his own person that created the rift; and according to all three of the Synoptic Gospels, the scribes condemned Jesus for what he said about his own person—for blasphemy, not for agreeing with Fosdick.

The Gospels leave no doubt that Jesus had, and communicated to others, a very exalted conception of himself, though he was mysterious about it. According to all three Synoptics, "he charged his disciples that they should tell no man that he was Jesus the Christ," which is, of course, the Messiah. After his crucifixion, his disciples might have remained a Jewish sect, revering the memory of their master while giving up that for which he had been crucified; or, if they wanted to make this the rallying point and cornerstone, they must make the mystery of his person more explicit. This is what Paul did in terms of an elaborate theology, and the author of the Fourth Gospel even went beyond him in fashioning Christianity almost into a mystery religion, complete with sacraments.

If Jesus had taken as light a view of the Jewish laws as liberal Protestantism has alleged, we could hardly account for the fact that the first martyr after the crucifixion, Stephen, was put to death for blasphemy, too—namely, for his utterances about the person of Jesus—and that the disciples at first kept all the laws, and that it was Paul, who had not known Jesus, and not Peter or one of the other disciples, who pressed for the waiving of the Jewish laws, and even that only, to begin with, as far as Gentiles to be converted were concerned.

If liberal Protestantism were historically right, one could hardly escape the conclusion that Jesus' disciples, St. Paul, and the four evangelists betrayed him as soon as he was dead by abandoning the unencumbered purity of his moral teaching and by introducing, successively, miracle stories, fantastic claims about Jesus, dogmas, and sacraments and—even more important—that the Greek Orthodox Church, the Roman Catholic Church, and quite especially also the founders of Protestantism confirmed this betrayal and bettered the instruction. Emphatically, Luther did not depreciate faith in favor of morality. On the contrary, he went far beyond Paul and expressly repudiated Paul's notion that among "faith, hope, and charity" charity is supreme. According to Luther, this is "a Turkish and Jewish error" (I, 948; IV, 2061).

Some liberal Protestants point to the parable of the Good Samaritan (Luke 10) and to the passages on charity in the Fourth Gospel. A brief look at the context is rewarding. Before he tells the parable, Jesus is asked by a "lawyer": "What should I do to inherit eternal life?" He retorts: "What is written in the Torah?" and the lawyer replies: "Thou shalt love the Lord thy God with all thy heart, and with all thy soul, and with all thy strength, and with all thy mind; and thy neighbor as thyself." Jesus is said to have accepted this answer as "right," adding: "This do, and thou shalt live." Nor is there any disagreement after Jesus has told the parable as to who acted right. No doubt, the "lawyer" here presents the teaching of the best of the Pharisees; but the Gospels generally differ decisively from this Jewish view, and the Gospel according to John actually reads like a sustained repudiation of the dictum, "this do, and thou shalt live."

According to John, Jesus said: "Unless one is born of water and the Spirit, he cannot enter the kingdom of God" (3.5). "He who does not believe is condemned already, because he has not believed in the name of the only Son of God" (3.18). "He who does not believe the Son shall not see life, but the wrath of God abides on him" (3.36). "He who does not honor the Son does not honor the Father . . ." (5.23). "This is the work of God, that you believe in him whom he has sent" (6.29). "He who believes in me has eternal life" (6.47). "He who eats me will live because of me" (6.57). It would be tedious to keep adding to these samples from three chapters; one final quotation may suffice: "No one comes to the Father, but by me" (14.6).

Luther said of John "one might even call him alone an evangelist" (cf. § 57), and the other Gospels are certainly less emphatic, but they do not consider the two great commandments from the Torah sufficient either. Matthew speaks for all of them when he reports that Jesus said: "So every one who acknowledges me before men, I also will acknowledge before my Father who is in heaven; but whoever denies me before men, I also will deny before my Father who is in heaven" (10.32 f.; cf. Luke 12.8 f., Mark 8.38).

The sacraments and faith, including belief that various propositions are true, have been definitive of Christianity for over nineteen centuries. Charity has been stressed now and then, but before liberal Protestantism came along in the nineteenth century it would scarcely have occurred to anyone to find the mark of a Christian in charitable behavior. This suggestion is almost incomprehensible to Catholics and Confucianists, Buddhists and Jews, Taoists and fundamentalists, and nothing could have been further from the minds of Luther and Calvin. Until recently, everyone would have agreed that a Christian differs from a non-Christian by what he believes.

This preoccupation with beliefs rather than morals is amply attested by the endless disputes that have punctuated the history of the Christian churches down to Luther's disagreements with his fellow Protestants. The questions that were debated so ferociously were questions of dogma and the truth about the sacraments: it was these questions and not problems relating to love of one's enemies that were considered to be of sufficient importance to warrant schism after schism, each split generally being accompanied by the express conviction on both sides that their opponents were headed straight for eternal damnation, without possibility of reprieve. Not only the conviction but the explicit wish.

To the liberal Protestant it is an embarrassment that at the church councils and among the Reformers, too, fine points of dogma should have been debated with quite as much thoroughness and passion as the rabbis had ever devoted to points of law. The most striking difference only adds to the embarrassment: the Christian disputants lacked that spirit of charity and mutual respect, not to speak of the half-humorous tolerance, which distinguishes most of the Talmud. The Christian documents snort fire and brimstone.

The liberal Protestants feel sure that all this is most un-christian. But by what token can they condemn as unchristian Christianity as it has existed for nineteen centuries? Not only the Crusades and the Inquisition but Christianity's official and normative conception of itself fails to conform to the liberal Protestant view. The liberal Protestant bases his case on the beginnings. He claims that what he calls unchristian is contrary to the spirit of the Gospels and of Jesus. But is it?

To be sure, only the Gospel according to John gives un-equivocal support to those who claim that beliefs about Christ together with the sacraments are absolutely indispensable conditions for salvation. But do any of the other Gospels give half as much support as this to the opposite view, that of liberal Protestantism? The earliest of the four, that according to Mark, portrays Jesus first of all as a miracle man. And not one of the evangelists could be called a liberal Protestant or a Reform Jew, nor could the Jesus of any of the Gospels. Indeed, from the point of view of liberal Protestantism, not only Paul, Augustine, and Aquinas, as well as Luther and Calvin, but even the four evangelists and Jesus himself were deeply unchristian. (Cf. §§ 54–58 for this whole Section.)

Insofar as those who came to hear Jesus were not attracted by reports of miracles, they were men and women who lay awake nights worrying about salvation; and Jesus said that the end was at hand, and he told men what to do to gain salvation and what, conversely, would ensure damnation. According to the Gospels, Jesus did not evince any very great concern about the prospect that the mass of men would suffer everlasting torment: he often spoke of hell with all the accents of vindictiveness, and the rest of the time as a matter of fact. He knew of two ways: one wide and much-traveled, leading to hell, and another, narrower, path by way of which a few might gain salvation.

Those who think that morality was decisive with Jesus him-self and that, according to him, a man's conduct was to decide whether he would go to heaven or to hell are faced with the difficulty that, according to all the Gospels, Jesus was exceed-ingly vague about the conduct required of man. If he thought that those listening to him were headed for everlasting torment, but that some might be saved by following his directions, it remains deeply perplexing that he should have seen fit to give such equivocal directions.

Those disciples who had heard his every word felt much less sure of what was wanted than did Paul, who had never heard him preach, and confronted with Paul's impassioned certainty they were utterly unable to present any clear alternative. Later, Luther and others were able to say in all honesty that they thought Jesus' demands were meant merely to make man aware of his utter inability to do good and to teach man that his only hope lay in faith.

It is odd to find Jesus hailed as a moral genius and the greatest moral teacher of mankind when there is no agreement on his moral teachings, nor even on the question whether he thought that man could aspire to goodness at all. The prophets and the Buddha told parables, too, but their moral teachings were unequivocal and clear.

With Paul, specific beliefs were moved into the center as requirements for salvation: dogma became essential. The reason for the persistent Christian preoccupation with certain specific beliefs was that these beliefs were considered the gate to salvation. Indeed, Paul was so possessed with the hunger for salvation that he projected the same attitude into the Old Testament, as if the old commandments had been justified in terms of a similar concern, when in fact the very idea of a life after death was repudiated except in the very latest portions of the Old Testament where, though alluded to, it plays no important part.

Once salvation is moved into the center, the question of the alternative to salvation becomes important. It is generally bypassed in Jewish literature, where the rabbis speak of a share in the world to come. Even after the conception of a future life was accepted, charity prevailed and provided for God's blessings without at the same time creating a site of eternal torment. (Cf. § 55.)

It was otherwise in Christianity, and the difference was presumably due in part to Jesus' own preaching. He seems to have promised heaven and threatened hell, but his disciples evidently were not very clear in their own minds after his death what was essential to escape hell. Paul and John gave clear answers to that question: Christ came to save men, and those who believe various propositions about him, trust in him, and take the sacraments will be saved. The rest of mankind and all those who deviate from the essential dogma, all heretics and schismatics, will go to hell and everlasting torment. Hence the refrain of the church councils: "Let him be anathema!"

While the crucial question for modern Judaism is what remains of the Jewish religion if the traditional Halachah is abandoned (cf. § 64), the most crucial religious problem for the contemporary Christian is: What does it mean to be a Christian if one does not accept the traditional beliefs?

If one considers the traditional beliefs either false or meaningless or at best poetic, one dissociates oneself from historical Christianity as it has developed through the centuries and considers all the great Christians of the past, emphatically including the early Protestants, deeply deluded. Conceivably, a new religious movement might find a reason in spite of that for calling itself Christian, even Protestant. But liberal Protestantism has not brought off this feat, and the reason for its failure is not that it has been liberal rather than orthodox.

Liberal Protestantism has based its right on calling itself Christian, in spite of its repudiation of traditional Christianity, on its assumed continuity with the Gospels and with Jesus. It has condemned traditional Christianity as untruthful and has prided itself on its truthfulness and its refusal to be unscientific. But its crucial claim of its own continuity with the Gospels and with Jesus depends on a profound disregard for truthfulness and on reasoning which is quite as contemptuous of impartial scholarship as earlier Christians were of astronomy and biology.

In spirit, liberal Protestantism is dedicated to the truth and to truthfulness—and Christians generally have been—but at the very point where liberal Protestantism claims to be Christian, and to differ from other liberals who are not Christian, it overrides its own devotion to truth.

68. REINHOLD NIEBUHR AND TRUTH. This central failure of liberal Protestantism is shared by Reinhold Niebuhr, America's most vocal critic of liberal Protestantism—and that even in an early work in which Niebuhr's denunciation of all forms of liberalism, and particularly of liberal Protestantism, furnishes his point of departure. There is no need for a detailed analysis of the chapter on "The Ethic of Jesus" in Niebuhr's *An Interpretation of Christian Ethics;* we can confine ourselves to a single point which Niebuhr puts as follows:

"If there are any doubts about the predominant vertical religious reference of Jesus' ethic they ought to be completely laid by a consideration of his attitude on the ethical problem of rewards. Here the full rigorism and the non-prudential character of Jesus' ethic are completely revealed" (55). These are strong statements with their emphatic and repeated "completely"; but the Gospel texts give quite a different picture, and Satan has already cited some of them (§ 58, p. 240).

Niebuhr is not unaware of the many verses which seem to contradict his contention, which he reiterates many times with only slight variations, and soon he concedes: "It must be admitted that this rigor is seemingly qualified by certain promises of reward." This is an understatement reminiscent of some of Bultmann's similar concessions. Niebuhr goes on: "These rewards belong in two categories. The one is ultimate rewards 'in the resurrection of the just.' The other is probably a concession to a prudential morality" (56). What, then, remains of the complete revelation of "the full rigorism and the non-prudential character of Jesus' ethic"?

Another page later, Niebuhr tries to tone down his concessions: "Possibly Jesus thought of all these rewards only in eschatological terms. He may have meant to say only . . ." This is a far cry from the promise that all doubts "ought to be completely laid." But let us suppose Niebuhr's conjectures were correct and these rewards were meant "only" eschatologically: the fact remains that Jesus based his ethic on rewards and that his ethic was prudential. If you think that "the kingdom of God is at hand," any concern with noneschatological rewards becomes imprudent. And if you think that heavenly rewards are everlasting while earthly rewards are corrupted by moth and rust, any concern with rewards in this world would be thoroughly imprudent. Jesus' ethic, in short, was an ethic of prudence.

This conclusion is utterly unpalatable to most Protestant theologians. To their minds "prudence" is a word of reproach. And yet Guenther Bornkamm, a German professor of theology at Heidelberg who is close to Bultmann, has to admit in his monograph on *Der Lohngedanke im Neuen Testament:* "the New Testament does not know the idea of the good deed that has its value in itself" (8). *Lohn* can mean both reward and wages, and Bornkamm finds comfort in an anti-Catholic polemic which insists that the New Testament thinks in terms of a reward which the master freely gives to his slaves who have no right whatever to claim any wages, seeing that they are literally slaves whose bodies belong to their master. To an American audience this analogy is hardly helpful, and Niebuhr does not use it to soften the blow.

The crucial point is that Jesus' ethic, as presented to us in the Gospels, is based on a constantly reiterated appeal to the hope for reward. He preaches to those who want to enter the kingdom of heaven, and he tells them what they must do.

How, then, does Niebuhr proceed after his own admissions have completely undermined his initial claims? "All these promises of an ultimate reward are in no way in conflict with the rigor of the gospel ethic. They merely prove that even the most uncompromising ethical system must base its moral imperative in an order of reality and not merely in possibility" (57 f.). Even if we discount the untenable word "prove," are we to conclude that a consistently nonprudential ethic is impossible, and that any ethic which promises no rewards in this life must of necessity emphasize the certainty of rewards in the afterlife? Are genuine sacrifices impossible? If this is what Niebuhr claims by way of defending what he takes to be "the ethic of Jesus," he is certainly mistaken both logically and historically.

In view of the efforts of so many Protestant theologians to read an anti-prudential rigorism into the Gospels and to contrast this with the allegedly prudential ethic of the Pharisees, it should be noted that even if they were right about the Pharisees, the Sadducees did not believe in any afterlife or resurrection of the dead. Moreover, long before Jesus' time, Antigonus of Socho taught, according to Avoth, which is the most popular chapter in the Mishnah: "Do not be like servants who serve their master with the intention of receiving a gift, but be like servants who serve their master without any intention of receiving a gift; only the reverence of heaven be over you."

The prophets, too, did not base their moral demands on any promise of rewards. The individual was to subordinate his own desires to the will of God in order to help realize a society in which love and justice would prevail. The individual was promised no reward whatever.

It is therefore exceedingly odd for Niebuhr to begin his discussion with the claim that "The ethic of Jesus is the perfect fruit of prophetic religion" (43). In at least two respects the ethic of Jesus is the outright antithesis of prophetic religion: the prophets envisaged a social goal, including love and the abolition of war, while Jesus' ethic is asocial, if not antisocial; and the ethic of the prophets was not prudential while the ethic of Jesus is prudential. In both respects Niebuhr agrees with the prophets and disagrees with Jesus, but tries to persuade himself and us in the best manner of liberal Protestantism that what he himself feels strongly Jesus must, of course, have felt, too.

This disregard for the historical evidence and this deep-seated Protestant conviction that strong conviction is the best guarantee of truth finds its most astonishing expression when Niebuhr comes to argue that "The note of apocalyptic urgency is significantly lacking in many of the passages in which the religio-ethical rigor is most uncompromising" (58). This strange claim—even if this note were lacking in "many" of these passages but present in many others, this would hardly be very "significant"—is supported by a footnote which lists six references, which is hardly "many"; and these six are not quoted.

The first refers us to Matthew 5.29, which threatens "that your whole body be cast into hell," while the parallel verse in

Mark, which is not cited by Niebuhr, also refers specifically to the alternative that "it is better for you to enter the kingdom of God with one eye." (Cf. § 55.) Niebuhr's second reference takes us to Matthew 6.20: "But lay up for yourselves treasures in heaven, where neither moth nor rust corrupt, and where thieves do not break in and steal." The third reference is to Matthew 6.31; here the promise of reward comes two verses later in 6.33. The next two references are less striking but also prudential, while the final one refers us to Luke 18.22, which Satan cites to the theologian—a verse which is the very antithesis of the religion of the prophets.

This is surely strange support for an attempt to demonstrate "the full rigorism and the non prudential character of Jesus' ethic." No less than Kierkegaard in his comments on Socrates' attitude toward the immortality of the soul, in his *Concluding Unscientific Postscript* (180), Niebuhr defies the discipline of scholarship and rewrites history in accordance with the requirements of his own inwardness.

Kierkegaard's formula for this approach, "truth is subjectivity" (*ibid.*, 169–224), has been criticized in a previous section (35): it would be far less misleading to say that truth is sacrificed to strong conviction, and that Niebuhr, no less than most liberal Protestants, feels free to argue, in effect: this is my ethic; I feel deeply and strongly about it; therefore it must have been the ethic of Jesus. (Cf. §§ 55–58.)

The Protestant principle of the sovereignty of conscience leads to havoc in scholarship no less than in society. An *undisciplined* conscience is no safe guide, as Luther soon discovered when he was confronted with all kinds of doctrines and practices which he considered quite outrageous and which most of his modern critics, who condemn him for retracting his earlier principle, could not have condoned either. Murder cannot be tolerated when it is committed with a good conscience; neither should self-projection be condoned when it poses as history. A good conscience is a great help in sleeping soundly, but it is no substitute for laws. Neither can strong conviction justify defiance of the facts that parades as scholarship.

In the Niebuhr volume in The Library of Living Theology,

Niebuhr has said that he does "not claim to be a theologian,"
and that his primary concern is with ethics and apologetics
(3); and Paul Ramsey has pointed out that Niebuhr's apologetic strategy is to demolish the opposition (83). Daniel Williams has gone a step further and shown in some detail how
Niebuhr generally deals "with the point of view he is criticizing by using its most exaggerated, and sometimes even its most
fatuous, expressions to represent the entire position" (195 f.)
and how he employs his strategy in his critique of liberalism.
By dealing in some detail with Tillich, Bultmann, and Niebuhr,
as well as St. Thomas and Luther, the present critique of theology should avoid any similar charge. But the question remains
whether Niebuhr's treatment of Jesus, although scarcely unimportant or peripheral, is nevertheless uncharacteristic.

The essay on "The Ethic of Jesus" is not uncharacteristic of
Niebuhr though it represents an extreme example of his procedure. E. A. Burtt has furnished other examples to substantiate his charge that the value of Niebuhr's work is seriously
impaired by his lack of any "thoroughgoing respect for fact"
(356). In particular, he has protested againt "Niebuhr's frequent use of the phrase 'the Biblical view' or 'the Christian
view' when comparing a doctrine in which he believes with
positions he holds to be false. This use of language cannot help
making him appear to be indulging in an unconscious deception of himself and his readers" (357). Indeed, Niebuhr does
not hesitate "to reject doctrines clearly taught in the Bible as
'un-Biblical'" (358). In a similar vein, Gustave Weigel, S.J.,
says: "What puzzles the Catholic is how such a doctrine can be
proposed as the genuine Christian message. It is obviously a
frank negation of the clearly expressed beliefs of Christians for
centuries" (370 f.).

An obvious answer would be: of course, I gerrymander
(cf. § 56); I pick and choose from the Bible what seems right
to me and perhaps even read into it occasionally what is not
there; and I reject much that Christians have believed for centuries; but I nevertheless call my message true Christianity
because it agrees on all essentials with the Reformers. But
Niebuhr is wonderfully forthright in his devastating criticisms

of Luther and Calvin and even accepts the terrible indictment of both which his brother, H. Richard Niebuhr, has presented in his fascinating book on *The Social Sources of Denominationalism.* We must conclude: objectively, Niebuhr has no right to call his view "the Christian view," as he constantly does, or to call his ethic "The Ethic of Jesus." Again and again he exhibits the same shortcomings which we have found in liberal Protestantism (§ 67) and in theology generally (§§ 55–58). Subjectivity overrides objectivity, and passion, truth.

This is plain even in the few pages that he has devoted to "The Problem of Truth" in the second volume of his main work, *The Nature and Destiny of Man.* These pages profess to be "dialectical," and Arthur Murphy has published a sharp attack on this dialectic. But the whole dialectic of these pages depends on a spurious "paradox" which Niebuhr formulates: "The truth, as it is contained in the Christian revelation, includes the recognition that it is neither possible for man to know the truth fully nor to avoid the error of pretending that he does." The first insight certainly requires no revelation, while the second point, on which the "paradox" depends, is, like so many of Kierkegaard's false generalizations, a piece of gratuitous self-projection. Men as diverse as the Buddha and Socrates (neither of whom is ever mentioned in *The Nature and Destiny of Man*) or Hume and Hesse show, as does every agnostic, by definition, that it is quite possible for man to avoid this error. (Cf. §§ 5–10, 25, 37.)

Niebuhr goes on to say: "it is also possible to carry this insight into our interested thoughts and actions so that it creates some sense of pity and forgiveness for those who contend against our truth and oppose our action." Those who have avoided the error which Niebuhr considers unavoidable may be barred by their humility from following Niebuhr to those heights from which alone such condescension is possible. On the other hand, when Niebuhr concludes that "Mercy to the foe is possible only to those who know themselves to be sinners" (217), he overlooks the objective truth that mercy to the foe can also be prompted by decency, pride, or vanity.

Examples may be found in Mozart's *Entführung aus dem Serail* and Goethe's *Iphigenie*.

On the following page Niebuhr says: "Sin is the refusal to admit finiteness." Now there *is* a paradox, albeit not in any technical sense of that word. If this conception of sin were accepted, some agnostics would have to be judged free of sin! (Cf. Freud's comment on man's sense of his finiteness, cited in § 33.)

The oddity of Niebuhr's conception of sin is no small matter, seeing that his insistence on man's sinfulness is at the heart of his difference with liberalism and altogether central in his work and thought. Elsewhere, however, he uses the word "sin" differently. Gustave Weigel has aptly summarized Niebuhr's strategy: "He points to the undisputed fact that every human action is the action of a self. This truth is restated in the truism that every action of man is selfish, which from then on is understood in a non-truistic sense" (374).

So much for Niebuhr. Although he is occasionally hailed as America's greatest thinker, his apologetics will surely prove to be ephemeral, and unlike Harnack and Schleiermacher (cf. § 57) he has not made a mark as a scholar. What inspires and merits the highest regard and admiration is his unflagging and impassioned concern with the rectification of social evils. But there is, to put it gently, no logical connection between this and his neo-orthodox Paulinism. (Cf. § 55.) On the contrary, his apologetics has involved him in endless errors, contradictions, and injustices. The primary concern of the great religions is not with mundane truths; and when Christian apologists have forgotten this, the result has generally been deplorable —not only in the natural sciences.

The romantic notion that truth is beauty has been succeeded by the no less sentimental superstition that a good heart is the best warrant of truth. (Cf. § 40.) But it was one of the greatest insights of the founders of the American republic that untrue religious beliefs need not prevent men of good will from working together for the common good.

The question remains whether Niebuhr's essay on "The Ethic of Jesus" is utterly out of line with the procedure of other Christians. It is not. In the case of the Talmudic rabbis it is obvious to us today that their concern with truth and their mode of scholarship differed substantially from those now accepted in a secular context. In the case of Protestant discussions of Jesus, the same point does not meet the eye: Fosdick is a case in point no less than Niebuhr, and so is Pierre Van Paassen with his socialist Jesus. These men project their own ethic onto Jesus and are never at a loss to contrive an erudite rationalization: subjectivity overrides objectivity; conviction comes first and scholarship second, as the handmaiden of faith.

The rabbis had their own rules of argument, but these Protestant writers do not. They persuade themselves and others that they are following the usual rules of scholarship when in fact they defy impartial scholarship. Unconsciously and involuntarily they evince an enmity to reason and its rules which has been prominent in Christianity from the beginning.

69. A PLATONIC ERROR, REASON, AND CHRISTIANITY. It is in Christianity more than in any other religion that conflicts with nonreligious truths have been encountered again and again. It is customary to think of Copernicus, Galileo, and Darwin in this connection, and perhaps also of Freud; and conflicts with history and philology have just been considered. But no summary of this kind could possibly get to the heart of the anti-intellectual tradition in Christianity. At its center we find the Christian inversion of a fateful Platonic error.

When Plato distinguished knowledge and belief, he made the grave mistake of assuming that belief is completely undisciplined and permits of no criteria at all. Or, if criteria for judging beliefs should be *possible,* Plato at the very least deemed any question concerning them beneath consideration. Since he correlated knowledge with eternal objects, such as his "Forms" and mathematical objects, and belief with the world of sense experience, his influence helped to delay the development of the natural sciences: any disciplined study of the changing objects of sense experience was ruled out.

In philosophic questions, too, Plato sometimes reached the

point where certain knowledge was not available; and in such cases—most notably in the *Timaeus*—he sometimes introduced myths, explaining that this was the best that could be done under the circumstances. Many readers consider these myths oases in the desert of philosophy and are in no mood to question their propriety. But the dichotomy of knowledge and myth is unsound. As Aristotle already pointed out, different degrees of certainty are appropriate to different kinds of inquiry. From the plain fact that mathematical certainty is not obtainable in other fields it does not follow that all we may legitimately ask for are myths.

This, however, is precisely what Plato comes close to suggesting sometimes. Whether his myths are ancient or inspirations of the moment, or perhaps poetic conceptions for which he is happy to find a place in his dialogues, they are never examined critically. He readily grants that they cannot be proved to be true, but there is no discussion of favorable and unfavorable evidence and no careful consideration of rival myths, but only awed or charmed assent.

In some contexts—for example, in the cathedral scene in Kafka's *Trial*—myths are surely unobjectionable. The charge against Plato's myths concerns not the myths themselves, which are usually of great beauty, but their relation to reason and observation. They tend to take the place of the latter and are offered even where observation is available up to a point. If myths were used to sum up the most likely theory, there might be no rational objection; but Plato's myths are not always so coldly calculated: they are sometimes wonderful poetic inspirations that do not wait for reason to inform them. They tend to supplant empirical evidence and rational inquiry.

Possibly because he realizes that his myths are unforgettable and stay in the mind long after arguments have been forgotten, Plato permits himself excessive liberties in argumentation, and the Socratic impulse to question everything is slowly paralyzed. Against Plato's arguments for his two-world theory in the *Republic* there is much that could be said; but his magnificent myth of the cave tends to reduce all possible objections to the level of pedestrian trivialities that are not worthy of mention: once this myth is told, you *see* the two worlds.

It does not follow that philosophers must espouse drabness. But in a philosopher a strong poetic impulse represents a danger and heightens responsibility. In Plato the poetic gift was more highly developed than in any other great philosopher, saving only Nietzsche; and in the work of both myth came to encroach on evidence and reason in a fateful manner. (Cf. the chapter on "Philosophy versus Poetry" in my *From Shakespeare to Existentialism.*)

Plato's error was magnified by the Christian transvaluation of Plato. Plato had valued knowledge far above belief and myth, and had insisted that knowledge was available in regard to most of the questions that mattered most. His failure to examine myths critically was consistent with his high regard for reason; we can almost imagine him saying: what is not capable of being known rationally is somewhat childish, and in such matters we have no right to expect more than fairy tales.

Christianity reversed Plato's estimation of knowledge. Reason came to be considered impotent in all that mattered most and was exiled from the regions which, as Plato saw it, belonged to reason by birthright. These regions were handed over to what Paul, at the beginning of his First Epistle to the Corinthians, calls, over and over again, "foolishness." The modern Christian is tempted to discount Paul's triumphant glorification of foolishness and his scorn of "the wisdom of the wise" and "the wisdom of the world." But when Paul said disparagingly that "the Greeks seek after wisdom" and when he boasted that his own teaching was "to the Greeks foolishness," his transvaluation of wisdom and reason made history.

Luther went to even greater extremes in his denunciation of that "whore" reason, and one could compile a little anthology of the pretty compliments he paid her.

"The devil's bride, *ratio*, the beautiful whore, comes in and thinks she is clever" (XII, 1530). "Stay at home with your ugly devil's bride and do not elevate and praise her so much, but think and speak thus of her: Lady Reason does not fear God, does not love him, does not trust in him, but freely and without all embarrassment despises him and has no care of all his threats and promises; moreover, his word and will give her no pleasure and she does not love them but grumbles and mumbles, rages and blusters against them, especially when things go badly. In sum, she is God's worst enemy. Romans 8.8" (VIII, 2048). "There is on earth among all dangers no more dangerous thing than a richly endowed and adroit reason, especially if she enters into spiritual matters which concern the soul and God. For it is more possible to teach an ass to read than to blind such a reason and lead it right; for reason must be deluded, blinded, and destroyed" (V, 1312).

"Whether reason considers the doctrine of the holy Trinity foolishness, what do we care about that? It requires no great art to argue cleverly about such matters: I could do that as well as others; but, thank God, I have the grace of not desiring to dispute much here. . . . Thus every Christian should do, too, in all the articles of our holy faith: one should not argue and dispute much about it whether it is also possible, but solely see to it and ask whether it be the word of God" (XII, 859).

"Behold, this is what St. Paul in his epistles wants to show Christians: that these high and divine matters, which means both his divine being and also his will, his government and work, are altogether above all men's thoughts, understanding, wisdom, and in brief, for the whole of human reason incomprehensible, unfathomable, and completely concealed, and must remain that way, and that all is in vain and mere darkness and lies that reason might dare and try to inquire and teach and say about it" (XII, 838).

"Christ says: Take, eat; this is my body; Drink ye all of it; this is my blood. No, no, they say; it is not his body and blood; for Christ sits on the right side of God. They would judge the word according to their reason. Fie on you! That is like teaching hens to lay eggs, and teaching cows how to calve, trying to teach our Lord God how to preach. Would we like it so well if our servants and maids behaved like this towards us" (XIII, 1688)?

This is not the soft-spoken Luther of the motion picture sponsored by the Lutheran churches of America—a fastidious democrat who would have bitten his tongue off before indulging in the earthy profanities which Martin Luther relished. But the real Luther was no boor either: the power of his prose and the spontaneous authority of his images are almost without equal among Christian writers and invite comparison with Shakespeare and the prophets.

Never was intellectual honesty attacked with such impassioned and relentless honesty. Is this attack less honest than the dialectical praise which some modern theologians lavish on reason and intellectual honesty? The man who made the Reformation did not want to eat his cake and have it, too. He spoke with the elemental power of a cataclysm. But what he said, not only about reason, is as frightening as it is magnificent. Indeed, more frightening.

"Faith must trample under foot all reason, sense, and understanding, and whatever it sees it must put out of sight, and wish to know nothing but the word of God" (III, 215). "Here we learn to blind reason when we reach the point where faith begins, and we give her a vacation" (XI, 1850). "I have often said and wish powerfully that we might sever these two realms: the word and reason. For reason, however beautiful and glorious she may be, belongs nevertheless only in the realm of this world: there she has her dominion and regions. But in the realm of Christ, there God's word alone is supreme" (III, 1321).

For Luther there are two worlds as there were for Plato; and Luther, like Plato, disparages this world in favor of a supersensible world to which the soul belongs. But for Plato this higher world was the world of reason, and for Aristotle, too, man's dignity depended on his capacity for rational inquiry and philosophic discourse. Luther banishes reason from the supersensible world and links it contemptuously with "the wisdom of this world."

Luther's formulations are, of course, extreme. Others, notably including Thomas, have spoken in more conciliatory accents, insisting on the continuity of Christianity and philoso-

phy. But the cry of triumph voiced by Paul and Luther calls
attention to a transvaluation of Plato which, once noted, is
apparent in other traditional Christians, too.

Thus Aquinas writes in his *Summa Theologica* (II–II, Question 2, Article 4): "Human reason is very deficient in things
concerning God. A sign of this is that philosophers, in their
inquiry into human affairs by natural investigation, have fallen
into many errors, and have disagreed among themselves. And
consequently, in order that men might have knowledge of God,
free of doubt and uncertainty, it was necessary for divine
truths to be delivered to them by way of faith, being told to
them, as it were, by God Himself who cannot lie." St. Thomas
adds specifically (Article 10) that one "ought to believe matters of faith, not because of human reasoning, but because of
the divine authority." To be sure, "when a man has a will
ready to believe, he loves the truth he believes, he thinks out
and takes to heart whatever reasons he can find in support
thereof."

Here, too, Plato is turned around: reason cannot give certainty; certainty can be had only by way of belief and submission to authority. But instead of emphasizing like Luther
that reason is apt to produce reasons against this authority,
St. Thomas emphasizes that reason can be employed to think
up reasons in support of what the church teaches authoritatively.

"The reasons which are brought forward in support of the
authority of faith are not demonstrations which can bring intellectual vision to the human intellect. . . . But they remove
obstacles to faith. . . ." What, then, is the status of reasons
brought forward against the authority of faith? "Whatever is
in opposition to faith, whether it consists in a man's thoughts,
or in outward persecution, increases the merit of faith in so
far as the will is shown to be more prompt and firm in believing. . . . The wise have greater merit of faith, through
not renouncing their faith because of the reasons brought forward by philosophers or heretics in opposition to faith." In
sum, reason can be used both to contest and to defend faith,
and in neither case yields certainty. Certainty can be had only

by way of "the authority of faith"; and those who use their reason to think up arguments in support of this authority, and thus try to neutralize the objections mustered by the opposition, accumulate merit. Those, on the other hand, who use their reason to produce objections against faith must be "exterminated from the world by death." (Cf. § 45.)

What sounds strange in Paul and Luther is the jubilant candor of men who did not feel constrained to worship reason, evidence, and intellectual integrity as well as Christ. What is disturbing in Aquinas is his calm determination to use reason "in support of the authority of faith," thinking out "whatever reasons he can find in support thereof," while threatening with death and damnation all who follow reason in any other direction. Reason is toppled from the heights where Plato had enthroned it and confronted with the choice of slavery or death.

In conjunction with sense experience, reason enjoys a limited freedom as long as it does not presume to deal with anything of genuine importance. In its long struggle with science, Christianity has yielded position after position with the claim that it did not matter because the truly vital realms were as safe as ever. For the traditional Christian, whether Catholic, Protestant, or Orthodox, this has been and still is nothing less than a criterion: whatever reason and observation can deal with is not of ultimate importance.

Today many Christians consider morality vitally important and close to the core of their religion and therefore oppose rational discussion of moral questions as well as appeals to observation. Most Christian ideas about sexual ethics are certainly not based on the wisdom of this world, and would have seemed "to the Greeks foolishness." Rational examination is only opposed that much more. To be sure, reason and observation alone cannot settle moral problems; but this does not establish their irrelevance. To suppose that where reason cannot dictate it is powerless, is to fall back into the fallacious dichotomy of Plato.

The spurious dichotomy of mathematical certainty and myth is the gate to barbarism. Reason cannot dictate a way of life to us: should we therefore abandon our way of life and our most vital decisions to myths?

In one way, morality will soon go the way of astronomy, physics, and biology: to be sure, it will not become a science; but Christians, too, will soon concede the need for rational discussion of moral questions as well as the relevance of observation—and then Christianity will adopt the position that morality is not of ultimate significance. Today, some Christians may still object: if morality is not of ultimate significance, what is? But it is far from self-evident that rules about permissible and impermissible sexual relations should be more crucial for religion than whether the earth revolves around the sun or whether man is a cousin of the gorilla.

Reason and observation alone will never tell us what to do and how to live; whom, if anybody, we should marry; or how many, if any, children we should want. But it does not follow that religion must answer these questions. Nor does it minimize the crucial difference between informed and uninformed decisions or between responsible and irresponsible choices.

Christianity has been right in insisting on the limitations of reason and observation; but it has vastly exaggerated them while failing to recognize its own limitations: again and again it has claimed competence in areas where it had none. And from the very beginning it has conceived itself as an enemy of reason and worldly wisdom; it has exerted itself to impede the development of reason, belittled the achievements of reason, and gloated over the setbacks of reason.

In principle, many outstanding Roman Catholic thinkers have maintained that reason and religion need not be enemies but could be complementary. But the peace effected by Roman Catholicism was based on the enslavement of reason, upon its employment in the service of propositions which it was not allowed to question. The vaunted synthesis of reason and faith depended on the stake. When the stake lost its tyrannical effectiveness, the revolt of reason and the long war between reason and faith came to dominate the intellectual history of the West for centuries.

Traditional Christianity has been deeply authoritarian in

matters of truth. It has made a supreme virtue of unquestioning docility. Though Luther was initially opposed to authoritarianism, his truculent disparagement of reason drove him back into this tradition; for he soon discovered that where conscience and conviction are supreme no safeguard remains against fanaticism, stupidity, and immorality. Many a modern Protestant has looked upon the later Luther with embarrassment, thinking: "What a falling off was there!" But it was not caprice that led to Lutheran authoritarianism: the issue on which Luther had staked his Reformation had been unsound. The dichotomy between authoritarianism and the anarchy of the supremacy of conscience is pernicious. But what alternative remains where reason and observation are ruled out of court?

70. CHRISTIANITY AND TRUTH. In Christianity, as in no other major religion, faith is central, and this includes belief that certain propositions are true. These propositions and belief in their truth are considered far more important than any result of rational inquiry. Presumably because the articles of the Christian faith do not stand up well under rational investigation, reason has been declared, again and again, incompetent to judge that which must be believed. Traditionally, Christianity has been suspicious of reason; and except at times when reason was safely enslaved by faith and rendered harmless by the potent threat of certain persecution of all heresies, reason was denounced.

The liberal Protestants have allayed the fears of reason by paying generous tributes to it and by insisting that Christianity is singularly rational and reasonable. Liberal Protestantism has made a prophetic Reform Jew out of Jesus, a great liberal and Idealistic philosopher of Paul, and a mild-mannered, modest, reasonable man of Luther, who is portrayed as a champion of freedom and democracy against the superstitions and corruptions of the Church of Rome. In sum, liberal Protestantism has courted reason by rewriting history in defiance of reason and evidence.

The ultimate concern of Christianity has never been with truth in any ordinary sense of that word. On the contrary, Christianity has come into conflict with truth from the days of Paul to the days of Fosdick and Niebuhr. The ultimate concern of Christianity has been with Jesus Christ—and those who accept Jesus' saying according to John (14.6) "I am the way, the truth, and the life: no man comes to the Father, but by me" may, of course, claim that their ultimate concern *is* with the truth; but in that case they must accept a doctrine of double truth and depreciate the truths of this world for the greater glory of Jesus Christ. Involuntarily, the liberal Protestants, too, have done this.

The men of the Enlightenment and their philosophic progenies have tried to show how many of the supposed truths of Christianity were superstitious; but in holding them up to ridicule, the critics have sometimes made themselves ridiculous by assuming all too smugly that their discoveries were new and that everybody before them had been either crafty or tricked. Like the iconoclasts of the Reformation, they rashly assumed that all images were merely manifestations of superstition. For thousands who had idolized these images, they had been precisely that; but for hosts of intelligent people they had been wonderful creations of the human spirit, part of an atmosphere that lifts the mind above its everyday concerns. The images in the old cathedrals can be revered as works of art; and the dogmas, too, can be revered as poetry.

The view that the dogmas of Christianity are poetry is irreconcilably at odds with the position taken by Paul and Augustine, by the church councils and Aquinas, by Luther and Calvin. Nor do the liberal Protestants consider their moralistic Jesus a poetic fiction. As soon as we view the dogmas and scriptures of various religions as more or less magnificent works of the human imagination—some with a historical kernel, like *Richard II;* others with little or no basis in historic fact, like *King Lear*—we refuse to take seriously the rival truth claims of different religions and agree to contemplate all these religions more or less on the same plane. There is no longer any reason in that case why our admiration for one need entail a lack of admiration for another: we may be catholic in our tastes and profoundly moved by many.

The three religions we have considered—even Buddhism—would protest any such approach. Before we consider the question how religious scriptures should be read, we should therefore ask what any such view of religion leaves out of account. What is the core of religion?

IX. THE CORE OF RELIGION

71. CLAIMS FOR MYSTICISM. Many writers find the core of religion in mysticism. This provides an experiential basis for religion and an excuse for the conflicts between religion and common sense, faith and reason. Religion, it is said, represents an attempt to do justice to a singular kind of experience which is ignored by common sense and by the sciences: at the very least, religion supplements the partial world views that are based on sense and reason; and some writers even claim that the world of sense and reason is a phantom while mysticism affords us a glimpse of ultimate reality.

It would follow that there are two kinds of religion: the genuine religion of the mystics, and the secondhand religion of the rest of mankind. The mystics are said to have experienced something to which religious scriptures, dogmas, rites, and propositions try to give form, however inadequately. The mystic himself does not need these aids: they are for the rest of us who must, alas, get our religion secondhand.

Some think that all the mystics agree on essentials, which is, on the face of it, patently false; but the term can be defined so narrowly that it insures uniformity: those who do not agree are not called real mystics. Even to the extent to which there is agreement, there is doubt about its significance. Against those who assume that, if the mystics agree, they must be right, Bertrand Russell has argued in an essay on "Mysticism": "From a scientific point of view we can make no dis-

tinction between the man who eats little and sees heaven and
the man who drinks much and sees snakes. Each is in an abnormal physical condition, and therefore has abnormal perceptions."

In a similar vein, Santayana has repeatedly called mysticism
"a religious disease." Although Santayana and Russell, usually
poles apart, are in partial agreement on this point, their view
is decidedly a minority view. Catholics think of some mystics
as saints, while most Protestants are thrilled by the individ-
ualism of so many mystics. Those who are not religious often
feel that for the mystic it is reasonable to be religious because
he is after all a kind of empiricist.

There is more agreement among authors who have written
on the subject that mysticism is admirable than there is about
what precisely it is. In 1899, Dean Inge selected for critical
discussion twenty-six definitions of mysticism, and since then
many further suggestions have been made. The difficulty here
is not merely one of definition, on the same plane with the
problem of defining religion or philosophy. In the latter case,
we might agree that Plato, Aristotle, Descartes, Hume, Hegel,
and Mill have all been notable philosophers, but we might
be perplexed if asked to state briefly what they had in common. It is similar with religion, where we can agree that
Buddhism, Christianity, Judaism, Hinduism, and Islam, for
example, are religions. In both cases, there are borderline phenomena, but we have no doubt about the chief representatives.
In the case of mysticism it will not do to speak of Elijah and
the prophets, or of Jesus and St. Paul, as borderline phenomena; but according to some writers they were mystics, and according to others, not. There is no agreement what is meant
by mysticism. There are a few clear-cut cases, like Meister
Eckhart and Plotinus; and many more, from the Buddha to
Buber, who present a problem.

72. INEFFABILITY. In his chapter on "Mysticism" in *The
Varieties of Religious Experience*, William James proposed
"four marks which, when an experience has them, may justify

us in calling it mystical." These four criteria were: ineffability, noetic quality, transiency, and passivity. After briefly discussing each, James reiterated: "These four characteristics are sufficient to mark out a group of states of consciousness peculiar enough to deserve a special name." Yet the last three criteria afford us no grounds whatever for distinguishing the mystic experience: sense experiences also yield knowledge, do not last, and find us receptive rather than active. It would seem therefore that it must be ineffability that sets apart mystic experiences.

In his emphasis on ineffability, James is far from alone. On the basis of many assertions in this vein by mystics themselves, other writers have stressed this point, too; most emphatically, perhaps, Walter Stace in his attempt to show that mysticism is the core of all religion. This claim of a unique ineffability deserves closer scrutiny.

The first objection that comes to mind is that so many mystics have been downright garrulous. A sympathetic immersion in the texts, however, suggests that their effusions often issued from dissatisfaction with any single statement they could make.

The second objection is that this criterion might exclude the major figures of the Bible from Moses to St. Paul: they did not take refuge in any claim of ineffability, and their own statements apparently struck them as adequate and clear. This objection may be answered by saying that these men were indeed no mystics.

The third objection is more detailed and involves some analysis of the assertion that the mystic experience is distinguished by its ineffability. What is supposed to be ineffable? Is it the experience or its object? Let us begin by supposing that it is the *experience*.

There are two aspects of an experience that might well lead a person to call it ineffable: first, direct acquaintance; secondly, emotion. Suppose you have long known a description or even a picture of the temple of Poseidon at Paestum in southern Italy; and then you see the temple for the first time. This experience might well be ineffable in a sense. What

you can say about the temple after this experience might be
nothing new at all. What you now describe, you could have
described before, too. But the difference between reading a
description or even seeing a picture and seeing the temple itself may be overwhelming. If it is, the second element comes
into play, too: you have an emotional experience; and emotional experiences are extremely difficult to describe. (Cf. §§
28 ff. and 63.)

James cites many analogous examples from the mystics.
Saint Ignatius Loyola suddenly understood "the deep mystery
of the holy Trinity" without being able to say anything about
it that he could not have said before. But according to a life of
the saint which James quotes, "This last vision flooded his
heart with such sweetness, that the mere memory of it in
after times made him shed abundant tears" (401). In a similar vein, James cites Santa Teresa: "On another day, she relates, while she was reciting the Athanasian Creed—'Our Lord
made me comprehend in what way it is that one God can be
in three persons. He made me see it so clearly that I remained
as extremely surprised as I was comforted, . . . and now,
when I think of the holy Trinity, or hear It spoken of, I understand how the three adorable persons form only one God
and I experience an unspeakable happiness.' On still another
occasion, it was given to Saint Teresa to see and understand
in what wise the Mother of God had been assumed into her
place in Heaven" (403).

Pratt is surely right: "the mystics are by no means always
unable to communicate the truths which they have intuitively
perceived during their ecstasy, although it must be noted that
the 'revealed' truths which they can communicate are always
old truths which they knew (though in a much less living
form) before" (410). And two pages later Pratt adds: "Possibly *all* the mystical 'revelations' may be accounted for as
being first carried into the ecstasy by the mystic, and derived
originally from social education, and all except this sense of
presence may possibly be mere conclusions which the mystic
comes to after reflecting upon his experience by a process of
ordinary discursive thought; a number of mystics will be found

to admit this. . . ." Later on, Pratt cites Coe's critique of
James in which this point is briefly epitomized: "The mystic
brings his theological beliefs to the mystical experience; he
does not derive them from it" (450). And elsewhere Pratt
himself argues that "The visions of the mystics are determined
in content by their belief, and are due to the dream imagination working upon the mass of theological material which fills
the mind" (403). A fundamentally similar view was developed by J. H. Leuba, who was much less sympathetic toward
mysticism than Pratt.

Both the element of acquaintance and that of emotion are
present in all of our experiences, and neither is entirely ineffable. The element of acquaintance can be communicated,
and usually is, simply by the statement that we saw something, or heard, or smelled, or felt something with our own
eyes, ears, nose, or body. The element of emotion is generally
communicated by means of an approximate label: I was
thrilled, excited, disappointed, desperate, or possibly dum-
founded. To achieve greater precision requires art. If utterly
unimaginative declaratory sentences could do full justice to all
our nonmystic experiences, there would be no need for poetry
and painting, for the subtle prose of Joyce and Faulkner, or
for music. But these problems have already been discussed
at length in Chapter III.

The frequent claim in discussions of mysticism that language is adapted only to the realm of subject-object experiences, while the mystical experience transcends this realm
uniquely, overlooks that even the simplest subject-object experience involves an element of acquaintance which is not
fully describable. The claim further ignores emotional experience.

All experience has a trans-scientific dimension which it
takes art to communicate. The inadequacy of ordinary propositions to the mystic's experience does not set his experience
apart. Some mystics are unpoetic souls who require special
exercises and an eventual trance to see anything but the everyday world.

The mystic's insistence on the unique ineffability of his experience may prove no more than that he has never known any other intense experience. He may even have gone into a monastery to make sure of that.

Now it may be claimed that the mystic differs from other men by having a kind of second sight which enables him to perceive an ineffable *object*. Where the mystic himself claims something of this sort, we must consider three possibilities.

First, his experience may actually have no object at all; it may be intransitive like the experience of hunger, bliss, despair, or ecstasy. If we realize that we are hungry and that some food would allay our discomfort, we are not likely to be very puzzled by our experience or to think of it as ineffable, though, if we concentrated on what we actually feel, we should find that it was exceedingly hard to describe. But if we are hungry, as occasionally happens, without realizing that we are hungry, we are quite apt to consider our experience ineffable. It is similar with homesickness when a child does not diagnose its own condition. It cannot rightly say what it feels. Words fail the child: it must depend on the intuitive understanding of a person who has had the same experience and knows how it feels.

Bliss, despair, and ecstasy present fundamentally the same picture. They are all ineffable in a sense but amenable to an imaginative attempt at communication. When we know what prompted the experience, we are less apt to emphasize its ineffability; when we feel elated or dreadfully depressed without quite understanding our own condition, we are more apt to stress the inadequacy of words.

Secondly, it is possible that an experience has a definite object which *is* describable, and that it is only the element of acquaintance or the emotional aspect which all but defies description. In that case, my description will sound like the descriptions I used to read; it will miss what I had always missed —and what my audience will miss until and unless they have the experience themselves. As in all of the preceding cases, there is no essential difference between mystic and nonmystic experience.

Thirdly, let us imagine a case in which a person desires to

have a particular experience of which he has some preconception. He may, for example, crave a vision of the Virgin Mary. He may go into seclusion, forgo sleep, fast, practice austerities, pray and meditate, and hope for his vision all the time. When the moment of his vision comes, we should hardly expect him to see Shiva in his glory, dancing. Lutherans do not usually see the Virgin Mary, and Catholics do not see Martin Luther, unless it were in hell. On the nonreligious level, a man who desires passionately to evoke the vivid picture of a loved one who is either dead or distant will usually find, if he succeeds, that the image conforms, at least in important respects, to the image he expected.

Now, if a man desires the experience of an ineffable object, whether Brahma or the One or God, then any experience that is not ineffable will be ruled out as not yet the ultimate experience. If, on the other hand, the man has an experience which is in important respects indescribable, he will be inclined to insist that it was ineffable even if it belonged in one of the categories considered above. If he was determined all along to experience something timeless and eternal, he will construe his oblivion of time during his experience as an indication that he has experienced something timeless. If he wished for the experience of the One, he will take the absence of plurality in his experience for a proof that its object was the One.

One such tradition of ineffability has been considered at length in the section on "Zen Buddhism and truth" (63). Here the ineffability of experience is stressed from generation unto generation, and any attempt to describe it is, to put it mildly, discouraged from the outset. Yet the Zen Buddhist admits that *all* experience has a trans-scientific dimension; and on this he concentrates. Those modern writers who insist that the religious experience differs from the so-called aesthetic experience posit a distinction which the great mystics would have failed to understand.

Many modern writers banish religion to some special province of experience. But the concept of religion is lacking in the great religions to begin with: it appears only as religion becomes problematic.

If those who decided what books to include in the Hebrew canon had accepted the modern distinction between the religious and the aesthetic, or if they had assumed, as so many writers do today, that the religious experience is *sui generis*, they would not only have omitted the Song of Songs—which later exerted a greater influence on Christian mysticism than any other book of the Bible—but more than half of the Scriptures. And if the early Christians or the Reformers had accepted these false modern ideas, they would have thrown out of the Bible most of the Old Testament.

Some people think that the Old Testament *is* a medley of religious books, secular history, love songs, laws, and all kinds of things that have little or nothing to do with religion. But all of it has a great deal to do with religion and actually *was* religion not only for the ancient Hebrews but also for millions of Jews and Christians down to our time.

Defenders of religion who, never having had a mystical experience, would identify religion with the experience of the great mystics would save it by placing it in protective custody: in a reservation, museum, or grave.

The eulogists of mysticism may reply that some of the mystics have emphatically insisted that the mystical experience is ineffable in a way in which no other experience is ineffable; and that any attempt to assimilate mysticism to other experiences disregards this testimony. To this a threefold answer may be made.

First: for every mystic who insisted on the apartness of the mystical experience one could probably cite two who did not.

Second: mysticism is a name for a vast variety of phenomena. William James follows a personal preference in concentrating disproportionately on eccentrics and downright crackpots. Meister Eckhart presents a very different picture; and the serene sages of the Upanishads have little in common with Santa Teresa.

Third: mysticism, though encountered in all religions, is not encountered in all religions at all times; it is a historical phenomenon which belongs to a particular stage in the development of a religion. This last point deserves special emphasis and needs to be developed further.

73. MYSTICISM AS A HISTORICAL PHENOMENON.   If the plea of ineffability is considered a definitive criterion of mysticism, the religion of the Old Testament was nonmystical, and prophetic religion represents a powerful alternative to mysticism. By the same token, there would be little mysticism in the New Testament. The prime example of mysticism would have to be found in the Upanishads. The Buddha, on the other hand, would have to be considered the leader of an anti-mystic movement. In the West, the great age of mysticism would have to be found in the late Middle Ages, carrying over into the seventeenth century. In short, mysticism that claims ineffability is a phenomenon confined to rationalistic ages, and its plea is meant as a defense against rationalistic attacks or as a protest against theology, or both.

The Hebrew prophets were not subjected to critical questioning about the nature of their experience; the sages of the Upanishads were. Upanishads means something like "seminars"; and the typical situation is that a teacher answers the questions of a student. The plea of ineffability is a last resort. The student asks whether the experience was like this? Like this? Like this? He always misunderstands. The situation invites comparison with an older brother telling his younger brother that he has fallen in love for the first time. What is it like?—I am all excited.—Oh, the way one feels during an examination?—No, very happy.—Oh, the way one feels at the circus.—Not at all; I am upset and do not feel like eating.—Oh, I had an upset stomach once not long ago.—Not like that; and I can't sleep at night either.—Oh, you have insomnia like Uncle Wilbur.—No, no, no; I could sing all the time, but when I see her I suddenly can't get out a word.—Oh, like Aunt Prudence the night when she had stage fright and suddenly could not sing.—No, not this, not that.

This is the schema of many an interrogation in the Upanishads. An older man tries to describe an experience to a younger man who has not had the experience and who keeps asking bright questions which are overliteral and show no imaginative understanding whatsoever until the teacher finally exclaims *"neti! neti!"* Not this, not that.

What is decisive is not that the experience is mystical but that it is subjected to persistent unsympathetic questions. Where that condition is met, the concluding line can always be: not this! not that! And the modern writer concludes: the experience is clearly ineffable.

In the late Middle Ages, systematic questioning was the order of the day. The man who wanted to make a point of his religious experience could not speak the language of the prophets; he spoke that of the mystics.

The mystic feels that the theologian's descriptions miss the crucial element of acquaintance which in many cases did not come to the mystic easily but only as the result of much effort. Also, the theologian's intellectualism misses the element of emotion which means so much to the mystic. And so he insists that what matters most is left out: it is ineffable.

The Buddha's experience of enlightenment was no less ineffable than that of the sages of the Upanishads; but since he was protesting against their esoteric coterie and wished to emphasize four truths that could be rather baldly stated, he did not stress the ineffability of his experience. Amos' experience of God's call had its ineffable aspect, but he was more concerned to state unequivocally what he thought of the morals of his contemporaries than to be coy about his experience.

The plea of ineffability, far from being proof of singular profundity, is a plea of impotence, if it is not a polemic as in Zen. The poet who can communicate his experience need not plead that it is indescribable; that is the poor poet's excuse. Shakespeare finds words where lesser poets would not.

The claim of ineffability expresses a negation—sometimes of one's own power to communicate; sometimes of the questioner's power to understand; and sometimes of the profundity of theology. The claim is essentially critical and belongs to critical ages.

To say it once more: great art and philosophy begin on the other side of ineffability.

74. CRITERIA OF MYSTICAL EXPERIENCE. We have found William James' set of four criteria utterly inadequate: what sets apart mystical experiences is not that they are, unlike other experiences, ineffable, noetic, transient, and passive. Other similar attempts are little better; and many are a great deal worse.

Evelyn Underhill, for example, in one of the best-known studies of *Mysticism,* offers an effusive tribute rather than objective criteria when she stipulates five points in Chapter IV, following up each with a little paean. In the original, all five sentences are italicized. "(1) Mysticism is practical, not theoretical. . . . (2) Mysticism is an entirely spiritual activity. . . . (3) The business and method of Mysticism is Love. . . . (4) Mysticism entails a definite Psychological Experience. . . . (5) True Mysticism is never self-seeking."

These suggestions came out of years of study which issued in other books, too, and they have some evocative power; but they do not offer adequate criteria. In fact, Miss Underhill seems to imply that the experience itself has no distinctive criteria and can be judged to have been an instance of "True Mysticism" only in the light of its fruits: mysticism—that appears to be the implication—is a psychological experience which affects a person's life and leads him to engage in "entirely spiritual activity" which is marked by the prominence of "love" and the absence of "self-seeking." The emphasis on love excludes the sages of the Upanishads and the Zen Buddhists. Nor did Miss Underhill realize that her five points fit the Hebrew prophets rather better than many of the most-renowned mystics, for example, Plotinus. Clearly, she was thinking of certain Christian mystics whom she admired especially.

Miss Underhill was perhaps the best-known English writer on mysticism. Her American counterpart was Rufus Jones. He defined mysticism as "the type of religion which puts the emphasis on immediate awareness of relation with God, on direct and intimate consciousness of the Divine Presence" (xv). But this definition would restrict mysticism to theistic religions, which is hardly reasonable. Again, the Zen Buddhists would be left out.

What James and Jones and Underhill, among others, overlook is this: what sets apart the mystic experience is not anything given, but the interpretation and evaluation which the person who has the experience accords to it. And this interpretation need not be theistic.

To be considered mystical, an experience must, first, be considered different from everyday perception. It stands out, it is uncommon, it marks a break in the everyday world. James' four criteria take no note of this. It may seem to be a highly elusive criterion, but it is not. Two men may have two very similar experiences: if one of them feels that it was part of the everyday world and really not at all extraordinary, he rules out the suggestion that it might have been a mystical experience; while the other man, if he feels that it was an uncommon experience, leaves open the possibility that it might have been mystical.

The second criterion is that the experience is considered much more important than our everyday perceptions. If a man says that while crossing the street and being narrowly missed by a car he had an uncommon experience, but that he attaches no importance to it, then he is implying that it was not a mystical experience.

The third criterion is that the person who has the experience finds no objective correlative for it in nature. The conception of the objective correlative was popularized by T. S. Eliot, who took the idea—and not only this idea—from Santayana's *Interpretations of Poetry and Religion* (277); and Eliot's use of it was anything but propitious. He argued that Shakespeare's *Hamlet* "is most certainly an artistic failure" and then tried to back up this extraordinary judgment by finding "the grounds of *Hamlet's* failure" in the lack of an objective correlative. It will be best to quote Eliot's own explanation of his term from "Hamlet and His Problems" (1919): "The only way of expressing emotion in the form of art is by finding an 'objective correlative'; in other words, a set of objects, a situation, a chain of events which shall be the formula of that *particular* emotion; such that when the external facts, which must terminate in sensory experience, are given, the emotion is immediately evoked." To give an example, Eliot claims that "the words of Macbeth on hearing of his wife's death strike us as if, given the sequence of events, these words were automatically released by the last event in the series. The artistic 'inevitability' lies in this complete adequacy of the external to the emotion; and this is precisely what is deficient in *Hamlet*. Hamlet (the man) is dominated by an emotion which is inexpressible, because it is in excess of the facts as they appear."

A short critique of Eliot will provide a helpful perspective for our third criterion of the mystical experience. In the first place, there is a very important sense in which Hamlet's emotions are fully warranted by the facts. His father, whom he worshiped, has been murdered. If Hamlet's feelings toward his father were deeply ambivalent, this would complicate his emotion and make it harder for him to express it. His mother, whom he loves, has remarried almost immediately—a man whom Hamlet loathes, and of whom he suddenly hears that he was the murderer. Moreover, his murdered father was king, he himself is the heir, and his loathsome uncle is now the head of the state: even without going into Hamlet's relation to Ophelia, it should be clear that Hamlet's emotions are *not* "in excess of the facts as they appear." And yet there is a sense in which they *are:* a less sensitive person would feel less emotion even under such extraordinary provocation; it is only in conjunction with Hamlet's sensibility that the objective correlative is adequate for his emotions.

It is a commonplace that Hamlet is highly sensitive; and highly sensitive people, by definition, feel emotions which are, if one insists on putting it that way, "in excess of the facts"—from the point of view of less sensitive people. The average person would not have broken out into the words of Macbeth either, even if he had heard of his wife's death under the very same circumstances; and one might with more justice question the unity of Shakespeare's conception of Macbeth—even though Eliot considers *Macbeth* one "of Shakespeare's more successful tragedies"—than the emotion of Hamlet. (Cf. § 87.)

There is, in sum, no objective correlation of fact and emotion in such a way that one could say generally that certain facts warrant a certain amount of emotion, unless we include among the facts of the case the sensibility of the person who has the experience. If we apply this result to experiences which may or may not be mystical, it appears that a highly emotional experience in a situation in which most men would not feel nearly so much emotion does not establish the absence of an objective correlative: if the person who has the experience is extremely high-strung and excitable and has possibly even worked himself into a state of hypersensitivity by fasting, going without sleep, and praying fervently, then there is an objective correlative even for an enormous amount of emotion. Our criterion, however, is that the person who *has* the experience finds no objective correlative for it in nature; that he himself feels that his experience is in excess of what is warranted by the naturalistic facts. If he does find an objective correlative for it in nature, then he rules out the suggestion that it might be a mystical experience.

The fourth criterion is that the person who has the experience finds the objective correlative either beyond nature or in nature as a whole, as opposed to any conjunction of things *in* nature. Which of these two alternatives he embraces and what name he gives to the objective correlative will generally depend on the religious tradition in which he stands. The man of the Upanishads will speak of Brahma; the Taoist of the Tao; some Buddhists of Nirvana; some Christians of God, others of the Trinity, and still others of the Virgin; and some who stand outside all denominations may speak of nature or the cosmos.

These four criteria are meant to be taken in conjunction: where all four are satisfied we are confronted with what is usually called a mystical experience. It does not at all follow from all this that mystical experiences must be particularly hard to explain: the Society for Psychical Research keeps records of experiences which few, if any, would call mystical, but which are far harder to explain in terms of modern science than most of the experiences of the great mystics. (Cf. § 39.)

If the fourth criterion were qualified further to demand that the person who had the experience must feel afterward that he was altogether one with the non-naturalistic objective correlative we mentioned—if, in short, we should restrict mysticism to experiences of a so-called *unio mystica*—we should exclude altogether too much that is generally included in discussions of mysticism. "Numerous mystics, Jews as well as non-Jews, have by no means represented the essence of their ecstatic experience, the tremendous uprush and soaring of the soul to its highest plane, as a union with God." Scholem (5) has shown this in considerable detail as far as Jewish mysticism is concerned; but there can be no doubt that he is right about non-Jewish mystics, too.

Mystical experiences are by no means all the same, and the differences are not reducible to the interpretations which the mystics offer afterward. The experiences themselves are molded by the personality and the prior beliefs and expectations of the mystic. Suzuki does not have the same experience as Santa Teresa.

In one way, however, the mystic experience might well be narrowed down further. There is an experience which might be called mystical in accordance with the four criteria offered but which in fact we generally do not call mystical and which I should prefer to distinguish from the mystical experience. The Hebrew prophets are among the most outstanding representatives of this other type of experience and one might therefore call it prophetic. Against this term one may urge at least three objections.

First, it is apt to suggest falsely that the experience usually issues in some forecast of the future. Secondly, it may be better not to associate this experience primarily with the prophets. Else, the question arises immediately whether all the prophets had essentially the same experience. Perhaps the experiences of Amos and most of the earlier prophets, but also the Second Isaiah, were very different from those of Ezekiel, Zechariah, and other visionaries. Also, some might feel that the Hebrew prophets represent a unique phenomenon rather than a typical experience. Therefore, a more neutral term seems preferable. Thirdly, Friedrich Heiler has contrasted mysticism and prophetic religion along somewhat different lines in his book on *Prayer* (Chapter VI ff.), and use of the same terms for a similar contrast might lead to confusion. Let us therefore call the other type an experience of inspiration.

75. THE EXPERIENCE OF INSPIRATION. In his letters from Muzot (114), Rilke offered a brief description of his experience in writing the *Duino Elegies* and the *Sonnets to Orpheus* and spoke of "a nameless gale (a hurricane in the mind)." But the most detailed account of such an inspiration which is not given a religious interpretation is found in Nietzsche's *Ecce Homo,* in the chapter on "Zarathustra."

"Has anyone at the end of the nineteenth century a clear idea of what poets of strong ages have called *inspiration?* If not, I will describe it.—If one had the slightest residue of superstition left in one's system, one could hardly reject altogether the idea that one is merely incarnation, merely mouthpiece, merely a medium of overpowering forces. The concept of revelation—in the sense that suddenly, with indescribable certainty and subtlety, something becomes *visible,* audible, something that shakes one to the last depths and throws one down—that merely describes the facts. One hears, one does not seek; one accepts, one does not ask who gives; like lightning, a thought flashes up, with necessity, without hesitation regarding its form—I never had any choice. . . . Everything happens involuntarily in the highest degree but as in a gale of a feeling of freedom, of absoluteness, of power, of divinity.— The involuntariness of image and metaphor is strangest of all; one no longer has any notion of what is an image or a metaphor: everything offers itself as the nearest, most obvious, simplest expression. . . . This is *my* experience of inspiration."

This experience is not half as rare as Nietzsche thought it was: many an adolescent writing poetry has surely had much the same experience. It may have a different coloring when it is storm and stress and when it is romantic; but in large strokes it is the same experience. Is there any doubt that a religious person having such an experience would interpret it religiously? Or that, if such a person lived in a religious age and confronted his contemporaries with his "revelations," he would often be hailed as a prophet?

76. MYSTICISM, INSPIRATION, AND RELIGION.   What sets apart the mystical experience is in part what the man who has it thinks of it. And he will generally give his experience a religious interpretation, or even have his experience in religious terms, only when he stands in a religious tradition. *The mystical experience is not the core of religion but a phenomenon in the history of religion.*

Inspirational experiences, too, can be given a nonreligious interpretation by the person who has the experience, depending on his prior outlook. But while the mystical experience is frequently mild and impersonal and at least superficially at odds with the traditional anthropomorphism of popular religion, the inspirational experience is typically violent and suggests to the person having it that he encounters a being not altogether unlike himself, only more powerful. It is therefore likely that this type of experience had more to do with the origin of the major religions than the mystical experience. This thesis would have to be tested by careful historical research, but an initial probability in its favor may be established by reference to the Hebrew Scriptures and to the Vedic literature, both of which are inspirational rather than mystical.

The major religious teachers of mankind have had experiences which more or less approximated one or the other of these two types; but millions of religious people have never had any experience which closely approximated either type. So we may conclude that mystical and inspirational experiences have played a central role in all of the major religions and sacred scriptures of mankind, but these two types of experience cannot be said to be the core of religion; rather they constitute two central phenomena in religion. There are others as well.

77. CONTRA FROMM: RELIGION AND TRAGEDY. In his stimulating book on *Psychoanalysis and Religion*, Erich Fromm offers a very different contrast between two "types of religious experience": the distinction which he considers "the most important" is "that between *authoritarian* and *humanistic* religions." This contrast is rooted in Fromm's earlier work and introduced with almost four pages of straight quotations from his own *Man for Himself*.

Fromm maintains that his contrast allows a significant modification of Freud's critique of religion: there are two kinds of both psychoanalysis and religion, and the good kind of psychoanalysis is compatible with humanistic religion, though not with authoritarian religion. The incompatibility with authoritarian religion, of course, Freud would have granted: Fromm's thesis depends on whether there really are humanistic religions which are compatible with psychoanalysis. If there are not, and if authoritarianism is present in all religions, we should find another central factor of religion and advance our analysis of the core of religion.

Fromm's contrast is illuminating but untenable. "The essential element in authoritarian religion and in the authoritarian religious experience is the surrender to a power transcending man. The main virtue of this type of religion is obedience, its cardinal sin is disobedience" (35). Fromm finds what he considers a splendid example in Calvin and then proceeds: "Authoritarian secular religion follows the same principle. Here the Führer . . . becomes the object of worship" (36). The suspicion that Fromm is treating us to a black-white contrast is confirmed immediately: "Humanistic religion, on the contrary, is centered around man and his strength. Man must develop his power of reason. . . . The prevailing mood is that of joy, while the prevailing mood in authoritarian religion is that of sorrow and of guilt. . . . Illustrations of humanistic religions are early Buddhism, Taoism, the teachings of Isaiah, Jesus, Socrates, Spinoza, certain trends in the Jewish and Christian religions (particularly mysticism), the religion of Reason of the French Revolution" (37).

These examples are highly questionable. Did Lao-tze, Isaiah —in Fromm's subsequent enumerations "the Prophets" take the place of Isaiah—and Jesus and the mystics insist that man must develop his reason? And is the prevailing mood of early Buddhism, the prophets, and Jesus really one of joy? Nor can we follow Fromm when he writes: "The human reality, for instance, underlying the teachings of Buddha, Isaiah, Christ, Socrates, or Spinoza is essentially the same. It is determined by the striving for love, truth, and justice" (63). (The following sentence again lumps Calvin with the totalitarians.) Are Fromm's humanists concerned with "love, truth, and justice" in the same sense, or are they "for" these things in the same way in which all politicians are against sin?

Their attitudes toward truth have been considered in the last chapter. Are Isaiah and the Buddha concerned with "love" in the same sense—and with "justice"? Is there not an important sense in which the Buddha was *not* concerned with justice and preached *against* love? (Cf. § 92.) Nor is "the human reality" underlying the teachings of the Buddha and the prophets and of Christ and Socrates the same: they represent four very different visions of what man might and should be. Neither Christ nor Isaiah ever conceived of rational inquiry as a way of life; and the Buddha, too, would have felt that Socrates had given insufficient attention to "the one thing needful" while distracting people with frivolous dialectic. And what might Socrates have asked Isaiah or Jesus? Surely, he would have been more conscious than Fromm of their authoritarianism.

At first, many a reader may merely feel that Fromm has cleverly spirited Jesus and the prophets across the border into his own camp—a brilliant feat which assures his victory over Luther, Calvin, and Catholicism, who suddenly find themselves alone with Hitler and Stalin, deserted by their own leaders. This debater's triumph is not based on any argument but on bald assertion: "That early Christianity is humanistic and not authoritarian is evident from the spirit and text of all Jesus' teachings" (48). This claim is certainly preposterous. Not only the Gospel according to John, which after all is an important document of "early Christianity," is full of authoritarianism, but the other three Gospels are, too. The Sermon on the Mount ends: "And it came to pass, when Jesus had ended these sayings, the people were astonished at his doctrine: For he taught them as one having authority, and not as the scribes." The same characterization would be applicable to most of Jesus' teaching. And this impression is greatly reinforced by the pervasive emphasis on miracles which are clearly meant to establish Jesus' authority. The Jesus of all four Gospels stresses obedience and not the development of reason, and he relies on dire threats rather than arguments.

What is wrong with Fromm's dichotomy is not merely that he assigns to the humanistic camp a few well-selected authoritarians: he also encumbers his contrast with another dichotomy which neither logically nor historically coincides with it. With authoritarianism Fromm seeks to link not only an emphasis on obedience but also a lack of concern for love and justice which he considers essentially humanistic. As a matter of historic fact, however, the emphasis on love and justice—both words taken in Fromm's sense—found its classical expression in the prophets, who did not tell man to "develop his power of reason" but rather demanded obedience to God.

Nothing could be more antiauthoritarian than the wonderful story which Fromm tells of the Buddha and the hare (38 ff.). The hare, sleeping under a mango tree, was suddenly awakened by a loud noise and in his fright supposed that the world must be coming to an end. He tried to run away and, asked by the other hares why he was running, told them that the world was coming to an end. Soon all the animals were in a wild stampede. As they passed the Buddha, he, too, asked why they were running and was told, like everybody else before him, that the world was coming to an end; but he did not start running. Rather he asked his informants *why* they supposed that the world was coming to an end. Each animal referred him to the authority of another, but the Buddha was not content till he had traced the chain all the way back to the hare who had started it all. The Buddha asked him why *he* thought that the world was coming to an end, and when the hare told him of the great noise, the Buddha asked him where he had been at the time, ventured the hypothesis that perhaps he had been startled by the noise of a mango fruit hitting the ground; and then the Buddha retraced the steps back to the mango tree and verified his hypothesis by finding a big fruit on the ground a foot from the place where the hare had slept.

The contrast with the Gospels speaks for itself, though Fromm ignores it. This story is antiauthoritarian and, in a sense, humanistic. But does it entail any great concern with love and justice? Amos was much more authoritarian than the Buddha but also much more concerned with love and justice. And to deny Luther and the Catholic Church all concern with love merely because they are authoritarian involves a plain logical and historical error.

Are there really any completely nonauthoritarian religions? If, of Fromm's initial list, only Socrates, Spinoza, and the thinkers of the French enlightenment remain, the answer would be: No. Freud would not have been surprised if Fromm had told him that these men were less vulnerable to his strictures than traditional Christianity and Judaism. Let us then consider some of the remaining examples of supposedly nonauthoritarian religion.

First, there is "early Buddhism." There are stories like the one about the hare which are through and through nonauthoritarian. Perhaps the Buddha himself was, too, though he established monastic orders. But there is no evidence that early Buddhism was completely nonauthoritarian; rather there is some evidence that as soon as it was institutionalized it became somewhat authoritarian.

About early Buddhism little is known; but Fromm also adduces Zen Buddhism. This is perhaps as nonauthoritarian as any religion has ever been. It repudiates dogma and insists that every man must find his own enlightenment—but certainly not by developing "his power of reason." Zen Buddhism evolved in monasteries with a rigid line of command, and the stories reported in a previous section (63) show how the relationship of master and pupil was anything but nonauthoritarian. There is still a great difference between the spirit of Zen Buddhism and the spirit of Calvin or Catholicism; but for all that Zen Buddhism is certainly not completely nonauthoritarian.

Similarly, there is unquestionably a strongly antiauthoritarian element in Judaism, and one of its finest expressions may be found in the glorious story of Rabbi Eliezer which Fromm relates (45 ff.). According to the Talmud (Baba Mezia 59b), Rabbi Eliezer disagreed with some other rabbis about a point of law and, unable to convince them, said, "If the law is as I think it is, then this tree shall let us know." Immediately the tree jumped a hundred yards, but the other rabbis said: "One does not prove anything from a tree." Rabbi Eliezer then appealed to a brook, which immediately began to flow upstream, but his colleagues replied: "One does not prove anything from a brook." Rabbi Eliezer said: "If the law is as I think, then the walls of this house will tell." And the walls began to fall. Rabbi Joshua reprimanded the walls: "If scholars argue a point of law, what business have you to fall?" Then the walls stopped midway: to show their respect for Rabbi Joshua, they did not fall further; and in deference to Rabbi Eliezer they did not straighten up. Then Rabbi Eliezer appealed to heaven, and a voice said: "What have you against Rabbi Eliezer? The law is as he says." Rabbi Joshua, however, replied: "It is written in the Bible [Deut. 30.12]: It is not in heaven. What does this mean? Rabbi Jirmijahu said: The Torah has been given on Mount Sinai, so we no longer pay attention to voices, for on Mount Sinai already thou hast written into the Torah to decide according to the majority." Some time after this dispute, Rabbi Nathan met Elijah, the prophet, and asked him what the Holy One, blessed be His Name, had done in that hour. And Elijah replied: "God smiled and said: My children have won against me, my children have won."

Although these rabbis lived a generation later, this story illuminates the Pharisees' attitude toward Jesus rather better than most books on that subject. It also brings out some striking differences between traditional Jewish and Christian piety and illustrates the sense of intimacy and the pervasive sense of humor which have characterized so much of Judaism. God is the father as in Christianity, but a father with a sense of humor.

For all that, the story does not point to a completely antiauthoritarian attitude. No appeal to miracles is tolerated, and decisions must be based on arguments—but these arguments must be based on citations and interpretations of an absolutely authoritative text, and no critical questions about the text are allowed any more than an appeal to other books or independent observation. (Cf. § 64.)

In this story the rabbis were arguing about what was, and what was not, "clean"; and they subordinated their lives as well as the lives of other Jews to the ritual laws of the Torah. Fromm's book provides a welcome antidote against the popular notion that the Talmudic rabbis could not have been humane because they were authoritarian; but he assumes that, having been humane, they could not have been authoritarian.

The remainder of the story, which Fromm omits, is worth quoting, too: "It is related that on that day the rabbis brought together everything that Rabbi Eliezer had pronounced clean and burned it in a fire. Then they voted on him and placed him under the ban. Then they asked: Who will go and tell him? Rabbi Akiba said: I will go; else an unsuitable person might go and tell him, and then he would destroy the whole world. What did Rabbi Akiba do? He put on black clothes and shrouded himself in black; then he sat down four yards away from him. Rabbi Eliezer asked him: Akiba, why so different today? He replied to him: Master, it seems to me that our colleagues have withdrawn from you. Then Rabbi Eliezer, too, tore his clothes and took off his shoes and sat down on the ground, and tears fell from his eyes. Then the world was struck one third in olives, one third in wheat, one third in barley. It is said: There was great woe that day, for every spot toward which Rabbi Eliezer directed his eyes was burned." In the end "he rose to his feet"—it is not entirely clear whether Eliezer is meant or Akiba—"and said: Lord of the world, to you it is evident and known that I have not done this for my honor nor for the honor of my father's house, but for thy honor, that quarrels shall not grow in Israel. Then the sea ceased to rage."

There is a profound humanity even in this part of the story: one has a sense of compassion rather than vindictiveness. This impression is supported by what we are told of Rabbi Eliezer's death, many years later. "When Rabbi Eliezer got sick, Akiba and his companions went to see him." And on the day of his death, some of the other rabbis asked him about the ritual purity or impurity of various objects. He died, saying, "pure." And when he died, Rabbi Joshua rose and said: "The ban is lifted." Akiba was not present at that time, but when he learned of Eliezer's death, he exclaimed, as Elisha had done when Elijah went up into heaven: "My father, my father, the chariot of Israel and the horsemen thereof" (Sanhedrin 68a). Later on, when some other rabbis argued against one of Eliezer's dicta, none other than Rabbi Joshua said to them: "One does not refute the lion after his death" (Gittin 83a). And according to the Talmud of Jerusalem, "So long as Eliezer lived, Joshua's decision was followed; but when Eliezer died, Joshua insisted that his opponent's views be accepted" (Niddah 1.3, 49a).

These men were not intimidated by miracles and did what they considered right after searching their hearts; but of free and untrammeled inquiry outside the framework of the Torah, there was no thought. In a previous section (64), I compared Akiba with Socrates, but also noted the striking differences between the two men. Socrates might well have accepted Akiba's maxim: "Not he who answers quickly is worthy of praise, but he who can support his views" (Finkelstein, 175). But Akiba's ideas about legitimate support for a statement were worlds apart from Socrates' methods and unquestionably

authoritarian. Like his colleagues, Akiba looked for support
in Scripture; and his habit of basing his case, if need be, on
the repetition of a word or on a single letter occasionally made
him the butt of his friends' jokes.

It has been argued that "the rules which he derives through
his curious and intricate logic are so reasonable that when we
examine them we are even more impressed with his judgment
as a jurist, than with his skill as debater. It is obvious that he
considered the interpretation of the written law merely a form
which had to be followed in the derivation of desirable rules
from the scriptural text. . . . He was trying to change the
complexion of the inherited Law. To accomplish this he had
to find an authority superior to that of his predecessors and
accepted by everyone. Only one instrument could fulfill these
requirements—Scripture itself" (Finkelstein, 171, 173). But
his attitude was not as calculated as these quotations make it
sound when they are taken out of context: Akiba believed passionately that whatever was reasonable and right must be in
the Torah. And he would not brook any argument that was
not based on Scripture, any more than his colleagues would.

In sum, he was a very humane authoritarian—one more instance of the plain historical and logical fact that humanism
and authoritarianism are not mutually exclusive alternatives.
Or, if one should care to insist that the authoritarianism of
Akiba and the Zen masters detracts from their humanism,
then one must face the fact that there never has been any
completely humanistic religion.

Fromm's book makes a real contribution to our understanding of religion by focusing attention on humanistic elements
in various traditions; and the illustrations he adduces are so
superb that it is no insult to remark that his quotations constitute the best part of the volume. His central dichotomy,
however, is misconceived, and he generally finds in a text only
what he has believed all along. Thus he simply does not see
the authoritarian elements in Hassidism and in early Christianity. Hegel's neglected essay on "The Positivity of the Christian Religion," written over 150 years earlier, but equally

concerned with authoritarianism, offers a far more perceptive analysis of the Gospels.

It would be tedious to keep caviling at *Psychoanalysis and Religion*. Fromm's tendency to find nothing in books but corroborations and illustrations of what he has been saying all along is much plainer in his book on symbolism, *The Forgotten Language*. Here he deals with single books and the unsoundness of his approach is unmistakable. More important: the focal points of the following discussion—ambiguity and tragedy—should throw further light on the core of religion, though this may not be immediately obvious.

In Fromm's interpretation of Kafka's *Trial*, no place at all remains for anything Kafkaesque: a rich and deliberately ambiguous novel is reduced to a didactic allegory which teaches what Fromm has long said far more clearly. Fromm depends heavily on the double meaning of "he was arrested" in the first sentence of the novel: arrested can mean "stopped in one's growth and development." The original German *"wurde er eines Morgens verhaftet"* makes this reading much less plausible than the English translation. The hero's fault, according to Fromm, was that he was arrested in his development and "knew only the 'authoritarian conscience,' to which obedience is the greatest virtue and disobedience the greatest crime." He did not know the "humanistic conscience," for which Fromm refers us to a chapter in his book, *Man for Himself*. The nightmare disappears: it can be cured by reading a chapter of Fromm.

The priest in the cathedral, who tells the haunting parable "Before the Law" and then shows how its ambiguity is irreducible and no univocal translation is tenable, becomes to Fromm a representative of the humanistic conscience; but of the parable and the memorable discussion about it there is no hint in Fromm's account. As if the ambiguity of the parable were not representative of the whole novel!

Fromm's section of more than thirty pages on three of Sophocles' tragedies similarly turns these plays into untragic tracts that say obscurely what Fromm has long said plainly.

Fromm gives no indication that Sophocles wrote over 120 plays, that his *Antigone* was first performed as part of a trilogy about 442 B.C., *Oedipus Tyrannus* as part of another trilogy about 425 B.C., while *Oedipus on Colonus* was written shortly before the poet died at ninety in 406 B.C. Fromm treats the three plays as a trilogy, as if the *Antigone* were the last play of three. Only in a footnote is there even a hint of the facts just mentioned, and it is barely a hint: "While it is true that the trilogy was not written in this order and while some scholars may be right in their assumption that Sophocles did not plan the three tragedies as a trilogy, the three must nevertheless be interpreted as a whole. It makes little sense to assume that Sophocles described the fate of Oedipus and his children in three tragedies without having in mind an inner coherence of the whole" (202).

The last sentence shows little understanding of poetry. Why shouldn't a poet deal with a myth three times in a different way? (Cf. Chapter X.) If he lived to be ninety and wrote over 100 plays, he might well have reverted to related themes to express his current experience of life, without feeling that his hands had been tied by his previous efforts.

One of the most memorable features of Freud's discussion of Sophocles' *Oedipus Tyrannus*, in the first edition of his *Traumdeutung* (1900), was a footnote on *Hamlet* which Ernest Jones later expanded into a book. Freud's interpretation of *Hamlet* is by now much better known than the conclusion of his footnote: "Just as, incidentally, all neurotic symptoms—just as even dreams are capable of overinterpretation [*Überdeutung*], and indeed *demand nothing less than this before they can be fully understood,* thus *every genuine poetic creation, too,* has presumably issued from more than one motive and more than one stimulus in the poet's soul and *permits more than one interpretation.* What I have attempted here is merely an interpretation of the deepest layer of impulses in the soul of the creative poet" (II, 267 f., italics mine).

To return to Sophocles, Fromm writes: "We find that *the* theme running through the three tragedies is the conflict between father and son. . . . The problem of incest exists neither in the relationship between Oedipus's sons to their mother [who is also their grandmother, and commits suicide while they are small] nor in the relationship between Haemon and his mother, Eurydice. If we interpret *King Oedipus* in the light of the whole trilogy, the assumption seems plausible that *the real issue* in *King Oedipus*, too, is the conflict between father and son and not the problem of incest" (204, italics and parenthesis mine). Even if the three plays Fromm has in mind did form a trilogy, the assumption that a Sophoclean tragedy—or even three of the seven we know—should dramatize a single real issue is exceedingly implausible.

That the problem of incest is not present in *all* relationships proves nothing. The conflict between father and son cannot by its very nature be present in all relationships either, and in the *Antigone* the father-son conflict is plainly a side issue. On the other hand, the fate that overtakes the sons born of Oedipus' marriage with his mother and the fate of Antigone herself, too, can obviously be viewed as the nemesis of incest. Moreover—though the word incest sounds too crude for this— it should not be overlooked, as it usually is, that Antigone's conduct is partly influenced by her love of her brother. Since her brother is dead, she has no wish to live on: she does not want Haemon's love; she wants to die.

In its context, the wonderful hymn on Eros is profoundly ambiguous; and this is underscored by Antigone's outcry in her immediately following dialogue with the chorus.

> *Woe, my mother's outrage in the bed!*
> *Embraces with him she herself had born,*
> *with my father—the wretched mother*
> *of whom, hapless, aweless, I was begotten!*
> *To them, accursed, unwed,*
> *to dwell with them, I return.*
> *Woe, unhappy wedlock*
> *that felled my brother*
> *who, dying, destroys me, surviving, too!*

The Greek words with their tremendous weight, already noted by Aristophanes in one of his comedies, are worlds removed from transparent prose and abound in ambiguities. To give two examples: the word I have translated "outrage" can also mean delusion, guilt, punishment, misfortune; and the word rendered with two words, "hapless, aweless," may hint that even as her parents committed a wretched deed, without seemly fear, Antigone, born of this union, is herself wretched and fearless.

Any claim that incest is "the real issue" of the play would be almost as ridiculous as Fromm's claim. But there is a sense in which we can identify "the real issue" of *all* tragedies, that which makes them tragedies. And that is the inadequacy of the kind of humanism represented, for example, by Erich Fromm.

There are situations in which one cannot act, nor abstain from action, without incurring guilt: that is the common theme of *Oedipus* and *Antigone,* and of *Hamlet,* too. How one gets into such situations is not altogether clear, but at times, as in the case of Antigone, it may happen without any moral fault of our own. And what the great tragic poets suggest is that in the attempt to avoid such guilt by inaction (like Ismene in the *Antigone*) there is something small. Greatness and guilt belong together. Without surrendering moral sensitivity, tragedy celebrates guilt.

How is tragedy related to religion? The Book of Job is not a tragedy. First, it has a happy end; and even if we omitted the last few verses, which contrast so sharply with the sensibility of the preceding speeches—conceivably, these offensive verses formed part of the original folk tale—the end would still not be tragic. Second, Job is not meant for the stage but essentially didactic. Third, there is no connection between suffering and character, no guilt: Job is innocent.

Nor *can* there be any Jewish or Christian tragedy. Both religions emphasize morality to the point of being incapable of celebrating guilt. Even where it is clearly seen that the experience of guilt raises a man higher, repentance and reconciliation close the cycle, as in David's case and Jacob's. And in Christianity the conception of heaven and the lack of sympathy for the damned militate against tragedy: hell is not experienced as tragic but as part of a divine comedy.

In the Old Testament, Jacob and Samson, Saul and David, come very close to being tragic figures, and it is not only the moralistic outlook that bars tragedy: the interest in history is too great. For all its interest in individuals, the Old Testament is not individualistic: it is ultimately concerned with a people who are to perform a task assigned to them by God. But where the individual stands in the service of an idea which will triumph eventually, there can be no tragedy. Tragedy occurs where society dissolves and man stands all alone, like Oedipus, Antigone, and Hamlet. Tragedy occurs where men have come to see that even an exemplary devotion to love, truth, justice, and integrity cannot safeguard a man against guilt.

Tragedy opens up the possibility of a profound alternative to religion. The tragic outlook can be the religiousness of the irreligious. There is little in world literature that can equal the pathos of the great religious scriptures, except the great tragedies. *Oedipus, Antigone,* and *Lear* move the heart like the best of the Bible. Even in Captain Ahab in *Moby Dick* there is still more of a religious dimension than in Starbuck or in Sunday school.

What the great religious scriptures and tragedies know, and what popular religion and such humanists as Fromm and Dewey (in *A Common Faith*) ignore, is the sheer misery of being human and the experience that only self-immolation can redeem this misery. For the downfall and death of the tragic hero was originally, if we remember the genesis of tragedy, a self-sacrifice. The guilt which the hero takes upon himself transcends his own person: by accepting the guilt as his own and paying for it with his own destruction he sacrifices himself for others. By destroying himself, Oedipus lifts the curse that had descended on Thebes. He accepts as his own a guilt that was by no means only his. Antigone, by sacrificing herself, cleanses the city of the guilt that would rest on it if she left her brother unburied, and she also lifts the curse of

Creon's tyranny. Hamlet sacrifices himself, frees his country from his uncle's rule, and cleanses it from horrible guilt.

In Lao-tze, in early Buddhism, and in Zen, we do not find this emphasis on self-sacrifice; but we encounter an at least equally pervasive disillusionment and an utter lack of faith in the kind of progress championed by Fromm and Dewey. Indeed, in these Oriental religions no less than in the tragic world view, there is no belief in progress at all.

The Hebrew prophets taught that progress *was* possible, and this was a profoundly original idea. But they believed that it was possible only through self-sacrifice. In their reinterpretation of this ancient notion of self-sacrifice, they again showed a profound originality: one could sacrifice oneself, living; self-sacrifice could be a matter of suffering for others without necessarily dying for others. A similar idea appeared much later in Mahayana Buddhism.

Jesus did not unequivocally exemplify this novel insight and was soon said to have *died* for men's sins. As a result, this conception of living self-sacrifice has never been as clearly envisaged in Christianity as in some of the prophets—most notably, the Second Isaiah.

The magnificence of these somber world views is alien to modern man, and the emphasis which a few theologians today would place on original sin represents a pitiful alternative to Fromm and Dewey. *Antigone* is more profound than either humanism or neo-orthodoxy.

People think of *Antigone* as a play, if at all; and a few know that line which defies adequate translation into English: "Not to hate with those who hate, but to love with those who love, I live." The modern reader finds Antigone almost Christian. But what great Christian ever defied his age instead of making concessions to it and sharing its prejudices to the point of reinforcing and sanctifying them? What great Christian did what he considered right, like Antigone, without hope of any reward whatever, and without any vengefulness toward those he defied?

Traditional Judaism was a religion by which one could live and for which one could die. Early Christianity was a religion by which one could not live, but for which one could die. By Buddhism one can live, though one cannot die for it. But by what is today called religion one cannot live, nor could one die for it. How much more profound is the outlook of the great tragic poets! What is there to prevent a man from living and dying like Antigone?

What we find in Sophocles is an outlook which will probably never be understood by many. But the vast majority who do not understand him are likely to have a very limited notion of religion, too. Fromm is paradigmatic: his lack of feeling for Sophocles throws light on his discussion of religion. It is epitomized by his mistranslation of the first line of the most celebrated chorus in the *Antigone:* "Wonders are many, *and none is more wonderful than man"* (223). The same line is used as a motto for a chapter in Fromm's *Man for Himself* (210).

The words which Fromm renders "wonders" (τὰ δεινά) usually mean terrors, danger, misfortune, distress; while δεινός can mean any of the following: venerable, terrible, bad, dangerous, extraordinary, astounding, sublime, strong, clever, unheard-of, outrageous, strange, uncanny. Hölderlin, in his German translation of the play, solved the problem beautifully: *"Ungeheuer ist viel. Doch nichts/Ungeheuerer als der Mensch."* In English, "uncanny" would certainly be much better than "wonderful." But what matters here is not the discovery of a perfect English equivalent, but that Sophocles is not voicing "the humanistic principle" (223); he is saying something profoundly ambiguous, and this ambiguity is underlined by the context: the vaulting ambition which has led man to triumph over nature does not prevent him from coming to grief faced with other men. For this profound irony Fromm has no ear any more than for the ambiguity of Kafka or of the religions he discusses. None of them share Fromm's optimism any more than Freud did, or the prophets.

There never has been any "humanistic religion" in Fromm's sense: there have only been humanistic tendencies in most religions, and occasionally, but rarely, these humanistic tendencies have found clear and striking expression in some tale, a page of a Scripture, or a marginal figure. Some Hassidic tales furnish wonderful examples—Fromm cites a couple and Martin Buber has collected hundreds—but, for all that, Hassidism was also deeply authoritarian, and the Jewish opponents of the Hassidim, the so-called Mitnaggedim, were put off as much by the Hassidim's authoritarian cult of the Zaddik, the rabbi, as by their touch of mystic libertarianism.

Personal religious experience has sometimes played a prominent role in religion—for example, in Hassidism—but to prevent it from eroding the tradition, and to preserve a cherished continuity, all religions have cultivated a strong authoritarian undercurrent. Individual religiousness is possible without any touch of authoritarianism; but no historic religion has dispensed with it completely.

Those who would renounce authoritarianism entirely must renounce religion, though they may wish to keep religiousness. Whether such religiousness without religion can be passed on from generation to generation is very doubtful. Probably, it can exist only on the fringes of the historic religions and is unable to survive without them.

Even the profound prophetic conception of the remnant cannot dispense with an authoritarian touch. But our popular spokesmen for religion pin their hopes on all whom best-sellers can reach. Their optimism is shallow compared to the deep disillusionment not only of the prophets, Jesus, and Calvin, but also of Nietzsche, Freud, and Hermann Hesse. The idea of a spiritual but nonauthoritarian mass movement is utopian.

The hope that spirituality may be nourished by a few scattered individuals with no commitment to each other but a common respect for the great spirits of the past, in whose works they seek comfort and strength and to whose achievements some of them add in turn, is compatible with a pervasive resignation. It requires no faith in religion. Those who believe that religion has a future, not merely as a vulgar mass movement or a mess of chronic superstitions, should reflect on the idea of the remnant.

78. RELIGION AND LOYALTY. Religious faith cannot be understood apart from faithfulness, fidelity, loyalty. It is loyalty that determines allegiance to Judaism, Christianity, Hinduism, or Buddhism. Acceptance of specific propositions as well as religious experiences, whether mystic or prophetic, are secondary. What is primary is not a dedication to any humanistic ideal, but loyalty to a tradition and acceptance of its authority, at least up to a point.

Why are most believers so reluctant to specify the meaning of the religious propositions they cherish? There are at least three reasons. First, there is security in obscurity. Precision invites refutation.

Secondly, many religious propositions, including almost all statements about God, are not reducible to any one meaning but essentially ambiguous. The believer feels that the original proposition is more profound than any translation he could ever hope to furnish: there is somehow more to it—namely, though he is not likely to think of it in these words, an indefinite number of other possible interpretations.

The third point is intimately connected with this ambiguity. The believer senses, however dimly, that previous generations, and even other believers today, associate widely different meanings with the same propositions. What determines his acceptance of religious propositions is not primarily their peculiar adequacy to his own intentions and ideas but a desire for continuity. As soon as a particular translation of a religious proposition is accepted as completely adequate, the continuity both with past generations and with one's own disappears.

Intellectually, the apparent agreement of believers is apt to be verbal rather than real. Many believers are far closer to many nonbelievers than they are to many of their fellow believers, provided we concentrate on what they really believe. But intellectual tenets are not the primary consideration when it comes to deciding to what community one wants to belong.

There is a close analogy between religion and marriage. We do not choose a person to live with by seeing with whom we can agree on the most propositions. A certain amount of agree-

ment enters into the decision, but what is central is the will
to stay together in spite of any disagreement.

There is a unity of will rather than intellectual agreement.
The phrase "a unity of purpose" suggests itself, but "purpose"
suggests a specifiable aim, and just this is usually lacking.
Neither in marriage nor in religion are we likely to find any
such specifiable aim; rather, the will to belong together, for
better or for worse. Loyalty to a religion, too, may be rooted in
love.

It is no accident that the moving words of Ruth in adopting
a new religion are so often cited at weddings, even though she
was not speaking to a man: "Whither thou goest, I will go;
and where thou lodgest, I will lodge: thy people shall be my
people, and thy God my God."

79. THOMIST VERSUS NON-THOMIST.   Even the difference between Thomist and non-Thomist is apt to be a matter of temperament and loyalty as much as a matter of belief. This, of
course, takes our argument a step further, and what has been
said so far does not stand or fall with this extension. For
Thomism involves acceptance of an unusually articulate and
comprehensive theology.

Consider a book which is in many respects at opposite poles
from St. Thomas' *Summa Theologica*: Genesis. A resourceful
philosopher should be able to present all of his thought in the
form of a commentary on Genesis. This would be a tour de
force, but not impossible. It is a reflection of our current climate of thought that those who write philosophy at all prefer
to sail under their own colors—or under those of a previous
philosopher, like Thomas.

A great deal of the present book could have been presented
in the form of a commentary on the Book of Job. A quotation
from Job 13, in my own translation, may show what I mean:

> *Behold, my eye has seen all this,*
> *my ear has heard and understood.*
> *What you know, that I also know . . .*

But you, you beautify with lies,
idol-physicians, that you are. . . .
Would you speak wickedly for God
and deceive for his sake?
You think, you favor him?
You think, you take his side? . . .
Be still and leave me that I speak,
and let come on me what will.
Wherefore? I will take my flesh between my teeth,
and my life I will put in my hand.
He will slay me? For that I hope.
But my ways I will maintain to his face.
And let this be my salvation
that no hypocrite comes to face him. (Cf. § 65.)

My critique of theology, and my polemics against finished philosophic edifices and the finding of dubious reasons for what we believe anyway, could have been forced into the mold of a commentary on Job.

In that case, the verse "I only am escaped alone to tell thee" might have evoked the reflection that beasts earn survival by being fit while men must justify their survival after the event. And this might have led to a revision of the quotation from Gide's *Counterfeiters*, used early in the Preface: What *right* has a survivor to do over again what other people have done already or might do as well? A commentary on Job need not be dry or impersonal.

The man who chooses Genesis or Job has much more freedom than the Thomist; even those who take off from Plato will encounter less constraint. Thomism furnishes an extreme case, but even the decision to be a Thomist cannot be understood in terms of agreement alone.

The decision is made before one has studied all of Thomas' writings and is not meant to be provisional. A Thomist does not adopt Thomism as a working hypothesis. He is not prepared to renounce it the first time he comes across a sentence which seems false. Rather he decides that he will interpret apparently false sentences in such a way that they will not be false. And he finds his reward in hundreds of surprises: Thomas already knew this, and Thomas anticipated that.

The same attitude is feasible in relation to Plato, Aristotle, Kant, or Hegel, and some have adopted it; but no other philosopher can offer a sense of community with as many others as St. Thomas. And this sense of being part of a living tradition, of not standing alone, of belonging, is part of the meaning and inspiration not only of a man's acceptance of Thomism but of adherence to any religion.

80. LOYALTY AND TRUTH. Religions do not so much offer truths as a common language in which to express truths as well as superstitions. Whitehead once said that "religion is what the individual does with his own solitariness" (16). This definition tells us more about the age in which it was written than about religion. Religion offers man a way out of his solitude. Even when it does not lure man into church or visible fellowship with others, *religion offers man a language which makes real loneliness impossible.*

The language of religion may be ritual, prayer, or an idiom based on Scripture: the man who speaks this language breaks out of the solitary confinement of his mute emotions, transcends the isolation of his boredom or despair, and becomes part of a community. He belongs.

That acceptance of traditional statements may lead to conflicts with truth is obvious; but such conflicts may arise even where such statements are scrupulously avoided and only a language is accepted. Protestants do not agree about sexual morals, but they agree that their own conclusions, whatever they may be, are dictated by the spirit of Christianity. Instead of "decent" they say, "Christian"; in place of "immoral," "un-Christian"; and "Christ would have considered this an outrage" or "this is the very sort of thing which Christ denounced" become synonyms of "*I* consider this an ourage." Eventually the language molds the man and affects his attitude toward history and philology, philosophy and science. (Cf. §§ 37, 40, 55 ff., 67 ff.)

The language—"this is what Jesus meant"—dictates conclusions to autonomous sciences and undermines discussion with an arbitrary appeal to authority. Loyalty assumes that whatever is false or unworthy cannot have been said by Jesus or by Moses or Mohammed, and that what is true and profound cannot have escaped them.

The choice of a language may make some kinds of discussion impossible. Exegesis takes the place of a study of relevant evidence, and homilies supplant a critical analysis of reasons. In a certain climate of thought, inventiveness and ingenuity occupy the position of the intellectual conscience. (Cf. § 64.)

Loyalty may expressly override respect for truth. Suppose a man says: I have complete faith in John. This statement may be analyzable into a series of propositions which rest on reasonable evidence: in one situation John could be counted on to do this and in another not to do that. But a declaration of faith is not always meant to sum up such a string of propositions. To make this clear, the speaker may have recourse to a paradoxical proposition: Even if I saw John do this with my own eyes, I should refuse to believe it. Or perhaps: No matter what the evidence might be, I stick to my position.

In rare cases even such statements may be based on very strong evidence, particularly if they are qualified in some way. Few of us would hesitate to say of some people whom we know well that they would under no circumstances steal money for their own gain, even if all the evidence pointed toward it: "He is the kind of person who could not possibly have acted that way: if he did it, he must have been told that, if he refused, some terrible harm would come to someone else; or else he must have been broken completely first." Such sentences have an empirical ring and might be uttered about a man toward whom we feel no special loyalty.

An unqualified statement of faith belongs to an altogether different realm. It formulates a personal commitment, the way in which a person chooses to live, a loyalty which matters more than truth. "This is precisely what Jesus opposed; I do not care what he said."

In some cases it is not immediately obvious whether a statement that expresses a loyalty claims that anything is the case. Dean Acheson's "I shall not turn my back on Alger Hiss" is a case in point. If this means "I still believe that he is innocent," then this belief must be judged in terms of the evidence; and if there were conclusive proof of guilt, we should have to conclude that loyalty had led Acheson into conflict with the truth. But if Acheson meant, "even if Hiss should be guilty, I should not turn my back on him," then truth is out of the picture. The question becomes: What are the values of the man who says this? There is still room for different evaluations. Some would say: Anyone who is unwilling to turn his back on a man who has done what Hiss was accused of is unfit to hold high office. Others might say: Any man who would speak otherwise has no business calling himself a Christian. But the issue now is no longer the truth of a proposition but the values revealed by a loyalty.

In evaluating any loyalty one must ask whether it involves any conflict with truth. Patriotism furnishes an obvious example of loyalty and often leads people to override the truth. American teachers feel quite free to assert that the American form of government is by far the best without feeling the least obligation to acquire any knowledge of the workings of other forms of government. They may even say that all kinds of particular liberties and equalities are more perfectly realized in the United States than anywhere else on earth. Confronted with data about Switzerland or Sweden, Mississippi or Mayor Curley, such people readily become involved in untrue statements, illicit argumentation, and impatience with facts.

Loyalty to a political party furnishes another example. If a man feels bound to assent to every party platform and every statement made by a candidate for office, he gets involved in untruths. It is quite another matter if he chooses a party as a congenial vehicle for action; but even then he is tempted to discount inconvenient truths about his own party while readily believing slanderous rumors about his opponents.

"My country, right or wrong" is not an objectionable motto if it is coupled with the strong determination to fight wrongs. It may be an expression of the will to assume responsibility and to speak out against the wrong and to work for the right here more than anywhere else. But even such a loyalty poses a threat to intellectual integrity which can be warded off only by continual concern.

Wherever a loyalty is based on a deliberate choice among alternatives, evidence is relevant. The man who is loyal to the Nazi Party is open to criticism even if he studiously avoids making false statements. A loyalty can be irresponsible, blind, uninformed.

In Germany in 1933, some men decided to oppose Hitler through the Social Democratic Party. Others considered the Communist Party a more promising vehicle. Still others felt that only opposition from within stood any chance of success and joined the Storm Troopers. Such decisions do not only reveal what kind of men we are; they strongly affect what kind of people we become.

Most men are born into their religion and accept it without investigation. A study of other religions is generally considered irrelevant, and a knowledge of one's own is rare. Most people know what they like, without *knowing* what they like.

One picks and chooses, discounts some parts of the tradition, and emphasizes others. But all this is usually done erratically and rather irresponsibly.

One inherits a religion like a house and makes some slight changes to make it more comfortable. One keeps some old beliefs as one keeps old pictures to which one is used from childhood: one does not really like them but they seem to belong there; one is hardly conscious of them, but if they were removed the house would no longer be our childhood home. But one also *believes,* if only a little, without being at all sure in one's own mind what these beliefs might mean. At that point irresponsibility begins: a belief that is believed, even if only half, is no longer a picture, and it compromises honesty if we treat it like a picture.

We are responsible for our beliefs. We are also responsible for our loyalties, even if they do not involve us in beliefs. Adherence to a religion may be the choice of a vehicle for living, the acceptance of a tradition and a way of life. But men who have left a lasting imprint on their religion are rare indeed, and even they were usually more influenced by the tradition than they influenced it. In general, the great religions have molded man; and after his childhood is over, a man is responsible for what he allows to mold him.

81. RELIGION, ASPIRATION, AND THE HOLY.   Man is the ape that wants to be a god. Perhaps there is a thrust beyond the present, beyond itself, in all life; possibly even in lifeless matter. In man this thrust has become conscious aspiration, conscious self-contempt. Man is unhappy in his skin and cannot shed it. He wants to abandon himself and attain a higher state of being. He is only too willing to believe that this longing will be satisfied upon his death, but he will not be put off until then. In love he seeks abandonment, transcendence of his everyday existence, another state of being. The Greek myth that man is a fragment and yearns to be one with his beloved gives expression to this longing. So do art and morality, philosophy and religion.

Man is the rational animal; but what is reason? A thrust beyond the present and an education in self-contempt. From this presence and this and this, man projects the concept "crimson" and "circle" and "courageous." Then he can say: this is not a circle though I tried to draw one. And he can say: I was not courageous. He can criticize himself. For general concepts are so many norms, and every norm is a rebuke and can be a spur. Reason enables man to strive consciously to transcend himself.

Primitive moralities may be partly superstitious, partly utilitarian; they are also expressions of man's dissatisfaction with humanity, of his aspiration to be other than he is. While most human activity is found wanting, like the winter, some of it, like the spring, is experienced as a promise of immortality and the conquest of imperfection. What man craves is a break with his everyday existence; but the ecstasies of the dance and the transports of love do not last. Religion is an attempt to make bliss enduring, and ritual is frozen rapture.

That spontaneity which, like the thawing wind, cracks the ice of custom and is felt to be the herald of a more exalted life becomes tradition: a tune or a dance that was the gift of abandon, evanescent as the wind, is repeated religiously; and a figure, carved from wood, or a graven image, enduring monuments of unprecedented creation, are worshiped as living symbols of a higher state of being and become idols.

The mystical experience becomes a conscious goal to be reached through breathing exercises and a detailed regimen, and the stammerings of the ecstatic become normative for future generations. The prophetic seizure is induced by dances, and the prophet's poems are canonized.

Religion is rooted in man's aspiration to transcend himself. It does not merely satisfy needs—many more needs than most psychologists give it credit for—religion has, if not created, cultivated needs which no longer allow man to feel at home among the other animals.

William James turned to religion because he wanted to feel at home in the universe. But *the greatest accomplishment of religion has been that it did not allow man to feel at home in the universe,* that it raised a hope in man's heart which the world could not quench, and that instead of telling man to abandon such a foolish hope, religion staked its life on it.

Some religions exhort men to become as gods, whether only after many incarnations or immediately upon death or even in this life. Both Hinduism and Buddhism know of a state of being in which man before death surpasses the gods. The Yogi makes the gods tremble, and the Buddha spurns Mara's offer of dominion over four continents, saying: "I am about to cause the ten thousand worlds to tremble with my becoming a Buddha."

In the Hebrew Bible this higher state of being—boundless creative power and love everlasting—is represented by God. But this conception of God is not experienced as the incarnate futility of man's aspiration, as perfection from which man is cut off by original sin, as power before which man must grovel in the dust. God is the great promise: "Ye shall be holy: for I the Lord your God am holy."

Of the four evangelists, two no longer had any place for this challenge; and of the two who repeated it, one changed "holy" to "merciful." Only one kept the radical old meaning, though he changed "holy" to "perfect." Soon it became the distinction of Christ that he alone among men had achieved perfection; and he was God to begin with: perfection was now envisaged as being beyond the power of man.

What is holiness? The concept of the holy is found in most religions and means essentially a contrast to the everyday world. In recent times it has become restricted to holidays; and now that the holidays, too, have become profane, some writers on religion seek the holy solely among the mystics—who are dead. Gradually, the holy has become a memory or a matter of hearsay—something at which T. S. Eliot hints when he writes about the experiences which he believes other people to have had. But in its inception the idea of the holy is anything but safely dead or remote: it is encountered here and now, like a clearing in the jungle of existence—a difference, a challenge, a promise.

Rudolf Otto has become famous for his account of this experience, which he calls numinous and a *mysterium tremendum*. His attempt suffers from many flaws: it is encumbered with Christian, even Lutheran, apologetics; it is used to support a fallacious proof of God's existence; and the account itself is not only needlessly weighted down with an excess of Latin phrases but also unnecessarily stark. Many a reader feels: if that is what is meant by being religious, then I am not. In spite of these faults, the book concentrates on a root experience of religion; and the one religious experience on which Otto concentrates is more important than all of William James' "Varieties."

Otto's emphatic supernaturalism is uncongenial to many a modern mind, but there is a sense in which religion is essentially antinaturalistic, and the holy is the antinaturalistic concept par excellence. It is the extraordinary. Otto tries to locate it as given in a certain experience which he tries to describe. This is a serious mistake. He half realizes this himself and adds later in his book that the experience would be impossible if the holy were not an a priori category of the mind. In Kant's sense, of course, the holy is not a category of the understanding, constitutive of all experience; and the postulation of an a priori category in the mind for every distinctive experience—why not also for love or the experience of red?—approximates the obscurantism of Molière's doctor: opium induces sleep by virtue of a *virtus dormitiva*.

What is wanted is not Latin terminology but an indication of what is roused to consciousness by what is given in experience. What is *given* does not transcend nature, but the aspiration it awakens does.

A human being, a work of art, a dream, a burning bush can arouse and crystallize in our consciousness a deep dissatisfaction with the world of facts and with ourselves, a sense of something other than all this. Otto's and Barth's phrase "wholly other" is but half true. There is a sense in which a radiator is more nearly wholly other than we are than is the God in whose image we are made. What is so deeply disturbing about the experience of the holy is not the stark drama of the encounter, which Otto stresses though it is the exception rather than the rule, but the sense that this otherness, though different from the everyday world, is by no means "wholly other" but tantalizingly close. It is a reproach to our present state.

There are two kinds of religions. The first says: "Ye shall be holy." Judaism does, and adds: "for I the Lord your God am holy." Early Buddhism does, too, and adds, in effect: even as the Buddha became holy who, like you, was born mere man. The other kind of religion says: All your efforts are doomed and will never make you holy; therefore, adore that which is holy. This is the essence of idolatry; and in this, a great deal of traditional Christianity is close to idolatry.

There are many other ways of classifying religions; and in many ways Buddhism and Judaism are antithetical, and the contrast between Christianity and idolatry is obvious. In many respects, Buddhism is closer to Christianity than to Judaism, and Christianity is closer to Judaism than to idolatry. Clearly, both tendencies are encountered in most religions, and in

Christianity, too, the aspiration for self-perfection has found persistent expression: indeed, this is the aspect of Christianity of which the modern Christian is most conscious, and as a result he is either perplexed by the moral and social ineffectuality of Christianity in the course of history or, more often, attributes to Christianity social achievements, like the birth of democracy or the abolition of slavery, of which it might well be argued that Christianity has, in fact, delayed them. Certainly, there is no very close connection either logically or historically between the New Testament, Augustine, Aquinas, and Luther on the one hand and these social developments on the other. We cannot understand historic Christianity if we see in it only the aspiration toward self-perfection; we must also recognize the strong element of idolatry that has characterized it from the beginning.

From the start, Christianity has tended to *objectify* the holy in a variety of ways. The Protestant will think of the Catholic's regard for relics and images, if not of the Virgin; while the Catholic may recall Luther's insistence that all Biblical commandments were given only to make man aware of his utter inability to do good and to teach him to worship Christ instead. In Jesus Christ the holy becomes objective for the Christian; it becomes flesh, an article of faith. But not only Christolatry is idolatry of a sort—in the wide sense of that word here suggested—but God himself, too, is objectified and becomes another article of faith.

The God who was unending love and sustained creative power, who had made man in his image and bidden him to become holy like his creator, is hypostatized and adored and ceases to be a challenge, a commandment, an imperative. The law is abrogated and supplanted by faith; and with the conception of hell, cruelty is projected into a mien that had never been cheerful, and the divine countenance is surrounded with an aura of magic, miracles, and superstition. In the end, man lies in the dust before his own graven image.

This is a more sinister aspect of Christianity than those usually emphasized, and something corresponding to this can be found in all religions: as a tendency and a menace, idolatry is found in all of them, and in popular religion it is the rule. But the leading figures in some other religions have condemned this tendency much more unequivocally than the leading spirits of Christianity, who have not been altogether free of this tendency themselves. The Buddha, Moses, and the prophets opposed idolatry much more radically than the great Christians.

Religion can channel man's aspiration to transcend himself into many different ways of life: on the one hand, there is asceticism, ranging from stern demands on oneself to systematic and elaborate austerities, and there is moral effort, ranging from a sustained attempt to perfect oneself to a devotion to social reform; on the other hand, there is inactive adoration of that which transcends the self, ranging from meditation to prayer and hope for grace, and there are beliefs and rites and sacraments.

The basic choice is this: either man hypostatizes the object of his profoundest aspirations, projects his boldest hopes, and in the most extreme case strips himself of all that distinguishes him from the apes, and then the ape that remains grovels on his belly; or man seeks to leave the ape behind on the ground and tries to raise himself to a higher level of being. Whether he worships idols or strives to perfect himself, man is the God-intoxicated ape.

82. OTHERWORLDLINESS. Otherworldliness is the child of disenchantment with this world. Having made room for the possibility of another world in his *Critique of Pure Reason,* Kant believed in this other world as a place where one might find what could not be found in this world: freedom, immortality, a proportion of virtue and happiness, and God. This is paradigmatic.

In the ancient world, otherworldliness gained ground as more and more people were deprived of control over their own affairs and lost all hope for this world. Alexander's conquests gave a boost to otherworldliness, and as Rome's rule spread and was solidified, the emphasis on another world became more and more prominent in ever more religions.

What of Plato's otherworldliness? Many writers suppose that the experience of alienation is distinctively modern. Yet Plato felt deeply alienated from his world, his class, his people. His hypostatization of another world was not required by logic. (See § 16.) It must be understood in conjunction with his disenchantment with this world. But Plato's disillusionment was still accompanied by a prophetic temperament: the philosopher who has had a vision of the other world must return to this world and remake it. Plato was true to Socrates no less than the other Socratics in maintaining the master's moral pathos, insisting that men perfect themselves.

More often than not, however, the belief in another world has served to make the holy into something wholly other. It has cut the moral nerve of a deeply upsetting experience by interpreting this experience as cognitive, as giving knowledge of another world, of something that is the case, of objects. A tremendous tension is allayed: the hunger of the heart is stilled before it has fully developed. It becomes possible to tell man, when he is dissatisfied with himself and this world, that there is no hope of changing either, and that he might better occupy himself in contemplating God and another world.

83. RELIGION AND POETRY.   Religion is not some one thing but the primeval chaos out of which different phenomena have gradually developed. Hegel, in his system, placed religion between art and philosophy. Art he considered more primitive; in religion a first attempt is made to spell out the hidden meaning of art; and in philosophy, finally, ultimate clarity is sought, and truth is no longer adulterated with sensuous elements. But it is more illuminating to view religion as the ancient matrix of both art and philosophy; and the separate existence of both in the modern world makes the position of religion precarious.

The very conception of a work of art is more dangerous to religion than any scientific conception. Before art became self-conscious and autonomous, in the centuries when architecture and sculpture, poetry and music, were all part of the religious life, religion alone could offer the mass of men lasting bliss. There are those who are nostalgically longing back for such an age. It is therefore well to remember that among the Greeks we have to go back beyond Homer for this: the whole of the flowering of Greek civilization belongs to a later epoch; and this lesson was not lost on the men of the Renaissance. To understand the soul of religion, one must go back to the age before the Renaissance, or before Homer, or to communities in which even today the conception of a work of art is unknown.

If you go to a cathedral to see the building, to admire the splendid sculptures, and to see the carvings in the choir; if you know the organ music because you have heard it on the radio or perhaps own it on records; if you then go on to another cathedral, and perhaps have beautifully illustrated books on all of them, or to a museum—how can you hope to do justice to religion? You must first of all imagine an existence quite different from your own: an essentially drab life in which sex, war, and religion offered man the only ecstasy he knew. Into such a life the cathedral introduced a touch of the sublime, and some of the sculptures an inkling of beauty: here a young soul was awakened to some sense of a higher existence than could be found between one's daily bread and nightly bed, or in circuses and autos-da-fé.

Shakespeare and Beethoven pose at least as profound a problem for the future of religion as Copernicus and Darwin. The great artist answers to the aspiration which before had to turn to religion: in Beethoven's music the hunger of the soul and its jubilation cease to be religion. What, then, remains to religion? If a museum in Florence offers you a room full of some of Michelangelo's most moving sculptures, what is any church to offer?

As long as poetry is religious poetry—the Bible, for example —the question whether religion is essentially poetry cannot arise. But with the advent of the great secular poets the question becomes inescapable. How is religion related to poetry?

Philosophy is poetry become self-critical. Is religion poetry that still mistakes itself for something else? Philosophy is poetry with an intellectual conscience, poetic vision subjected to rational scrutiny. Positivism is scrutiny without vision; poetry, vision without rational scrutiny; and religion, poetry turned authoritarian.

Not only dogma is poetry turned authoritarian, but ritual, too. What could be more poetic than lighting candles on the eve of the Sabbath? Or not boiling the kid in his mother's milk? Or the Christian sacraments? Or a touch of monastery? Or a day in the life of an itinerant Buddhist monk? What was poetry when it was done once spontaneously, becomes religion when it is enforced.

Whenever dogma and ritual are liberated from authority and routine, and their original spontaneity is re-experienced, they become poetic again. In the experience and utterance of the mystic, religion manifestly becomes poetry, and its essentially nonliteral character is made evident.

The utterances of the prophets were poetic, too, and they did not claim that their experiences were either ineffable or *sui generis*. They did not claim ineffability because in their time poetry was accepted without rational scrutiny. And they did not claim that their experience was essentially different from the creative or the receptive aesthetic experience or from moral indignation or simple despair, because it was not: for them every intense experience that involved the whole man and fused the aesthetic and moral was religious. They had no separate words for religion, art, and morality.

Hosea's experience of the unfaithfulness of his wife and of his anguish and love was for him a profoundly religious experience which shed light on the relationship of Israel to the God of Abraham, Isaac, and Jacob. Jeremiah, seeing the potter's wheel, does not ask himself whether his experience is aesthetic, moral, or religious; nor does Amos pose such questions when his moral indignation sweeps him away from the herdmen of Tekoa to cry out in magnificent poetic cadences.

What makes such poetry not merely religious poetry, comparable to Dante's, Milton's, or Blake's, but the very stuff of religion itself, is its acceptance as authoritative and canonical.

With that it ceases to be "mere" poetry and becomes binding.

Religious reformers often want to recapture the poetry of their religion and oppose the degradation of blind routine, but they take the language of the emotions for the word of God; and by appealing to authority, they insure the eventual failure of their effort.

Those who would take the poetry out of religion kill religion if they succeed; and if they do not kill it, that is because they do only half the job. The Jesus of most liberal Protestants and Unitarians is not the historical Jesus but a moral fiction, a poetic conception. Nor do they realize the essential ambiguity of the conception of God. Their religion recalls Plato's expurgation of Homer: what remains is moralistic poetry which seems thin, even if slightly less incredible, to anyone who has ever loved the unexpurgated original. As Santayana said in the Preface to his early *Interpretations of Poetry and Religion:* "Mythology cannot become science by being reduced in bulk, but it may cease, as a mythology, to be worth having."

Santayana's objection is best understood when applied to his great hate, Luther. By discarding a great many beliefs as superstitious, Luther barred any possibility of accepting the remaining beliefs in a very free spirit—as deeply moving, as poetic, as capable of a great many interpretations. He could not accept, for example, Zwingli's symbolic interpretation of the Eucharist—and thus precipitated the splintering of Protestantism. For if the beliefs he kept could be treated in this fashion, any justification would be lost for rejecting the beliefs he denounced: were the beliefs of Dante unpoetic or less moving than those Luther kept?

The Protestant who believes in the Trinity, the virgin birth, and the resurrection, but prides himself on his rejection of the latest Catholic dogma which he considers pagan, idolatrous, or superstitious, displays prejudice. Surely, Protestant theologians could think up no less edifying interpretations of this latest dogma than they lavish on beliefs made dogmas a few centuries earlier.

Moses, unlike Luther, did not "reduce in bulk" the mythology of the religion he rejected. When he threw out belief in the afterlife and the scores of gods of Egypt, this was not a quantitative reduction but a rejection of myth as such. Unlike Ikhnaton, the monotheistic pharaoh, Moses protested against any objectification of the divine whatsoever and offered an altogether new conception of the divine as essentially an embodied—or rather, *unembodied*—moral challenge. Moses tells no stories about God in the Egyptian or Greek manner. Moses' God is nonmythical: he has no private life, no objective existence; in the language popularized by Buber, Moses' God is no It but *only* a Thou. He is not seen—an experience in which he would be a passive object—but heard: he is active, he addresses us, he challenges us. Visual representations of God are expressly ruled out. God is not an object of contemplation, reflection, or even thought: always and essentially he is associated with a challenge to man. What is to be taken literally is only this challenge; there is no myth that is to be believed.

The one apparent exception is the story of the creation in Genesis. It is hard for us today to read it as it surely wants to be read. It is too familiar and at the same time too ornate in most English versions: the contemporary reader associates it with Sunday school or with the Tennessee monkey trial. It seems a myth which has no place in adult everyday life; for the challenge has been heeded so long ago that one is no longer aware of it. Yet this is not a myth about God but an address to man. It explodes the myth, still championed by Plato centuries later, that the sun and moon and other objects in this world are gods; it tells man that no object whatsoever is divine; that the only one in the whole world who breathes the spirit of the divine is man—not any king or priest or race, but man as such—and women, too. Man should not bow before anything in this world nor before any man; he should raise himself above the things in this world, above the animals: he is to become like the Creator, who is unlike anything in this world, and should rest on the seventh day every week lest he ever become wholly absorbed in the world of objects and routines.

If this should sound homiletic, that can hardly be helped: the beginning of Genesis *is* hortatory. It is not a myth. "Why was man created a solitary human being, without a companion? So that it might not be said that some races are better than others," says the Talmud (Sanhedrin 37a). That does not exhaust the riches of Genesis 1 and 2: there is more to them; but this is an essential part of their plain meaning.

This is how the beginning of Genesis was understood even in Biblical times. Witness Malachi, the prophet: "Have we not all one father? Has not one God created us? Why is one man faithless against the other" (2.10)? And Amos says, in a more famous verse: "Are you not as children of the Ethiopians to me, O children of Israel? says the Lord. Have I not brought up Israel out of the land of Egypt? and the Philistines from Crete, and the Syrians from Kir" (9.7)? And Job says: "If I did not respect the right of my manservant or of my maidservant, when they contended with me, what should I do when God appears, and what reply to him when he calls to account? For he who made me in the womb, made him, and One fashioned us in the womb" (31.13–15). In an essay on "Judaism and the Democratic Ideal," Milton Konvitz has collected many similar exegeses of Genesis 1 and 2 from rabbinical literature.

Moses and the Buddha brought off the unique feat of offering a moral, nonmythical religion that is not thin but powerful in its radicalism which in both cases appears in radical rejections and demands. Original Buddhism and Judaism represent the two pure types of nonidolatrous religion. All the other great religions are adulterated with eclecticism.

Hinduism furnishes the prime example of tolerant syncretism, Christianity of intolerant syncretism. From the start, Christianity made it a principle to bite the hands that fed it, whether Jew or Greek. In China, syncretism was carried to the point of altogether dissolving the individual religions. And in all these cases, superstition and idolatry gained ready entrance. In Judaism, too, superstitions have often been rife, but they never became authoritative. In Buddhism, superstition and outright idolatry have all but obscured the purity of the original doctrine; only Zen Buddhism recovered the Buddha's freedom from idolatry.

Liberal Protestantism and Unitarianism lack the radicalism of Moses and the Buddha. They seem thin because, unlike Moses and the Buddha, they offer nothing new, and their rejections tend to be equivocal. Whitehead said well that Unitarians believe in at most one god.

Moses and the Buddha defied their age by rejecting what all the world believed. The liberal Protestants and Unitarians make concessions to their age by giving up beliefs that might give offense and keeping those which at the moment seem relatively innocuous. They profess belief in God, assuming that God is innocuous.

Santayana, who realized that "mythology cannot become science by being reduced in bulk," wanted "a mythology . . . worth having." What is so curious about his writings on religion, very much including his later work, *Reason in Religion*, is his attitude toward mythology. In his early *Interpretations* he finds fault with "The Absence of Religion in Shakespeare" (Chapter VI). He cites Macbeth's speech from "To-morrow, and to-morrow, and to-morrow" down to "Signifying nothing," only to exclaim at the end: "How differently would Homer or Dante have answered that question" (155)! But when T. S. Eliot comes along later and compares Shakespeare with Dante to show how the philosophy behind Shakespeare's poetry was inferior, Santayana is exasperated and writes an essay on "Tragic Philosophy" to take issue with Eliot: "We can understand why Mr. Eliot feels this to be a 'superior' philosophy; but how can he fail to see that it is false" (274)? Santayana prefers the Catholic mythology to the impoverished mythology of Protestantism and regrets "The Absence of Religion in Shakespeare"; but he has no patience with anyone who believes, or writes as if he believed, the Catholic mythology.

Though one may sympathize with Santayana, his peculiar detachment approaches smugness. Religion fascinates him, but his attitude toward it is somehow deeply irreligious. One old etymology derives "religion" from *religare*, to tie. I have tried to show that it is of the essence of religion to claim authority and impose some obligation: it asks for a commitment.

Santayana's perspective is aesthetic: for him religion offers a spectacle which he contemplates.

Santayana thought that at their best religion and poetry become one: religion is simply the most grandiose poetry that deals with the most serious themes. On paper it seems a small point indeed to insist against this that the poet throws his creations into the face of the world for men to take them or leave them as they see fit. That applies even to *Lear* and *Faust*. The philosopher, too, speaks without authority. Some philosophies, including those of the Socratic schools and of Spinoza, are offered to like-minded individuals to live by; but they make no claims on men. Let those who wish to do so adopt them! The most profound poets and philosophers were resigned to being misunderstood. They decided to speak at their own level, and they thought—but only Jesus and his followers ever meant this literally—that those who did not understand should go to hell.

There is the difference, and it is anything but a small point: the poet and the philosopher do not greatly care about those who do not understand or accept what they have to offer; but religion says at the very least: "Choose life or death this day!"

Religion is poetry, but not "mere" poetry. Prayers, for example, can be poetic outbursts or, as in the Hebrew liturgy, time-hallowed poetry that makes men conscious of the essentials of man's condition, the same now as two thousand years ago, and of man's need to rise above the everyday routines that threaten him with spiritual death—or else prayers, and quite especially prayers for others spoken in that special tone of voice that instantly reveals the preacher, imply a conception of God which would make him unworthy of worship. A god who, able to make the sick well, did so only if asked often enough or ardently enough, would be a sentimental devil who occasionally traded an ounce of mercy for a ton of sycophancy.

Prayer is poetry or blasphemy. It can be a spontaneous outcry. It can be ancient poetry that lifts us out of our immediate situation, establishes a bond with some of our fellow men and with previous generations, and makes us think about human life as a whole and about our own existence in particular:

it can make us more thoughtful. But prayer can also be, and
usually is, an expression of incredible thoughtlessness, an un-
reflective petition directed toward a being who, if he were as
the prayer implies he is, would deserve anything but adoration.
Most often, prayer is the absent-minded mumbling of embarrassed conformists.

Where prayer is more than this, where it is poetry, it is
clearly not "mere" poetry. It has religious significance only
insofar as it is not contemplated aesthetically with aloof appreciation. It is poetry in which a man involves himself with
all his heart, soul, and power. And religion is even more than
that.

Religion begins as youthful aspiration with a lively sense of
wonder, but soon gets set in its ways and suspicious of youthful aspirations. And when it is old and conservatism itself, it
boasts of the deeds of its youth and complains how the times
have changed.

Religion is authoritarian poetry, but it is also mysticism and
morality, loyalty and aspiration—and its claim to truth is its
heel of Achilles.

Religion is nourished by mysticism and inspiration and holds
out similar experiences to those who are loyal to it; its demands
are partly moral, but the ritual, too, aims to transform man's
life; and at its best religion kindles and cultivates man's dissatisfaction with himself and helps him to raise himself higher.
But when it mistakes itself for some sort of science, it deserves
disparagement. It is closer to poetry.

Religion does not have a single function, even as man does
not have a single function. Religion is unlike mysticism and
morality, poetry and loyalty, in its multiplicity which makes
any analysis exceedingly difficult. It is more like man himself.

X. SCRIPTURES
AND POETRY
or
HOW TO READ THE BIBLE

84. INEXHAUSTIBILITY. Why are some works of literature read again and again? Some abound in information, memorable formulations, or subtle observations. The sound may be beautiful, too—the texture of the words, the rhythm, rhymes perhaps, or assonance. But the books that are most re-readable are those which offer something new on every reading.

When we go on to ask why some works of literature give rise to ever new interpretations and a vast secondary literature, it is hardly an answer if we say: because they are inexhaustible. Obviously, such books must offer a wealth of insights and untold possibilities of interpretation. It is only another way of putting the last point if we say that such books must be in some way exceedingly difficult.

What constitutes the difficulty of such works? It may be darkness. Rare old words whose meaning is not clear, lacunae in the ancient manuscripts, preservation of mere fragments, or even deliberate mysteriousness may invite ever new conjectures. Usually, however, there is yet another feature which spurs the imagination: apparent inconsistencies. Kafka furnishes some excellent recent examples.

Proponents of the concept of artistic truth have often argued that consistency is an essential feature of artistic truth no less than of other truth; but in novels, dramas, poems, and religious scriptures inconsistency is compatible with the highest excellence and almost a necessary condition of it. More often than not, inexhaustibility is partly a function of inconsistencies.

85. THE PSYCHOLOGY OF INTERPRETATION. To understand why some books elicit so many interpretations, one must consider not only the books but also those who interpret them. There are hosts of people who want to write—either because they enjoy it or because their career depends on it—but who have little of their own to say. So they write about what others have said.

In giving an interpretation one indulges one's will to power —both over the text and over rival exegeses. Though one did not start with any great originality, one grows creative as one works out a new interpretation, pitting one's skill and perception against that of previous readers.

Above all, men feel a delight in finding meaning. Meaninglessness is a synonym of futility. Many men do not know what to do with themselves: they reel from purpose to purpose, spend half a day driving to a ball game, scramble for seats, freeze while they watch, scramble for their cars before the game is over to beat the worst rush, and reach home late at night, having spent another day off to which they had looked forward during the week.

Many are appalled that their life does not come to them neatly labeled with a clear-cut meaning, and conclude that they are doomed to bleak futility.

A work of literature that bears no label that spells out its meaning in a tidy moral is like life itself, and if it contains a variety of clues that point to different possibilities of interpretation, that only increases the similarity. Man can indulge his craving for meaning, plan, and purpose by going to work on the microcosm provided by a book. He feels impotent confronted with what he cannot explain. The more original his interpretation is, the greater the satisfaction that it gives; and the more he excels his rivals by discovering clues that they have overlooked, by finding flaws in their interpretations, and by being able to make sense of things which they could not explain, the greater is his sense of power.

There is even a sense of timelessness in giving a new but plausible interpretation. It will continue to be cited and live on together with the work that prompted it—not as a parasite: it may help the work to greater glory. Even if it is not remembered indefinitely, there is a finality in the achievement which seems timeless: it towers out of the chaotic sea of purposes that are too.ill-conceived to yield any feeling of lasting fulfillment and gives a sense of permanence.

86. EXPLANATION.   Given the will to explain, there are many modes of explanation. What they have in common is that they all try to make plain and understandable what was not altogether comprehensible at first. Explanations answer questions.

These questions may have been discovered by the interpreter, who in that case must begin by making them plausible and, if possible, urgent. In answer, he must point to something new and relevant. If it is not altogether new, at least its relevance must be newly seen: else nothing has been explained.

Some interpreters point to new things which are irrelevant. A book on Kafka, for example, tells us of a great many of his nouns whether they are male or female symbols. This explains nothing. The same is true of a good deal of historical and biographical material supplied by critics of one kind and of much formal analysis presented by critics of another school.

The most obvious kind of explanation is the sort of causal explanation common in natural science: it points to events which, if repeated, would presumably produce the same effect.

Historical explanations are similar but introduce a new kind of cause: intention. To explain why Brutus conspired against Caesar, the historian tries to unravel Brutus' intentions, his thoughts.

Psychoanalytic explanations are also similar but introduce a new kind of intention: "unconscious" intentions. A psychoanalytic explanation of Brutus' behavior would involve Brutus' unconscious attitude toward Caesar and the question, for example, whether Brutus acted out an unresolved Oedipus complex.

These are three kinds of explanations; but how does one explain a work of literature? What problems are posed by books?

There is, first, the writer's relation to his work. We can inquire about biographical events which are reflected in the work and about the poet's intentions, both conscious and unconscious.

There is, secondly, the reader's relation to the work. How does the work achieve its effect on us? Here one may concentrate on the sensuous means, such as rhyme, meter, or assonance, or on the images. Or one may ask why the experiences, attitudes, or ideas expressed in the work affect us as they do. To give a specific example: why do so many readers admire and even love some of Shakespeare's heroes who, without the poet's art, might well evoke a negative reaction? The poet employs three devices. In the first place, he gives them enemies against whom we side immediately, thus sympathizing with the hero. Lear is the outstanding instance of "a man more sinned against than sinning"; but the same device is enlisted in behalf of Hamlet and Coriolanus. Secondly, there is the appeal of courage, older than poetry itself. The cunning Odysseus would seem loathsome if he were a coward, but his daring elevates him to the status of a hero. Courage is the tragic virtue par excellence. If the hero or heroine lacked it, the play would be no tragedy. Finally, Shakespeare's tragic heroes speak as we should like to be able to speak, and the conjunction of this power with courage makes them beings of a higher order who in important ways are as we should like to be.

Having asked how a work of literature achieves its effect on us, we can go on to ask why it impresses different readers differently, and especially why it has produced different effects in different ages. But the most interesting problems are generally concerned neither with the poet's relation to his work nor with the work's relation to the reader.

There remain the problems posed by the work itself. They

are primarily of two kinds: either obscurities, grounded in expressions, lacunae, and allusions; or inconsistencies, whether real or apparent. To try to explain such inconsistencies is the most fascinating part of literary exegesis.

87. INCONSISTENCIES. The frequency of vital inconsistencies in the most widely admired works of literature is generally vastly underestimated. It reduces to absurdity the thesis that consistency is a requirement of literary excellence in works of the imagination.

The most obvious example is furnished by the four Gospels. It would scarcely be credible if it were not such a well-established fact that the vast majority of readers are, and have been for centuries, quite unaware of the scores of vital contradictions between the four Gospels as well as the far fewer, but no less interesting, contradictions in each of the four. Moreover, the fascination of the Jesus of the Gospels is due in large measure to these inconsistencies, even though most readers are not conscious of them. It is these inconsistencies that have invited literally thousands of "Lives" of Jesus and almost as many diverse portraits of him.

There are those who suppose that consistency is the first condition of achieving verisimilitude or a likeness of life. No doubt, some measure of coherence is essential, but not nearly as much as most readers suppose. A measure of inconsistency liberates us from a sense of remote abstraction and restores fluidity and possibilities and, therefore, life itself.

There is a verisimilitude that achieves the opposite of its intention: it seeks lifelikeness and yet kills. Art achieves the greatest sense of life when it escapes such verisimilitude.

Would the ancient Greek torsos gain in beauty or vitality if we added arms? Or heads? Should we admire any number of them half as much if we could see them as their makers made them? Only the passage of five thousand years brought out that haunting look on the face of Zoser who built the step pyramid at Saqqara, the world's first large stone structure. Looking at a statue that is broken, we feel the texture of the stone, vibrant with life and with uncertainty. It makes us muse, whether we think of it that way or not, over human possibilities.

It would be too bold to say that inessentials have disappeared. One could hardly stipulate what is essential. What matters is that what remains calls into question our previous notions, and the artist's, too; and something new is seen. There are works of literature that would be vastly more impressive if only a few large fragments were left. That is even truer of sculptures. There is something offensive in a sculpture: it is an attack on the human body and face which after all are not simply stone—hard, inflexible, and smooth.

A face and a body are never finished while they are alive. That is why Michelangelo's unfinished sculptures are more alive than those he finished.

Look at two sculptures of Ikhnaton and of Sesostris III. In both the tip of the nose is broken. Nothing worth while seems lost. Rather the breach reminds us unconsciously that these are not passing likenesses which some such flaw might well reduce to worthlessness. These faces are not functional. That little loss is liberating. Unobtrusively it does what modern artists often go to such great lengths to do. The break frees us from bondage to the facts and is a triumph of the spirit.

What a break does sometimes for a sculpture, inconsistency may do for literary works. In neither case would it make sense to offer such a flaw as a reliable prescription. The Elgin marbles do not need their heads, but knocking the heads off other sculptures would not turn them into equals of the Elgin marbles. Nor is inconsistency in literature a panacea. But it does not necessarily constitute an objection and may even enhance the excellence of a work and increase its fascination.

In his most famous monologue, Hamlet speaks of death as "The undiscovered country from whose bourn no traveller returns"; and yet the whole action of the play is set in motion by the ghost of Hamlet's father who returned from death. Should we think of Hamlet as being fat, as we are told to at one point? Surely, he was thin. Or as being thirty, as we are told in another scene? Surely, he was younger. What has exerted the greatest fascination is the apparent contradiction between his callousness, evinced after Polonius' death and in relation to Rosencrantz and Guildenstern and even toward Ophelia, and his sensitivity; his rashness and his hesitation.

In *Macbeth* the Lady says in one of her most striking speeches:

> *I have given suck and know*
> *How tender 'tis to love the babe that milks me:*
> *I would, while it was smiling in my face,*
> *Have plucked my nipple from his boneless gums,*
> *And dashed the brains out, had I so sworn as you*
> *Have done to this.*

Yet later on, after the murder of Macduff's children, Macduff says of Macbeth: "He has no children."

This apparent inconsistency was noted by Goethe in a conversation with Eckermann, April 18, 1827. It did not trouble him in the least: "These words of Macduff contradict those of the Lady; but that does not bother Shakespeare. He is concerned with the power of each speech, and even as the Lady had to say, to lend the utmost emphasis to her words, 'I have given suck,' Macduff, too, had to say for the very same reason, 'He has no children.'" Goethe sums up his point by saying "that the poet always lets his characters say what in some particular place is fitting, effective, and good, without worrying a great deal, or anxiously calculating, whether these words might not perhaps offer an apparent contradiction to another passage." Christmas, 1825, Goethe told Eckermann that he considered *Macbeth* "Shakespeare's best play."

If there is one thing wrong with Goethe's analysis, which, incidentally, defends the artist's right to inconsistency quite generally and takes off from a Rubens canvas which features inconsistent shadows, it is Goethe's failure to note how deep the contradiction in *Macbeth* cuts. After all, the question whether Macbeth has children is anything but irrelevant to the plot. His rage at the prospect that Banquo's progeny are to inherit the throne from him and his attempt to prevent this, and even his intentions in seeking the throne, are intimately bound up with the issue whether he has children. Any hypothesis that the Lady was previously married or had a child from Macbeth which died in childhood would merit Goethe's scorn and overlook that Shakespeare was mysterious about one of the central points of the play.

The inconsistencies in Goethe's *Faust*, the most widely read and analyzed work of German literature, are legion. Consider two. One is slight but illustrates the poet's attitude. Some of the speeches are ascribed to "Gretchen" and some to "Margarete." They were written at different times, and Goethe felt no desire to level the difference: he associated some scenes with the full name and others with the diminutive. Nor did Goethe change Faust's great monologue in the scene "Forest and Cave" where Mephistopheles is described as an emissary of the Earth Spirit, after the Prologue in Heaven was added and Mephistopheles dispatched by God. himself. One can try to create an artificial harmony, but the poet would have despised any such attempt. His conversations are full of pertinent remarks:

Goethe expressly admired Shakespeare's "leaps and sudden transitions" (#1187); and on another occasion he said: "In poetry there are no contradictions. These exist only in the real world, not in the world of poetry. What the poet creates, that must be taken as he has created it. As he has made his world, it is. What issues from a poetic mind wants to be received by a poetic mind. Any cold analyzing destroys the poetry and does not generate any reality. All that remains are potsherds which are good for nothing and only incommode us." (#625) And Goethe's friend and executor von Müller reports: "I often heard him say: a work of art, especially a poem, that leaves nothing to be guessed is no true or entire work of art. Its highest calling is always to excite reflection; and it can become really dear to the beholder or reader only if it forces him to interpret it according to his own bent and, as it were, to complete it by recreating it." (#2280)

In a similar vein, Goethe wrote his friend Zelter on June 1, 1831, less than a year before his death, that the Second Part of *Faust* was practically completed, but that he still had to "wrap a few mantle folds around the finished product that it may altogether remain an evident riddle, delight men on and on, and give them something to work on." The most extreme statement is found in one of Goethe's most important conversations with Eckermann, dated May 6, 1827, and italicized by Eckermann: "The more incommensurable and incomprehensible for the understanding a poetic production is, the better."

88. QUELLENSCHEIDUNG. Nowhere have inconsistencies elicited more excitement or a greater secondary literature than in the case of sacred scriptures. In this genre interpreters for the past hundred years have not been satisfied to deal with evident contradictions: they have searched for inconsistencies, hunted for them, and not infrequently invented them. And one of the axioms of this so-called Higher Bible Criticism, which originated in Germany but soon spread to England and the United States where it is almost universally accepted today, except among fundamentalists, is that whenever two statements are inconsistent in any way they must have been written by different authors. The absurdity of this axiom is covered up by the fancy name of *Quellenscheidung*: discrimination of sources.

Imagine a Higher Critic analyzing Goethe's *Faust*, which was written by a single human being in the course of sixty years. The scenes in which the heroine of Part One is called Gretchen would be relegated to one author, those in which she is called Margarete to another; the conflicting conceptions of the role of Mephistopheles would be taken to call for further divisions, and the Prologue in Heaven would be ascribed to a later editor, while the Prelude on the Stage would be referred to yet a different author. Our critic would have no doubt whatsoever that Part Two belongs to a different age and must be assigned to a great many writers with widely different ideas. The end of Act IV, for example, points to an anti-Catholic author who lampoons the church, while the end of Act V was written by a man, we should be told, who, though probably no orthodox Catholic, was deeply sympathetic to Catholicism.

Where do we find more inconsistencies in style and thought and plan: in Goethe's *Faust* or in the Five Books of Moses?

In his book on *Die Philosophie der Inder*, Helmuth von Glasenapp, one of the foremost students of Hinduism, Jainism, and Buddhism, says of the Bhagavadgita, the most venerated and most popular Indian scripture: "Repeatedly, attempts have been made to construct an '*Urgita* [an original version of the Gita]' and to discriminate the earlier portions of the poem from the later ones. It is my considered judgment that all such attempts can at most be subjectively persuasive; for the contradictions and leaps of thought which serve the European scholar as clues that show how the text must have been expanded need not at all have been experienced as leaps and contradictions by an Indian, 2,000 years ago." One alleged inconsistency which von Glasenapp singles out for comment is that between theism and pantheism which has prompted the hypothesis that an originally theistic work was later revised from a pantheistic point of view. One of his objections to this argument is that the European notion of the opposition and mutual exclusiveness of theism and pantheism has never been accepted in India (170).

In the case of the Bible, the practice of *Quellenscheidung* is further vitiated by several other theories of which the most fantastic is what might be called the mosaic theory of creation.

89. THE TWO MOSAIC THEORIES.   Until the nineteenth century, the most popular conception of the origin of the Five Books of Moses was the Mosaic theory which maintained the authorship of Moses. This theory was based on a Jewish tradition that reaches back into pre-Christian times without, however, having any clear foundation in the texts themselves. Indeed, the final verses of the fifth book which relate the death of Moses were ascribed to Joshua by the Jewish tradition; but Genesis, in which Moses is not mentioned at all, was ascribed to Moses.

Spinoza, in his *Theological-Political Treatise*, listed reasons for disbelieving Moses' authorship, and approximately 100

years later, in 1753, a French physician, Jean Astruc, published an anonymous work entitled *Conjectures sur les mém-
oires originaux dont il paraît que Moyse s'est servi pour com-
poser le livre de la Genèse,* in which he suggested that there
must have been two main sources which Moses used in writing
the Book of Genesis.

The so-called Higher Criticism developed more than another 100 years later and bears the stamp of the second half
of the nineteenth century. It was one of the myriad forms of
popular Darwinism, an attempt to understand everything in
terms of evolution and—a widely prevalent confusion—progress.

Albright, in *From the Stone Age to Christianity* (88),
blames popular Hegelianism rather than Darwinism. These
two suggestions are not mutually exclusive, and in view of
the evidence Albright adduces, there can be no doubt that
Hegelianism, too, played an important part. In the Introduction to his *Prolegomena* (1878), which spearheaded the
Higher Criticism, Wellhausen named Vatke as the man from
whom he had "learned the most and the best"; and Vatke was
"an ardent Hegelian" whose "most important book on biblical
theology (1835) is saturated with Hegelian terminology. Wellhausen and his school, to which belonged in the last decade
before the World War practically every Protestant Old Testament scholar of standing in the world, reflect their Hegelian
background in various ways." Albright lists many salient He-
gelianisms in the Higher Criticism, concluding with "the Hegelian view that the fully developed religion of Israel unfolded
gradually from primitive naturalism to lofty ethical monotheism."

Surely, this evolutionary idea was greatly reinforced by popular Darwinism. And the most distinctive thesis of the Higher
Criticism was quite un-Hegelian: namely, its essentially novel
mosaic theory.

That many traditions had developed before the Five Books
of Moses were written down, few will doubt. Both Goethe and
Shakespeare drew on old traditions, and these were not always
consistent. In the case of the Bible, even a man who did not
deliberately set out to study various traditions must often have

heard the same stories, or similar stories, about the creation, the flood, and the patriarchs in slightly different ways from, let us say, his two grandmothers. If he sat down to record these stories, or even if he merely passed them on by word of mouth to his own children and his children's children, is it reasonable to assume that he would make a choice in every case between the rival versions and suppress one for the sole sake of consistency? It is far more likely that he would either mix both or tell both—sometimes one right after the other, and sometimes the first on one occasion and the second on the next Sabbath or perhaps a year or two later.

The Higher Criticism went far beyond such reasonable assumptions and proposed to view the Five Books of Moses as quite literally a mosaic, though this word was not used. It was assumed that the editor or editors had worked, as it were, with scissors and paste, and the Higher Critics vied with each other in assigning verses, even half verses, to different sources and outdid each other in "discovering" sources. This was supposed to be a belated scientific approach to the Bible, but was really deeply unscientific: it depended on highly implausible assumptions which were not examined critically, and the procedures of the critics as they dealt with specific texts were excessively arbitrary.

The point of departure for the division of sources was the use in the Bible of two different designations for the deity which are rendered in the English Bible as, respectively, "God" and "Lord." The first of these is in Hebrew Elohim, while the Hebrew word for the second presents a problem. In the texts without vowel signs it consists of four letters and is therefore sometimes called the Tetragrammaton. These letters can be transcribed variously, depending on whether we use a J or a Y, a V or a W; e.g., J H V H. At an early date, centuries before the time of Jesus, the Jews ceased pronouncing the name and began to say Adonai, my Lord, instead. Later, when the text was sometimes written with vowels, the Tetragrammaton was given the vowels of Adonai since the reader was supposed to read Adonai: and a medieval Christian misinterpretation of this practice gave rise to the Christian form Jehovah. Most modern scholars now think that the original pronunciation was probably Yahweh.

About the derivation and meaning, if any, of this name there is no agreement. But there is agreement that Exodus 3.14 is intended as an interpretation: "And Moses said to God: When I come to the children of Israel, and say to them, The God of your fathers has sent me to you; and they ask me, What is his name? what shall I say to them? and God said to Moses, EHYEH ASHER EHYEH: and he said, say this to the children of Israel, EHYEH has sent me to you." The King James Bible renders the first phrase "I AM THAT I AM" and the second "I AM."

Martin Buber has argued most persuasively (82 ff.) that the question which Moses anticipates depends on the Egyptian assumption that one can conjure a god if one knows his name, while God's reply means: "I shall be present as whoever I shall be present." I shall be there, but you cannot predict the mode of my presence. "In sum: you do not have to conjure me, neither can you conjure me." The Tetragrammaton, with the initial J or Y which indicates the third person, would then mean: HE IS PRESENT.

The Higher Criticism starts with the assumption that verses which contain the word Elohim must have been written by one author, and verses which contain the Tetragrammaton by another. The first author is called, for want of any other evidence, the Elohist or E for short; the second, the Jahvist or J. It is assumed that the same person could not have written the verses which in the English Pentateuch refer to God and those which refer to the Lord. Indeed, this is widely taken for granted today by nonfundamentalist students of the Bible, and people forget how utterly implausible this assumption is on the face of it.

If we treat it as a hypothesis, the question becomes how it works: What happens if we move into two different columns the verses with "God" and the verses with "Lord"? Do we get two independent narratives? Do we find that there are differences in style and sensibility and attitude? The answer to all these questions is No. Moreover, there are many verses, beginning in Genesis 2, where God is called "The Lord God" (JHVH Elohim). The hypothesis requires a great many auxiliary hypotheses. To our two hypothetical authors, J and E, two further hypothetical authors are added: P, a supposed "priestly" author, and D, who is credited above all with the fifth Book of Moses, Deuteronomy. Nor is this sufficient: as the literature grew and more and more young scholars had to make original contributions to knowledge, more and more "sources" were discovered: J_1 and J_2 as well as E_1 and E_2, and so forth.

That there are such different authors as these is one of the conventions of the game and has been widely accepted by laymen; but on the detailed analysis of specific chapters there is wide disagreement. Even where there is a large area of agreement, as in the case of the flood story in Genesis 6–9, the basic presuppositions deserve to be examined. The interested reader will find a visual representation of the mosaic in Karl Budde's *Geschichte der althebräischen Litteratur* (49 ff.) and a brief summary of the claims in S. R. Driver's *An Introduction to the Literature of the Old Testament* (14 f.).

The most detailed and impressive critique of the Higher Criticism is unfortunately little known: it is a tall volume of over 1,000 pages, published in Germany in 1934 in a small edition: *Das Erste Buch der Tora Genesis übersetzt und erklärt von B. Jacob.* Throughout, the commentary is written against the background of the Higher Criticism, showing its inadequacy and proposing an alternative, and in the end an Appendix of 100 pages deals specifically with *"Quellenscheidung."*

According to the Higher Criticism, the editors of the Biblical books took all kinds of liberties and carved up the received texts, moving half a sentence here a few sentences down, and three and a half sentences there a few sentences up, while altogether suppressing and omitting large portions of each source which could not be fitted into this mosaic. But *on this hypothesis, though it is prompted by both real and alleged inconsistencies, such inconsistencies are all but inexplicable.*

That the editor arrogated the right to leave out parts of

both the manuscripts from which he allegedly copied his account is explicitly admitted by Driver and his colleagues and
cannot be denied by any Higher Critic, seeing that we do not
find two complete reports of the flood, for example; and the
detection of the most highhanded transpositions of sentences
and half-sentences is the forte of the Higher Critics. *On these
assumptions, the editor would have had to be an idiot* if he
ended up by offering a text as full of inconsistencies as the
Higher Critics find it.

The gross materialism underlying the Higher Criticism has
perhaps never been duly noted. Nowhere else do we find a
comparable example of the mechanistic outlook which Bergson criticized: these men literally believed that artistic creation could be explained in terms of a purely spatial construction out of separate particles. We know of no major work of
literature that originated in any such fashion, even if we waive
the requirement that the artist who put the work together
must have been an idiot. And Genesis, with its less than 100
pages, need not fear comparison in content and form, in its
inexhaustibility and in its impact on human thought and art,
with any other book of any length in any tongue.

How are we to read this book? Any suggestion of the close
affinity of religion and poetry is generally met with the retort
that a religious scripture is not mere poetry, which is true
enough. But at the very least one might accord a religious
scripture the same courtesy which one extends to poetry and
recall Goethe's dictum: "What issues from a poetic mind wants
to be received by a poetic mind. Any cold analyzing destroys
the poetry and does not generate any reality. All that remains
are potsherds which are good for nothing and only incommode us." (Cf. § 87.)

The Higher Criticism must be understood as a revolt against
the long-unquestioned authority of the Old Testament, and
some of its chief exponents were clearly motivated in part by
the wish to debunk the book and its god. Really, some Higher
Critics seem to be saying, this god is not so great or mysterious
—we don't mind calling him Yahweh to make clear that he is

no better than Jove or Aphrodite—and as for the book, any one of us could have done much better.

It is an iconoclastic movement, as blind to the beauty of the Hebrew Scriptures as the iconoclasts of Luther's time were to the beauty of the sculptures they destroyed. The Higher Critics, of course, have not literally destroyed the texts, but they have taught several generations to see only the potsherds.

In recent years many Biblical scholars have given up the major presuppositions of the Higher Criticism, but their work has not yet been noted sufficiently. Nyberg has argued that in the Orient tradition is predominantly oral and that "no Muslim scholar ever looks up any verse in his copy of the Koran; the book must be learned by heart and is used and cited only in this manner." He tells of a Parsi priest who recited the Yasna fluently from beginning to end without understanding a word of it. "He did have a book, I admit; but, asked about the pronunciation of this or that written word, he first had to spell out, with some difficulty, the first word of the page; and, only after having found the thread in this way, he would recite till he came to the desired word" (7 f.).

Nyberg also points out that the unsound methods of the Higher Criticism were developed at a time "when good taste had reached a lower point than perhaps during any other period in the history of European culture" (5) and when classical philologists, too, were in the habit of offering bold but baseless emendations and conjectures. He mentions a scholar who made 700 revisions in Horace and claimed that *Paradise Lost* was full of later interpolations. Another Latinist proposed enough ingenious emendations of Horace to be able in the end to publish a volume which contained, in effect, a revised version of the poems which, while hardly improved, had become rather amusing (1 ff.).

Regarding Old Testament criticism, Nyberg writes: "The most insane arbitrariness in this field is slowly beginning to recede, but we are still far from any clear reflection on the problem of principles. The first step to such reflection, however, must be the recognition of the errors in method that have so

far been made in the treatment of the texts" (13). And few
readers will differ with Nyberg's conclusion: "In the end, we
should remember a good old philological rule: when one does
not understand something, one should first mistrust oneself and
not the text" (16).

Another Scandinavian scholar, Aage Bentzen, whose *Introduction to the Old Testament,* in two volumes, is beginning
to attract some attention in the United States, is a little less
radical than Nyberg. He sums up the new temper by citing a
conversation between two Old Testament scholars in which the
first differs with past practice by saying, "We must not use
conjectures unless it is absolutely necessary," and the second
replies: "And then, too, it is best not to use it" (97). After a
sixty-page survey of the traditional "Massoretic" Hebrew text,
the Samaritan text, and other ancient texts and translations,
notably including the Septuagint, he arrives at the conclusion:
"*Veritas Hebraica* in the reliability of its tradition stands above
all other witnesses. Of course its value is not the same in all
its parts. The Torah is relatively well preserved. . . . The
handing down of the Law probably has been attended to with
special care" (101). Of special interest is Bentzen's very detailed survey at the beginning of the second volume of the
whole history of Bible criticism down to, and including, the
work of Nyberg and another important Scandinavian scholar,
I. Engnell.

"All this shows that the history of the older documentary
theory from ca. 1800 is repeating itself: *The New Documentary Theory is tending towards self-dissolution*" (II, 16). But
most of the post-documentary scholars still approach Genesis
and the rest of the Torah too much as if they were straight
history and with too little feeling for their poetic character or
their homiletic intent.

In explaining "The Documentary Hypothesis, Its Basis and
Its Methods," not without sympathy, Bentzen writes: "Continually we encounter perplexing *repetitions,* e.g. the double
tradition of the creation, containing *contradictions* which seem
to exclude the possibility of one man as originator of both"
(24). Even in view of the many examples he adduces, this

inference depends on the assumption that the primary intent of Genesis is to tell us "how it actually happened," to use Ranke's celebrated formula. But this is hardly the purpose of the story of the creation (cf. § 83), notwithstanding the final sentence in the following quotation from Bentzen:

"It is true that such variants and contradictions do not prove the documentary hypothesis, and not even always that there are different traditions behind the books. Oral tradition works with repetition. But it is an exaggeration, when *Cassuto* tells us that his supposed 'maestro di altissimo genio' who has collected the old traditions has built them up as a harmonious whole, forming a narrative which is 'an organic and well-to-gether-welded unity.' The two creation stories cannot be reconciled . . ." (25).

Neither the last sentence nor Bentzen's assertion that "There are differences in the conception of God" (26) refutes Cassuto (393 f.)—unless, of course, we are prepared to say that neither *Macbeth* nor *Faust* is "an organic and well-together-welded unity" and that therefore they cannot be ascribed to any *maestro di altissimo genio.*

Anyone who has ever written with any feeling for literary form must have felt a real regret at having to eliminate one of two inconsistent statements or passages, assuming that both were exceedingly well put and that each also said something worth saying. A modern philosopher will generally feel that he must do something to eliminate the inconsistency; a modern poet or preacher may not consider it necessary; and the assumption that the author of Genesis should have felt any such constraint is downright fantastic.

The Sabbath commandment in the Decalogue is worded differently in Exodus (20.8 ff.) and Deuteronomy (5.12 ff.). There is no troubling inconsistency here unless we insist on asking what the Lord really said. The rabbis, of course, did ask that question and gave the only sensible answer, provided one asks the question at all: God, unlike man, was able to say both at once. And if it were asked which explanation was given on the two tablets of the law—assuming that there was space for all this—one might conjecture that the words of Exodus were found on the first set which Moses smashed in his anger, while those of Deuteronomy appeared on the second set. This suggestion is meant in somewhat the same spirit in which another rabbi answered the question what God did before the creation: he made switches for people who ask such questions.

There are convincing reasons for denying that Moses wrote the Pentateuch (summarized ably by Bentzen, II, 10 ff.) and for ascribing Isaiah 40 ff. to a prophet who lived during the exile rather than the Isaiah who lived in the eighth century, almost 200 years earlier. These as well as many other findings of a similar sort enhance our understanding of the texts. But the Higher Critics were much more literal-minded than many fundamentalists: they assumed that the flood story was meant as straight history and were terribly distressed when they found mutually contradictory statements. Certainly, the later books of the Bible contain a great deal of history, and even the Torah makes abundant use of historical traditions; but the primary intent of the Five Books of Moses is not to offer us positivistic historiography. And any textual criticism which is based on this assumption is obtuse.

It may be objected that modern archaeology has proved that the Old Testament narratives are by no means mere poetry. But for that matter Heinrich Schliemann and Sir Arthur Evans were able to use Homer to find clues for the discovery of propitious sites for excavations, and they have shown that Homer's poems as well as many Greek myths made ample use of historic memories. We can also read Shakespeare to inform ourselves about Elizabethan mores or to find out how English was pronounced in his time. There cannot be the least objection against reading the Bible in an effort to find out all sorts of things. What is untenable, however, is any approach that assumes implicitly that the Bible, and Genesis in particular, was written by men whose prime motive it was to give us information of this sort.

Goethe's previously cited statement goes too far in its all-out opposition to analysis. By all means, be analytic, too. Analysis may be prompted by reverence. For that matter, a lot can be said in favor of irreverence. But Goethe was surely right when he said: "What issues from a poetic mind wants to be received by a poetic mind."

90. RELIGION AND PROGRESS.   At the beginning of his book on *The Modern Use of the Bible,* Harry Emerson Fosdick claims with unconcealed satisfaction: "The total consequence of all the work of the Higher Criticism is that at last we are able to see the Bible a good deal as a geologist sees the strata of the earth; we can tell when and in what order the deposits were laid down whose accumulated results constitute our Scriptures" (6). It might be objected that the geologist's approach is hardly appropriate, but Fosdick goes on to explain the reasons for his delight.

"It means that we can trace the great ideas of Scripture in their development from their simple and elementary forms, when they first appear in the earliest writings, until they come to their full maturity in the latest books. Indeed, the general soundness of the critical results is tested by this fact that as one moves up from the earlier writings toward the later he can observe the development of any idea he chooses to select, such as God, man, duty, sin, worship. Plainly we are dealing with ideas that enlarge their scope, deepen their meaning, are played upon by changing circumstance and maturing thought, so that from its lowliest beginnings in the earliest writings of the Hebrews any religious or ethical idea of the Bible can now be traced, traveling an often uneven but ascending roadway to its climax in the teaching of Jesus."

That the Old Testament must be read as a story of progress is not one of the results of the Higher Criticism but one of its dubious presuppositions. What is at stake is the question to what extent the conception of progress is applicable to religions.

In the case of the Hebrew Scriptures we do not know, to begin with, what is early and what is late; but, if there were overwhelming evidence in the case of other great religions that they rise gradually from humble beginnings and slowly get better in some sense, it would be reasonable to ask whether this same pattern might not be found in the Old Testament, too.

What we find in other great religions, however, is the very opposite of all this. Where we have data, we often find a towering figure, possibly never equaled since, in the beginning, and it is therefore entirely reasonable to suppose that some of the most impressive ideas of the Old Testament might have originated with Moses.

That there is progress in another sense, we need not doubt. Ideas which first occur to one man and are understood by few are gradually disseminated to a growing minority until eventually they become common property. That this happened with the religion of Moses is stressed emphatically in the Old Testament, which makes a great deal of the stiff-necked generation which was not prepared to absorb Moses' ideas; and the same theme runs through Judges, Kings, and Prophets.

It does not detract from the glory of the prophets if we suppose that they meant it when they said: "You have been told, man, what is good." To have insisted so uncompromisingly and with such an utter lack of egotism on what their people had been told before and to have grasped so clearly the moral and social implications; to have insisted on them to the point of disparaging in no uncertain terms the cult and ritual—much more unequivocally than Jesus ever did—that would be original enough. The idea that war is evil, that nation should not lift up sword against nation, that swords should be made into plowshares and spears into pruning hooks, though it is implicit in the old idea that all men are brothers, descended from a single couple and made in the image of God, appears in any case to have originated with Micah and Isaiah; and to have seen and forcefully stated this implication, untutored by the horrors of two world wars with poison gas and atom bombs, shows as much moral originality as is to be found anywhere in recorded history.

The popular construction of a gradual evolution of monotheism, on the other hand, which is supposed to have been far beyond the ken of Moses and to have been fully attained only by the Second Isaiah, depends on the arbitrary ruling that all the hundreds of emphatically monotheistic passages in apparently pre-exilic texts must be of a later date.

The tremendous emphasis of the Second Isaiah that there is only one God who has created both light and darkness must be understood in terms of his time: he prophesied as the Persians conquered the Babylonian empire, and he insisted that there were not two gods, a god of light and a god of darkness, as the Persians believed, but that Cyrus, the king of the Persians, had been sent by the one and only God to put an end to the exile of Israel.

The monotheism of the first prophet, Amos, was no less pure when he cried out: "Are you not as children of the Ethiopians to me, O children of Israel? says the Lord. Have I not brought up Israel out of the land of Egypt? and the Philistines from Crete, and the Syrians from Kir?"

Still further back, we find Elijah. Julius Wellhausen, who is widely considered the greatest of the Higher Critics, hailed Elijah as a lone exception: "Solitary, this prophet, the most grandiose heroic figure of the Bible, towered above his age." But only a page later, Wellhausen has to admit: "At that time the idea of God began to rise in a few individuals, as it seems, above national borders. Of a similar spirit as Elijah's, and no less solitary than he, was his contemporary Micaiah ben Yimlah" (77). As a matter of fact, Kings is full of prophets, both solitary ones and groups. Can we rule out the possibility that King Solomon, a century before Elijah, might really have said when consecrating the temple, as he is reported to have said in I Kings 8: "Behold, the heaven and heaven of heavens cannot contain thee; how much less this house that I have built?"

The most probable hypothesis is that both monotheism and exalted moral demands were offered by Moses in the thirteenth century B.C., and that he appealed to and interpreted still earlier traditions; that for a long time neither his monotheism nor his moral demands were absorbed by the mass of the people though in nearly every generation there were at least one or two who recalled the children of Israel to Moses' teaching, while many of the rest handed on their ancient heritage from generation to generation without fully comprehending it and without much grasp of its radical moral implications; that for 200 years, beginning in the eighth century, there was a rapid

succession of towering figures whom we call the prophets; and
that by the end of that time, as the exile drew to a close, the
heritage of Moses and the prophets had in principle been absorbed by the whole Jewish people, though, of course, they
did not always live up to it. A similar view has been defended
in detail by Albright, who is a devout Christian and the leading Biblical archaeologist.

From the Mosaic-prophetic point of view, then, there was
progress in two ways. First, ideas initially held by a minute
minority gradually became common property. Second, as these
ideas were reiterated by the few in a relentless effort to impress the recalcitrant majority, these ideas had to be related
to ever new situations; and in this process new facets were
emphasized and hidden implications spelled out. In retrospect
this explication is easily underestimated; it is better appreciated
by those who live through part of it. Americans, for example,
may think of the arduous road from the "self-evident" truth
that "all men are created equal and endowed by their Creator
with certain unalienable rights" to the abolition of slavery and
hence to equality for the Negro, effectively guaranteed by law.

To enable us to speak of progress, two conditions must be
fulfilled. First, there must be some continuity rather than a
disjunction. Second, and this is crucial, one must adopt a point
of view and pass a value judgment to speak of progress. Progress is not a purely descriptive concept but always involves
some norm.

It is therefore very doubtful whether it makes sense to speak
of progress in poetry or in art generally. It does make sense to
speak of *development*—for example, from Byzantine art to
Simone Martini and Giotto, and hence to Masaccio and Michelangelo, Tintoretto and the Baroque, and from that to the
Rococo. Whether one considers this development an instance of
progress is quite another question. Some might call it progress
up to Giotto, others up to Michelangelo, and few all the way
to the Rococo. One might also view this evolution as an instance of decline, at least from a certain point on; or one might
accept Ranke's dictum: "Every epoch is immediate to God,

and its value rests not at all on that which issues from it, but in its existence itself, in its own self."

These words from Ranke's preface to his *Epochen der Neueren Geschichte* (1888, p. 5) could scarcely be more applicable to religion and religious scriptures. As long as we read the Rig-Veda mainly as the foundation for the Upanishads; or the latter as the steppingstone of Buddhism; or the Dhammapada and other early Buddhist scriptures as important background material for the understanding of the Bhagavadgita, we remain deaf to what these scriptures have to say to us. Exactly the same is true of the fashionable approach to the Old Testament: it is profoundly obtuse. What is most unfortunate about this is that, even conservatively estimated, few books have so much to offer us.

91. THE GOSPELS AND POETRY.   Those who are willing to admit that Genesis no less than the Bhagavadgita and the Dhammapada is poetry may still have qualms about the Gospels. These, they feel, are not poetry but history. One could make the same claim with rather more justice regarding large portions of the Old Testament; but let us look briefly at Christ's words from the cross, which are sometimes compiled in a single sequence and given to children to learn by heart.

According to both Mark and Matthew, Jesus cried out with a loud voice about the ninth hour: "Eloi, Eloi, lama sabachthani." Matthew has "Eli" instead of "Eloi." Both translate the Aramaic outcry which means "My God, my God, why hast thou forsaken me?" In Hebrew, it is the beginning of the 22nd Psalm, and the whole account of the crucifixion abounds in allusions to this Psalm. After this, according to Mark and Matthew, Jesus "cried again with a loud voice, and yielded up his spirit" or "uttered a loud voice, and gave up the ghost." Neither of these two evangelists, of course, had been present at the crucifixion, nor does either of them claim that any of Jesus' disciples were anywhere near at the time. Their very close and often quite literal agreement is due to the fact that Mark "was *the* most important source of the First Gospel," i.e., Matthew's (Major, 6).

Luke begins his Gospel by referring to "many" other Gospels with which he is not satisfied and explains how it seemed good to him to write an account of his own. According to Luke, Jesus did not cry out, "My God, my God, why hast thou forsaken me?" But he did say three other things. First, "Father, forgive them; for they know not what they do." This sentence is missing in many ancient manuscripts (see the Revised Standard Version) and "must be considered more or less doubtful" (Enslin, 208). Then Luke added a little conversation between Jesus and the two robbers who, according to both Mark and Matthew, were crucified together with him. After some dialogue between the two malefactors—this is what Luke calls them—Jesus says to one of them: "Truly, I say to you, today you will be with me in paradise." Finally, "when Jesus had cried with a loud voice, he said, Father, into thy hands I commend my spirit; and having said this, he gave up the ghost."

How likely is it that Luke was guided by better information, extracted from a man who had spoken to an eyewitness who had been closer to the cross? Even Thucydides, the greatest ancient historian, who is still admired by modern historians for having possessed the true historian's spirit and for having set an example of sound method, felt free to put into the mouths of historical figures speeches which were meant to express in graceful literary form what, he supposed, these men must have thought in a given situation and might fittingly have said. May we not suppose that Luke did the same? Surely, he omitted the Aramaic outcry recorded by Mark and Matthew because he considered it unfitting and offensive. Whether Jesus had ever cried out those words, I should not make bold to say, particularly in view of the many other references in the story to the 22nd Psalm—which Luke kept, presumably because they were not offensive. "Father, forgive them" seemed more fitting to Luke than "My God, why hast thou forsaken me." And given the situation of Christ crucified between two robbers, Luke wondered what might have gone on in their minds and added a conversation. Nor was he satisfied to record that Jesus should

have merely cried out with a loud voice and given up the
ghost. It seemed more fitting that he should have said, "Father,
into thy hands I commend my spirit"—a fine antithesis to Mark's
and Matthew's version of Christ's last words.

John, coming latest in time, has Jesus say four things, not
including any of the words offered by the other three. John—
or rather the writer who adopted the name of John, the disciple, whose oral tradition he may have used—has Jesus see
John. "When Jesus saw his mother, and the disciple whom he
he loved standing near, he said to his mother: Woman, behold, your son! Then he said to the disciple: Behold your
mother! And from that hour the disciple took her to his home.
After this, Jesus knowing that all things were now accomplished, said, that the Scripture might be fulfilled: I thirst." In
accordance with Psalm 69.21, he is then given vinegar to drink
and, having received that, "he said: It is finished; and he
bowed his head and gave up his spirit."

The words from the cross are a paradigm of the attitude
of the four evangelists toward their subject matter. Here is a
tremendously important story which all four of them tell.
Clearly, their attitude is not that of the rigorous modern historian as he is supposed to be, ascetically sacrificing sentiment
to fact and preference to truth. Matthew's and Luke's stories
of Jesus' birth furnish even more extreme examples. (For an
excellent discussion of the Gospels and Acts by an outstanding
Christian scholar who corroborates many of my suggestions
without going into precisely the same problems, see Morton
Scott Enslin's *Christian Beginnings,* especially pp. 418–451.)

Are the evangelists, then, writing "mere" poetry? No, they
are preaching. They want to obligate men and demand a commitment. And the difference between religious scriptures and
poetry is not, as is usually supposed, either that poetry is relatively trivial or that religious scriptures claim to be true. Both
claims are untenable. Some religious scriptures are unimpres-
sive, too, and *King Lear* and *Faust* are not trivial. An excellent
performance of *Lear* is as deeply moving as any religious
scripture; and many people are much more affected by Keats
than by the Apocalypse or even by John. Nor do religious

scriptures necessarily claim to be true in a sense in which poetry is not true; certainly, they do not always claim to be literally true.

What makes a work of literature a scripture is that it is accepted as obligatory. Not all scriptures were intended by their writers to be accepted in this way, but the Gospels were. Their primary intent was plainly not to entertain nor to move deeply a few scattered individuals here and there through the centuries. The evangelists felt free to employ what we today might call poetic license whenever it seemed fitting to get across their message. Matthew had no qualms about assembling Jesus' most striking teachings and making a single sermon of them, but his intention in doing this was clearly not merely poetic but homiletic. And Luke did not hesitate to invent appropriate situations and conversations in which he might place some of these very same dicta.

Tolstoy's intent in writing *Resurrection* was also primarily homiletic, though it is a fine novel. What keeps the book from being a sacred scripture is that it has not been adopted as canonical or authoritative by any church or community. What makes the Song of Songs a sacred scripture rather than "mere" poetry is the fact that it has been canonized first by the Jews and then by the Christians. If we should recover any of the ancient Hebrew works referred to in the Bible, they would be examples of old Hebrew literature but not scriptures, unless we found that some sect had at one time adopted them as part of their canon.

Not all scriptures preach. To accept them as scriptures means accepting them as somehow authoritative and assuming that they have something important to tell us. And to read scriptures that one does not oneself accept, not as mere poetry but as scriptures, that involves asking about their homiletic content, about the demands they make on those who do accept them. To do justice to a scripture we must ask how it would have us change our lives.

Those who accept a scripture as canonical do not necessarily agree about its homiletic implications, but they do agree in principle that they must concede it some authority over their lives. If Luther, for example, does not accept the Sermon on the Mount as obligatory, he nevertheless does not objectify it as something very interesting or as the product of a moral genius: he is convinced that this Sermon is there to teach him something—namely, man's utter inability to do good or to satisfy God by works.

Scriptures can be read "as living literature" or as historical documents, or for clues to propitious sites for excavations. We can also read them to study the stylistic forms, or simply for enjoyment. But as long as we do not allow the texts to address us, we read with a closed heart.

To hear the message does not necessarily involve accepting it; but until we hear it our reading has been obtuse and our nonacceptance irresponsible.

Not all poetry should be read as "mere" poetry either. We can let the experience of life that found expression in it address us; we can allow it to change us as an encounter with a human being sometimes changes us.

92. A BUDDHIST TEXT.   Most translations give no adequate idea at all of Buddhist scriptures, and those in most anthologies are especially inadequate. The originals are so exceedingly long and repetitious that the translator or editor usually feels forced to omit most of the text, keeping the bare plot and at best indicating the omissions with dots. The result is as alien to the original as if we changed the tempo of a piece of music, speeding up a slow movement, and making up for omissions by syncopation.

Here is a story from the so-called medium collection, Majjhimanikayo, of the Pali canon of early Buddhist scriptures. I follow the German translation of Karl Eugen Neumann, who made no omissions and even followed the rhythms of the original. The chapter, Number 87, which I quote in full, is entitled "What is dear to one."

"This I have heard. At one time the Sublime One dwelt at Savatthi, in the Forest of Triumph, in the garden Anathapindikos.

"At this time, some father's only, much beloved little boy had died. And now that he was dead, the father did not care to work or eat. Again and again he went back to the corpse and moaned: 'Where are you, only little boy? Where are you, only little boy?'

"Then this father went to the place where the Sublime One dwelt, greeted the Sublime One reverently, and sat down sideways. And to this father who was sitting there sideways, the Sublime One now turned thus:

" 'Your features, father, are not those of a man spiritually composed: your features are disturbed.'

" 'How, O Lord, should my features not be disturbed? After all, O Lord, my only, much beloved little boy has died! And now that he is dead, I do not care to work or eat. Again and again I go back to the corpse and moan: "Where are you, only little boy? Where are you, only little boy?" '

" 'Thus it is, father; thus it is, father. What is dear to one, father, brings hurt and misery, suffering, grief, and despair, which comes from what is dear.'

" 'Who, O Lord, could possibly think: "What is dear to one, brings hurt and misery, suffering, grief, and despair, which comes from what is dear"? What is dear to one, O Lord, brings joy and satisfaction, which comes from what is dear.'

"And the father, indignant and annoyed at the word of the Sublime One, rose from his seat and went away.

"Now, at that time, there were assembled together, not very far from the Sublime One, many dice-throwers who were throwing dice. Then this father went to them and spoke thus:

" 'I, O Lords, had gone to the ascetic Gotamo, had greeted him reverently and sat down sideways. And as I sat there, O Lords, the ascetic Gotamo turned toward me thus: "Your features, father, are not those of a man spiritually composed: your features are disturbed." Thus addressed, O Lords, I replied to the ascetic Gotamo: "How, O Lord, should my features not be disturbed? After all, O Lord, my only, much beloved little boy has died! And now that he is dead, I do not care to work or eat. Again and again I go back to the corpse and moan: 'Where are you, only little boy? Where are you, only little boy?' "—

"Thus it is, father; thus it is, father. What is dear to one, father, brings hurt and misery, suffering, grief, and despair, which comes from what is dear."—"Who, O Lord, could possibly think: 'What is dear to one, brings hurt and misery, suffering, grief, and despair, which comes from what is dear'? What is dear to one, O Lord, brings joy and satisfaction, which comes from what is dear." Thus I spoke, O Lords, indignant and annoyed at the word of the ascetic Gotamo, rose from my seat and went away.'

"'Thus it is, father; thus it is, father! What is dear to one, father, brings joy and satisfaction, which comes from what is dear.'

"Then the father said: 'Then I am right according to the dice-throwers!' And he went away.

"Gradually, this conversation became known all the way to the court of the king. And King Pasenadi of Kosalo turned to his wife Mallika:

"'Hear, Mallika, your ascetic Gotamo has said: "What is dear to one, brings hurt and misery, suffering, grief, and despair, which comes from what is dear."'

"'If that is, great king, what the Sublime One has said, then it is thus.'

"'Whatever the ascetic Gotamo may say, this Mallika always concedes everything, simply everything: "If that is, great king, what the Sublime One has said, then it is thus." Even as, whatever the teacher may say to the pupil, the pupil always agrees with everything, "Thus it is, Master; thus it is, Master," even so you, Mallika concede everything, simply everything, whatever the ascetic Gotama may say: "If that is, great king, what the Sublime One has said, then it is thus." Let it be, Mallika, stop it!'

"Then Queen Mallika turned to the Brahmin Nalijangho and asked him:

"'Go, Brahmin, to the Sublime One and at his feet bring the Sublime One my greetings and wish him health and freshness, cheerfulness, strength, and well-being: "Mallika," thus speak, "O Lord, the Queen, offers the Sublime One at his feet greetings and wishes him health and freshness, cheerfulness, strength,

and well-being." And then add: "Is it true, O Lord, that the
Sublime One has spoken this word: 'What is dear to one, brings
hurt and misery, suffering, grief, and despair, which comes
from what is dear'?" And how the Sublime One replies to you,
that remember well and report to me. For the Perfected do
not speak imperfectly.'

" 'Yes, Mistress!' Nalijangho, the Brahmin, replied obediently
to Mallika, the Queen. And he went to where the Sublime One
was dwelling, exchanged polite greetings and friendly, memorable words with the Sublime One, and sat down sideways.
Sitting sideways, Nalijangho, the Brahmin, spoke thus to the
Sublime One:

" 'Mallika, O Gotamo, the Queen, offers the Lord Gotamo
greetings at his feet and wishes him health and freshness, cheerfulness, strength, and well-being; and she added: Is it true, O
Lord, that the Sublime One has spoken this word: "What is
dear to one, brings hurt and misery, suffering, grief, and despair, which comes from what is dear"?'

" 'Thus it is, Brahmin; thus it is, Brahmin. What is dear to
one, Brahmin, brings hurt and misery, suffering, grief, and despair, which comes from what is dear. Therefore, Brahmin, one
must always judge according to the circumstances how what is
dear to one brings hurt and misery, suffering, grief, and despair, which comes from what is dear. One day, Brahmin, some
woman's mother had died here in Savatthi. Frenzied and deranged in her mind by this death, she ran from street to street,
from market to market, and cried: "Have you not seen my
mother? Have you not seen my mother?" Therefore, Brahmin,
one should judge according to the circumstances how what is
dear to one, brings hurt and misery, suffering, grief, and despair, which comes from what is dear.

" 'One day, Brahmin, some woman's father had died here in
Savatthi—brother, sister had died; son, daughter had died; husband had died. Frenzied and deranged in her mind by this
death, she ran from street to street, from market to market,
and cried: "Have you not seen my husband? Have you not seen
my husband?" Therefore, Brahmin, one should judge according to the circumstances how what is dear to one, brings hurt

and misery, suffering, grief, and despair, which comes from what is dear.

" 'One day, Brahmin, some man's mother had died here in Savatthi—father had died; brother, sister had died; son, daughter had died; wife had died. Frenzied and deranged in his mind by this death, he ran from street to street, from market to market, and cried: "Have you not seen my wife? Have you not seen my wife?" Therefore, Brahmin, one should judge according to the circumstances how what is dear to one, brings hurt and misery, suffering, grief, and despair, which comes from what is dear.

" 'One day, Brahmin, some woman had come into the house of her relatives here in Savatthi. And these relatives forbade her to live with her husband and wanted to marry her to another man; but she did not want him. And she implored her husband: "These relatives, O husband, tear me away from you and want to marry me to another man; but I do not want him." And the husband killed his wife and took his own life: "Dead, we shall be together." Therefore, Brahmin, one should judge according to the circumstances how what is dear to one, brings hurt and misery, suffering, grief, and despair, which comes from what is dear.'

"And Nalijangho, the Brahmin, pleased and satisfied with the speech of the Sublime One, rose and returned to Mallika, the Queen, and related to her, word for word, the entire conversation which the Sublime One had had with him. And Queen Mallika now went to King Pasenadi and spoke thus:

" 'What do you think, great king: is your daughter Vajiri dear to you?'

" 'Certainly, Mallika, my daughter Vajiri is dear to me.'

" 'What do you think, great king: if something happened to your daughter Vajiri, if something harmed her, would you feel hurt and misery, suffering, grief, and despair?'

" 'If, Mallika, something happened to my daughter Vajiri, if something harmed her, my own life, too, might well be done for: how then should I not feel hurt and misery, suffering, grief, and despair?'

" 'But this, great king, is what he considered, the Sublime

One, the Prober, the Seer, the Holy One, the Perfectly Awakened One, when he said: "What is dear to one, brings hurt and misery, suffering, grief, and despair, which comes from what is dear." What do you think, great king: is the Princess Vasabha dear to you?'

"'Certainly, Mallika, the Princess Vasabha is dear to me.'

"'What do you think, great king: if something happened to the Princess Vasabha, if something harmed her, would you feel hurt and misery, suffering, grief, and despair?'

"'If, Mallika, something happened to the Princess Vasabha, if something harmed her, my own life, too, might well be done for: how then should I not feel hurt and misery, suffering, grief, and despair?'

"'But this, great king, is what he considered, the Sublime One, the Prober, the Seer, the Holy One, the Perfectly Awakened One, when he said: "What is dear to one, brings hurt and misery, suffering, grief, and despair, which comes from what is dear." What do you think, great king: is General Vidudabho dear to you?'

"'Certainly, Mallika, General Vidudabho is dear to me.'

"'What do you think, great king: if something happened to General Vidudabho, if something harmed him, would you feel hurt and misery, suffering, grief, and despair?'

"'If, Mallika, something happened to General Vidudabho, if something harmed him, my own life, too, might well be done for: how then should I not feel hurt and misery, suffering, grief, and despair?'

"'But this, great king, is what he considered, the Sublime One, the Prober, the Seer, the Holy One, the Perfectly Awakened One, when he said: "What is dear to one, brings hurt and misery, suffering, grief, and despair, which comes from what is dear." What do you think, great king: am I dear to you?'

"'Certainly, Mallika, you are dear to me.'

"'What do you think, great king: if something happened to me, harmed me, would you feel hurt and misery, suffering, grief, and despair?'

"'If, Mallika, something happened to you, harmed you, my

own life, too, might well be done for: how then should I not feel hurt and misery, suffering, grief, and despair?'

" 'But this, great king, is what he considered, the Sublime One, the Prober, the Seer, the Holy One, the Perfectly Awakened One, when he said: "What is dear to one, brings hurt and misery, suffering, grief, and despair, which comes from what is dear." What do you think, great king: is your realm of Benares and Kosalo dear to you?'

" 'Certainly, Mallika, my realm of Benares and Kosalo is dear to me: it is by virtue of the power of my realm of Benares and Kosalo that we own silk and sandalwood, jewelry and sweet-smelling salves.'

" 'What do you think, great king: if something happened to your realm of Benares and Kosalo, if something harmed it, would you feel hurt and misery, suffering, grief, and despair?'

" 'If, Mallika, something happened to my realm of Benares and Kosalo, if something harmed it, my own life, too, might be done for: how then should I not feel hurt and misery, suffering, grief, and despair?'

" 'But this, great king, is what he considered, the Sublime One, the Prober, the Seer, the Holy One, the Perfectly Awakened One, when he said: "What is dear to one, brings hurt and misery, suffering, grief, and despair, which comes from what is dear." '

" 'Wonderful, Mallika, extraordinary, Mallika, is the way in which he, the Sublime One, sees, wisely penetrating, wisely. Well then, Mallika, praise on!'

"And King Pasenadi of Kosalo rose from his seat, bared his shoulder, bowed reverently in the direction where the Sublime One was dwelling, and thrice sounded this greeting:

> *"Reverence to the Sublime One,*
> *The Holy Awakened Lord!*
>
> *"Reverence to the Sublime One,*
> *The Holy Awakened Lord!*
>
> *"Reverence to the Sublime One,*
> *The Holy Awakened Lord."*

To the Western reader this story seems intolerably long and repetitious: he is eager to get on to something new and begins to skip in the hope that something different may be ahead, but is disappointed. If he does not want to take the time to listen slowly, the Buddha might say, it will take him a long time to attain salvation; he may be reborn many times and repeat the same experiences over and over and over again until one day he may be ready to take the time to listen.

The story was not written to give information or to fill a gap in an anthology, or to be sampled. That the reader gradually loses interest constitutes no objection whatsoever to the story: its whole point is to make the reader lose interest. In the beginning we share the father's grief as he loses his only son; but before long, we do not care any more. It is the point of the story to get us not to care any more.

The story is indigestible: that is why it must be quoted in full. The reader who lets this one story address him may understand more of Buddhism than a reader who skims through a whole anthology, streamlined for quick reading.

The perfect antithesis of this story, and especially of the early paragraphs which relate how the "father's only, much beloved little boy" died, may be found in Genesis 22:

"After these events God tested Abraham and said to him: Abraham! And he said: Here I am. Then he said: Take your son, your only one, whom you love, Isaac . . ."

Few stories in world literature are as laconic as this story in Genesis which takes up scarcely more than a page and yet makes the reader feel all of Abraham's emotions. If we retold this story after the manner of the Buddhistic story, we should falsify its style, sensibility, and impact as completely as most English versions falsify the scriptures of Buddhism. The narrative style of the Hebrew Scriptures is generally characterized by superlative economy, and the same applies to the Talmud, as our quotations have shown. The style of the Buddhistic scriptures goes to the opposite extreme.

The Jewish religion emphasizes the unique, that which happened once only. There is only one God and he created only

one world, once. We live only once, and in most of the Old
Testament there is no life after death.

Buddhism denies the unique and tries to show us that our
sufferings are anything but unique. What grieves us has grieved
others before us and will grieve us again as long as we live,
many times, and in lives to come, over and over again.

Some scientists tell us that in our own galaxy there are at
least 100,000, and more likely 1,000,000, planets like the earth
which might well support life and beings like ourselves; and
that our galaxy is by no means the only one: even if we confine ourselves to galaxies which are within reach of our telescopes, there are about 100,000,000 galaxies. To Jews and
Christians this is a bizarre idea. The idea of ten trillion cruci-
fixions on ten trillion planets is out of keeping with the spirit
of the Bible. Mahayana Buddhism, on the other hand, has
long indulged in similar conceptions. In the Saddharmapun-
darika Sutra (in Volume X of the American edition of the
Sacred Books of the East), a ray of light from the Buddha's
forehead illuminates 18,000 Buddha fields, and 80,000 bodhisattvas are beheld; and a story is told of two Buddhas who
once put out their tongues for 100,000 years. There have been
many, many Buddhas in the past, and at one point one is recalled who is said to have lived 5,400,000 myriads of 10,000,-
000 cycles ago.

What matters is not the literal truth of these stories any
more than the question whether the long story quoted here
happened precisely as it is told: what matters is the world
feeling, the rhythm of breathing and living, the involvement or
detachment.

Buddhism does not offer 102 great ideas which are waiting
for a compiler or a synthesizer who will check off the ideas
also encountered in the West and amalgamate the remainder
with the Occidental outlook. Buddhism offers four truths which
are the theme of our story: the universality of suffering, its
causation by attachment which in turn is due to ignorance,
and the thesis that the removal of the cause will remove suffering, too. The fourth truth is that adherence to the Noble
Eightfold Path will lead to this end—and our story is part of

that path. It tries to lead to detachment by way of knowledge—
not some esoteric gnosis but the simple knowledge, available
to all, that suffering is universal. But it will not do to jot this
truth down on a file card, or to record it in the mind along
with other things: we must accustom the mind to dwelling on
these truths—for example, by taking the time to read the whole
story without omissions, more than once, and by meditating
on it.

93. AGAINST ECLECTICISM.   The eclectic collects; he builds a
museum; he is sovereign. He does not go behind the work of
art, the idea, the philosophy, to reach the disturbing experience
that prompted it: he stays at home. His taste may be excellent,
but something is lacking. He is like a man who assembles snapshots of works of art and prides himself on the catholicity of
his appreciation, but knows only the surfaces: what is lacking is dimension, depth, going out of one's own safe world to
enter into what is strange.

Those who insist on the fundamental agreement of all the
great religions, no less than those who arrange them on a scale
with their father's at the top, share the faults of the eclectic.
They, too, stay at home.

Fromm claims that on essentials there is agreement among
"early Buddhism, Taoism, the teachings of Isaiah, Jesus, Socrates, Spinoza, certain trends in the Jewish and Christian religions (particularly mysticism), the religion of Reason of the
French Revolution." (Cf. § 77.) What are these essentials?
"Man must develop his power of reason." But is this true of
Taoism, Isaiah, Jesus, and the mystics? "He must develop his
power of love for others as well as for himself and experience
the solidarity of all living beings." Of the solidarity of all living
beings, presumably including animals if not plants, we find little in Jesus and Socrates, in Spinoza or the French Enlightenment; and "love for others" obscures the vast difference between early Buddhism and Robespierre, Isaiah's concern with
social justice and Jesus' otherworldliness. "Virtue is self-realization." But were the Buddha and Jesus really concerned with

self-realization? The Buddha preached emancipation from the self, and Jesus the kingdom of God. "And if your hand causes you to sin, cut it off; it is better for you to enter life maimed than with two hands to go to hell" (Mark 9.43)—that is hardly the epitome of an ethic of self-realization. Picture a youth who is troubled about his sexual desires seeking advice from Jesus, Socrates, the mystics, the Buddha, Lao-tze, and Freud: would they all tell him essentially the same thing? And how many of them would equate virtue with self-realization?

These men were radicals, not eclectics. They emphasized their *dis*agreement with their predecessors and their fellow men. Most men refuse to expose themselves to any such radicalism. They rest content with glittering phrases like love, truth, and integrity. They feel secure in the knowledge that all the greatest men are essentially at one. But this is like finding comfort in the thought that all of them were against sin.

If you study the religions of the world to find corroboration for what you believe anyway, the inquiry is sterile. You are trying to bolster your ego with the agreement of the great. But is the only alternative to this to show what fools the great men of the past have been—another attempt to bolster the ego?

In the study of art, religion, and philosophy, we ourselves are the clay, and the biggest question is what becomes of ourselves. If we stay at home or play God, giving good and bad marks, instead of letting ourselves be formed, we bury that one talent which is death to hide.

Paul Elmer More once wrote that the Buddha was a stuttering Christ and found it difficult to put his message into words because Christ had not yet come; presented with the words of Christ, the Buddha would have said: that is what I was trying to say! But, alas, the Buddha never met Mr. More.

Whoever reads a major work of literature without in any way becoming different or changing his outlook on the world has missed what matters most. To find confirmation of one's prior beliefs is futile: there is scarcely any error, prejudice, or outright idiocy that could not be buttressed with a few quotations from great men. The thing to look for is disagreement.

We should ask what evidence suggests that our previous

position was wrong and how we propose to deal with such evidence. What rival hypotheses are there, and how, if at all, is ours superior? How must we modify it? Such questions are fruitful, while the hunt for corroboration and the edifice of an eclectic museum are at best edifying and dull the critical faculties.

In studying the great religions we should ask what lies behind the scriptures and traditions, what experiences, ideas, attitudes, or deeds appeared central to the Buddha, Jesus, Micah, and the men of the Upanishads, and what was the distinctive message of each. Similar ideas and experiences may have found expression in our own traditions, too; but what is barely suggested here, incidentally, may have been felt to be absolutely central elsewhere. By exposing ourselves to the slings and arrows of diversity we should be changed.

We do not simply appreciate Mozart, agree with him, or classify him as a stammering Wagner: he makes us aware of possibilities that would never have occurred to us; he affects our tastes, not only in music; he influences our attitudes, our values, our aims.

We are not in safe possession of the truth or of knowledge of good and evil or of the right standards, and able to apply them with sovereign wisdom to Mozart or Moses, Shakespeare or the Buddha, Michelangelo or Paul. It is through our encounters with them that our standards are formed.

Luther once said that sacred scriptures want humble readers who always say: Teach me, teach me, teach me! And he added that the Spirit resists the haughty. Luther's friend Melanchthon insisted that in the encounter your spirit must become transformed. And Karl Barth, after citing both (50), adds that I cannot fully understand any text whatever "unless I find myself asked by it in the greatest possible openness."

But with how much openness have these men read the Epistle of James in the New Testament? Or the scriptures of other religions? Or the *Apology* of Socrates? What is wanted is a continual openness that does not hide behind the first text— the Epistle to the Romans, for example—that has really spoken to it. What is wanted is not the citation of a few convenient verses out of context, but a wholehearted attempt to re-experience, for better or for worse, the total impact of St. Paul and of the Jesus of each of the four Gospels, of Aquinas and the Buddha, of the prophets and Akiba, and of Shakespeare, Sophocles, and Mozart.

Ultimate convictions are often inconsistent and can be refuted. They cannot be proved. But they can be responsible or irresponsible. They are irresponsible if they are arbitrary and blind. They are responsible if they have grown out of encounter after encounter. And in the end we can only ask others to expose themselves to the same encounters—and, if after having done this they do not agree with us, expose ourselves to their criticisms.

XI. REASON AND EROS

94. PLATO AS EDUCATOR.   Plato's central importance for a humanistic education—and "humanistic education" is really tautological—is due to the fact that a prolonged encounter with Plato changes a man. It will not change every reader in the same way, but on the whole it is likely to make a man less dogmatic, more cautious and critical in his thinking, aware of endless possibilities, and alive to the delights of sustained reflection.

Plato makes us think of a problem as a promise of joy, and he inspires dissatisfaction with most subsequent philosophy, not only stylistically. Beyond that, he confronts us with the personality of Socrates, whose impact on all who ever felt it—from Alcibiades, Antisthenes, and Plato to our own time—has at least equalled that of any other man. And there are Plato's hosts of insights.

Among these insights the most valuable to us are those which are furthest from corroborating our own prior beliefs. In his political philosophy, for example, it is precisely his critique of democracy and the case he makes out for an authoritarian state and for censorship that deserve our attention. Many of his propositions about these matters are untenable, but he saw many things that we generally overlook.

Those who accept what they take for Plato's doctrines will frequently find their position challenged as the dialogue moves on or, failing that, in another dialogue. And there is always the *Apology* of Socrates to haunt them. What Plato teaches is not Platonism but philosophy: impatience with confusions and the passion to reflect.

Rare is the inquiry that leaves the true philosopher unscathed. He spurns the safety of a sluggish intellectual and moral imagination, which is the original sin of humanity though it likes to hide behind the superstition that original sin is associated with sex.

Philosophy can be used, and has often been used, to construct an edifice, a comfortable home for the philosopher himself and other congenial individuals in future generations. What is wrong with that? The lack of intellectual imagination which mistakes an asylum for the world.

There are many such edifices, some exceedingly odd and some very impressive, but we should be fools to exchange even the most beautiful among them for the earth and sky and sea. *That those who prefer freedom to the existence of the intellectual shut-in must of necessity be unable to make up their minds or to act with a will is a myth popular in institutions.* It is exploded by the earliest masterpiece in the history of philosophy that has come down to us intact: Plato's version of the *Apology* of Socrates.

95. THE UNCLOISTERED VIRTUE. The great insight of modern philosophy that goes beyond Plato and is chiefly associated with existentialism, but also with the theory in analytic philosophy that goes by the name of emotivism, is that ultimate convictions can be based neither on intellectual intuition nor on proofs which must after all depend on premises. But the positive suggestions offered by emotivists and existentialists are far from satisfactory. Both pay insufficient attention to the great distinction between responsibility and irresponsibility.

That our valuations are tied up with our emotions and not grounded in a rational vision of absolute values is surely right, but we should not ignore the difference between untutored emotion and cultivated emotion. Nor is "cultivated emotion" merely a euphemism for the emotions of those who share our value judgments.

No amount of reading, study, and research can obviate the ultimate necessity for choice, but again there is a vast difference between an informed and an uninformed choice, a responsible and irresponsible decision. This difference has been insufficiently appreciated by the existentialists, beginning with Kierkegaard.

The popular secondhand versions of existentialism and emotivism are forms of anti-intellectualism, while the nonemotivist analytical philosophers are all too often intent on rationalizing the philosophy of their nurseries. The appeal to ordinary language is, more often than not, an appeal to the unquestioned wisdom of our elders.

The point against Plato was far better stated by Milton in *Areopagitica.* "I cannot praise a fugitive and cloister'd vertue, unexercis'd and unbreath'd, that never sallies out and sees her adversary, but slinks out of the race where that immortall garland is to be run for, not without dust and heat. Assuredly we bring not innocence into the world, we bring impurity much rather: that which purifies us is triall, and triall is by what is contrary." And half a dozen pages later Milton says of Adam: "when God gave him reason, he gave him freedom to choose, for reason is but choosing."

This conception of reason is anti-Platonic, as Milton well knew. Indeed, he discusses Plato before offering his own dictum about reason. For Plato, reason was a kind of second sight; Milton's idea comes from the Bible. And his idea that we bring impurity into the world and are purified by trial comes from his religion, too.

Choosing is not necessarily irrational, but not choosing is subrational, and choosing without trial *is* irrational. If we cloister ourselves in the beliefs of our elders, our language, our own tradition, and look elsewhere only to find confirmation or pass judgment from our point of view, then we clip the wings of our reason.

Those who only expose the follies of their elders harness reason, also clip its wings, and put it to work. Left to itself,

reason has no greater passion than to sally forth and explore.
It finds faults in the cloister and outside, in its childhood religion and in its adolescent revolt. But it does not find faults
only, it finds much else. Nor is it satisfied to study philosophies
only; most philosophies are much more cloistered than the
sacred scriptures of the great religions. It explores them and
cannot accept them in their totality but finds itself enriched
more than by any other reading.

What else is an invitation to rationality but a challenge that
men should expose themselves to many views, exploring them
critically but also willing to learn? If we find ourselves disagreeing with others on important moral principles, we can try
to convict our adversaries of confusions, inconsistencies, or erroneous information, and we can re-examine our own position
to see if it is open to similar objections. Often this will prove
sufficient; sometimes more information may be needed. Such
information is not always reducible to statistics; sometimes
what is required above all is an extension of the imagination,
an awareness of possibilities: possible norms, possible feelings,
possible developments. And apart from the experience of a
lifetime, the medium in which we encounter human possibilities
is history, and above all the history of art, literature, religion,
and philosophy.

Strictly speaking, reason can certainly not be identified with
choosing, but Milton's paradoxical formulation is pedagogically
superior to the dogmatic dichotomy of the realm of reason and
the realm of choice. Reason can participate in a choice, and
the greatest contribution it can make comes long before the
choice itself is made: reason can criticize the cloister in which
we are raised and extend our horizon by persistent questioning.

96. KANT AND FREUD.   It was during the Enlightenment, in
the eighteenth century, that this conception of reason as essentially critical first became popular, and Kant's essay *What
Is Enlightenment?* was an appeal to man to leave the cloister:

"Enlightenment is man's emergence from his self-incurred
minority. Minority is the incapacity for using one's understand-

ing without the guidance of another. And this minority is self-incurred when it is caused by the lack, not of understanding, but of determination and courage to use it without the guidance of another. *Sapere aude!* Have the courage to avail yourself of your own understanding—that is the motto of the Enlightenment."

The great enlighteners, including Kant and Freud, possessed this courage to a high degree, but they have failed to construct an image of man in which this aspiration to emerge from our minority has any place. To link Kant and Freud in this manner may seem strange, seeing that Kant is sometimes held to have banished psychology from philosophic reflection. In fact, he lectured on anthropology every winter semester for over thirty years and eventually, in his seventies, published an *Anthropology* (1798) of which he even brought out a revised edition two years later.

In Kant's *major* works, too, we find an image of man. His elaborate anatomy of the human mind offers a philosophical psychology which is based on inference rather than observation. In the *Critique of Pure Reason,* for example, he develops a detailed hypothesis to account for the form of some, but by no means all, of our experiences and for the possibility of Newtonian science. This is a kind of metapsychology, to use Freud's term for his own account of the mind in terms of ego, id, and superego. But while Freud was concerned mainly to account for man's errors, Kant tried to account for his truths.

With his great gift for coinage, Freud called his contribution: psychoanalysis. To locate his contribution historically, one might call it Freud's critique of unreason.

Kant helps us very little if we want to understand the psychopathology of everyday life; Freud helps us no more if we want to understand the mental foundations of science. This is fairly obvious and may not constitute any ground for serious criticism. But both men tried to illuminate morality, religion, and art, and the shortcomings of these attempts are due in part to their inadequate images of man.

The limitations of Kant's ethics are connected with his assumption that moral problems can always be reduced to a con-

flict between reason and inclination. He did not realize that
what he analyzed was not the moral mind as an eternal datum,
but merely one type of spirit or, to use a Hegelian phrase, one
phase of the phenomenology of the spirit. What Kant described
was neither, as he himself supposed, moral man in general nor,
as some of his critics have supposed, merely the morality of
Prussian pietism: it was one type of moral conflict, which is
epitomized in the Gospel according to Matthew: "The spirit is
willing, but the flesh is weak." Where reason and inclination
conflict, a man knows his duty but would rather not do it.
Kant presupposes a mentality for which, to cite his own words
in his Introduction to the *Metaphysics of Ethics* (1797, p.
xxiv), "a collision of duties or obligations is altogether unthinkable." The type of man that Kant discusses cannot even imagine a genuine moral perplexity. There have been such people
long before eighteenth-century pietism, and there are such
people today; but they constitute merely one type of humanity.

The limitations of Kant's conception of man become even
more evident in his aesthetics, in the *Critique of Judgment.*
Aesthetic judgments, according to Kant, cannot be colored by
any interest whatsoever. The idea of interest is introduced at
the outset and defined in Section 2 as "that approbation which
we connect with the representation of the existence of an object." Kant distinguishes three cases: approbation of the agreeable, which corresponds to what Kant, in his ethics, calls
pathological interests; approbation of the good, which he elsewhere calls moral interest and finds profoundly puzzling; and
approbation of the beautiful, which is, as Kant expressly claims,
"devoid of any interest whatsoever." This phrase is repeated by
Kant in Section 5.

Much later in his *Critique of Judgment* (§§ 41–42), Kant
suddenly speaks of an empirical and an intellectual interest in
the beautiful, but without any genuine inconsistency. Having
once been judged beautiful in the absence of any interest whatever, an object may then inspire an empirical, clearly "pathological," interest: it becomes an object of desire simply because it
has been judged beautiful. This happens, Kant adds, only in
society: isolated from society, nobody would take any such

interest in the beautiful, and Kant himself says that this kind
of interest is "of no importance to us here."

Intellectual interest, too, is pictured as a mere epiphenome-
non of the aesthetic judgment and, according to Kant, restricted to the beauty of nature: here it supports in some
measure our innate moral sense by holding out hope of its
objective validity. If parts of nature are beautiful, who knows
whether there might not be a moral world order after all?
The intellect, discouraged by the refutation of the teleological
argument for God's existence, perks up, as it were, and takes
an interest when told that beauty has been found in nature.

Regarding works of art, Kant sees only two possibilities of
interest: "Either they are such successful imitations of nature
that they achieve deception, and then they have the effect of
supposed natural beauty; or they are instances of art that is
intentionally and visibly directed at arousing our approbation."

It is customary in aesthetics, and plausible up to a point in
a critique of judgment, to concentrate on the spectator's experience rather than the artist's; but a moment's reflection on
the artist's experience might have convinced Kant that the primary intention of an artist need not be either to achieve deception or to arouse the public's approbation: he may be
motivated by an interest which explodes Kant's scheme. And
it is really no different with the spectator or audience: far from
having no interest whatever in the work of Shakespeare,
Michelangelo, or Beethoven, many of us feel an interest that
far surpasses in intensity any interest in the merely agreeable.
Parts of the works of these men are downright disagreeable
and unpleasant, but our "approbation" is by no means "devoid
of any interest whatsoever."

What Kant saw was that we do not have a prudential or
utilitarian interest in works of art—assuming for the moment
that our interest is not in buying or selling, or in impressing
our neighbors—but Kant jumped to the false conclusion that
we have no interest in them at all. Actually, we have a surpassing interest in works of art, and this interest is closely related to our determination to emerge from our "self-incurred
minority" and to our religious quest. Though himself deeply

imbued with it, Kant failed to take into account man's aspiration to be other than he is, to transcend himself, to be "as God."

97. FREUD AND ASPIRATION.   In his failure to do justice to that
aspiration which is central in art and religion, philosophy and
science, and which gained such notable expression in his own
work, Freud is at one with Kant. He accepts the dichotomy of
reason and inclination but, unlike Kant, concentrates on inclination. He realizes, in effect, that Kant was wrong when he
claimed that we have no interest whatever in the beautiful, but
Freud jumped to the false conclusion that this interest develops
faute de mieux.

At the end of his twenty-third lecture in *General Introduction to Psychoanalysis,* Freud offered a brief psychology of art.
What the artist really wants is to "attain honor, power, wealth,
fame, and the love of women; but he lacks the means to achieve
these satisfactions." He tends toward introversion, is close to
neurosis, turns his back to reality, and concentrates on "the
wishful constructs of his fantasy life." So far, he does not greatly
differ from a mental case. "The way back to reality, however,
the artist finds in the following way. He is after all not the
only one that leads a fantasy life. The intermediate realm of
fantasy is approved by common human consent, and everyone
who suffers a privation expects some alleviation and comfort
from this realm. But for the nonartists the attainment of pleasure from the sources of fantasy is very limited. The inexor-
ability of their repressions forces them to content themselves
with the wretched daydreams which are still allowed to reach
consciousness." The artist makes the most of this situation. He
purges his daydreams both of what is too personal and of what
is too obscene or offensive, and presents them in a form that
gives great pleasure. And Freud concludes his lecture:

"If he can achieve all this, then he makes it possible for
others to draw comfort and alleviation again from the sources
of pleasure in their own unconscious which had become in-
accessible; and thus he gains their gratitude and admiration
and has attained by means of his fantasy what at first he at-

tained only in his fantasy: honor, power, and the love of women."

Art is here understood as a substitute gratification which may also incidentally procure for the artist the satisfactions which he really wants most of all: honor, power, and the love of women. The implication is that if all of us could reap the kind of honor, power, and love that the lucky artist is accorded, there would be no need for art.

In his essay on "The Interest in Psychoanalysis," Freud argued that we must also regard "myth, religion, and morality [*Sittlichkeit*] as attempts to create for ourselves some compensation for satisfactions lacking in reality." (IV, 311 ff. Jones, II, 214–218, offers a summary.) And in the second section of *Civilization and Its Discontents* a similar explanation is given of science: "Life, as it is imposed on us, is too hard for us: it brings us too many hurts, disappointments, insoluble tasks. To endure it, we cannot do without palliatives. . . . There are perhaps three such means: powerful diversions which make us esteem our misery lightly, substitute gratifications which lessen it, and intoxicants which render us insensitive. Something of this sort is indispensable. Voltaire aims at such diversions when he ends his *Candide* with the advice that we should cultivate our gardens; all scientific activity, too, is such a diversion."

In the immediately following sentence, art is again characterized as a "substitute gratification." Later in the same section, Freud complains that, though he cannot praise art too highly as a source of pleasure and consolation, "the mild narcosis which art induces in us can but fleetingly remove us from the troubles of life and is not strong enough to make us forget real misery." Religion tries to remedy this insufficiency by altogether turning its back on reality, and Freud concludes that "We must characterize the religions of mankind as a mass delusion."

If the image of man implicit in these judgments were correct, we should have to conclude that, given a life free of hurts, disappointments, and insoluble tasks, a life rich in honors and appreciation by others, and above all an entirely unrepressed sex life, we should have no need of art, myth, religion, morality,

or science: we should have the real satisfactions that man
wants and should not need diversions or substitute gratifications. But this seems as wrong about Freud as about men in
general. Consider two of Freud's letters, cited by Ernest Jones
(II, 396 f.). The first dates from 1910:

"I could not contemplate with any sort of comfort a life without work. Creative imagination and work go together with me;
I take no delight in anything else. That would be a prescription for happiness were it not for the terrible thought that
one's productivity depends entirely on sensitive moods. . . . I
secretly pray: no infirmity, no paralysis of one's power through
bodily distress. We'll die with harness on, as King Macbeth
said." And Freud did die with harness on, working till the end,
though he had cancer for sixteen years, suffered thirty-three
operations, and was in almost constant pain.

The second letter dates from 1925: "No one writes to achieve
fame, which anyhow is a very transitory matter, or the illusion
of immortality. Surely, we write first of all to satisfy something
within ourselves, not for other people." Surely, one may add,
the artist does not write or create for the sake of honor, appreciation, and the love of women. Nor does either the artist
or the scientist seek mere substitute gratifications or diversions.

The crucial fact that Freud never took into account sufficiently in his books and papers is how insufficient for lasting
happiness not only fame and honor are but also the love of
women. Given all these satisfactions, a man might still feel
deeply dissatisfied, if not bored and desperate. When we seek
lasting bliss in artistic creation, science, or philosophy, we are
not looking for distractions or substitutes but for the very thing
we want most and which fame, honors, and a happy sex life
cannot give us, owing to their very nature.

It would be far truer if we said that it is the hunt for fame,
honors, wealth, and women that is likely to be a search for
diversions, narcotics, and substitute gratifications, provided we
add immediately that most men need a measure of approbation, too, especially, though not only, to tide them over their
uncreative spells or, more often, to reconcile them to their lack
of creative power.

Occasionally, for example at the very end of Section IV of *Civilization and Its Discontents*, Freud makes a hesitant concession: "Sometimes one thinks one recognizes that it is not only the pressure of civilization but something in the nature of the sexual function itself that denies us full satisfaction and pushes us on other paths. It may be an error, it is hard to decide." In a footnote Freud speculates, much as he had done almost twenty years earlier in a paper published in 1912, whether this failure to achieve complete satisfaction in sexual relations might be explainable in terms of man's bisexuality—perhaps one cannot fully satisfy both one's masculine and one's feminine desires with "the same object"—or in terms of our sadistic tendencies which we cannot fully indulge, or possibly in terms of an insuperable embarrassment at the unedifying location, and possibly also the smell, of the genitals.

If Freud means that it is impossible for anyone ever to achieve complete sexual satisfaction in intercourse, he is surely wrong; but if he means that even the most complete sexual satisfaction does not completely satisfy a man and does not provide him with sufficient content for his life, then Freud's three tentative hypotheses are irrelevant and his initial statement is an almost incredible understatement.

In his little-known early paper on "The Most Common Degradation of Love Life" (1912), Freud adduced one further hypothesis to account for the limitations of sexual satisfaction: owing to the incest taboo in our early years "the final object of the sex drive is never the original one but always a mere surrogate. Psychoanalysis, however, has taught us: when the original object of a wish has been lost owing to repression, it is often supplanted by an unending series of substitute objects of which none satisfies fully" (V, 210). Again, the same objection applies: would sexual relations with mother or sister have satisfied a man "fully"? Surely, not in the sense that a Sigmund Freud would have been content to spend his life in bed!

In the passage just quoted, Freud recognized that "the final object of the sex drive is . . . always a mere surrogate"; but his positive suggestion that it is a substitute for sexual relations with the parent or siblings of the opposite sex is quite unsatisfactory, though not for the kind of reason usually given. Many a critic has argued like Palmström in Christian Morgenstern's poem, "The Impossible Fact":

> *Because, he argues, razor-witted,*
> *that can't be which is not permitted.*

> (*Weil, so schliesst er messerscharf,*
> *nicht sein* kann, *was nicht sein* darf.)

The real objection to Freud's suggestion is that, even if we grant the existence of an early incestuous desire, there is no reason whatsoever to believe—and Freud himself adduces none —that gratification of this early desire would markedly change later behavior. After all, early incestuous relations between brothers and sisters are by no means unheard of, and many of the pharaohs of Egypt lived in lawful wedlock with their sisters; yet there is no evidence that such unions provided gratifications far surpassing those possible in nonincestuous sexual relations, nor were these pharaohs so satisfied that they felt no need for art or religion. In sum, Freud is right that "the object of the sex drive" cannot satisfy all our desires and is even to some extent a "surrogate"; but he is wrong in thinking that this is true only of "the final object" and that the thing really wanted is sexual intercourse with one's closest relatives.

On the question what it is that is really wanted, Freud sheds more light than he seems to have realized when, two pages before the passage quoted, he makes a crucial concession, prompted by his sheer honesty. Like his two letters, it undercuts his position:

"But unrestricted sexual freedom from the beginning does not lead to any better result. It is easy to show that the psychic value of the need for love goes down at once, as soon as its satisfaction is made easy. It requires an obstacle to drive the libido up to a high point, and where the natural obstacles to satisfaction are not sufficient, men have at all times interposed conventional ones to be able to enjoy love. This is as true of individuals as it is of nations. In ages in which the satisfaction of sexual desire did not encounter any difficulties, as, for example, during the decline of classical antiquity, sexual love became worthless and life empty, and strong reactive constructions were needed to re-establish the indispensable emotive values. In this context one may claim that the ascetic current in Christianity has created psychic values for sexual love which pagan antiquity had never been able to confer on it. It attained the highest significance among ascetic monks whose life was almost solely taken up with the struggle against libidinous temptation."

Sexual satisfactions by themselves cannot fill a man's life because he has other needs besides sexual needs. This does not amount to saying that man's sexual needs are unimportant: without food and drink man dies; yet full gratification of these relatively primitive needs still leaves a man dissatisfied. Among the less primitive and distinctively human needs, there is one which was insufficiently recognized by Freud as well as by Kant, and for that matter by most heirs of the Enlightenment, and to this need we must now turn our attention. (Cf. §§ 23, 81.)

98. MAN'S ONTOLOGICAL INTEREST. John Dewey once observed, in his *Theory of Valuation* (34), that "valuation takes place only where there is . . . some need, lack, or privation." Man's profoundest and most interesting privation, however, which helps to explain his valuation of works of art, and his development of morality, religion, science, and philosophy, has received insufficient attention from philosophers and psychologists, although Plato, Nietzsche, and Sartre have shown some awareness of it. Its classical formulation is found in Genesis.

Man and woman were in paradise, naked and unashamed, when the serpent asked the woman with exceeding cunning: "Indeed, did God say, Ye shall not eat of all the trees of the garden?" In fact, there was only one tree of which they had been told not to eat, but it is this one privation on which the serpent fastens. The woman explains: "we may eat of the fruit of the trees of the garden"; it is only a single tree that is forbidden to us. And the serpent replies that if the man and woman will only eat of the fruit of that one tree, "ye shall be as God."

When the woman and the man ate of that fruit they were not prompted by hunger or sexual frustration, but by the mere existence of a prohibition, an obstacle, a difficulty—the only one in sight—and the conviction that by overcoming that they would be as God. Man's profoundest privation is that he is not as God, and many other privations are mere foreground privations which, in Platonic language, "participate" in the ultimate privation.

What does it mean to be as God? It has a negative as well as a positive meaning. Negatively, it means: not being as we are. There is no single feature that can be picked out as the prime objection to our present state of being: different features are experienced as intolerable at different times and by different people. For the woman in paradise what was insufferable was that there should be a single prohibition and that she should be excluded from the knowledge of good and evil. The Buddha was shocked into sudden dissatisfaction with his luxurious and sheltered existence in his father's palace when he encountered in a single day old age, sickness, death, and an ascetic: the vision of the ascetic suggested a possible triumph over old age, sickness, and death. Prohibitions, concealment, deceptions, physical infirmities, and death can all arouse a deep dissatisfaction with our being—by no means *only* death, as some of the existentialists would have us believe. Nor is this negative side all there is to the desire to be as God.

Positively, it means above all else creativity. Immortality, omnipotence, omniscience, and the like are all at bottom negative concepts which mean primarily the absence of certain defects; but creative activity is a positive experience and, according to the first chapter of Genesis, the essence of divinity.

Creativity is not a substitute nor a narcotic; it is spontaneity itself. The child that plays is creative. "Work," it says, "is something other people think of for you to do; play is what you think of yourself." The child's play, the child's improvisations, the child's play-acting and pretending, are not mere compensations for parental prohibitions. If it turns a chair or empty space into a horse, that is not necessarily because its parents have not given it a horse: what the child wants is not so much a real horse as the ability to create a horse out of nothing and—very important—to make the horse vanish into nothing again as soon as it is no longer required. The child wants to be as God.

The privation for which the child refuses to settle is not imposed arbitrarily by its parents or by civilization; it is the privation of being merely human. Denied something it wants badly, whether a toy or, as Freud would emphasize, a sexual satisfaction, the child would gladly use its divine powers to overcome that privation, too—but, as it were, incidentally. The prohibition, by making man conscious of his limitations, awakens an interest out of all proportion to the object: it arouses the desire to overcome our limitations.

Man has *physiological* needs, whether he is aware of them or not: he needs food and drink, calcium and thyroid, and a measure of sexual satisfaction. Man has *psychological* needs, whether he is aware of them or not: he needs to be loved and appreciated, he needs some security (which Thomas Hobbes emphasized, but much too exclusively), some sphere of his own which one might call property (as did Locke, who stressed *this* need much too exclusively), and he needs some pleasure (which is what Bentham insisted on exclusively).

Man also experiences an *ontological* privation, whether he is aware of it or not: he needs to rise above that whole level of being which is defined by his psychological and physiological needs and their satisfaction; he needs to love and create.

None of these needs can be disproved by pointing to the plain fact that many men are not aware of them. Few men indeed know that they need calcium. The test in all three cases —physiological, psychological, and ontological (or spiritual) —is that verifiable frustration results where the need is not satisfied, and that this frustration disappears with gratification. In this way, man's need to love and be creative is quite as verifiable as his need for calcium or security.

The classical story of a man whose every physiological and psychological need is fulfilled as he reels from pleasure to pleasure without getting rid of a pervasive sense of frustration is *The Picture of Dorian Gray* by Oscar Wilde. Not only the typical pattern of a ceaseless hunt for satisfactions that cease to satisfy as soon as they are attained usually points to an unsatisfied ontological interest, but a good deal of aggressive behavior does, too. The man whose need to rise above his own unsatisfactory self and the routines of the everyday world remains unsatisfied by love and creativity is likely to find comfort in the prejudice that at least he is better than Negroes, Mexicans, or Jews. If his frustration is so great that this mere thought affords small comfort, he may seek satisfaction in some nonroutine activity, like a lynching or an auto-da-fé.

It is hardly a sufficient explanation of the fire Nero set to Rome or of Hitler's massacres that both men were frustrated artists who had found that they lacked the ability to create as they wanted and needed to create; but that this was one crucial factor which it would be easy to underestimate we need not doubt.

From men's submission to totalitarian governments it has often been inferred that men, far from feeling any deep need to create or love, have a profound need to submit. But totalitarianism has never yet succeeded where creative freedom was the alternative. When an oppressive Czarist regime was losing a war, a small but determined minority opted for Communism, which at that time did not seem to involve totalitarianism. In Germany, after fourteen years of economic hopelessness that had begun with a lost war and a disastrous inflation and culminated in widespread unemployment, a very large minority was prepared to try Hitler, again without any clear idea of the consequences. Other totalitarian successes have been of a similar nature and prove nothing against men's ontological need.

The relation of this need to love deserves special attention. In his postscript to *Pygmalion*, Shaw says: "Landor's remark that to those who have the greatest power of loving, love is a secondary affair, would not have recommended Landor to Eliza." If Landor was right it was because love is only one expression of man's ontological need: those in whom this need is strongest and who therefore have the greatest power of loving seek other ways, too, to satisfy this need, and usually become creative.

Not only Shaw's Eliza has faced this problem, but also Alcibiades in Plato's *Symposion* (218 f.). The whole dialogue deals with the relation of love to man's ontological interest. Aristophanes, noting that each of us is but a fragment of what he would like to be, explains love as our longing for our other half. Socrates understands love in terms of an ontological predicament, a tension between the human and the divine. Eros, he says, is the child of Poros and Penia, of Plenty and Poverty, and Poros, unlike Penia, was a god. Love, says Socrates, is of immortality. In other words, it is the striving to be as God. And in the *Theaetetus* (176) Socrates actually exhorts man to "become like a god, as far as he is able to."

In the *Symposion*, immortality may be sought through physical generation which "always leaves behind a new existence in place of the old"; but it may also be pursued in another way: "Who, when he thinks of Homer and Hesiod and other great poets, would not rather have their children than ordinary human ones? Who would not emulate them in the creation of children such as theirs?" According to Plato, Socrates went on to speak of contemplation of pure and absolute beauty. We may well doubt whether Socrates hypostatized another world as Plato did after him. But we have no reason whatsoever for doubting what Alcibiades says toward the end of the dialogue: that Socrates stirred men's souls even more than Pericles and made them angry at the thought of their own slavish state until they could hardly endure the life they were leading; and that physical love was for him, to cite Landor once more, "a secondary affair" whose satisfaction could not possibly quench his aspiration.

Historically, it has been religion above all that has awakened and cultivated men's ontological interest and raised the sights of the mass of men to some idea at least of a higher level of being. In the form of gods it has hypostatized this higher being and represented it, more or less visibly, as a possibility; and in the name of these gods it made demands on the mass of men to change their mode of existence, to be dissatisfied with a life on the physio-psychological plane, and to aspire to something higher.

Unadorned sex offers small satisfaction. Hence men have tried for thousands of years to make an art of sexual relations with embellishments and subtleties. The art of love is the poor man's art, the one avenue to ecstasy open to those who lack all other talents. But its bliss does not last and soon gives way to boredom and depression unless the lovers share a higher aspiration and can be creative in some way and fashion something apart from their intimate relation.

The conception of gods provides a setting for an aspiration that reaches out beyond all physical objects. It makes possible a language in which superhuman love and gratitude, despair and grief, can be expressed. A heart fuller than seems warranted by any event in this world can relate itself to the divine and voice passions that seem to transcend human relations.

In prayer an intensity of devotion can be achieved which in a dialogue with other human beings would scarcely ever be possible. Solitude ceases to be mute and gains dimension. Passionate feelings, inhibited in speech with others, find an outlet in jubilations, thanksgiving, complaints, and accusations for which suddenly there is an ear. What formerly was blighted in the bud and withered undeveloped, now unfolds. The soul takes wing and soars.

Jeremiah cries out: "Cursed be the day when I was born; the day my mother bore me be unblessed! Accursed the man that brought glad tidings to my father, saying: A son was born to you—and made him glad. . . . That he slew me not from the womb! And that my mother were my grave. . . . Wherefore came I forth out of the womb? To see suffering and grief, that my days are consumed with shame" (20.14 ff.). To what human being could one say words like these? And it is only because the 90th Psalm is addressed to God that it is an outpouring of the heart and an accusation rather than a literary and not wholly sincere description of the miseries of life.

What could equal the pathos of the cry: "My God, my

God, why hast thou forsaken me?" To be able to utter these words with a whole heart and not as a mere trope is almost reason enough to accept the religion of the Bible.

If it were not for the absence of religion in Shakespeare, one might wonder whether ultimate passion is possible only in relation to a god. The Greek tragedies present no clear evidence one way or the other since the gods loom in the background; Goethe's Prometheus addresses Zeus, and in *Faust* the Lord is introduced to add dimension to the drama. Little if anything in modern poetry can equal the intensity of passion in religious scriptures. In Dostoevsky's novels we find the utmost in passion and devotion—and God.

In all religions, aspiration and demands have been countered to some extent by a quietistic tendency which has earned them Marx's contemptuous epigram "Religion is the opiate of the people" as well as Freud's scornful opinion that religion is an illusion. But in no religion has this palliative note of comfort held exclusive sway; in every religion we also find an appeal to man's ontological interest.

In the Hebrew Scriptures it is by no means only the serpent that says: "ye shall be as God." At the very center of the Law of Moses, in Leviticus 19, the Lord himself demands: "Ye shall be holy: for I the Lord your God am holy."

In the two immediately following verses, we find the commandments "keep my sabbaths: I am the Lord your God. Turn not to idols, nor make yourselves molten gods: I am the Lord your God." To keep the Sabbath is to be like God, who rested on the seventh day. The Sabbath is the great symbol that man's life should not be exhausted by his everyday existence. Once a week he should stop altogether and concentrate entirely on another level of being. And man should not objectify the divine by turning to idols or making himself molten gods. The divine is not an object, it is a challenge.

When later generations turned God into an object of their cult, the prophets rose to remind them that God was not to be objectified, neither in visible images nor by being spoken about and being made the object of worship: God represents a challenge to man to change his life and to become loving and just out of the overflow of a higher, fuller, more godlike existence. "Ye shall be holy."

Where the divine is objectified—as it is, for example, in Christ and in the Christian creeds—the palliative strain in religion immediately comes into prominence and threatens to turn religion into an opiate. In its inception theology is understandable enough as an anti-authoritarian attempt to understand what is believed; yet it is of the attempt to understand that belief is born in the first place; and *belief is a misunderstanding that objectifies what defies objectification.*

Those truculent antitheologians from Tertullian to Luther and our own time whom Gilson once lumped together as "the Tertullian family" (10) realized, as Gilson does not, that theology is somehow an incongruity, a frivolity, and an impiety; but they failed to see that the same objections apply to belief itself. Their authoritarian anti-intellectualism and their insistence on absolutely blind belief, in what Tertullian called "impossible" and modern theologians "absurd" or a "paradox," fail to get to the root of the matter and would have us jump from the frying pan into the fire.

The Old Testament opposes all mythical thinking about the origin of the world (cf. § 83) and has God say, "Let there be . . . and there was." Centuries later, in another age, in the Apocrypha (II Maccabees 7), we find a Jewish mother and her seven sons defying the inhuman tortures of the king of Syria, and she exhorts her last son: "Look upon the heaven and the earth and all that is therein, and consider that God made them from what was not; and so was mankind made likewise. Fear not this tormentor." And in yet another age the theologians come along and discuss how precisely God created the world from nothing and try to objectify God, the process of creation, and the Nothing.

The Old Testament opposes that superstitious thinking which supposes that the deity sees, as it were, what goes on outdoors but can be deceived by him that hides inside. The prophets denounce that smug conceit which fancies that we can rely completely on what we have built and that our security is flawless, and they comfort those whose despair is bot-

tomless: Is there anything, their God says, that is too hard
for me? And a later age comes along and objectifies God and
ascribes predicates to him: he is omniscient and omnipotent.
And a yet later age tries to understand these beliefs by offering increasingly farfetched interpretations of these puzzling
attributes.

That the Old Testament never mentions creation out of
nothing in so many words, that it offers no nonpoetic discourse
about God at all, that the Book of Job specifically repudiates
all attempts at such discourse—all that is of no avail. Sentences
are torn from their context, at first in Greek translations which
frequently differ decisively from the Hebrew originals (as
Buber has shown in *Two Types of Faith*, regarding Paul's
quotations from the Old Testament), and later in Latin
translations.

In these foreign tongues, verses are ripped out of stories and
poems and treated like so many single authoritative deliver-
ances, without the least regard for their original context, and
without any feeling for its sensibility. Of the spirit of the God
of Abraham, Isaac, and Jacob, many theologians have felt no
breath, but they play games parting his garments among them
and casting lots for them.

The original sin of religion is to objectify the divine and to
accept as final some dogma, sacrament, or ritual. The original
sin of philosophy is to be satisfied with isolated propositions
and to champion or oppose the milestones of a flight without
any effort to raise men's sights.

99. REASON AND ASPIRATION.   Reason is not the great adversary of inclination and passion: it is allied with man's profoundest passion, the aspiration to be as God. Reason is creative: it fashions general concepts—so-called universals—which
permit criticism of the given, of being, and especially of our
own being.

Reason, confronted with a few deeds we admire, forms the
concept "courage" and burns it as a norm into the flesh of our
cowardice. It forms the concept "love" and cuts it as a re-

proach into our inclinations. It forms the concept "honesty" and sets fire to our self-deceptions.

Reason can be used to weave beliefs into a hair shirt which is euphemistically called theology. Reason can also be used to dissociate beliefs from the tangled experiences out of which they have been woven and to adduce ingenious arguments for beliefs foisted on us in the nursery or come by later; and with some luck this may pass as philosophy. But theology is not religion, and philosophy need not be, though much of it has been, rationalization.

If its wings are not clipped, reason will always soar beyond belief.

Reason can never be at home in this world. On the wings of searching questions, it transcends beliefs and facts and all that is. It seeks another dimension.

Reason is said to be cold. The air in the upper regions is colder. But there is no more excitement, passion, or joy in the dust than between glaciers and rocks, or still higher up, soaring and seeing everything in new perspectives.

Gods and Ideas are potent reminders of man's dissatisfaction with all that is given in this world—spurs to reach out beyond. But when gods and Ideas become facts or objects of belief, when the dimension reason requires is peopled with them, reason rebels.

Reason can never stop with facts, whether in this world or another; it cannot abide beliefs without subjecting them to criticism. Finding the dimension it sought peopled, too, reason has sometimes been persuaded to return humbly to the dust. But reason cannot accept dust any more than gods. It must criticize beliefs without loss of dimension.

Reason is often employed to criticize beliefs without seeing what they are pointing to. But reason can also criticize beliefs because *they* are blind and inadequate. Beliefs profane the uninhabited dimension.

No religion has paid sufficient respect to reason, and some have made war against it. But if we are made to choose between reason and religion, the choice is between criticism and idolatry. Whatever in religion cannot stand up to criticism is not worth having—and that means a great deal, but it does not mean everything. Among the things that remain is the aspiration which is the soul of religion.

100. EPITAPH
(1939)

Alles starb in meinem Herzen
was nicht reines Feuer war:
in den Gluten meiner Qualen
bracht ich's Gott im Himmel dar.

Nur das flammenhafte Sehnen,
das sich grad am Brande nährt,
hat die Gluten überstanden
noch nachdem sie Gott verzehrt.

BIBLIOGRAPHY

Only books referred to in the text are listed here. This Bibliography is intended to take the place of footnotes by indicating the editions to which the citations in the text refer; it is not intended as a list of works consulted, which would be far longer without serving any very useful purpose.

In the text, figures in parentheses represent page references. IN THE BIBLIOGRAPHY, FIGURES IN PARENTHESES REFER TO THE SECTIONS OF THE PRESENT VOLUME IN WHICH THE TITLE IS CITED. IN THIS WAY, THE BIBLIOGRAPHY SUPPLEMENTS THE INDEX.

Classics available in many different editions are not listed. That explains the omission of Plato and Maimonides, Hume and Kant, Sophocles and Shakespeare, Milton and Shaw, among others.

Some of the translations from the Greek and Hebrew and all translations from German titles are mine. That includes the Goethe poem in Section 7.

References in the text are to the original editions listed below, even where English translations are listed, too, for the convenience of students.

Albright, William Foxwell; *From the Stone Age to Christianity: Monotheism and the Historical Process;* The Johns Hopkins Press 1940, 1946. Rev. ed. with a new introduction; Anchor Books, N.Y. 1957. (50, 58, 89, 90)

——; "The Biblical Period" in *The Jews: Their History, Culture, and Religion;* ed. Louis Finkelstein; 2 Vols.; 2nd ed.; Harper & Brothers, N.Y. 1955. Ten pages of notes and a four-page bibliography add to the great importance of this essay. (50, 90)

Aquinas, Saint Thomas, *Basic Writings of;* ed. Anton C. Pegis; 2 vols.; Random House, N.Y. 1945. *Imprimatur,* Archbishop of New York. (45, 52, 54, 69)

Austin, J. L.; "Other Minds" in *Logic and Language: Second Series;* ed. Antony Flew; Basil Blackwell, Oxford 1953. Flew's volumes (see also under Ryle, below) are anthologies of articles that are representative of analytic philosophy. Austin's essay is generally acknowledged to be one of the best in this genre. (36)

Baeck, Leo; "Romantische Religion" in *Aus drei Jahrtausenden;* destroyed by the Gestapo before publication, except for less than half a dozen copies; English version in Baeck's *Judaism and Christianity;* translated by Walter Kaufmann; Jewish Publication Society; Philadelphia 1958. (57)

——; *The Pharisees and Other Essays;* Schocken Books, N.Y. 1947. (55)

——; *Das Wesen des Judentums;* 6th ed.; J. Kauffmann, Frankfurt a. M. 1932. English translation by Victor Grubenwieser and Leonard Pearl, revised by Irving Howe; Schocken Books, N.Y. 1948. (55)

Barth, Karl; *Rudolf Bultmann: Ein Versuch, ihn zu verstehen;* Evangelischer Verlag, Zollikon-Zürich 1952. (55, 93)

Bentzen, Aage; *Introduction to the Old Testament;* 2 vols.; 2nd rev. ed.; G. E. C. Gad, Copenhagen 1952. (89)

Bettenson, Henry; *Documents of the Christian Church;* Oxford University Press 1943, 1947. For the original texts, see Schaff, below. (54)

Billerbeck, Paul, and Herman L. Strack; *Kommentar zum Neuen Testament aus Talmud und Midrasch;* 4 vols. in 5; C. H. Beck, München 1922–28; 2nd ed., unchanged but with Rabbinical Index vol., 1954–56. Strack is usually named first as coauthor because his reputation was established, but almost all the work on Vol. I was done by Billerbeck, and Strack died before the later vols. were attacked. (55)

Bornkamm, Guenther; *Der Lohngedanke im Neuen Testament;* Heliand-Verlag, Lüneburg 1947. (68)

Bradley, F. H.; *Appearance and Reality;* Clarendon Press, Oxford 1893, 1930. (1)

Briffault, Robert; "The Origin of Love" from his book, *The Mothers,* Macmillan, N.Y., included in *The Making of Man: An Outline of Anthropology;* ed. V. F. Calverton; The Modern Library, N.Y. 1931. (29)

Broad, C. D.; *Five Types of Ethical Theory;* Harcourt, Brace & Co., N.Y. 1930. (17)

——; *Religion, Philosophy and Psychical Research;* Routledge & Kegan Paul Limited, London 1953. (45)

Buber, Martin; *Die Chassidischen Bücher;* Schocken Verlag, Berlin, n.d. Preface dated 1927. English in 2 vols., arranged differently: *Tales of the Hasidim: The Early Masters* and *The Later Masters;* translated by Olga Marx; Schocken Books, N.Y. 1947–48. (65, 77)

——; *Königtum Gottes;* 2nd rev. ed.; Schocken Verlag, Berlin 1936. (89)

——; *Die Schrift und ihre Verdeutschung* (essays by Buber and Franz Rosenzweig); Schocken Verlag, Berlin 1936. The relevant pages from the preceding title are reprinted in this book, pp. 338–41; so are two items on the name of God by Rosenzweig. (89)

——; *Zwei Glaubensweisen;* Manesse Verlag, Zürich 1950. English translation by N. P. Goldhawk; entitled *Two Types of Faith;* Macmillan, N.Y. 1951. (65, 98)

Cf. also my essay on "Buber's Religious Significance" in *The Philosophy of Martin Buber;* The Library of Living Philosophers; ed. Paul Schilpp; Tudor Publishing Company, N.Y. 1962.

Budde, Karl; *Geschichte der althebräischen Litteratur;* C. F. Amelangs Verlag, Leipzig 1906. (89)

Buddha; *Die Reden Gotamo Buddhos,* aus der mittleren Sammlung, Majjhimanikayo, des Pali-Kanons zum ersten

Mal übersetzt von Karl Eugen Neumann; 3 vols.; R. Piper
& Co., München 1922. (92)
  The citation in § 81 is from Jataka, I.63 (271), as quoted
in Nathan Söderblom; *The Living God* (Gifford Lectures
1931); Oxford University Press 1933, 1939, p. 89.
Bultmann, Rudolf; *Die Erforschung der synoptischen Evan-
gelien;* Töpelmann, Giessen 1925. English translation by
Frederick C. Grant in *Form Criticism: A New Method of
New Testament Research;* Willett, Clark & Co., Chicago
and N.Y. 1934. (57, 58, 59)
——; "Neues Testament und Mythologie: Das Problem der
Entmythologisierung der neutestamentlichen Verkündi-
gung" (1941), reprinted in *Kerygma und Mythos*, Vol. I
(1948). English translation of *Kerygma and Myth* by R. H.
Fuller; S.P.C.K., London 1954. (54, 55)
——; *Theologie des Neuen Testaments;* Mohr, Tübingen
1953. English translation by K. Grobel, entitled *Theology
of the New Testament;* 2 vols.; Charles Scribner's Sons,
N.Y. 1951–55. (55, 57)
——; *Das Urchristentum im Rahmen der antiken Religionen;*
Artemis Verlag, Zürich 1949. English translation by R. H.
Fuller, entitled *Primitive Christianity;* Living Age Books,
Meridian Books, N.Y. 1956. (55, 57)
—— and Karl Jaspers; *Die Frage der Entmythologisierung;*
R. Piper & Co., München 1954. (55)
——; See also under Gogarten and under Harnack.
Burnet, John; *Early Greek Philosophy* (1892); 4th ed.; A. & C.
Black, Ltd., London 1930. Reprinted by Meridian Books,
N.Y. 1957. (14)
Burtt, E. A.; "Some Questions about Niebuhr's Theology" in
Reinhold Niebuhr; ed. Kegley and Bretall; see below. (68)
Cassirer, Ernst; *An Essay on Man;* Anchor Books, N.Y. 1953.
(53)
Cassuto; *La Questione della Genesi;* 1934; cited in Bentzen,
q.v. (89)
Chesterton, G. K.; *Saint Thomas Aquinas;* Image Books, N.Y.
1956. (45)

Collingwood, R. G.; *An Autobiography;* Oxford University Press 1939, 1951. (12)

Copleston, Frederick, S.J.; *A History of Philosophy,* Vol. II, *Mediaeval Philosophy: Augustine to Scotus;* Burns Oates & Washbourne Ltd.: Publishers to the Holy See, London 1950; *Imprimatur,* Archiepiscopus Birmingamiensis. (52)

——; *Aquinas;* Penguin Books 1955. (45)

Coulton, G. G.; *Five Centuries of Religion,* Vol. I; Cambridge, At the University Press 1923. (55, 59)

Daube, David; *The New Testament and Rabbinic Judaism;* The Athlone Press, University of London 1956. (58)

Davids, T. W. Rhys; *Buddhism: Its History and Literature;* G. P. Putnam's Sons, N.Y. 1896, 1909. (64)

Davies, W. D.; *Paul and Rabbinic Judaism: Some Rabbinic Elements in Pauline Theology;* S.P.C.K., London 1948, 1955. (58)

Demos, Raphael; "Are Religious Dogmas Cognitive and Meaningful?" in *Academic Freedom, Logic, and Religion;* ed. Morton White; University of Pennsylvania Press. (37)

Dewey, John; A *Common Faith;* Yale University Press 1934. (77)

——; *Theory of Valuation;* University of Chicago Press 1939. (98)

Driver, S. R.; *An Introduction to the Literature of the Old Testament;* Meridian Library, Meridian Books, N.Y. 1956. (89)

Eliot, T. S.; "Hamlet and his Problems" (74) and "Shakespeare and the Stoicism of Seneca" (83), both reprinted in *Selected Essays 1917–1932;* Harcourt, Brace and Company, N.Y. 1932.

With the second essay I have dealt more fully in Chapter 13 of my *From Shakespeare to Existentialism.*

Enslin, Morton Scott; *Christian Beginnings;* Harper and Brothers; N.Y. 1938. Reprinted in 2 paperback vols., the second (Part III) under the title *The Literature of the Christian Movement;* Harper Torchbooks 1956. The references are to the latter volume. (91)

Finkelstein, Louis; *Akiba: Scholar, Saint and Martyr;* Covici Friede, N.Y. 1936. (55, 77)

Fosdick, Harry Emerson; *The Modern Use of the Bible;* Macmillan; N.Y. 1940. (90)

Foss, Martin; *The Idea of Perfection in the Western World;* Princeton University Press 1946. (46)

Freud, Sigmund; *Gesammelte Schriften;* Internationaler Psychoanalytischer Verlag 1925 ff. (2, 33, 42, 53, 97)

Most of the books and articles cited are available in English translations. For some further criticisms of Freud as well as a general estimate, see Chapter 16 of my *From Shakespeare to Existentialism,* and my review of Ernest Jones' biography (see below) in *Judaism,* Winter 1958.

Fromm, Erich; *Psychoanalysis and Religion;* Yale University Press 1950. (77, 93)

———; *The Forgotten Language;* Rinehart & Co., Inc., N.Y. 1951. The Grove Press has published a paperback edition with the same pagination. (77)

———; *Man for Himself;* Rinehart & Co., Inc., N.Y. 1947. (77)

Gide, André; *Corydon: Four Socratic Dialogues;* translated by P. B.; Secker & Warburg, London 1952. (21, 24)

———; *The Counterfeiters with Journal of "The Counterfeiters";* translated by Dorothy Bussy and Justin O'Brien; Alfred A. Knopf, N.Y. 1952 (Preface).

Gilson, Étienne; *The Christian Philosophy of St. Thomas Aquinas;* Random House, N.Y. 1956. *Imprimatur,* Archbishop of Toronto. (45)

———; *God and Philosophy;* Yale University Press 1941. *Imprimatur,* Episcopus Hartfordiensis. (45)

———; *History of Christian Philosophy in the Middle Ages;* Random House, N.Y. 1955. *Imprimatur,* Archbishop of Toronto. (45)

———; *Reason and Revelation in the Middle Ages;* Charles Scribner's Sons, N.Y. 1938. (98)

———; *The Spirit of Mediaeval Philosophy* (Gifford Lectures 1931–32); Charles Scribner's Sons, N.Y. 1940. (45)

———; *The Unity of Philosophical Experience;* Charles Scribner's Sons, N.Y. 1937. (45)

Glasenapp, Helmuth von; *Die Philosophie der Inder;* Alfred Kröner, Stuttgart 1949. (88)

Goethe, Johann Wolfgang von; the poem in § 7 is from *West-östlicher Divan;* the conversations are cited according to Ernst Beutler's *Gedenkausgabe der Werke, Briefe und Gespräche;* Artemis-Verlag, Zürich 1949. (87)
See also my *From Shakespeare to Existentialism.*

Gogarten, Friedrich; "Die christliche Wahrheit" in *Festschrift Rudolf Bultmann;* Kohlhammer, Stuttgart und Köln 1949. This essay contains interesting quotations from Bultmann's "Untersuchungen zum Johannesevangelium: Ἀλήθεια" in *Zeitschrift für die neutestamentliche Wissenschaft,* 1927, and from Hans von Soden's *Was ist Wahrheit?* Marburger Rektoratsrede 1927. (26)

Green, Thomas Hill; *Lectures on the Principles of Political Obligation;* Longmans, Green and Co. 1937. (1)

Harnack, Adolf; *Das Wesen des Christentums;* J. C. Hinrichs, Leipzig 1900. English translation by T. B. Saunders, entitled *What is Christianity?* with an introduction by Rudolf Bultmann; Harper Torchbooks, Harper & Brothers, N.Y. 1957. (54, 55, 57)

Hay, Malcolm; *The Foot of Pride;* Beacon Press, Boston 1950; retitled, *Europe and the Jews,* with new preface by Walter Kaufmann, "History and Honesty"; Beacon paperback, 1960. (55)

Hegel, G. W. F.; all quotations for which no source is given are from the preface (*Vorrede*) to the *Phänomenologie des Geistes;* Bamberg 1807. English version by J. B. Baillie, entitled *The Phenomenology of Mind;* Macmillan, N.Y. 1931. (7, 12, 14, 25)

———; "Die Positivität der christlichen Religion" (ca. 1795) in *Hegels theologische Jugendschriften,* ed. H. Nohl; J. C. B. Mohr, Tübingen 1907. English version by T. M. Knox in Hegel's *Early Theological Writings;* translated Knox and R. Kroner; University of Chicago Press. (77)
See also my *From Shakespeare to Existentialism.*

Heidegger, Martin; cf. my *Existentialism from Dostoevsky to Sartre;* Meridian Books, N.Y. 1956; and Chapters 17 and 18 of my *From Shakespeare to Existentialism.* (13, 24)

Heiler, Friedrich; *Prayer: A Study in the History and Psychology of Religion;* translated and edited by Samuel McComb; Oxford University Press 1932. (74)

Herford, R. Travers; *Judaism in the New Testament Period;* The Lindsey Press, London 1928. (55)

——; *The Pharisees;* Macmillan, N.Y. 1924. (55)

Hoffmeister, Johannes; *Wörterbuch der philosophischen Begriffe;* 2nd rev. ed.; Felix Meiner, Hamburg 1955. (24)

Huizinga, Johan; *Homo Ludens: Vom Ursprung der Kultur im Spiel;* Rowohlt, Hamburg 1956. An English translation of the original edition, first published in German in Switzerland in 1944, is available as a paperback: *Homo Ludens;* Beacon Press, Boston 1955. (58, 64)

Inge, William Ralph; *Christian Mysticism;* Methuen and Co., London 1899. Appendix A, pp. 335–348, quotes and discusses 26 definitions. The Appendices are omitted in the paperback edition, Living Age Books, Meridian Books, N.Y. 1956. (71)

Interpreter's Bible, The: The Holy Scriptures in the King James and Revised Standard Versions with General Articles and Introduction, Exegesis, Exposition for Each Book of the Bible; 12 vols.; Abingdon-Cokesbury Press, N.Y. and Nashville 1951 ff. (55, 65)

Jacob, B(enno); *Das Erste Buch der Tora, Genesis, übersetzt und erklärt;* Schocken Verlag, Berlin 1934. (89)

Jaeger, Werner; *The Theology of the Early Greek Philosophers* (Gifford Lectures 1936); Clarendon Press, Oxford 1947. (14, 58)

James, William; *A Pluralistic Universe;* Longmans, Green & Co., N.Y. 1909, 1943. (37)

——; *The Varieties of Religious Experience* (Gifford Lectures 1901–2); The Modern Library, N.Y. (40, 72)

——; "The Will to Believe," reprinted with an important note by the editor in *Selected Papers on Philosophy* by William James; ed. C. M. Bakewell; Everyman's Library 1917, 1918. (37)

Jannasch, W.; *Deutsche Kirchendokumente: Die Haltung der Bekennenden Kirche im Dritten Reich;* Evangelischer Verlag, Zollikon-Zürich 1946. (55)

Jaspers, Karl; *Einführung in die Philosophie;* Artemis-Verlag, Zürich 1950. English translation by R. Mannheim, entitled *The Way to Wisdom;* Yale University Press 1951. (13)

——; *Nietzsche und das Christentum;* Fritz Seifert, Hameln, n.d. (13)

　　Some of the criticisms in the text are developed more fully in my *Existentialism from Dostoevsky to Sartre;* Meridian Books, N.Y. 1956; and, above all, in my *From Shakespeare to Existentialism.*

——; See also above under Bultmann.

Jones, Ernest; *The Life and Work of Sigmund Freud;* 3 vols.; Basic Books, N.Y. 1953, 1955, 1957. All quotations are from Vol. 2. (97)

Jones, Rufus M.; *Studies in Mystical Religion;* Macmillan, London 1923. (74)

Kafka, Franz; "Before the Law" and the ensuing discussion of this myth—all from *The Trial*—are reprinted and discussed in my *Existentialism from Dostoevsky to Sartre;* Meridian Books, N.Y. 1956. (53, 55, 69, 77)

Kaplan, Abraham; review of *Dilemmas* by Gilbert Ryle (1954) in *The Philosophical Review,* LXIV, No. 4 (October 1955). (18)

Kaufmann, Walter; *From Shakespeare to Existentialism;* Beacon Press, Boston 1959; rev. ed., Anchor Books, N.Y. 1960. Part B of the Bibliography of this book lists some of my other publications in which some of the themes of the *Critique* are developed more fully. (35, 69)

——; See also under Baeck, Buber, Hay, and Nietzsche.

Kegley, Charles W.; see below under Niebuhr and Tillich.

Keynes, John Maynard; *Essays and Sketches in Biography;* Meridian Books, N.Y. 1956. (17)

Kierkegaard, Søren; *Concluding Unscientific Postscript;* translated by David F. Swenson and Walter Lowrie; Princeton University Press 1944. (35, 68)

　　The criticisms in the text are developed more fully in Chapter 10 of my *From Shakespeare to Existentialism.*

Konvitz, Milton R.; "Judaism and the Democratic Ideal" in

Bibliography 441

The Jews: Their History, Culture, and Religion; ed. Louis
Finkelstein; 2 vols.; 2nd ed.; Harper & Brothers, N.Y. 1955.
(83)

Leuba, James H.; *A Psychological Study of Religion;* Macmillan, N.Y. 1912. An Appendix, pp. 337–361, offers 48
"Definitions of Religion and Critical Comments." In § 33
I make use of some of these definitions and accept Leuba's
threefold classification; but I also introduce two additional
classes and classify some definitions differently than he does.
My comments, of course, are different, too. (33)

——; *The Psychology of Religious Mysticism;* Harcourt, Brace
& Co., N.Y. 1925. (72)

Lovejoy, Arthur O.; *Essays in the History of Ideas;* The Johns
Hopkins Press 1948. (18)

Luther, Martin; *Sämtliche Schriften;* ed. Johann Georg Walch;
24 vols.; printed in Halle, Germany, in the 18th century,
and reprinted in St. Louis 1881–1910. (55, 57, 65, 67, 69)
Satan, in § 58, cites Luther according to Troeltsch. (See
below.)

Major, H. D. A.; T. W. Manson; C. J. Wright; *The Mission
and Message of Jesus: An Exposition of the Gospels in the
Light of Modern Research;* E. P. Dutton and Co., Inc., N.Y.
1938, 1946, 1947. (38, 55, 91)

Manson, T. W.; see Major.

McKeon, Richard; "Propositions and Perceptions in the World
of G. E. Moore" in *The Philosophy of G. E. Moore;* ed.
Paul Schilpp; The Library of Living Philosophers 1942.
(12)

Montefiore, C. G., and Loewe, H.; *A Rabbinic Anthology;*
Macmillan & Co., London 1938. (55)

Moore, G. E.; "Autobiography" in *The Philosophy of G. E.
Moore;* ed. Paul Schilpp; The Library of Living Philoso-
phers 1942. This volume contains also a Bibliography of
Moore's writings. 2nd ed., Tudor Publishing Company,
N.Y. 1952. (12, 17)

——; "Wittgenstein's Lectures in 1930–33" in *Mind,* LXIII,
No. 249 and 251 (January and July 1954), and LXIV, No.

253 (January 1955), pp. 1–27. Only the last number is quoted. (19)

Moore, George Foot; *Judaism in the First Centuries of the Christian Era;* 3 vols.; Harvard University Press 1927–30. (55, 65)

Murdoch, Iris; *Sartre: Romantic Rationalist;* Yale University Press 1953. (15)

Murphy, Arthur E.; "Coming to Grips with 'The Nature and Destiny of Man'" in *The Journal of Philosophy,* LX, No. 17 (August 19, 1943); reprinted in *Religious Liberals Reply;* The Beacon Press, Boston 1947. (68)

Muschg, Walter; "Zerschwatzte Dichtung" in *Die Zerstörung der deutschen Literatur;* Francke, Bern 1956. (13)

Niebuhr, H. Richard; *The Social Sources of Denominationalism;* Henry Holt, N.Y. 1929; reprinted by Living Age Books, Meridian Books, N.Y. 1957. (68)

Niebuhr, Reinhold; *An Interpretation of Christian Ethics;* Harper & Brothers, N.Y. 1935; reprinted with a new Preface, Living Age Books, Meridian Books, N.Y. 1956. (68)

——; "Humour and Faith" in *Discerning the Signs of the Times: Sermons for Today and Tomorrow;* Charles Scribner's Sons, N.Y. 1949. (65)

——; *The Nature and Destiny of Man* (Gifford Lectures 1939); 2 vols.; Charles Scribner's Sons, N.Y. 1941–43. (68)

——; *His Religious, Social, and Political Thought;* ed. Charles W. Kegley and Robert W. Bretall; The Library of Living Theology; Macmillan, N.Y. 1956. (68)

Nietzsche, Friedrich; *The Portable Nietzsche;* selected and translated, with an introduction, prefaces, and notes, by Walter Kaufmann; The Viking Press, N.Y. 1954. (7, 25, 42, 49, 62, 63)

Cf. also my *Nietzsche;* Princeton University Press 1950; rev. ed., Meridian Books, N.Y. 1956; my opuscula listed on p. 363 of the Meridian edition; and my article on him in the *Encyclopaedia Britannica.*

Nyberg, H. S.; *Studien zum Hoseabuche: Zugleich ein Beitrag zur Klärung des Problems der alttestamentlichen Textkritik;* Uppsala Universitets Arsskrift 1935:6. (89)

Otto, Rudolf; *Das Heilige;* Klotz, Gotha 1917, 1926; English translation by J. W. Harvey, entitled *The Idea of the Holy* ("The *Experience* of the Holy" would have been far more accurate); Oxford University Press 1923, 1946, 1950. (43, 81)

Pascal, Blaise; *Pensées* translated as *Thoughts* by W. F. Trotter and available in several editions. The wager is found in Section 233. (49)

Passmore, John; "Professor Ryle's Use of 'Use' and 'Usage'" in *The Philosophical Review,* LXIII (January 1954). (32)

Pratt, James Bisset; *The Religious Consciousness;* Macmillan, N.Y. 1940. (39, 72)

Raglan, Lord; *The Origins of Religion;* Thinker's Library, Watts & Co., London 1949. (33)

Ramsey, Paul; "Love and Law" in *Reinhold Niebuhr;* ed. Kegley and Bretall; see above. (68)

Rilke, Rainer Maria; *Briefe aus Muzot 1921 bis 1926;* Insel-Verlag, Leipzig 1937. (65, 75)

Cf. also Chapters 12 and 13 of my *From Shakespeare to Existentialism.*

Russell, Bertrand; *Religion and Science;* Home University Library, Oxford University Press 1935, 1947. (71)

———; "The Cult of 'Common Usage'" in *Portraits from Memory and Other Essays;* Simon and Schuster, N.Y. 1956. The other two essays which contain similar material are "Philosophical Analysis" in *The Hibbert Journal,* July 1956, and "Logic and Ontology" in *The Journal of Philosophy,* LIV, No. 9 (April 25, 1957). (20)

Ryle, Gilbert; *The Concept of Mind;* Hutchinson's University Library, London 1949. (29, 32)

———; *Dilemmas;* Cambridge University Press 1954. (18)

———; "Ordinary Language" in *The Philosophical Review,* LXII (April 1953). (32)

———; "Systematically Misleading Expressions" (1931–32), reprinted in *Logic and Language: First Series,* ed. Antony Flew; Basil Blackwell, Oxford 1951. (18)

Santayana, George; *Character and Opinion in the United States;* Anchor Books, N.Y. 1956. (37)

——; *Interpretations of Poetry and Religion;* Charles Scribner's Sons, N.Y. 1900, 1927. Reprinted as a paperback by Harper & Brothers, N.Y. 1957. Same pagination. (71, 74, 83)

——; *Reason in Religion* in *The Life of Reason;* one-vol. ed., rev. by the author in collaboration with Daniel Cory; Charles Scribner's Sons, N.Y. 1954. (83)

——; "Tragic Philosophy" in *Essays in Literary Criticism of George Santayana;* ed. Irving Singer; Charles Scribner's Sons, N.Y. 1956. (83)

Schaff, Philip; *The Creeds of Christendom with a History and Critical Notes;* 3 vols.; 6th rev. ed.; Harper & Brothers, N.Y. 1877 ff., 1931. (54)

Scholem, Gershom G.; *Major Trends in Jewish Mysticism;* Schocken Publishing House, Jerusalem 1941. (65, 74)

Schweitzer, Albert; "Die Idee des Reiches Gottes im Verlaufe der Umbildung des eschatologischen Glaubens in den uneschatologischen" in *Schweizerische Theologische Umschau* (23.1/2), February 1953. English version in E. N. Mozley, *The Theology of Albert Schweitzer;* Macmillan, N.Y. 1951. (55)

Soden, Hans von; see under Gogarten.

Stace, Walter T.; *Religion and the Modern Mind;* Lippincott, Philadelphia and N.Y. 1952. (53)

——; *Time and Eternity;* Princeton University Press 1952. (53, 72)

Stebbing, Susan; "Moore's Influence" in *The Philosophy of G. E. Moore;* ed. Paul Schilpp; The Library of Living Philosophers 1942. (12)

Strack, H. L.; see Billerbeck.

Suzuki, D. T.; *An Introduction to Zen Buddhism;* The Philosophical Library, N.Y. 1949. (63)

Talmud; In addition to a 6-vol. ed. of the original, published in Wilno 1931, I have consulted the annotated 12-vol. ed. of *Der Babylonische Talmud;* translated by Lazarus Goldschmidt; Vol. I, Verlag Biblion, Berlin 1929; and Vols. II–XII, Jüdischer Verlag, Berlin 1930–36. There is also an annotated English edition of *The Babylonian Talmud* in 34 vols., The Soncino Press, London 1935–48, plus index vol., 1952. (24, 52, 54, 55, 64, 65, 77, 83)

Taylor, A. E.; *Plato: The Man and His Work;* Meridian Books, N.Y. 1956. (44)

Tillich, Paul; "The Concept of God" in *Perspective: A Princeton Journal of Christian Opinion,* II, No. 3 (January 1950). (50)

——; *The Courage to Be;* Yale University Press 1952. (57)

——; *The Protestant Era;* University of Chicago Press 1948. (53, 57)

——; *Systematic Theology;* 2 vols.; University of Chicago Press 1951–57. All references are to Vol. I. (50, 53, 57)

——; *The Theology of;* ed. Charles W. Kegley and Robert W. Bretall; The Library of Living Theology; Macmillan, N.Y. 1952. (53)

Times Literary Supplement; January 8, 1954. (40)

Torczyner, Harry (now Tur-Sinai); *Die Heilige Schrift, neu ins Deutsche übertragen;* J. Kauffmann, Frankfurt a. M. 1937. (65)

Toynbee, Arnold J.; the remarks about him in §§ 24, 25, 26, 41 are backed up in Chapters 19 and 20 of my *From Shakespeare to Existentialism;* and in *Collier's Encyclopedia.*

Troeltsch, Ernst; *Die Soziallehren der christlichen Kirchen und Gruppen;* Mohr, Tübingen 1912. English translation by O. Wyon, entitled *The Social Teachings of the Christian Churches;* 2 vols.; Macmillan, N.Y. 1931. (58)

Underhill, Evelyn; *Mysticism;* Meridian Giant, Meridian Books, N.Y. 1954. (74)

Van Paassen, Pierre; *Why Jesus Died;* Dial Press, N.Y. 1949. (68)

Vaughan, The Very Reverend Roger Bede, O.S.B.; *The Life and Labours of S. Thomas of Aquin;* 2 vols.; Longmans & Co., London 1871–72. (45)

Weigel, Gustave, S.J.; "American Catholic Intellectualism: A Theologian's Reflections" in *The Review of Politics,* 19, No. 3 (July 1957). (53)

——; "Authority in Theology" in *Reinhold Niebuhr;* ed. Kegley and Bretall; see above. (68)

446 Bibliography

Wellhausen, Julius; *Israelitische und Jüdische Geschichte;* 4th ed.; Georg Reimer, Berlin 1901. (90)

Whitehead, Alfred North; *Religion in the Making;* Macmillan, N.Y. 1926. (80)

Williams, Daniel D.; "Niebuhr and Liberalism" in *Reinhold Niebuhr;* ed. Kegley and Bretall; see above. (68)

Wisdom, John; *Philosophy and Psycho-Analysis;* Blackwell, Oxford 1953. This is a collection of his essays. (19, 20, 32)

Wisdom, John Oulton; *The Unconscious Origins of Berkeley's Philosophy;* The Hogarth Press and The Institute of Psycho-Analysis, London 1953. (40)

Wittgenstein, Ludwig; *Logisch-Philosophische Abhandlung; Tractatus Logico-Philosophicus;* Kegan Paul, London 1922, 1933. Published with C. K. Ogden's English version on facing pages. I have made my own translation. (11, 13, 32)

——; *Philosophische Untersuchungen; Philosophical Investigations;* Macmillan, N.Y. 1953. Published with G. E. M. Anscombe's English translation on facing pages. I have made my own translations and refer to sections, not pages. (11, 19, 20)

——; the references to *AJP* refer to the article on "Ludwig Wittgenstein" in *The Australasian Journal of Philosophy,* XXIX, No. 2 (August 1951), signed by D. A. T. G. [Gasking] and A. C. J. [Jackson]. (19, 20)

Wright, Georg Henrik von; "Ludwig Wittgenstein, A Biographical Sketch" in *The Philosophical Review,* LXIV, No. 4 (October 1955). (19)

INDEX

What follows is no more than the third part of an Index of which the detailed Table of Contents and the Bibliography form parts one and two. In the Bibliography, every title is followed by the numbers of the sections of this book in which the title is cited; and when *all* references to an author are listed in the Bibliography, he is not listed again in the Index.

Numbers refer to the *sections* of this book; *M* to the mottos at the beginning; *P* to the Preface.

A. Some Names and Subjects

B. Some Scriptural Books and Names

1. OLD TESTAMENT

2. NEW TESTAMENT